ERSITY OF WINNIPEG
BALMORAL
DISCARDED
CANAD

SOVIET AND EAST EUROPEAN STUDIES

BOOKS IN THE SERIES

A. Boltho *Foreign Trade Criteria in Socialist Economies*
Sheila Fitzpatrick *The Commissariat of Enlightenment*
Donald Male *Russian Peasant Organisation before Collectivisation*
P. Wiles, ed. *The Prediction of Communist Economic Performance*
Vladimir V. Kusin *The Intellectual Origins of the Prague Spring*
Galia Golan *The Czechoslovak Reform Movement*
Naum Jasny *Soviet Economists of the Twenties*
Asha L. Datar *India's Economic Relations with the USSR and Eastern Europe, 1953–1969*
T. M. Podolski *Socialist Banking and Monetary Control*
Rudolf Bićanić *Economic Policy in Socialist Yugoslavia*
S. Galai *Liberation in Russia*
Richard B. Day *Leon Trotsky and the Policies of Economic Isolation*
G. Hosking *The Russian Constitutional Experiment: Government and Duma 1907–14*
A. Teichova *An Economic Background to Munich*
J. Ciechanowski *The Warsaw Rising of 1944*
Edward A. Hewett *Foreign Trade Prices in the Council for Mutual Economic Assistance*
Daniel F. Calhoun *The United Front: the TUC and the Russians 1923–28*
Galia Golan *Yom Kippur and After: the Soviet Union and the Middle East Crisis*
Maureen Perrie *The Agrarian Policy of the Russian Socialist-Revolutionary Party from its Origins through the Revolution of 1905–1907*
Paul Vyšný *Neo-Slavism and the Czechs, 1894–1914*
James Riordan *Sport in Soviet Society: Development of Sport and Physical Education in Russia and the USSR*

The Precarious Truce

ANGLO-SOVIET RELATIONS

1924–27

SOVIET AND EAST EUROPEAN STUDIES

The National Association for Soviet and East Europ
Studies exists for the purpose of promoting study
research on the social sciences as they relate to
Soviet Union and the countries of Eastern Europe
Monograph Series is intended to promote the pu
tion of works presenting substantial and original re
in the economics, politics, sociology and modern
of the USSR and Eastern Europe.

The Precarious Truce

ANGLO-SOVIET RELATIONS

1924–27

GABRIEL GORODETSKY
Lecturer in Russian History at Tel-Aviv University
and
Senior Research Fellow of the Russian and East European Research Center, Tel-Aviv University

CAMBRIDGE UNIVERSITY PRESS
CAMBRIDGE
LONDON · NEW YORK · MELBOURNE

Published by the Syndics of the Cambridge University Press
The Pitt Building, Trumpington Street, Cambridge CB2 1RP
Bentley House, 200 Euston Road, London NW1 2DB
32 East 57th Street, New York, NY 10022, USA
296 Beaconsfield Parade, Middle Park, Melbourne 3206, Australia

First published 1977

Printed in Great Britain by
Western Printing Services Ltd, Bristol

Library of Congress Cataloguing in Publication Data
Gorodetsky, Gabriel, 1945–
The precarious truce.
(Soviet and East European studies)
Bibliography: p.
Includes index.
1. Great Britain – Foreign relations – Russia
2. Russia – Foreign relations – Great Britain. 3. Great Britain – Politics and government – 1910–1936. 4. Russia – Politics and government – 1917–1936. I. Title.
II. Series.
DA47.65.G67 327.41'047 76–2279
ISBN 0 521 21226 X

Contents

Abbreviations

Arcos	All-Russian Co-operative Society Limited
ARJAC	Anglo-Russian Joint Advisory Council
AUCCTU	All-Union Central Council of Trade Unions
BOT	Board of Trade
Comintern	Kommunisticheskii Internatsional (Communist International)
CPGB	Communist Party of Great Britain
CPSU	Communist Party of the Soviet Union
FO	Foreign Office
GC	General Council of the Trades Union Congress
IFTU	International Federation of Trade Unions
IKKI	Ispolnitel′nyi Komitet Kommunisticheskogo Internatsionala (Executive Committee of the Communist International)
KPD	Kommunistische Partei Deutschlands (German Communist Party)
MFGB	Miners' Federation of Great Britain
Narkomfin	Narodnyi Komissariat Finansov (People's Commissariat of Finance)
Narkomindel	Narodnyi Komissariat Innostranykh Del (People's Commissariat for Foreign Affairs)
NMM	National Minority Movement
Profintern	Krasnyi International Professional′nykh Soyuzov (Red International of Trade Unions)
TUC	Trades Union Congress

Preface

Lenin's death at the beginning of 1924 coincided with an exhaustive search by the USSR for a *modus vivendi* with the capitalist world. A relaxation of international tension was considered a prerequisite for the construction of socialism in one country, a policy dictated by the decreasing likelihood of imminent revolution on a world scale.

In laying the foundations of peaceful coexistence priority was given to the cultivation of relations with Britain. It was axiomatic with the Russians that reconciliation with Britain, the spearhead of the military efforts to crush the Soviet regime in its infancy as well as the post-war arbitrator of European affairs, would set the pace for acceptance by the rest of Europe. This study examines the British Government's various responses to the Soviet overtures. The scope of the work ranges from Labour's *de jure* recognition of the Soviet Union at the beginning of 1924 to the Conservatives' severance of relations in May 1927. The bulk of the study is set against the background of rapidly-deteriorating relations and traces the unsparing measures employed by the Russians to forestall an open breach.

Notwithstanding the pre-eminence which the Russians attached to relations with Britain, no comprehensive scholarly study of Anglo-Soviet relations in the 1920s has been undertaken. The neglect probably stems from the impact of the Second World War, which led historians to concentrate on the events immediately leading up to it and to pay little attention to a more remote but nevertheless significant period of international friction. Valuable research has been pursued on Anglo-Soviet diplomacy, but this has not extended to cover the period in which Soviet diplomacy took shape. The few studies which focus on Anglo-Soviet relations are either ideologically inspired or confined to dramatic incidents like the 'Zinoviev letter' affair and the Arcos raid. Intriguing as such events are, they reflect the symptoms rather than the substance of the relations.

The opening for research of the British Government's archives after thirty years, rather than fifty years as previously, lays bare the process of policy-making towards Russia throughout the period under investigation. Traditional patterns of policy-making and strict definition of spheres of activity within the Government departments secured for the Foreign Office almost total authority over the formulation and execution of this policy. Its records are particularly enlightening for the Conservatives' term in office, when the lion's share of decisions concerning Russia were formulated, debated and executed within the Foreign Office. However, Labour's suspicion of the Office, especially on the issue of Russia, meant that much of Labour's policy was arrived at informally.

An examination of some invaluable collections of private papers served to restore the balance. D. Marquand, M.P., kindly allowed me access to MacDonald's papers which are at present in his possession, while Lord Ponsonby of Shulbrede was most helpful in providing me with copies of entries in his father's diary concerning Russia, and other correspondence not included in the collection deposited in the Bodleian. I am no less indebted to Mr M. Gilbert, who allowed me to consult Churchill's private papers, of which he temporarily has custody. Extensive use has also been made of Austen Chamberlain's and Baldwin's papers which are available for research. Other collections consulted have either produced corroborative evidence or provided insight into the *dramatis personae*; full reference is made to them in the bibliography.

The archives of the Home Office, which periodically assumed a significant role in Anglo-Soviet relations, are unfortunately closed for a hundred years; the correspondence of Joynson-Hicks, Home Secretary under the Conservatives, is also unobtainable. However, after repeated entreaties I was permitted to consult selected Home Office material which was particularly helpful for the study of the Arcos raid.

The TUC archives, which have not been previously used for research in Anglo-Soviet trade union relations, presented an enormous amount of material. I am grateful to the late Lord Feather, former General Secretary of the TUC, for permission to study the archives, and to Mr J. Murphy, the librarian, who helped me to sift the material. It produced unpublished records of the Anglo-Russian Joint Advisory Committee's meetings and correspondence with the Soviet trade unions, and also illuminating information on the TUC's decision-making.

The patterns of Soviet foreign policy are very much more intricate than the British. The overwhelming tendency of students of Soviet diplomacy has been either to overlook the interlocking relations between Comintern and Narkomindel or to treat the two separately. It is generally assumed that Comintern was a millstone around the neck of Soviet diplomacy rather than one of its fundamental elements. This misconception ensues partly from disregard of the peculiarities of Soviet conduct of foreign affairs at the time, a phenomenon which incidentally the Russians were anxious not to emphasize, and partly through evaluation of Soviet foreign policy in terms of conventional diplomacy.

The present study does, of course, deal with Narkomindel's straightforward diplomatic moves, indispensable for communication with the capitalist world. However, it devotes equal attention to complementary activities under the auspices of Comintern and the Soviet trade unions, rallying support for the USSR without regard to frontiers or international protocol. On the surface these three institutions appear to have little in common; the increasingly firm control of the Soviet communist party, however, ensured a coordinated policy.

In contrast with the mass of British primary sources available for examination, Soviet archives remain virtually closed to the Western student of foreign affairs. The only published primary material is the useful official series of documents on Soviet foreign policy. Yet it by no means provides an adequate basis for a comprehensive survey of the period. Only a few studies, however, have attempted a systematic review of the ample Soviet contemporary publications in the form of newspapers, periodicals, pamphlets and booklets. Though obviously not a substitute for a survey of policy-making at its rudimentary stages, these publications often served as the mouthpiece of the regime and an instrument for implementing policy. The advantage for the researcher of the 1920s is that despite the conformity of the Press, it still expressed the diverging views prevailing among the leadership.

Records of congresses of the Soviet communist party and

trade unions, Comintern and Profintern are equally important and in addition demonstrate the interaction between these institutions.

The failure in the 1920s to appreciate the significance of contemporary Soviet publications is reflected in their absence from British libraries. The largest collection of periodicals and newspapers, that of the British Museum, is unfortunately limited and incomplete. The Library of the International Labour Office in Geneva, however, provides an excellent collection of such sources. This was supplemented by shorter visits to the Institut für Weltwirtschaft of Kiel University and several libraries in Paris. Miss A. Abley, then librarian of St Antony's College, Oxford, was most helpful in obtaining on loan rare publications from the Lenin Library in Moscow and photocopies of selected manuscripts from the Trotsky archives in Harvard.

While the British material is relatively homogeneous, the most serious methodological problem confronting the present writer was that of putting every aspect of Soviet policy-making under the same spotlight. Though it is possible to treat Profintern and Comintern together, it is at times impossible to integrate them with the straightforward diplomatic issues. On such occasions it was necessary to present the tendencies in parallel fashion. The first half of the study, preserving a chronological approach, deals with the two aspects separately. They are then combined in an examination of Anglo-Soviet relations from the general strike to the severance of relations, which was accompanied by the termination of the united front in the trade unions

This work is the fruit of an extended stay in St Antony's College, Oxford, and my thanks are due to the Warden and Fellows for the pleasant and constructive atmosphere which I encountered there. I should like to express my sincere gratitude to Dr R. Kindersley of St Antony's for careful reading and useful criticism of the work, and for unstinted assistance on all occasions. I am deeply indebted to Professor M. Confino, Head of the Russian and East European Research Center of Tel-Aviv University, who in the first place made possible my stay in Oxford, and generously supplied my subsequent needs. My thanks are no less due to Professor E. H. Carr, who read the manuscript with close attention and gave me the benefit of several stimulating conversations.

Last, but by no means least, I would like to thank my wife Susan for painstaking editorial help at all stages of the preparation of the book.

Jerusalem
October 1975

G. G.

Introduction
Striving for acceptance

The Soviet regime emerged victorious from the civil war and intervention to face a country reduced to chaos, whose economy was in ruins as a result of seven years of continuous war and the virtual collapse of the old administration. With hopes of support from the expected revolutions in the advanced countries fading fast, the restoration of Russia had become essential for survival. The introduction of the New Economic Policy was matched by similar moves in the diplomatic field. The pressing need for a breathing space and the serious shortage of foreign capital and technical skill made it necessary to overcome the universal apprehension and distrust of the Bolshevik regime which had persisted after the failure of the attempt to overthrow it by force.[1]

The first decade of Soviet diplomacy was marked by two major drives to reach a *modus vivendi* with the capitalist world. The first, culminating in the conclusion of the Rapallo Treaty of 1922, laid down the principles of Soviet diplomacy and is undoubtedly the more impressive in its achievements. In the short space of two and a half years the Soviet Union had emerged from a totally insignificant position in international affairs to secure *de facto* recognition from Britain and full recognition from Germany, and trade agreements from both countries – certainly the strongest economic powers apart from the isolationist United States. Even more overwhelming was the Russians' success in the East in obtaining recognition and treaties from Turkey, Persia and Afghanistan. The second phase, with which this study is concerned, aimed for international formal recognition of the Soviet Union, the removal of the *cordon sanitaire* set up after the revolution and integration within Europe, but ended with only a partial success.

1 R. H. Ullman, *Britain and the Russian Civil War* (Princeton, 1968), Chap. VIII. On the overriding economic motives for the diplomatic moves, see V. A. Shishkin, *Sovetskoe Gosudarstvo i Strany Zapada v 1917–1923gg.* (Leningrad, 1969), pp. 19–62 and 240–49.

In both periods all eyes were on Britain, which was believed to be the key to the post-Versailles order in Europe. It was assumed that striking an accord with Britain, which had been the leading spirit in the intervention, would encourage other countries to follow suit.[2]

The initial success scored by the Russians in establishing relations should be largely attributed to Lloyd George's pragmatic approach and his shrewd realization that the Bolsheviks would not be toppled from power. His ingenuity in bringing about the *rapprochement* was all the more remarkable in view of the fact that most of the prominent members of the coalition Government he headed were ardent anti-communists and opposed to accommodation with the Moscow regime. Lloyd George, however, committed to a policy of reconstruction in Europe, was convinced that this could not be effectively executed while standing aloof from such a vast country as Russia. He was no less aware of the wide economic possibilities which the Russian market could offer Britain.

The first and unavoidable step towards regulating relations was boldly taken by Lloyd George in November 1919 when he publicly admitted the failure of the military intervention and announced the withdrawal of the last British troops from Russia. Within two months he had lifted the economic blockade imposed on Russia during the intervention by securing the approval of the Allied Supreme Council in Paris for the establishment of commercial ties with Russia. Trade was to be conducted through the Russian Co-operative Societies, which were nominally independent of the Soviet Government. Only a month later, on 12 February, diplomatic contacts were established when Maxim Litvinov, the Deputy Commissar for Foreign Affairs, met British officials in Copenhagen and successfully concluded an agreement on the exchange of prisoners of war.[3]

These early approaches were consolidated when the Russians were invited to negotiate a trade agreement with the British Government. A Soviet delegation, led by Leonid Krasin, one of

[2] O. F. Solov′ev, 'Iz Istorii Bor′by Sovetskogo Pravitel′stva za Mirnoe Sosushchestovanie s Angliei', *Voprosy Istorii* (1965), No. 2, pp. 54–64.

[3] E. H. Carr, *The Bolshevik Revolution 1917–1923* (London, 1953), Vol. 3, pp. 148–52 and 156; Ullman, *Britain and the Russian Civil War*, pp. 42–43.

the most brilliant of Soviet diplomats and an able economist, arrived in Britain at the end of May 1920. The negotiations dragged on for almost a year and were conducted almost entirely by Lloyd George, often against the express wish of the Cabinet. In addition, the negotiations were interrupted by the Soviet-Polish war, which at its critical stages in the summer of 1920 brought Britain to the verge of renewed intervention, and by frequent obstruction on the part of the French Government. Notwithstanding these difficulties, the negotiations proceeded surprisingly smoothly after the Russians had undertaken to curb propaganda activities in Britain and had agreed in principle to compensate former owners of property in Russia. They were brought to a successful conclusion by the signing on 16 March 1921 of a trade agreement in which Britain recognized *de facto* Soviet Russia and which provided for mutual trade facilities and the exchange of official representatives.[4]

The Soviet-Polish war, which marked the final attempt of the capitalist countries to unseat the communist regime by military intervention, had a long-lasting effect on Anglo-Soviet relations. The rallying of the divided Labour movement in defence of the Soviet Union under the slogan of 'Hands off Russia' was deeply appreciated in Moscow. The formation of a National Council of Action in London was followed up by the mushrooming of similar local councils in most industrial districts. These councils exerted effective pressure on the Government and a head-on collision was only averted by Polish successes on the battlefield, which rendered British intervention unnecessary. The Russians hastily dispatched L. B. Kamenev to Britain to divert support for Russia into pressure on the Government to conclude the negotiations. Kamenev's hasty and ill-disguised efforts, however, were unsuccessful and proved to be an impediment to the talks, whereupon he was ordered back to Moscow.

The 'Hands off Russia' movement, however, was not treated by the Russians as a passing episode: by tightening control over

[4] A coherent survey of these negotiations is in M. V. Glenny, 'The Anglo-Soviet Trade Agreement, March 1921', *Journal of Contemporary History* (1970), Vol. 5, No. 2, pp. 63–82. See also R. H. Ullman, *The Anglo-Soviet Accord* (Princeton, 1972), Chap. x. One of the few illuminating Soviet accounts of the period is in Shishkin, *Sovetskoe Gosudarstvo*, pp. 171–91 and 249–59. See also I. M. Maisky, 'Anglo-Sovetskoe Torgovoe Soglashenie', *Voprosy Istorii* (1957), No. 5, pp. 66–77.

Comintern and encouraging the infiltration of communist-oriented movements into the trade unions they were able to channel solidarity and fraternal feelings into a more subtle and effective diplomatic instrument. These tactics culminated in the formation of the Anglo-Soviet trade union committee, by 1925 a cornerstone of Soviet diplomacy which had lost much of its initial drive.[5]

The Russians, having concluded the trade agreement, wasted little time in proceeding to secure full recognition. In September 1921 Chicherin, who had replaced Trotsky as commissar for Foreign Affairs in 1918, urged Lloyd George, over the head of the persistently hostile Foreign Office, to summon a peace conference which would solve the outstanding issues between Russia and the Allies. Lloyd George's favourable reaction paved the way for the Genoa conference, which met in April and May 1922. The declared aim of the conference was to facilitate the recovery of the European economy. Lloyd George hoped to achieve this by setting Russia and Germany on an equal footing with the rest of the powers and re-opening the Russian market for extensive trade. His policy, however, had by now burnt itself out; not only did the French obdurately refuse to follow his course, but there were growing reservations at home.

The conference is better remembered as the scene of the conclusion of a German-Soviet treaty in Rapallo on 16 April, which *inter alia* granted the Soviet Union *de jure* recognition. The Russian policy was motivated by a wish to drive a wedge between Germany and the Allies, thereby forestalling the crystallization of an anti-Soviet bloc, while cultivating relations with both. The alliance of the two defeated powers, which was precisely what Lloyd George had attempted to avoid, further weakened his already precarious position in Britain and brought the accommodation in Anglo-Soviet relations to a temporary halt.[6]

[5] On 'Hands off Russia', see S. R. Graubard, *British Labour and the Russian Revolution 1917–1924* (Harvard, 1956), pp. 65–114; L. J. Macfarlane, '"Hands off Russia" – British Labour and the Russo-Polish War 1920', *Past and Present* (1968), No. 38; W. P. and Z. K. Coates, *A History of Anglo-Soviet Relations* (London, 1943), pp. 268–70.

[6] On Genoa and Rapallo, see L. Fischer, *The Soviets in World Affairs, 1917–1929* (Princeton, 1951), Vol. 1, pp. 318–54. See also R. H. Debo, 'George Chicherin: Soviet Russia's Second Foreign Commissar' (Univ. of Nebraska Ph.D. thesis, 1964), pp. 213–21, and G. Freund, *Unholy Alliance* (London, 1957, Chaps. IV and V.

The deteriorating position of Soviet diplomacy became evident in the ensuing Hague conference, an attempt by the Western countries to retrieve the damage done at Genoa. Although the conference achieved little, it provided Litvinov with a forum to expound principles for the next stage of encounters: he announced their willingness to compensate former owners of nationalized property in return for long-term credits.[7]

The formation of a Conservative Government under Bonar Law at the end of 1922 allowed Lord Curzon a free hand in the conduct of foreign relations, which was marked by a wave of anti-Soviet sentiments. The Curzon Ultimatum, which had threatened to repudiate the 1921 agreement unless demands concerning Comintern propaganda in the East, compensation claims and detained British trawlers were met by the Russians, hampered a *détente* in Anglo-Soviet relations during the summer of 1923.[8]

This phase, however, could not survive for long. The trade agreement had opened new prospects of relieving economic hardship and soaring unemployment. By 1923 the Russians maintained that the absence of proper political relations was entirely responsible for the failure of the agreement to fulfil its early promise. Increasing pressure from commercial interest groups of varying political shades was put on the Government to reconsider its Russian policy.[9] In October Chicherin, Soviet Commissar for Foreign Affairs, predicted that Curzon's hostile policy towards Russia would not endure and did not exclude an early recognition. He therefore outlined to Kh. Rakovsky, who was appointed to replace Krasin as the Soviet representative in Britain in September 1923, the principles which should guide him when the occasion arose. Rakovsky fully shared his confidence in an imminent improvement in Anglo-Soviet relations.[10]

[7] E. H. Carr, *The Bolshevik Revolution 1917–1923*, Vol. 3, pp. 426–32; B. E. Shtein, *Gaagskaya Konferentsiya* (Moscow, 1922), pp. 9–15.

[8] The ultimatum dated 8 May and the Soviet reply of 11 May are in *Dokumenty Vneshnei Politiki SSSR*, Vol. VI, pp. 282–302 (hereafter referred to as *Dok. Vne. Pol.*).

[9] E. H. Carr, *The Interregnum 1923–1924* (London, 1954), pp. 243–45; Shishkin, *Sovetskoe Gosudarstvo*, pp. 351–55.

[10] *Dok. Vne. Pol.*, Vol. VI, pp. 476–78, 15 Oct. 1923; Rakovsky interviewed in *Izvestiya*, 11 Nov. 1923. Rakovsky, of Rumanian origin, led the communist uprising in Bessarabia and was prominent in the foun-

Their hopes soon materialized. On 16 November the Conservative Government obtained the dissolution of Parliament, and on 6 December general elections were held in which the Conservatives lost their overall majority. Labour's manifesto pledged the resumption of 'free economic and diplomatic relations with Russia'; the Liberals' manifesto welcomed the 're-opening of full relations with Russia'.[11] The Russians, therefore, had ample grounds for optimism; the long-awaited full recognition seemed likely to follow shortly.

dation of Comintern. For some time he also acted as the chairman of the Council of Peoples' Commissars in the Ukraine. His mastery of languages and knowledge of the West soon launched him in a diplomatic career.

[11] Quoted in Coates, *A History of Anglo-Soviet Relations*, p. 129.

I

Soviet Russia and the First Labour Government

Recognition

The commitment of both Labour and Liberals to granting *de jure* recognition to Russia suggests that there was little to prevent Ramsay MacDonald from embarking on such a course once the arduous task of forming a Cabinet had been completed. However, hopes of exacting concessions in return for recognition, wide divergences of public opinion on the subject, and MacDonald's long-standing opposition to Bolshevism militated against prompt action. These obstacles were matched, however, by the Russians' determination to gain unconditional recognition, by constant pressure from Labour's left wing and by apprehensions that the Italians, currently engaged in negotiations, might steal a march on Britain in recognizing the Soviet Union. MacDonald, outlining Labour's programme in an Albert Hall rally on 8 January 1924, had undertaken to end the 'pompous folly of standing aloof from the Russians'.[1] He failed to make clear, however, whether recognition would be immediate or conditional on the solution of controversial issues with Russia. MacDonald had already tried to convince Rakovsky, through an intermediary, that in view of the precarious position of the future Labour Government an early settlement of the differences of opinion would hasten recognition. He had even proposed to send a representative to Moscow immediately to open negotiations.[2]

These early feelers were received coolly by Rakovsky. MacDonald's Albert Hall speech, however, encouraged him to make new approaches. In reaction to MacDonald's reference to propa-

[1] *The Times*, 9 Jan. 1924. At least one of his future ministers had conditioned his participation in the Cabinet on an immediate recognition; see Lord Parmoor, *A Retrospect: Looking back over a Life of Eighty Years* (London, 1936), p. 191.

[2] L. Fischer, *The Soviets in World Affairs, 1917–1929* (Princeton, 1951), Vol. 2, p. 473.

ganda, the *bête noire* of Anglo-Soviet relations, as an impediment to better understanding, Rakovsky agreed to give the British Government '*formal* assurances that if confidence is accorded to our country it, in its turn, will reciprocate by an act of confidence'.[3] MacDonald's prompt reply informed Rakovsky that recognition would be considered 'on its own merits' and that it was a 'great mistake' to mix it with economic discussions. At the same time, if Russia wished 'to find its way smoothed', the Labour Government should be able to announce at the moment of recognition that the 'first fruits' were already being reaped. For that purpose he proposed the appointment of a committee to deal with claims against Russia and to reach an understanding on the propaganda issue.[4] The Russians, however, remained adamant that recognition should be unconditional. After consulting Moscow, Rakovsky warmly welcomed MacDonald's statement on recognition, but put forward Soviet counter-claims and insisted that the absence of credits from Great Britain constituted the 'greatest hindrance in the development of Russo-British trade'. A few days later, in placatory mood, he informed MacDonald that the amnesty of Social Revolutionaries imprisoned in Russia was motivated by 'willingness to meet the wishes expressed by Labour Party circles'. MacDonald's failure to achieve an early agreement in principle brought the correspondence with Rakovsky to an end; a letter from the latter's secretary described him as 'head over ears in work at present' and excused him from writing personally.[5]

A variety of questions concerning recognition arose instantly upon the Labour Government's taking office on 23 January. A group of Labour back-benchers, headed by E. D. Morel and closely in touch with Rakovsky, pressed Arthur Ponsonby, Parliamentary Under-Secretary of State for Foreign Affairs, to grant immediate recognition, hinting at the imminence of Italian recognition.[6]

[3] P.R.O., Foreign Office Papers, Series 371, Vol. 10519, N7948/7948/85: 11 Jan. 1924.

[4] *Dok. Vne. Pol.*, Vol. VII, pp. 33–34. This remained the Foreign Office's opinion; see F.O. 371 10464 N804/10/38: minutes by Sir Eyre Crowe, Permanent Under-Secretary of State for Foreign Affairs, and J. D. Gregory, Head of the Northern Department in the Office, 31 Jan. 1924.

[5] F.O. 371 10519 N7948/7948/85: 16 and 19 Jan. 1924; MacDonald papers, 30/69 5/130: Rakovsky to MacDonald, 22 Jan. 1924.

[6] A. Duff Cooper, *Old Men Forget* (London, 1953), p. 123; *New States-*

Russian negotiations with Italy had been in progress since November 1923. Following Labour's election victory the Russians apparently regarded these negotiations as a bait to obtain recognition from Britain, to which they gave priority. Intensive attempts to secure recognition from other European countries were proving abortive, since these countries were reluctant to make an independent move but expressed willingness to follow a British example.[7] Mussolini, aware of this, declared in Parliament on 30 November 1923 that the conclusion of a trade agreement would carry with it *de jure* recognition. Although the Russians had no intention of succumbing to Italian demands for concessions in exchange for recognition, they welcomed Mussolini's initiative and spread the impression that the negotiations were making satisfactory progress.[8]

A completely unexpected obstacle arose when King George V expressed reluctance to accept at Court an ambassador representing the assassins of his cousin, Tsar Nicholas. MacDonald had already made known his intention of appointing as ambassador to Russia O'Grady, a veteran trade unionist, who had represented Britain in the initial contacts with the Bolsheviks in Copenhagen in 1919.[9]

In its first meeting the Cabinet agreed to postpone discussion on recognition until a later date to allow MacDonald to straighten matters out.[10] Anxious to gain the full advantages of recognition

man and Nation, 4 Aug. 1945, p. 74. As secretary of the Union of Democratic Control Morel had shared with MacDonald the basic concepts of foreign policy throughout the war. In 1924 he was expected to become Labour's first Foreign Secretary, but MacDonald preferred to fill the post himself.

7 *Dok. Vne. Pol.*, Vol. VII, pp. 11–13: report of Russian representative in Prague on conversation with Beneš, 3 Nov. 1923; pp. 39–41: Russian Ambassador in Germany on conversation with the Greek Ambassador, 21 Jan. 1924.

8 Leader in *Izvestiya*, 4 Dec. 1923; see also interview with Litvinov in *ibid.*, 6 Feb. 1924. For accounts of the Soviet-Italian negotiations see *Survey of International Affairs, 1924* (London, 1928), pp. 228–29, and I. D. Ostoya-Ovsynyi, *Leninskaya Diplomatiya Mira i Sotrudnichestva* (Moscow, 1965), pp. 85–105.

9 H. Nicolson, *King George the Fifth: His Life and Reign* (London, 1952), p. 385; P.R.O., Private Correspondence, Series 800, Vol. 227: minute by Ponsonby, 23 Feb. 1924.

10 P.R.O. Cabinet Conclusions, Series 23, Vol. 48, 7(24)19, 23 Jan. 1924 (hereafter referred to as Cab. 23).

and yet comply with the King's wish for the exchange only of *chargés d'affaires*. MacDonald sought to dissuade the Italians from sending an ambassador to Moscow. On 25 January Crowe told the Italian Ambassador in London that Britain would proceed towards recognition with the 'least possible delay', but owing to the circumstances would defer for a time the nomination of an ambassador. He then proposed that Italy 'adopt a similar procedure'. While further action was suspended until a reply came from Mussolini, MacDonald expressed optimism in Cabinet that recognition could be expected before Parliament met. The policy of resumption of relations, it was recorded, was being proceeded with 'as rapidly as circumstances permitted'.[11]

The way was cleared for recognition on 29 January, when Mussolini conveyed his 'cordial approval of the procedure suggested'. A draft Note of recognition prepared by the Northern Department was then circulated to different ministers, who were invited to comment on it. However, the circumstances dictated swift action; by the time the comments reached the Foreign Office, the letter of recognition had already been sent to Moscow.[12] Meanwhile, Labour back-benchers, refusing to accept that there 'should be an hour's delay' in the preparations for recognition, had misinformed Rakovsky that because of the advice of the Foreign Office MacDonald was inclined to attach conditions to recognition.[13] The Russians, hoping to hasten MacDonald's decision, went ahead with the negotiations in Rome, which had been held up on several points of principle. These were successfully resolved and an agreement on a draft treaty was reached on the night of 30 January.[14] Although Mussolini was prepared to announce recognition on the spot, the Russians adroitly persuaded him to defer the act until the date scheduled

[11] F.O. 371 10464 N840/10/38; Cab. 23/48, 8(24)10, 28 Jan. 1924.

[12] F.O. 371 10464 N840/10/38: Crowe on conversation with Italian Ambassador in London; F.O. 371 10465 N902/10/38: draft Note of recognition.

[13] Duff Cooper, *Old Men Forget*, p. 123; Feodor Rothstein, spokesman of Narkomindel, in *Pravda*, 6 Mar. 1924. See also R. W. Lyman, *The First Labour Government, 1924* (London, 1957), p. 185. In fact the decision was entirely MacDonald's, hardly involving the Foreign Office.

[14] F.O. 371 10465 N1032/10/38: British Ambassador to Rome on conversation with Mussolini, 5 Feb. 1924.

for the signing of the trade treaty.[15] The Russians apparently intended to see what effect the announcement of their agreement with Italy would have on the British position.

When MacDonald was informed of the Soviet-Italian agreement, he was advised to grant recognition before 2 February, the day on which the second congress of Soviets, then sitting in Moscow, was expected to disperse. This would ensure the acceptance of recognition not only by Chicherin but also by the 'representatives of the Soviets of all the Russians'. In view of the short time remaining, MacDonald acted in great haste and without consulting other members of the Cabinet.[16]

On the evening of Friday, 1 February the Note of recognition was dispatched to Sir Robert M. Hodgson, the official British representative in Moscow, who had served in various diplomatic capacities in Russia, mostly in Vladivostok and Omsk, since 1906. To forestall any Russian reservations, the Note had undergone last-minute alterations to make it appear as uncontroversial as possible. Hodgson was instructed to submit the text of recognition to Chicherin that night and ask him to refrain from 'definite appointments' to posts in London until he received a personal letter from MacDonald. This letter had not yet been dispatched because of the suddenness of the decision. Simultaneously, Ponsonby informed Rakovsky privately of the recognition, emphasizing the 'promptitude' with which the matter had been handled.[17] Hodgson, however, did not receive the telegram until the next morning and was unable to communicate it to Chicherin, who was absent from Narkomindel. Instead Hodgson was received by Litvinov in the early afternoon. By then all Governments had been notified of the British move, and the Note of recognition had been published in the Press. After the persistent wave of rumours from London on the improbability of

[15] *I Documenti Diplomatici Italiani*, Series VII, Vol. II, pp. 429–30: Mussolini to head of Italian Trade Delegation in Moscow, 4 Feb. 1924.

[16] Cab. 23/48 9(24)1, 4 Feb. 1924. There is no evidence to suggest whether news of the imminent Soviet-Italian agreement or the wish to allow the announcement to be made to the congress was the decisive factor. The Italian Ambassador conveyed his impression to Mussolini that the latter consideration was the uppermost; *I Documenti Diplomatici Italiani*, Vol. II, p. 440, 9 Feb. 1924.

[17] F.O. 371 10465 N902/10/38: letters by MacDonald to Hodgson and by Ponsonby to Rakovsky, 1 Feb. 1924.

recognition, Litvinov must have been sincere in expressing to Hodgson 'his profound satisfaction' at the step taken by the British Government.[18]

The same afternoon Litvinov read the Note to the congress, which received it with enthusiasm. A resolution was moved stating satisfaction at the 'historic step' which constituted 'one of the first acts of the first Labour Government in England'. It called upon other Governments to follow the example set by Britain.[19]

Mussolini, misled by his ambassador in London into believing that MacDonald had undertaken to coordinate with him on the question of recognition, was taken by complete surprise when he learnt from the Press about the British move.[20] Infuriated by the turn of events, he complained that the British had deliberately 'outmanoeuvred' him; he had attached personal importance to being 'first in the field of recognition'.[21] But he was soon to suffer more setbacks. The Russians now refused, in spite of his entreaties, to sign the agreement as it had stood when negotiations were adjourned. Litvinov explained that the Russians were given unfavourable terms by Mussolini, whose 'appetite grew with the negotiations'.[22] The Soviet Union finally received Italian recognition on 7 February. In a face-saving gesture, Mussolini capitalized on Britain's partial recognition by maintaining that his own, which involved the exchange of ambassadors and the conclusion of a treaty, had been granted in fact on 31 January.[23] However, by the time it came it had lost much of its weight, as pointed out by Kalinin, the President of the Soviet Union: 'The *de jure* recognition of the Soviet Union by Italy is a logical outcome of the fact of the recognition of the USSR by MacDonald's English Government. Had it occurred earlier, it would have had a greater political significance.'[24]

[18] F.O. 371 10465 N1398/10/38: Hodgson to MacDonald, 8 Feb. 1924.

[19] *Dok. Vne. Pol.*, Vol. VII, pp. 58–59.

[20] *I Documenti Diplomatici Italiani*, Vol. II, pp. 422–23 and 426: exchange of letters between Italian Ambassador in London and Mussolini, 30 Jan. and 2 Feb. 1924.

[21] F.O. 371 10465 N1032/10/38: British Ambassador in Rome to MacDonald on conversation with Mussolini, 5 Feb. 1924.

[22] *Izvestiya*, 6 Feb. 1924.

[23] *I Documenti Diplomatici Italiani*, Vol. II, p. 435: Mussolini's note to Chicherin, 7 Feb. 1924.

[24] *Izvestiya*, 9 Feb. 1924.

Despite the appearance of satisfaction with which the Soviet Government welcomed recognition, it was accompanied by misgivings. When Chicherin met Hodgson on 3 February, he was concerned with the terms of the Note. It suggested to him that complete recognition was conditional on the outcome of the proposed negotiations for the solution of outstanding issues.[25] MacDonald's letter, in which he reminded Chicherin that opinion in Britain was 'still sensitive' with regard to Russia, and therefore advised him to send to London a representative 'not involved in political issues and easy to accept', only added to his apprehensions. Chicherin's reply made it clear that he had no intention of considering MacDonald's delicate position *vis-à-vis* the Court. He strongly suspected that the delay in nominating ambassadors was not a result of 'technical considerations' but a calculated attempt to exert pressure on the Russians in the forthcoming negotiations.[26]

Indeed it soon became clear that Hodgson, despite his previous post as adviser to Kolchak in Omsk during the intervention, would continue to represent Britain in Moscow. Ponsonby was forced to admit that the appointment of O'Grady would have to wait for the successful conclusion of the negotiations.[27]

The Anglo-Soviet conference

The Russians' reservations about the recognition did not extend to the accompanying invitation to negotiate an Anglo-Soviet treaty. They seriously hoped to reinforce the 1921 agreement which, although a significant breakthrough, had proved to be a fragile cease-fire rather than the desired peace treaty.[28] The urge to regulate relations with the capitalist world received new impetus at the height of the NEP policy, the success of which largely depended on the expansion of trade and the elimination of threats to the existence of the Soviet Union.[29] Although the conference

25 F.O. 371 10465 N1398/10/38: Hodgson to MacDonald, 8 Feb. 1924.

26 F.O. 371 10465 N980/10/38: MacDonald to Chicherin, 4 Feb. 1924; F.O. 800/219: Chicherin to MacDonald, n.d.

27 R. Hodgson, 'Memoirs of an Official Agent', *History Today* (Aug. 1954), p. 524; F.O. 800/227: minute by Ponsonby, 23 Feb. 1924.

28 F.O. 371 10465 N902/10/38: Rakovsky to MacDonald, 8 Feb. 1924.

29 Karl Radek, authoritative spokesman on foreign policy, in a review of Soviet expectations from the conference, *Trud*, 8 Apr. 1924.

assumed a predominantly political character, economic motives were clearly the driving force behind the negotiations. Chicherin went so far as to maintain that recognition was significant merely as a practical step towards improving trade relations.[30]

The scarcity of foreign currency reserves in Russia made essential a positive balance of trade. This could be achieved through selective import of top-priority industrial and consumer goods indispensable for the reconstruction of industry in return for the export of agricultural products. However, the success of this policy depended on good harvests and the smooth operation of the trade machinery.[31] Opinion in the Politburo was that an agreement with Britain, the arbiter of world economic activity, was of 'the highest value' and would open the door to markets in other countries. This was disputed by Trotsky, who believed that the emerging power of the USA detracted from such an agreement.[32] Nevertheless, all were agreed on the importance of the conference and concurred that ideological differences with the British Government should in no way hinder the conduct of the negotiations.[33]

The Russians, however, determined to start negotiations on a *carte blanche* basis but without sacrificing their principles, approached the conference with no sense of urgency. The monopoly of trade, a stumbling-block in previous negotiations, had been resolutely defended by Lenin before his death and the Russians felt justified in presenting counter-claims concerning damage inflicted on Russia during the Allied intervention.[34] The Russians also maintained that, in contrast to former negotiations, an agreement held advantages for both sides. Their confidence

[30] *Dok. Vne. Pol.*, Vol. VII, pp. 605–608: speech by Chicherin, 7 Jan. 1924.

[31] A. Nove, *An Economic History of the U.S.S.R.* (London, 1969), p. 130. In three out of the five years 1923–28 there was a negative balance; see A. Baykov, *The Development of the Soviet Economic System* (Cambridge, 1950), pp. 74–75.

[32] *Dok. Vne. Pol.*, Vol. VII, pp. 597–604: Krasin's speech, 7 Jan. 1924; Trotsky archives, T-812: note to Krasin, 18 June 1924.

[33] *Trinadtsatyi S'ezd Rossiiskoi Kommunisticheskoi Partii* (*B*) (Moscow, 1963), pp. 33–34: speech by Zinoviev (hereafter referred to as *Trinadtsatyi S'ezd* (*B*)); Trotsky, *Trud*, 20 Apr. 1924.

[34] Speech by Trotsky in Baku, *Trud*, 16 Apr. 1924; Radek in *Pravda*, 11 Apr. 1924; Ukrainian Prime Minister on negotiations, *Izvestiya*, 13 Apr. 1924. On the monopoly of trade see Baykov, *Development of Soviet System*, pp. 71–73.

was reinforced by a partial solution of the 'scissors' problem. The disparity between industrial and agricultural prices, which had haunted Soviet economists during 1922–23, was reduced by two good harvests.[35] The Russians, therefore, were well prepared for the conference and had a clear notion of their expectations. As early as October 1923, Chicherin had briefed Rakovsky that if negotiations re-opened Russia would conduct them on the principles of the Genoa and The Hague proposals. This implied mutual cancellation of the Russian war debts and Soviet counter-claims, Russian compensation of private debts and long-term concessions to former owners of property in Russia.[36]

In an early correspondence between MacDonald and Rakovsky a general understanding had been established on issues which would be discussed by the conference.[37] To prevent another collapse in the negotiations because of French intransigence or divergence of interests, MacDonald rebuffed the Board of Trade's proposals to invite other Governments to participate in the conference. He agreed with the advice of the Foreign Office officials that Russia would offer no other Government the 'terms of greatest advantages' that it would to Britain. Further agreement was reached with Rakovsky, before he left for Russia to consult his Government, on breaking up the conference into political and economic subcommittees.[38] Early preparations undertaken by the British revealed discordance and confusion. Chapman, of the Board of Trade, who was charged with the direction of the economic committee, laid down the burden after he had reached the conclusion that the essence of the issues was political. It was therefore agreed with the Foreign Office that the delegation should be regarded as a single unit. Chapman accurately predicted that against expectations the plenary session would become the main instrument of the conference.[39]

[35] N. Jasny, *Soviet Economists of the Twenties* (Cambridge, 1972), pp. 17–19.

[36] *Dok. Vne. Pol.*, Vol. VI, pp. 476–78: Chicherin to Rakovsky.

[37] F.O. 371 10519 N7948/7948/85: exchange of letters between MacDonald and Rakovsky, 12 and 16 Jan. 1924.

[38] F.O. 371 10464 N841/10/38: minute by Gregory, 31 Jan. 1924; F.O. 371 10465 N1093/10/38: minute by MacDonald, 11 Feb. 1924; MacDonald to Rakovsky, 11 Feb. 1924.

[39] F.O. 371 10511 N2554/2554/85: Gregory to Chapman, 21 Mar. 1924;

Preliminary meetings of the British delegation failed to draw up a firm programme for the conference.[40] The closest MacDonald came to defining a policy was the speech to the last preliminary meeting in which he repeated his undertaking to Parliament in early February that 'the granting of direct credits to the Soviet Government was inadmissible'. MacDonald had recourse to the impracticable formula that a satisfactory solution of the outstanding problems would create the conditions for the Russians to raise loans in the City. He also insisted on the inclusion of a clause on propaganda.[41]

Even this vague outline, however, was invalidated before the conference convened. A memorandum from the leading City bankers on the conditions for restoring Russian credit was sent to MacDonald a few days before the conference opened. The demands made on the Russians – the restitution of private property to foreigners, changes in the Civil Code, guarantees against future confiscation, and abolition of the monopoly of trade – were clearly unacceptable; the future of the conference would be seriously endangered if MacDonald persisted in his views.[42] MacDonald, however, had already made known his intention of holding aloof from the conference, and the drafting of the opening speech was left to Owen O'Malley, an official in the Northern Department, who was highly sceptical about the outcome of the negotiations and believed that the only chance of success lay 'in giving the Russians a shock at the outset'.[43] MacDonald's opening speech at the conference on 14 April, despite its cordial tone, left no shadow of doubt that the successful conclusion of a treaty depended on adequate compensation of bondholders and former property owners in Russia. On the other hand,

F.O. 377 10511 N2665/2554/85: Chapman to Gregory, 24 Mar. 1924; F.O. 371 10513 N3098/3098/85: O'Malley on conversation with Chapman.

40 F.O. 371 10509 N1822 and 2766/1822/85: minutes of first and second preliminary meetings of British delegation, 28 Feb. and 27 Mar. 1924.

41 *Parl. Deb. H.C.*, Vol. 169, col. 769, 12 Feb. 1924; F.O. 371 10509 N2996/1822/85: minutes of third preliminary meeting, 3 Apr. 1924.

42 F.O. 371 10512 N3137/3028/85: Leaf, representative of the bankers, to MacDonald, 7 Apr. 1924.

43 F.O. 371 10513 N3297/3297/85: minute and draft speech for MacDonald by O'Malley, 11 Apr. 1924.

there was only a non-committal reference to the Russians' request for credit.[44]

His speech was lost in the chorus of Press comment on the Bankers' Memorandum, published on the same day. Doubts were cast on the authority and intentions of the Russian delegation. It is true that the delegation was broad-based; some delegates were chosen merely as a propaganda device to emphasize the working-class character of the delegation. Nonetheless its hard core, consisting of Mikhail Tomsky,[45] a prominent member of the Politburo and president of the central council of the Russian trade unions, A. Sheinman, the head of the Soviet State Bank, Rakovsky, and occasionally Litvinov, was fully competent to confer.[46] Neither the immediate response of Labour members nor the counter-memorandum by the CPGB could cancel the hostility of public opinion towards the negotiations. Suggestions were even made by *The Times* that the Bankers' Memorandum be adopted by the Foreign Office and put before the Russians.[47]

The fact that the conference quickly surmounted its initial obstacles should be attributed largely to Ponsonby, who relieved MacDonald in the chair from the second session and gained complete control of the proceedings.[48] The mainspring of his handling of the negotiations was not so much the solution of problems at hand as his aim of pacifying the European community by the inclusion of Russia on an equal footing.[49] Unlike

44 F.O. 371 10513 N3386/3377/85: record of first plenary session of conference, 14 Apr. 1924.

45 A veteran Bolshevik and genuine worker, Tomsky was primarily concerned with trade unionism and only secondarily with party politics. His clash with Trotsky in 1920 over the militarization of labour associated him with the right wing of the party and resulted in his exile. His standing improved during the introduction of NEP and his support of Stalin won him a powerful position in the Politburo.

46 F.O. 371 10508 N2976/1357/85: Hodgson to MacDonald, 29 Mar. 1924.

47 *Daily Herald*, 15 Apr. 1924; *Workers' Weekly*, 18 Apr. 1924; *The Times*, 7 and 15 Apr. 1924.

48 Ponsonby himself was surprised: 'I did not expect to have the whole guidance of the business so much in my hands.' See Ponsonby's papers (Ponsonby), Diary, 17 Apr. 1924. Rakovsky's satisfaction with Ponsonby's appointment was registered in *Pravda*, 30 Apr. 1924.

49 For Ponsonby's views see *Parl. Deb. H.C.*, Vol. 175, col. 1919, 7 July 1924. See also L. M. Weir, *The Tragedy of Ramsay MacDonald* (London, 1938), p. 171, and Ponsonby in *The Times*, 24 Sept. 1924.

MacDonald, Ponsonby continued active collaboration with the Union of Democratic Control through Morel, its secretary, with whom he shared a suspicion of the 'box', referring to the Foreign Office, and a distrust of secret diplomacy. However, Ponsonby, a highly disciplined man, was not so susceptible to pressure from the left wing of the Labour Party in spite of his political allegiance; he criticized its 'childish and blind confidence in anything that Bolsheviks say do & want'.[50] As a result the 'lion's share' of the negotiations fell to Ponsonby, who on his own admission preferred to solve the major differences of opinions by the unorthodox method of direct informal conversations.[51] This technique was successful not least because of the 'special personal relations' which developed between Rakovsky and Ponsonby and were maintained throughout the most difficult stages of the conference.[52]

The Bankers' Memorandum had seriously reduced Narkomindel's hopes of coming to terms with the City. This meant that a clause on a loan, which remained the Russian condition for the compensation of private claims, would have to be inserted into the negotiated treaty.[53] The Russians, therefore, proposed to raise the crucial questions for immediate discussion and defer the rest to a later date, but the British insistence on dealing simultaneously with the entire range of issues committed the conference to protracted deliberations. The plenary session then broke up into four committees, which were entrusted with the settlement of all groups of claims, the drafting of a treaty of commerce and navigation, the review of the question of territorial waters, and the revision of treaties of arbitration.[54]

The Russian desire to reach an agreement by the end of May now led Rakovsky to seek an interview with MacDonald. However, this meeting ended in a fiasco when Rakovsky found to his dismay that MacDonald obstinately refused to discuss the loan and offered stiff and uncompromising terms. The only concession

50 Morel papers, F.8: Ponsonby to Morel, 19 Apr. and 30 Aug. 1924.

51 *Parl. Deb. H.C.*, Vol. 176, col. 3013, 6 Aug. 1924; Ponsonby papers (Bodleian): Chapman to Ponsonby, 11 Aug. 1924.

52 Ponsonby papers (Bodleian): two letters from Rakovsky to Ponsonby, 12 Nov. 1925 and 19 Mar. 1926.

53 *Mezhdunarodnaya Letopis'* (1925), No. 1, p. 35; *Pravda*, 30 Apr. 1924.

54 F.O. 371 10513 N3589 and 3678/3377/85: records of third and fourth sessions of conference, 16 and 24 Apr. 1924.

that MacDonald would make was the authorization of a news black-out, in view of the biased representation of Russia in the Press.[55] This decision, however, also signified that the conference had entered troubled waters.

The Russians' incessant pressure for straightforward discussion of the controversial problems finally yielded results when Ponsonby agreed to present an agenda of the issues which his Government was prepared to discuss. The agenda adhered to demands for full compensation of claims but ignored the Russian counter-claims, request for a loan, and desire to discuss political questions.[56] It immediately provoked Russian alarm about the future of the negotiations. In the plenary session of 15 May, which was 'brought up against realities', in the words of Ponsonby, Rakovsky raised the Russian reservations about the British agenda. On the complicated question of claims Rakovsky stated that the British ones were 'insolubly connected with the Russian counter-claims'. Private claims, he believed, could be 'partly satisfied' on a pragmatic basis worked out by the conference but not by a 'formula' which would involve a recognition of claims in principle.[57] In a subsequent conversation between Ponsonby and Rakovsky which turned on the question of claims, the two sides retained uncompromising positions. Of the four groups – personal injury claims, bondholders, private properties and state debts – the second emerged as the bone of contention. Ponsonby's insistence on full unconditional compensation was rejected by Rakovsky, who in turn suggested that a lump sum be fixed by the two Governments provided that Russia received an annual loan of £20 million for three years.[58]

55 F.O. 371 10516 N4294/4294/85: minute by W. Selby, Private Secretary to the Foreign Secretary, on MacDonald's conversation with Rakovsky, 9 May 1924. The agreement was announced in *The Times*, 13 May 1924.

56 On Russian pressure see F.O. 371 10516 N4157/4157/85: Rakovsky to MacDonald, 14 May 1924; F.O. 371 10514 N4295/3377/85: British agenda, 15 May 1924.

57 F.O. 371 10514 N4295/3377/85: record of fifth plenary session. Tomsky informed the General Council of the TUC of the fragile state of the conference late on 14 May. The GC in turn undertook to prevent a collapse of the negotiations; M. P. Thomsky, *Getting Together* (London, n.d.), pp. 20 ff.

58 P.R.O., Cabinet Office, Series 24, Vol. 167, Cab. paper 310, 19 May 1924. The British stubbornness over the bondholders' issue is perplexing.

However, the first cracks in the British position became apparent on the next day when Rakovsky repeated his statement that a satisfactory settlement was 'inconceivable' without the active intervention of the Government to raise a loan. Ponsonby reiterated his refusal to do so but, anxious to find a way out, pledged the Government's 'moral support' if Rakovsky directly approached the City for a loan. Although Rakovsky was highly sceptical of the outcome of such a move, he nevertheless accepted it but refused to acknowledge this form of assistance as 'finally determined'.[59] Rakovsky came out of the session confident that the conference would end successfully for Russia 'without heavy material sacrifices'.[60] His optimism was not unfounded. By stipulating the loan as a *sine qua non* he left open three possibilities for the British Government. To demand from the Russians a declaration of intent on the British agenda as it stood would risk a breakdown and create dissatisfaction in Labour circles. On the other hand, to conclude an agreement without securing a Russian commitment to compensation would set the majority of the House against the Government. Their only option, therefore, was to reconsider the question of a loan.

The Russians were determined to force the Government to make a decision one way or the other. When the conference reassembled on 27 May, they turned down the British proposal of the previous meeting for direct negotiations with the bondholders. Instead Rakovsky produced the official Russian counter-proposals, which called upon the conference to determine a lump sum to settle the claims of small bondholders and fix the amount of compensation to be paid to other groups. In fact this was a repetition of their initial postulation that a solution should be sought on a practical basis.[61]

The British showed no sign of surrender; in an attempt to widen the area of discussion forced on them by the Russians, they sent Rakovsky new and more rigid proposals, which were

Unlike France, where the vast number of *rentiers* represented a political lobby to be reckoned with, in Britain the lion's share was held by institutional investors who had marginal political and electoral influence; see Ullman, *The Anglo-Soviet Accord*, pp. 107–108.

59 F.O. 371 10513 N4375/3377/85: record of sixth plenary session, 20 May 1924.

60 *Dok. Vne. Pol.*, Vol. VII, p. 305: Rakovsky to Chicherin, 21 May 1924.

61 F.O. 371 10513 N4594/3377/85: record of seventh plenary session.

however described by Ponsonby as modelled on the Soviet plan and 'aimed to avoid the conflict of principles'. Rakovsky, who had thought that the points of controversy were limited to the form of British Government assistance and the arrangements for compensation of bondholders, was suddenly confronted with a demand for full compensation of not only the bondholders but also the property owners. Without hesitation he rejected the proposals, which he believed to be a 'complete change of attitude' and a return to the demands made at Genoa and The Hague.[62]

The Russian technique in the negotiation was becoming clear; stating fully their requirements, they refused to be dug out of their positions by accepting compromises, even if this brought the talks to the point of rupture. The ball was returned to Ponsonby's court when a meeting of the Russian delegation decided to stand firmly behind Rakovsky's rejection of the 'shocking' proposals.[63] A meeting with Rakovsky on 2 June finally convinced Ponsonby that the Russians were determined to walk out if a loan were not forthcoming. A day earlier Rakovsky had stated to the Press[64] that the conference was in a 'perilous state' and depended on the readiness of the British Government to provide credit. Now, in a disguised ultimatum, Rakovsky made the compensation of former owners of property in Russia also dependent on a grant of credit, and urged Ponsonby to discuss the question with MacDonald. In return Rakovsky was persuaded to open negotiations with the bondholders and 'explore in the City', although he suspected that the prospects of both were 'far from reassuring'.[65]

For the Russians the fulfilment of private owners' claims was by far more advantageous than the compensation of the bondholders. It was hoped that a settlement with the private owners would encourage the re-establishment of the major concessions, thereby attracting capital and skill to selected branches of

62 F.O. 371 10513 N4698/3377/85: British proposals and covering letter from Ponsonby to Rakovsky, 30 May 1924; Rakovsky's reply, 31 May 1924.

63 The meeting of the Soviet delegation is described in F. D. Volkov, *Anglo-Sovetskie Otnosheniya, 1924–1929gg.* (Moscow, 1958), p. 51.

64 *The Times*, 3 June 1924.

65 F.O. 800/227: minute by Ponsonby on conversation with Rakovsky.

industry.[66] This was now discernible in the attitude of the Soviet negotiators to the bondholders.

In the first meeting Rakovsky and Sheinman drew their attention to the fact that they had not yet received a penny of compensation. They were, therefore, advised to present reasonable demands, taking into account Russia's poverty, as reflected by a deficit of £40 million, rather than its potential wealth. On the failure of the bondholders to make an offer in the second meeting, Rakovsky proposed that the figure of £40 million, mentioned in the Board of Trade memorandum as the estimated value of the bonds, should serve as a basis for discussion. After a long and detailed description of economic hardship in Russia, he offered to pay 16% of the nominal value of the bonds, which was double their current value.[67] This was rejected by the bondholders' chairman in the third and last meeting as 'inadequate and unsatisfactory'. Rakovsky, who apparently had no intention of prolonging these talks, ended the meeting with an ultimatum: if the bondholders failed to formulate a claim within a week, he would refer the issue back to the conference.[68]

In the meantime, Ponsonby, aware of the critical state of affairs, had decided that unless the Prime Minister reversed the decision concerning a loan, he would submit his resignation. This, however, was averted when MacDonald suddenly displayed impatience about the course of the negotiations and appeared determined not to 'let June slip past'.[69] To break through the *impasse*, MacDonald made new approaches to Rakovsky and Litvinov, who arrived in London at this crucial stage of the negotiations. He promised to use his influence to help the Russians to raise a loan in the City, provided an agreement in

[66] Trotsky archives, T–827 and T–830: exchange of notes between Trotsky and Krasin in Politburo meeting of 12 July 1924. On Soviet concessions to British firms see E. H. Carr, *The Bolshevik Revolution, 1917–1923*, Vol. 3, pp. 432–33, and *Socialism in One Country, 1924–1926* (London, 1964), Vol. 3, pt 1, pp. 415–16.

[67] F.O. 371 10509 N5377 and N5378/1822/85: record of first and second meeting with the bondholders, 12 and 23 June 1924. See also L. Fischer, *The Soviets in World Affairs*, Vol. 2, p. 484.

[68] F.O. 371 10509 N5490/1822/85: memorandum on third meeting, 27 June 1924.

[69] Ponsonby papers (Ponsonby), Diary, 7 June 1924; MacDonald to Ponsonby, 9 June 1924.

principle was reached with the bondholders. The Russians, however, although 'impressed' by the concession, were resolved not to accept any solution short of a fully guaranteed Government loan. Rakovsky, moreover, had meanwhile found out that financial circles remained adamant in their refusal to allocate credit to Russia.[70] The Russian rejection of MacDonald's proposals was soon demonstrated by the speedy rupture of the negotiations with the bondholders and Litvinov's sudden departure for Berlin on 'doctor's orders'. From there he announced that the 'course and tempo' of the negotiations depended entirely on the British decision concerning a loan.[71]

By the beginning of July the Government position had been made still more uncomfortable by severe criticism of the conspiratorial character and the stagnation of the negotiations.[72] To prevent a collapse of the talks and Ponsonby's resignation, MacDonald agreed in principle to reconsider granting a loan.[73] Ponsonby was now confident that the breaking of the deadlock would ensure a successful conclusion of the negotiations. He told the House that the only business left for the conference was 'picking up various threads that had been dropped'; he hoped to present the treaty to Parliament before it adjourned for the summer recess.[74]

In a memorandum of 18 July Ponsonby informed the Cabinet that the success of the conference depended entirely on its readiness to provide Russia with a £30 million loan. Any other decision, he believed, was bound to jeopardize the negotiations and hamper the policy of conciliation in Europe, thereby causing resentment in Labour circles, both in Parliament and in the

70 F.O. 371 10517 N5223/5233/85: minute on interview between MacDonald, Litvinov and Rakovsky, 19 June 1924. The correspondence of Steel-Maitland, Minister of Labour 1924–29, with the signatories of the 'Bankers' Memorandum' at the beginning of August verifies that with the exception of the Midland Bank none had retreated an inch; Steel-Maitland papers, GD 193/339.

71 *Pravda*, 28 June 1924.

72 See for instance Steel-Maitland in *Parl. Deb. H.C.*, Vol. 175, cols. 1817–18, 7 July 1924.

73 S. Webb, 'The First Labour Government', *Political Quarterly* (Jan.–Mar. 1961), p. 25. See also a survey of the negotiations by Chicherin in *Dok. Vne. Pol.*, Vol. VII, p. 498.

74 *Parl. Deb. H.C.*, Vol. 175, col. 1916, 7 July 1924.

country. He failed, however, to convey the advice of the other British delegates for a break in the negotiations.[75]

The Cabinet's discussion of the memorandum was nevertheless delayed on technical grounds.[76] The main reason for the delay was, however, a strong objection to the proposal by the Treasury, which had been kept in the dark about the latest stages of the negotiations. A meeting which was hastily arranged between Philip Snowden, the Chancellor of the Exchequer, and Rakovsky was unproductive. Rakovsky was told that a loan could be considered only after full compensation of the bondholders and private property owners. Snowden then countered Ponsonby's memorandum with one of his own in which, for the first time during the conference, the Russian proposals were dealt with purely on their economic merits. It described the prospects of revival of trade and relief of unemployment as 'not in sight' and dismissed the Russians' 'wholly ridiculous counter-claims'.[77]

When the Cabinet finally discussed the two opposing points of view on 30 July, it also had before it the complete draft treaty.[78] Snowden's arguments lost much of their force when it was realized that his memorandum had been written before he had seen the draft treaty, in which the loan was made conditional on a satisfactory solution of private claims. Ponsonby's insistence on the political significance of the treaty won to his side the majority of the Cabinet. The Cabinet on the whole appeared to be unaware of the danger which the loan might present as an electoral issue; most of the meeting was spent in discussing other provisions of the treaty, notably that on propaganda.[79] The Cabinet insisted that the draft treaty should represent the limit of British concessions and directed Ponsonby to conclude an agreement before the House rose for the summer recess on 8 August.[80]

However, one of the disconcerting revelations during the Cabinet meeting was that the Russians had not seen the draft

[75] F.O. 371 10517 N6035/6035/85: Ponsonby's memorandum; F.O. 371 10500 N8099/7016/38: O'Malley's account of the negotiations, 19 Jan. 1925.

[76] Cab. 23/48 43(24)2, 22 July 1924.

[77] Cab. 24/168 C.P. 415, 28 July 1924.

[78] F.O. 371 10517 N6267/6267/85: draft treaty.

[79] Cab. 23/48 44(24)6, 30 July 1924.

[80] F.O. 371 10500 N8099/7016/38: O'Malley's account.

treaty and were only familiar with its general outline. Ponsonby's recommendations to Cabinet were based on Rakovsky's repeated assurances that the refusal of a loan was the main obstacle to the conclusion of a treaty. He concealed from the Cabinet the embarrassing situation caused by Rakovsky's disapproval of the proposed terms of the treaty, which he had described as 'a considerable step backwards'. After receiving news of the possibility of a Government loan, Rakovsky stressed the Russians' refusal to compensate the former owners of nationalized property in Russia.[81] To add to Ponsonby's difficulties, MacDonald had once more yielded to rebukes from the Palace and, without consulting Ponsonby, had made an ill-timed representation to Rakovsky of the 'feeling of resentment among all classes of His Majesty's subjects against the utterances of the Soviet leaders'.[82]

Rakovsky, whose presence in London was now vital for the conclusion of the treaty, left unexpectedly for Moscow for consultations with his Government. This move also seems to have been calculated to exert last-minute pressure on the vacillating British Government to yield to the Russians' latest demands.[83] Ponsonby hastened from the Cabinet meeting to dispatch the draft treaty to Moscow and, using his 'personal influence', pleaded with Rakovsky in a private telegram to urge the Soviet Government not to miss 'the most favourable moment which was likely to occur for years', and sign the treaty.[84] However, doubts were creeping into Ponsonby's mind whether mere *rapport* with Rakovsky would ensure the conclusion. He therefore resorted to an unconventional method of diplomacy and approached Morel and George Lansbury, representatives of the back-benchers, to use their influence with Rakovsky to induce him 'to do his utmost' to secure the signature.[85]

Meanwhile Ponsonby had accidentally found out that J. R. Clynes, the Labour Party's deputy leader, had put forward the last session of Parliament to 6 August, and without consulting him had arranged for Ponsonby's statement to be made on

81 F.O. 371 10519 N8313/6267/85: Rakovsky to Ponsonby, 22 July 1924.

82 F.O. 800/291: Lord Stamfordham, King's secretary, to MacDonald, 22 July 1924.

83 Volkov, *Anglo-Sovetskie Otnosheniya*, p. 65.

84 F.O. 371 10517 N6267/6207/85: Gregory and Ponsonby to Hodgson and a private telegram from Ponsonby to Rakovsky, 30 July 1924.

85 Morel papers, F.8: Ponsonby to Morel, 31 July 1924.

4 August. It was only by pleading with the Conservative Chief Whip that Ponsonby managed to obtain a postponement of one day. A quick agreement with the Russians was now essential.[86]

Rakovsky, who was unaware of the change in the schedule, returned to London as determined as before. He was convinced that the 'decisive week' of negotiations ahead would yield successful results only if the question of the property owners could be settled without sacrificing Russia's revolutionary principles. A serious clash at this stage was unavoidable; indeed, grave obstacles arose when the British draft of the proposed treaty was reviewed by Ponsonby and Rakovsky on 2 August, the day of the latter's return from Russia.[87]

The plenary session of 4 August sat continuously for an arduous twenty hours in a last attempt to iron out the differences. The British draft treaty which was submitted to the meeting was stiffer than earlier ones presented by Ponsonby and was aimed at balancing the Cabinet's decision to grant a loan.

The procedure adopted was first to review the articles which were uncontroversial. The British gave way to minor Russian objections, which were inevitable when dealing with a British draft. The examination of the contentious articles was soon limited to articles 13 and 14, which provided for the conclusion of a further treaty after the Soviet Government's satisfaction of bondholders' claims, an agreement on the amount and method of payment of a lump sum for miscellaneous claims, and the compensation of property owners. This second treaty was to embody a British undertaking to guarantee a loan.[88] As might have been expected, Rakovsky objected to the inclusion of nationalized property in the same category as other claims. For his part he proposed that a treaty be signed when the British Government was satisfied that 'substantial progress had been achieved' in the negotiations with the property owners. Moreover, Rakovsky opposed the wording of the articles and demanded the substitution of the term 'losses' for 'claims',

[86] Ponsonby papers (Ponsonby), Diary, 14 Aug. 1924.

[87] Interview in *Pravda*, 31 July 1924; Volkov, *Anglo-Sovetskie Otnosheniya*, p. 65.

[88] *Parl. Pap. 1924*, Cmd. 2253: 'Text of Draft of Proposed General Treaty between Great Britain and Northern Ireland and the Union of Socialist Republics, as it stood when negotiations were suspended on August 5, 1924'.

explaining unequivocally that a settlement with the owners was a matter of expediency and not of obligation. However, Ponsonby, inhibited by the Cabinet decision not to alter these articles, sprang to the defence of the property owners. Tomsky, therefore, in a not unexpected Russian move, declared that the future of the treaty was 'more than doubtful' unless the Russian amendments were accepted, and retired with Sheinman to an adjoining room, leaving Ponsonby and Rakovsky to negotiate.

When the full conference reassembled at 5 a.m., the British had capitulated; but the Russians, who were determined to fight on every line of the treaty, raised new objections of principle. Sheinman now wished the words 'valid claims' to be replaced by 'claims the justice of which had been agreed upon by both Governments'. He admitted that such a clause was 'far more binding upon the British Government than on the Soviet Government'. This time Ponsonby was unwilling to agree to an arrangement which he feared would establish the Russians' right to arbitrary dealings with the claimants. However, even at the eleventh hour, Rakovsky still managed to gain an advantage. The treaty was to be divided into three main sections which ensured that even in the event of failure to settle the claims the rest of the clauses would remain in force. With neither side willing to make immediate concessions, a deadlock was inevitable. Therefore Ponsonby closed the meeting at 7.15 a.m. on 5 August, overtly regretting his failure to conclude a treaty.[89] An announcement to the Cabinet to that effect was made by Snowden later in the morning.[90]

The breaking off of the negotiations was mainly brought about by the time limit set for this phase of the talks, as well as the exhaustion of the two sides after twenty hours of negotiations. Ponsonby was therefore enraged when he found on leaving the Foreign Office that he had one more precious day for negotiations, as Clynes had again without his knowledge postponed for a day his speech to the House. However, the back-benchers, who had already been alerted by the Russians on 4 August to the serious situation, came to Ponsonby's assistance 'very usefully

89 F.O. 371 10513 N6555/3377/85: record of eighth plenary session, 4–5 Aug. 1924. See also a rather humorous but revealing account of the meeting in O. O'Malley, *The Phantom Caravan* (London, 1954), p. 67.

90 Cab. 23/48, 47(24)20, 5 Aug. 1924.

although of course they were a little inclined to take credit for having done the whole thing'.[91]

On the morning of 5 August,[92] the Russians approached the parliamentary committee of the Labour Party, a body recently created to keep watch on the Government which included a large number of back-benchers,[93] with a request to arrange a platform for Rakovsky to explain the reasons for the failure of the negotiations. In turn, in the early afternoon the committee met Ponsonby, who gave his version of the rupture and complained of Russian obstructiveness during the meeting, which he suspected was a result of last-minute instructions from Moscow to sabotage the conference.[94] Rakovsky met the committee and other prominent Labour leaders again the same evening and made a strong impression with his argument that the demand for compensation of the property owners was a repudiation of Soviet laws of nationalization with which the Russians could not comply. Some of the delegates voiced strong indignation against the Government.[95] A deputation consisting of Morel, Lansbury, Purcell and

[91] Ponsonby papers (Ponsonby), Diary, 13 and 14 Aug. 1924. O'Malley, who would have been only too glad to support Morel's account that the Government had yielded to his pressure, nevertheless accepts Ponsonby's version: 'Mr. Morel will no doubt be anxious to attribute the change in the Russian attitude to his own superior diplomatic skill'; F.O. 371 10500 N8099/7016/38. MacDonald also claimed later that he took advantage of the back-benchers to induce Rakovsky to re-open negotiations; *The Nation*, 4 May 1929. On the 'Tory mythology' of the back-benchers' pressure see also H. R. Greaves, 'Complacency or Challenge?', *Political Quarterly* (Jan.–Mar. 1961), pp. 56–61.

[92] The following account of the events of 5 August is based on a ten-page secret memorandum by Morel; Morel papers, F.8. Edited versions are in *Forward*, 23 Aug. 1924, and *Foreign Affairs* (Sept. 1924), pp. 51–53.

[93] Lyman, *The First Labour Government*, pp. 232–33. That the Russians initiated this approach is evident from I. Radchenko, *Sovremennaya Angliya i Anglo-Sovetskii Dogover* (Ekaterinoslav, 1924), pp. 15–17; he was a member of the Soviet delegation.

[94] Ponsonby did not hold this point of view for long; the diary entry for 13 Aug. reads: 'Sheinman & Tomsky looked at times *as if* they wanted to wreck the whole thing.' This belief was shared by O'Malley in his memorandum on the negotiations and by J. D. Gregory in *On the Edge of Diplomacy* (London, 1928), p. 148.

[95] According to *Pravda*, 9 Aug. 1924, some expressed readiness to resign their seats in Parliament and fight by-elections entirely on the issue of the treaty.

R. C. Wallhead, chairman of the ILP, 1920–23, then presented Ponsonby with a new Russian formula which was very much a repetition of their proposals of the night before. Ponsonby now authorized them to inform Rakovsky that he saw 'more clearly' their differences of opinion, accepted their principle, and believed that the textual difficulties could be overcome. The deputation rushed back to the terrace of the House of Commons, by now in darkness, and striking a match Morel read Ponsonby's proposal to re-open the negotiations, in which Rakovsky acquiesced.

Early in the morning of 6 August, Ponsonby met his colleagues in the Foreign Office and after a short examination of Rakovsky's proposal rejected it. A new formula was devised and transmitted through Gregory to Rakovsky, who could not accept it but returned yet another. In the meantime, as 'the sand was running out', Chapman had drafted another formula, which Ponsonby liked the best. He therefore hurried to Downing Street to obtain the Prime Minister's approval of it. There he met Snowden who, after a moment of hesitation, agreed to support the new formula 'as a mere face-saving device' to preserve the conference from complete collapse.[96] MacDonald, however, was busy discussing holidays with his daughter and Ponsonby, whose 'mutton and apple tart almost stuck' in his throat, had to waste precious minutes before he received the Prime Minister's approval of the new formula. Two hours before the House was due to meet Ponsonby left Downing Street and wisely decided to send the back-benchers instead of Foreign Office officials to Rakovsky. The formula, which finally became article 11 of the signed treaty, still insisted on 'an agreed settlement of property claims other than those directly settled by the Government of the Soviet Socialist Republics',[97] and the Russians were once more inclined to turn it down.[98] However, this time, under considerable pressure from the deputation, which was convinced of the conciliatory nature of the formula and impatient with the Russian obstinacy, the Russians gave way. A short plenary session ensued, in which

96 On his reaction to the formula see P. Snowden, *An Autobiography* (London, 1937), Vol. I, pp. 680–86.

97 *Parl. Pap. 1924*, Cmd. 2260: 'General Treaty between Great Britain and Northern Ireland and the Union of Soviet Socialist Republics.'

98 Ponsonby papers (Ponsonby), Diary, 14 Aug. 1924.

Ponsonby was formally notified of the Russian acceptance of the proposed article and readiness to sign the treaty.[99]

When Ponsonby finally rose to speak in Parliament, he 'cut a very sorry figure', in his own words. He had had only one interrupted hour to prepare his speech and, fatigued by the events of the last two days, was unable to explain the treaty to the House, which did not have the draft in front of it. McNeill, who spoke for the Opposition, exploited the confusion of the last stages of the conference and launched into an onslaught on Bolshevism, ending with an unprecedented demand that the Government withhold its signature of the treaty. Indeed, the next morning Ponsonby found Clynes and MacDonald, who was never an advocate of the treaty and was susceptible to Conservative pressure, toying with the idea of not signing. After persuasion by Ponsonby, MacDonald reluctantly took the floor and announced his intention of signing the treaty, while detracting from the significance of the signature, which would do no more than confirm the text agreement as long as Parliament had not ratified it.[100]

The treaty was punctually signed on 8 August, but MacDonald reminded the Russians that its full conclusion depended on Parliament's approval. He promised, nonetheless, that the Government would 'do its best' to carry through ratification but dwelt on the considerable opposition that was building up against the treaty. Rakovsky replied on the same lines, promising to do his utmost to secure Russian ratification. A further meeting took place on 12 August, in which Rakovsky declared Soviet policies regarding outstanding European problems; he and Ponsonby exchanged speeches expressing satisfaction at the outcome of the negotiations.[101]

Rakovsky, who wished to extract the maximum advantage from the conclusion of the talks, reminded MacDonald that a decision on the exchange of ambassadors had been put off pending the conclusion of a treaty.[102] O'Grady, who had been men-

[99] Morel papers, F.8, the secret memorandum; F.O. 371 10513 N6556/3377/85: record of ninth plenary session.

[100] *Parl. Deb. H.C.*, Vol. 176, Ponsonby, cols. 3012–19; MacDonald, col. 3136, 7 Aug. 1924. Ponsonby papers (Ponsonby), Diary, 14 Aug. 1924.

[101] F.O. 371 10513 N6557 and N6447/3377/85.

[102] F.O. 371 10495 N6622/2140/38: Rakovsky to MacDonald, 12 Aug. 1924.

tioned as the likely candidate for the post, also wasted no time in proposing himself for the appointment, believing that this would help 'to establish friendly relations between the peoples of the two countries'.[103] However, an earlier allegation from Hodgson in Moscow that spying on the delegation and conditions in general were intolerable provided the excuse for further delay.[104] MacDonald seized the opportunity to draft a very stiff letter to Rakovsky on 27 September, based on the Foreign Office's advice that the exchange should be delayed until the treaty had been ratified. Ponsonby, who had not been consulted about the draft, registered a strong protest with MacDonald, who eventually substituted a milder one. Rakovsky was informed that the maltreatment of the British delegation made it impossible for MacDonald to send an ambassador to Russia.[105] This was an unconvincing reason, for Hodgson had already written from Moscow that Chicherin had personally intervened to relieve the pressure on the mission.[106]

The treaty, which only provided for a further treaty which would secure a loan, was evaluated by Narkomindel as a final touch to recognition and a triumph for Soviet diplomacy of peaceful co-existence of different social systems.[107] It was justified as the only course open to 'Red diplomacy' as long as the capitalist encirclement persisted. However, among the cheers with which the treaty was welcomed, there was moderate criticism of its content. Radek drew attention to the fact that the British Government was willing to grant the credit only if Russia compensated the claimants for its 'crimes of history, for losses caused by the revolution'.[108] Even Rakovsky refused to accept the treaty as a victory and referred to it as a compromise which might lead to a successful conclusion once the second phase of negotiation

103 MacDonald papers, 30/69 1/2: O'Grady to MacDonald, 6 Aug. 1924.

104 F.O. 371 10495 N5948/2140/38: Hodgson to MacDonald, 15 July 1924.

105 F.O. 371 10495 N6622/2140/38: minutes by MacDonald, 14 and 30 Aug. 1924, and Ponsonby, 2 Sept. 1924; MacDonald to Rakovsky, 27 Sept. 1924.

106 F.O. 371 10495 N7216/2140/38: 29 Aug. 1924.

107 *Dok. Vne. Pol.*, Vol. VII, pp. 414–15: Narkomindel's announcement of the conclusion of the treaty, 10 Aug. 1924.

108 Leader in *Pravda*, 12 Aug. 1924; Radek in *ibid.*, 10 Aug. 1924.

was under way. This, he predicted, could be expected by November.[109]

A prolonged discussion on the 'substance and value' of the treaty in the plenum of the central committee of the CPSU ended with the decision to put off the question of ratification.[110] The Russians preferred to wait upon events which at this stage were beyond their control. However, a plenary session of the Moscow Soviet which assembled immediately after the plenum proved 'wildly enthusiastic for the treaty'. Kamenev, its president and a member of the ruling triumvirate, described it as 'a cornerstone in the development of the Soviet Union'. Unlike Rakovsky, Chicherin announced that even if ratification failed to materialize, the treaty was 'an international recognition of the October Revolution as a basis for a state structure'.[111]

The ratification of the treaty, and with it the future of the Government, depended largely on the tacit support of the Liberals. Their initial support had been forthcoming in the expectation that after Labour had demonstrated its incompetence to rule, the Liberals would be called upon to form a Cabinet. By the summer it had become clear that Labour was not only firmly in the saddle but disdainful of its allies, unwilling to admit the Liberals' share in its success. In view of this, the continuing support of the minority Government threatened the entity of a party already suffering from disunity.[112]

The conclusion of the treaty was seized upon by the Liberals as an appropriate issue for confrontation with the Government. Convinced that the time was ripe for 'throwing the Government out' Lloyd George rejected the treaty in Parliament as 'a fake', a contract in which a 'space for every essential figure [was] left blank'. Lloyd George's opposition carried particular significance

109 Rakosky interviewed in *Trud*, 11 Aug., and in *Pravda*, 19 Aug. 1924.

110 *Pravda*, 23 Aug. 1924.

111 Ponsonby papers (Bodleian): Susan Lawrence, a Labour back-bencher then on a visit to Russia, to Ponsonby on the mood of the session, Aug. 1924. For Rakovsky and Chicherin see *Pravda*, 29 Aug. 1924.

112 T. Wilson, *The Downfall of the Liberal Party, 1914–35* (London, 1966), pp. 280–98; B. Crisp, 'The Russian Treaty and the Liberals', *Foreign Affairs* (Oct. 1924), pp. 78–79. See also H. Wish, 'Anglo-Soviet Relations during Labour's First Ministry', *Slav. and East Eur. Rev.* (June 1939), Vol. XVII, pp. 389–403.

owing to MacDonald's insistence that only a vote of no confidence would prevent him from signing the treaty.[113]

MacDonald, discounting the signs of change of heart among the Liberals, was confident in his ability to 'face the House of Commons in a fighting spirit and defy them to turn it down'. In order to hasten ratification of the treaty, which the Government accepted as an integral part of its policy, it was decided to raise it for discussion when Parliament was recalled on 30 September to deal with the Irish boundary dispute.[114] In mid-September, Ponsonby was still 'entertained by cross currents in the Liberal Party' and convinced that Lloyd George had 'overdone it'. He predicted that the Liberals would neither seek elections, in which they surely 'would be split finally and irretrievably', nor reject the treaty, which was 'an unprecedented and most serious step to take'.[115]

Ponsonby's confidence, however, was mistaken. Ironically Lloyd George, the architect of the 1921 agreement, now fervently sought to rally all prominent Liberal leaders against the treaty. In doing so, he encountered little opposition; an open letter by Asquith made clear that the majority was finally converted to Lloyd George's point of view on the understanding that criticism should be limited to the loan.[116] However, the closing of ranks in the party hampered any agreement with the Conservatives, who were reluctant to oust the Government on a motion confined to the loan. Their objections were to the treaty as an entity. Nevertheless, wishing to exploit the widening rift between the Government and the Liberals, they left the door open for collaboration on a different issue.[117]

The occasion arose when Hastings, the Attorney-General, decided to drop proceedings under the Incitement to Mutiny Act against J. R. Campbell, a temporary editor of the communist

[113] *Parl. Deb. H.C.*, Vol. 176, cols. 3034 and 3136, 6 and 7 Aug. 1924.

[114] MacDonald papers, 30/69 1/2: MacDonald to Ponsonby, 13 Aug. 1924; Morel papers, F.8: Ponsonby to Morel, 28 Aug. and 6 Sept. 1924.

[115] MacDonald papers, 30/69 5/130: Ponsonby to MacDonald, 14 Sept. 1924: similar views in leader of *Daily Herald*, 10 Sept. 1924.

[116] Asquith in *The Times*, 22 Sept. 1924. See also Lloyd George and Grey in *ibid.*, 16 and 19 Sept. 1924.

[117] Churchill papers, 2/135: exchange of letters between Churchill and Horne, 2 and 30 Oct. 1924.

Workers' Weekly.[118] When Parliament was recalled on 30 September, MacDonald was accused of persuading the Attorney-General to withdraw the prosecution under pressure from his own left wing.[119] When Parliament met again on 8 October, the Conservatives, who had originally intended to table a vote of censure, decided to back a Liberal demand for a Select Committee of Inquiry. MacDonald, who chose to treat this as an issue of confidence, was defeated by the combined forces of the opposing parties. General elections were fixed for 29 October. Despite MacDonald's decision to go to the country over the Campbell affair, the underlying consideration seems to have been a reluctance to fight for the treaty after the Liberals' defection, reinforced by the rather fatalistic feeling frequently expressed in Cabinet that the Labour Government was a passing episode which could not last for long.[120]

Russia's satisfaction at the conclusion of the treaty soon gave way to a more cautious attitude. Unlike Ponsonby, they realized the precarious position of the treaty and the Labour Government as a whole. Mistrust of MacDonald gave rise to speculations in Narkomindel that he would either be overruled by the Foreign Office or seek to compromise the treaty in order to remain in power.[121] The Russians' stiffening attitude in preparation for the Parliamentary debate on the treaty was expounded by Kamenev, who dismissed suggestions that the future of the agreement was at the mercy of the British. The Russian Press underlined the 'heavy obligation' which the treaty imposed on Russia and advised the legal organs to study it 'most attentively' before ratification.[122] When the unexpected dissolution of Parliament took place without even mentioning the question of the treaty, the Russians returned to a 'wait and see' position. Although the central executive committee of the Soviets was clearly in favour

118 Campbell appealed to soldiers used for strike-breaking to disobey orders in *Workers' Weekly*, 25 July 1924.

119 *Parl. Deb. H.C.*, Vol. 177, cols. 8–10; interview with MacDonald in *Daily Herald*, 7 Oct. 1924. See also an account of the Campbell affair in P. Hastings, *Autobiography* (London, 1948), pp. 238–40.

120 *Parl. Deb. H.C.*, Vol. 177, cols. 619–23; Webb, 'The First Labour Government', p. 34.

121 Chicherin under pseudonym of M. Sharonov in *Pravda*, 27 Sept. 1924.

122 L. Kamenev, *Anglo-Sovetskii Dogovor* (Leningrad, 1924), p. 39; leader in *Pravda*, 25 Sept. 1924.

of ratification in spite of regarding it as the 'limit of concessions', it delayed the act by referring it to the presidium.[123]

The 'Zinoviev letter'

MacDonald had hoped to fight the elections on a minor judicial issue rather than the Anglo-Soviet Treaty, which might imply not only open support of Russia but also Labour's association with communism. These hopes were dashed when seditious instructions to the CPGB, allegedly emanating from Comintern, were published in the Press on 25 October at the height of the election campaign. Although suggestions have been made that the strain of the exhausting election campaign was mainly responsible for MacDonald's mishandling of the affair,[124] it seems that his growing dissatisfaction at the pattern of relations with Russia played no less a role. Recognition had marked the high point in MacDonald's acceptance of Russia, but this soon gave way to obstruction of the Anglo-Soviet negotiations. His hostility became particularly acute as a response to allegations that the treaty, of which he expressed disapproval in private,[125] was signed under the pressure of back-benchers manipulated by Moscow. This attitude became overt in September in connection with the Campbell affair and was apparent in the severe draft Note in Rakovsky of 27 September.

Copies of the instructions, purportedly sent by Grigori Zinoviev[126] to the central committee of the CPGB, were handed directly to Crowe and Gregory, as well as to four other Ministries, on 9 October by the Special Intelligence Service, which regarded the authenticity of the document as 'undoubted'.[127] The greater part of the letter called upon the CPGB to secure the ratification of the Anglo-Soviet Treaty and to press for the regulation of

123 *Pravda*, 21 Dec. 1924.

124 See for example H. Pelling, 'Governing without Power', *Political Quarterly* (Jan.–Mar. 1961), p. 51; Snowden, *An Autobiography*, p. 708; Gregory, *On the Edge of Diplomacy*, pp. 221–24.

125 Ponsonby papers (Ponsonby), Diary, 21 Apr. 1925.

126 Zinoviev was the President of Comintern and a member of the ruling triumvirate in the Politburo.

127 F.O. 371 10478 N7838/108/38: Special Intelligence Service to the Foreign Office, 9 Oct. 1924; F.O. 371 10478 N8105/108/38: Crowe to MacDonald, 26 Oct. 1924.

relations between the two countries. It was, however, the seditious latter part of the letter which made it remarkable. In it the Military Section of the CPGB was instructed to form cells in the Army which 'might be, in the event of an outbreak of active strife, the brain of the military organisation of the Party'.[128]

At the Northern Department, the letter was first examined by William Strang, a junior but perceptive official to whom it did not seem to be 'out of the ordinary run of these things'. He was about to pass on a short minute when, learning from Sir Neville Bland, Crowe's secretary, that the Permanent Under-Secretary attached extraordinary importance to the letter and favoured its publication, he substituted a long and detailed minute. The two questions confronting the Office were those of publication of the letter and remonstrations to Moscow. However, before presenting his suggestions, Strang issued the following warning: 'Anglo-Soviet relations are unfortunately an issue in domestic politics in this country and this fact on occasion – of which the present is one – renders it difficult for the department to advise.' Although he believed the letter to be authentic, Strang opposed publication on the grounds that it would only embarrass the Labour Government, as well as that part of the Soviet Government which was anxious for the normalization of Anglo-Soviet relations.[129] In spite of fresh evidence that the letter was genuine and that it had been received and discussed by the central committee of the CPGB, Gregory also doubted the wisdom of publication. Crowe, however, was adamant that the 'Russian machinations' should for once be exposed; it was the duty of the Government to inform the Soviet Government of breaches in the propaganda clauses of the 1921 trade agreement.[130]

The Red Box of Foreign Office documents which contained the Zinoviev letter found MacDonald in Manchester, during his absence from London on an extensive campaigning tour. On the morning of 16 October, before setting off for Birmingham, he composed a short minute adopting Crowe's proposals but warn-

[128] F.O. 371 10478 N7838/108/38: copy of a letter from Zinoviev to central committee of CPGB, 15 Sept. 1924.

[129] *ibid.*: minute by Strang, 10 Oct. 1924, which shows signs of the suppressed minute; see also W. Strang, *Home and Abroad* (London, 1956), p. 56.

[130] F.O. 371 10478 N7838/108/38: minutes by Crowe, 13 and 14 Oct. 1924, and Gregory, 13 Oct. 1924.

ing that a dispatch to Rakovsky would only be damaging unless the authenticity of the letter were established and the accusations well-founded.[131] Crowe, however, utterly convinced of authenticity, troubled neither to reconsider the matter nor to consult Ponsonby, who was responsible for Russian affairs. Nor did he consult Parmoor, who as Lord President of the Council dealt with foreign affairs in the House of Lords.[132]

On receiving the minutes from MacDonald on Friday, 17 October, Crowe instructed Gregory to prepare a draft Note of protest to Rakovsky, before retiring to bed for the week-end on doctor's orders. Returning to the Office on Monday, he extensively altered the draft Note and then sent it to Port Talbot, where MacDonald was speaking, suggesting that the Note and letter be published as soon as they had reached Rakovsky.[133] MacDonald, however, was not free to examine the draft until the early hours of 23 October. He then not only considered its dispatch but in fact redrafted parts of it which did not appear to him 'to be strong enough or pointed enough to meet the circumstances'.[134] On the other hand, having decided not to protest in earlier incidents of the same nature, MacDonald acted indecisively, approving the Foreign Office's policy in principle but delaying a final solution. He therefore did not initial the draft, which would thus have been authorized for dispatch. Instead the Foreign Office was requested to verify once again the authenticity of the letter and send him back a 'final form'.[135] On receiving the heavily corrected draft Note and directive on 24 October, Crowe, with Gregory and two other officials, overlooking the

131 MacDonald's account of the events in *The Times*, 27 Oct. 1924, and in *Parl. Deb. H.C.*, Vol. 215, cols. 47–51, 19 Mar. 1928.

132 Ponsonby papers (Bodleian), Crowe's secretary to Ponsonby, 28 Oct. 1924; Gregory to Ponsonby, 29 Oct. 1924. See also Parmoor, *A Retrospect*, p. 187.

133 F.O. 371 10478 N8105/108/38: Crowe to MacDonald, 25 and 26 Oct. 1924.

134 *Parl. Deb. H.C.*, Vol. 215, cols. 49–51, 19 Mar. 1928. Strang, *Home and Abroad*, p. 56, also mentions that MacDonald's corrected draft was 'in some respects stronger than Crowe's'.

135 This final draft and MacDonald's instructions have been removed from the Foreign Office's files, apparently unintentionally by 'weeders' in the early 50s. Chamberlain admitted that MacDonald had not sanctioned the dispatch of the Note; *Parl. Deb. H.C.*, Vol. 179, col. 673, 15 Dec. 1924.

absence of the initials on the draft and ignoring the specific instructions, decided to publish the letter and dispatch the protest Note with no further delay.[136]

The determination and haste of the Foreign Office in dispatching the Note, in contrast with their earlier leisurely handling of the letter, gave rise to accusations that they were acting deliberately to undermine the Labour Government. This was reinforced in 1928 when Gregory was implicated in a currency speculation case and new evidence seemed to support earlier rumours that he had an interest in the handling of the letter.[137] However, a Board of Inquiry established that Gregory's speculations had no connection whatever with the letter, and was satisfied that responsibility for the decision lay solely with Crowe. The board members did not go into questions of the motives which had brought about the publication of the letter. They merely expressed their confidence that Crowe had 'never anticipated the political consequences which in fact followed'.[138] It seems most likely, however, that Crowe's decision was dictated by the realization that the Press had a copy of the Zinoviev letter and that its contents 'would before long become generally known'. Crowe's main concern was to protect the Office from accusations of suppressing the information, while too little consideration was given to the political consequences. He was convinced that there was 'nothing to gain and something to lose' by delaying the Foreign Office's publication any further.[139]

It appears therefore that both MacDonald and Crowe are to be blamed in the different stages of dealing with the letter. Crowe, conscious of misjudging MacDonald's intentions, went to great pains to vindicate his handling of the affair and strengthen the evidence for authenticity. In a letter to Haldane, the Lord Chancellor, written the day after Labour left office, Crowe in-

136 *Parl. Pap., 1928*, Cmd. 3037: 'Report of the Board of Inquiry Appointed by the Prime Minister to Investigate Certain Statements Affecting Civil Servants', p. 217.

137 *Parl. Deb. H.C.*, Vol. 215, cols. 95–100: Thomas, 19 Mar. 1928.

138 *Parl. Pap. 1928*, Cmd. 3037, pp. 14–18. See also Ponsonby's papers (Bodleian): Gregory to Ponsonby, 29 Oct. 1924.

139 F.O. 371 10478 N8105/108/38: Crowe to MacDonald, 25 Oct. 1924. Marlow, the editor of the *Daily Mail*, claimed in the *Observer*, 4 Mar. 1928, that the Foreign Office 'had been forced' to publish the letter after he had informed it of his possession of a copy.

formed him with relief of fresh material which he believed proved beyond all doubt that a Politburo meeting had discussed the letter and the embarrassment that Zinoviev's activities caused to Chicherin.[140] But even Sir Wyndham Childs, the head of the Special Branch, who had communicated the information to Sir William Joynson-Hicks, the Home Secretary between 1924 and 1929, had reservations about the source of the information.[141] MacDonald always maintained that publication was the result of an 'error of judgement' by the Foreign Office officials, but significantly opposed an inquiry into the conduct of the civil servants.[142] Although MacDonald was 'staggered' when he learnt about the publication from a correspondent of the *Daily News*, he showed little intention of putting matters to rights.[143] Concerned rather with the prestige of the Government, he decided 'to handle gingerly' in order to demonstrate that the Government was 'not in Russian pocket'.[144] Understandably, both Crowe and MacDonald preferred to hush up the whole affair after the elections, once the Conservatives had agreed to do so.[145]

MacDonald's inconsistency and the liberty taken by Crowe are highlighted by the existence of other 'Zinoviev letters' in the Foreign Office files for 1924. It should be borne in mind that neither Strang nor Gregory was struck by the letter as being out of the ordinary.[146]

A copy of the first 'Zinoviev letter' was transmitted to the Home Office by the Special Branch and sent to the Foreign

140 Haldane papers, B 5916: 8 Nov. 1924; F.O. 371 10480 N9322/108/22: information received from the Intelligence Service, and submitted as memorandum to Cabinet, 21 Dec. 1924.

141 P.R.O., Home Office Series 45, file 13798, paper 52000/1, 8 Nov. 1924.

142 K. Middlemas (ed.), *Thomas Jones, Whitehall Diary* (Oxford, 1969), Vol. 1, p. 301; *The Times*, 5 Mar. 1928.

143 MacDonald papers, 30/69 5/126: account by Rosenberg, MacDonald's private secretary.

144 Ponsonby papers (Ponsonby): telegram from Rosenberg to Ponsonby, 25 Oct. 1924.

145 Haldane papers, B 5516: Crowe to Haldane, 14 Nov. 1924.

146 The account of the affair in Gregory, *On the Edge of Diplomacy*, pp. 216–17, supports this view: 'Why this particular rag should have been considered such a singularly tasty morsel I have never to this day been able to explain to myself. People could at any time have had a meal off Zinovieff letters.' Similar views are in W. Childs, *Episodes and Reflections* (London, 1930), pp. 246–48.

Office by the Home Office on 3 May. The letter, dated 7 April and allegedly addressed to the central committee of the CPGB and signed by Zinoviev, carried instructions to the Party to organize mass demonstrations on 1 May, which would 'assist the success of the work of the Soviet Delegation in England, but . . . also be a powerful step forward on the road of the development of the revolutionary movement in Great Britain'. In the event of an interruption in the course of the Anglo-Soviet negotiations, the Party was called upon to 'take all measures in order to call the wide working masses into the street'. Tomsky was named as the custodian of money allocated by Comintern for this purpose. The Home Office proposed that a demand for an explanation should be addressed to Rakovsky. Although none of the officials in the Northern Department were divided as to the authenticity of this letter they unanimously advised against any representations to Moscow. H. F. B. Maxse, an ex-naval officer who had been with the Northern Department since its formation in 1920, noted that the policy of the Government was not to create any 'unnecessary incidents' but rather to refrain from taking any action as long as they could. It was also suggested that representations could be made only about facts 'capable of clear proof and not on instructions to or intentions of Soviet agents secretly gleaned from documents'. Crowe also believed that agitation had to be caught '*in flagrante delicto*' before any steps could be taken against the Soviet Government. MacDonald summed up the discussion in a clear-cut directive: 'Unless and until we have evidence of *acts* we must wait and be watchful.' A reply along these lines was sent to the Home Office.[147]

The Home Office continued to exert pressure on the Foreign Office. Two weeks later, in connection with a Parliamentary Question concerning allegations of propaganda carried out by members of the Russian delegation to the Anglo-Russian conference, Arthur Henderson, the Home Secretary, passed to MacDonald the copy of another letter addressed to the central committee of the CPGB and signed 'Zinoviev'. The letter, dated 17 March, informed the CPGB that Tomsky was empowered by IKKI to deal with all questions concerning the Party during the

[147] F.O. 371 10478 N3844/108/38: Anderson, Home Office, to Ponsonby, 3 May 1924; minutes by Crowe and MacDonald, 6 May 1924; letter from Ponsonby to Anderson, 6 May 1924.

stay of the Soviet delegation in London. The letter also suggested that the visit of the delegation to Britain would help to revolutionize the British working class. Despite assurances from Scotland Yard and the Foreign Office Intelligence that the letter was genuine, MacDonald remained faithful to his previous decisions and shelved the file.[148]

The Foreign Office's disregard of the other letters when the notorious letter was discussed is particularly puzzling in view of the striking similarity between the documents. In fact it seems more than likely that all three letters emanated from the same source. The letters are similar both in style and content; most of the textual errors which suggest that the notorious letter was forged occur consistently in all the letters.[149] The conceptual consistency of the letters and their deep familiarity with Soviet politics suggests that their authors were in fact Russians who managed to unite plausibility with 'a tissue of absurdities'.[150] This combination of truth and falsehood made the letters appear genuine to the officials in the Foreign Office, who were not directly acquainted with Russian communist publications. The letter was widely accepted as genuine precisely because of a general belief that its substance was similar to Zinoviev's pronouncements throughout 1924.[151]

All three letters dealt with issues likely to compromise the Labour Government with regard to its Soviet policy. The first two clearly suggested that the Soviet delegation to the conference was carrying out subversive activities and spreading propaganda during its stay in Britain. All three implied that the delegation was working on strict orders from Comintern and interfering in

[148] P.R.O. Premier papers, Series 1, paper 49: Hurwood, Police Commissioner, to Henderson, 16 May 1924; Henderson to MacDonald, 19 May 1924.

[149] These consist mainly of the heading of the letters, 'Executive Committee, Third Communist International', instead of the formally used 'Communist International', and the initials IKKI and SSSR instead of the transliterations ECCI and USSR commonly used by the Russians.

[150] Ponsonby papers (Ponsonby): Rakovsky to Ponsonby, 25 Oct. 1924.

[151] *Parl. Deb. H.C.*, Vol. 179, col. 309: Joynson-Hicks, 10 Dec. 1924; the leader in *The Times*, 25 Oct. 1924, was typical: 'The substance of the instructions here given to the Communist Party is contained in hundreds of speeches, articles and leaflets published in Moscow and Petrograd during the last few years.'

British domestic affairs. The first letter, written shortly before the arrival of the delegation, instructed the Party to 'ensure free communication between the delegation and all revolutionary labour organizations for mutual informational assistance'. The second, during the course of the negotiations, encouraged demonstrations of sympathy towards Russia on 1 May, which would 'be useful in the sense of exerting a certain amount of pressure upon the Government'. The last letter, analysing the conclusion of the negotiations, stated that it was the 'weighty word' of the proletariat which had 'compelled the Government' to conclude the treaty. The letter also contained directives calling upon supporters of the labour movement to 'bring increased pressure to bear upon the Government' in favour of ratification.

The strikingly incongruous element in the letters is the idea that a successful conclusion of the Anglo-Soviet Treaty would revolutionize the British working class. The first letter described the arrival of the delegation as an event 'hastening the liberation of the British proletariat from the yoke of capitalist powers and the guardianship of pseudo-socialists'. The next letter stated that the 1 May demonstration in favour of the treaty would be 'a powerful step forward on the road of a development of the revolutionary movement in Great Britain'. The third one faithfully echoed this intriguing position: a settlement of Anglo-Soviet relations would 'assist in the revolutionizing of the international and British proletariat not less than a successful rising in any of the working districts of England'. Yet nowhere in the resolutions of Comintern, in its instructions to the CPGB or even in the numerous publications of the CPGB, do we find any desire that the issue of the treaty should generate any such revolutionary activity.

However, it is the seditious part of the 'Zinoviev letter' which casts most doubt on Comintern's authorship. While the fifth congress of Comintern stressed that the urgent task of the CPGB was to become a mass party through intensive work in the trade unions, no emphasis was laid on adventurist or military activities.[152] Only one vague reference to activities in the armed forces was included in one of the resolutions of the fourth congress of

152 *Pyatyi Vsemirnyi Kongress Kommunisticheskogo Internatsionala, Stenograficheskii Otchet* (Moscow, 1925), Vol. II, p. 81 (hereafter referred to as *Pyatyi Vsemirnyi Kongress*).

Profintern, calling upon its members to consolidate their connections with trade unionists in uniform with a view to preventing black-legging in industrial disputes.[153]

The actual instructions issued by IKKI to the CPGB on 10 October for their election campaign differed in character and substance from those in the 'Zinoviev letters'. The covering letter from O. W. Kuusinen, the secretary of IKKI, concerned itself with more modest targets, like the publishing of a daily paper, which he thought would demand the 'greatest efforts' from the Party and 'self-sacrifice' from working-class sympathizers. The instructions aimed at securing the full support of the Party for Labour candidates in the elections. The election slogans contained only one innocuous reference to the political rights of soldiers and military intervention in industrial disputes. The instructions and Kuusinen's letter do not display any of the textual peculiarities of the three letters.[154] The CPGB's election manifesto followed this line rather than the instructions of the 'Zinoviev letter'. Its main aim was to 'return a Labour majority in the election as a challenge to the capitalist class'.[155] The trade union delegation to Russia in autumn 1924 was permitted a thorough examination of Comintern's archives; it reached the conclusion that IKKI's correspondence with the CPGB was different in nature from the 'Zinoviev letter'.[156]

Accumulating evidence has illuminated to a great degree the controversy over the authenticity of the letter, despite the absence of a clear-cut proof.[157] The existence of two other 'Zinoviev letters' in the archives further supports the theory that the notorious letter was indeed a forgery. This theory is challenged by the suggestion that the letter was genuine and deliberately placed with the British Intelligence with a view to 'bringing about the fall of MacDonald'.[158] However, in spite of the great

[153] *Desyat' Let Profinterna v Rezolyutsiyakh* (Moscow, 1930), p. 140.

[154] *Parl. Pap. 1926*, Cmd. 2682, 'Communist Papers Seized during the Arrest of the Communist Leaders on 14 and 21 October, 1925', pp. 48–50.

[155] *Workers' Weekly*, 17 Oct. 1924.

[156] *The 'Zinoviev' Letter, Report of Investigation by British Delegation in Russia for the Trade Union Congress General Council, Nov.-Dec. 1924* (London, 1925).

[157] C. L. Mowat, *Great Britain since 1914* (London, 1971), pp. 199–212.

[158] N. Grant, 'The "Zinoviev Letter" Case', *Soviet Studies*, Vol. XIX (1967), pp. 264–81.

animosity displayed by Comintern towards MacDonald as leading spirit of the Second International, the CPGB was clearly called upon to back Labour in the election campaign. This theory also falls short by dating too early the struggle for power between Comintern, controlled by Zinoviev, and the CPSU, headed by Stalin, as well as by its wrong assumption that the letter was a *précis* of the resolutions of the fifth congress of Comintern.[159]

Zinoviev's strenuous denials of responsibility for the letter were ignored in the heat of the election campaign. Zinoviev's first reaction to the British Note was a telegram to the General Council of the TUC in which he dismissed the letter as a 'gross falsification'; 'there was not and could not be any such letter'.[160] In his address to the sixth congress of trade unions in Moscow in November Zinoviev expressed concern over the threat facing Russia as a result of the change of government in Britain. He held that the forged letter was exploited to secure a Conservative victory.[161]

The most comprehensive study of the 'Zinoviev letter' affair was prompted by a sensational disclosure by a Mrs Bellegarde that she had witnessed the forgery of the 'Zinoviev letter' by her husband and a group of White Russian *émigrés* in Berlin.[162] This work, written by the three journalists who had brought forward Bellegarde's evidence, collates all the material which has accumulated since the affair. However, a good deal of the new material reveals the Conservatives' involvement with the letter but contributes disappointingly little to the question of the actual forgery. Despite the shortcomings of Bellegarde's account, it must be considered most likely that the letter was forged by White Russian

159 It is even alleged by R. Fischer, *Stalin and German Communism* (Harvard, 1948), p. 463, that Zinoviev suspected that the GPU fabricated the letter to undermine his standing in Comintern.

160 TUC archives, B 51 18/2/7: Zinoviev's telegram, 26 Oct. 1924.

161 *Shestoi S'ezd Professional'nykh Soyuzov, 1924, Stenograficheskii Otchet* (Moscow, 1924), pp. 25–28 (hereafter referred to as *VI S'ezd Profsoyuzov*).

162 L. Chester, S. Fay, H. Young, *The Zinoviev Letter* (London, 1967). Bellegarde's evidence first appeared in *Sunday Times*, 18 Dec. 1966, and was provoked by misleading information in *The Times*, 12 Dec. 1966, that the carbon copy of the 'Zinoviev letter' was missing from the Foreign Office files.

émigrés in Berlin.[163] Copies of the letter were circulating in Europe, and American Intelligence had received it before it was released in England.[164] There is no consensus as to the precise identity of the forgers. Opinion in Russia has always been divided as to the origin of the letter; Zinoviev maintained that he had information that the letter was forged outside England[165] while Rakovsky presented ample documentary evidence that such forgeries were being manufactured in London.[166] As a result of the trial of Druzhelovski, a leading member of the Berlin circle, in Moscow in 1927, the forgery was attributed to this group.[167] However, a later work on Anglo-Soviet relations lays the forgery at the door of a certain Uexkuell, a Baltic Baron who had established a bureau of forgery inside the German Intelligence in Berlin.[168]

It seems very likely that the Polish Intelligence played a part in the intrigue. Zinoviev made this accusation in his interview to *Pravda* on 28 October 1924. This unsubstantiated accusation received a new impetus when Druzhelovski admitted in Moscow, in the summer of 1927, that the forged document was transmitted to Captain Paciorkowski of the Polish Intelligence, who planted it on the British Intelligence. Paciorkowski's name emerged in the same connection during the Leipzig trial of a German forger, Johann Schreck.[169] In the recently published diary of the Speaker of the Polish House of Deputies, in the entry for 9 November 1924, Maciej Rataj describes a meeting

163 A critical approach to Bellegarde's evidence in W. E. Butler, in 'Correspondence', *Soviet Studies*, No. 3 (Jan. 1970), pp. 395–400, is based on a comparison of her evidence with a Russian text of the 'Zinoviev letter' which has been in the Harvard Library since the twenties. See also Rothstein in *Morning Star*, 19 Dec. 1966.

164 Butler, 'Correspondence', p. 395, and in *Harvard Library Bulletin*, Vol. XVIII (Jan. 1970), p. 54.

165 *Pravda*, 28 Oct. 1924.

166 Narkomindel, *Antisovetskie Podlogi* (Moscow, 1926), pp. 20–24. The same publication devoted a chapter to the Berlin circle but did not associate it with the 'Zinoviev letter'; *ibid.*, pp. 13–14.

167 *Pravda*, 22 Mar. 1928.

168 Volkov, *Anglo-Sovetskie Otnosheniya*, pp. 104–105. This echoes an earlier theory elaborated by A. Sayers and A. E. Kahn, *The Great Conspiracy against Russia* (New York, 1946), pp. 45–48.

169 *Izvestiya*, 3 Jan. and 2 Mar. 1928; *The Times*, 30 Jan. 1928.

with Wladyslaw Sikorski, the Prime Minister, who intimated to him that the Polish Intelligence had a hand in the forgery.[170]

However, the main mystery remains the identity of those who provided the Foreign Office and the *Daily Mail* with copies of the letter. Chester and his co-authors pointed to Orlov, a member of the Berlin forgers' circle, as the source of the Foreign Office copy, but they later preferred the romantic figure of the master spy Sidney Reilly.[171] This seems very unlikely, for the information was described by Bland, Crowe's secretary, as being obtained from 'an absolutely trustworthy agent in Russia'. Reilly, however, was described by Bland as a 'rather double edged tool' who was inclined to 'exaggerate his own importance'. Bland refuted rumours then current that Reilly was employed by the Office.[172]

The forgers of the Zinoviev letter undoubtedly sensed that the political atmosphere at the beginning of October was suitable for the release of their product. The Labour Government had just been defeated on the issues of its handling of the Campbell case and the circumstances under which the treaty had been signed. It became clear that these issues would be prominent in the election campaign.[173]

The Conservatives, supported by four newspapers with a total daily circulation of 3 million, were constantly hammering home to the public information discrediting Labour's Russian policy. Labour was able to reply only with a single paper whose daily readership was 300,000. The *Daily Mail*, with a vast circulation of 1,779,000, edited by Thomas Marlow, an ardent anti-Bolshevik, was willing to render service to extremists within the Conservative Party in promoting a Red scare. Sir Arthur Steel-Maitland, Minister of Labour in the ensuing Conservative

170 Chester *et al.*, *The Zinoviev Letter*, pp. 60–61.

171 *Sunday Times*, 18 Dec. 1966; Chester *et al.*, *The Zinoviev Letter*, pp. 183–95, following an earlier suggestion by Sayers *et al.*, *The Great Conspiracy*, pp. 45–48. Since then it has been repeated by B. Lockhart, *Ace of Spies* (London, 1967), pp. 125–29.

172 F.O. 371 10478 N8105/108/38: 27 Oct. 1924; F.O. 371 12605 N3088/3088/38: 21 Jan. 1927.

173 C. Higbie, 'The British Press in Selected Political Situations, 1924–1938' (London Univ. Ph.D. thesis), pp. 34–35; R. D. Warth, 'The Mystery of the Zinoviev Letter', *South Atlantic Quarterly* (Oct. 1950), Vol. XLIX, p. 446.

Government, was continuously supplying Marlow with anti-Russian material which he believed was 'of great use to the "Daily Mail" in its campaign against the Russian Treaty'.[174] Referring to the 1924 elections Lord Rothermere, the proprietor of the paper, admitted later that 'by skilful propaganda' it was possible 'to play upon a phase of British mentality in a way which results in a tremendous vote for the party of the Right'.[175] The *Daily Mail*'s editorials attacked Russia in vituperative terms. The credit promised to Russia, for instance, was described as 'cash for the purpose of financing a gang of thieves and murderers who repudiated all social and financial morality'; the money would be used to destroy the British Empire.[176] Churchill described the promised loan as an 'insult to the honour of the nation'. Lloyd George too now gave vent to his feeling, suggesting that Russia was doing its best 'to plant its dagger in the heart of Britain'.

Attempts by MacDonald to emphasize that the loan was conditional and was to be floated on the London market were drowned in the sea of anti-Soviet pronouncements.[177] In this atmosphere, a letter from Zinoviev inciting the CPGB to act against the Government which was responsible for the Anglo-Soviet *rapprochement* was immediately taken up and incorporated in the election campaign, now in its last days. The reactions to the letter were characterized by *The Times*'s leader of 25 October: 'It is hardly credible that the nation will entrust the conduct of great Imperial affairs to a leader who has, on his own confession, allowed himself to be cajoled and outwitted by the worst enemies of our country.' Conservative speakers exploited the letter to impress upon the public the close association between Labour, Russia and Communism.[178] Labour ministers, on the other hand, who learnt about the letter from the morning papers, were taken by surprise. Snowden hurried to contact MacDonald but found him unconcerned, unable to realize what

174 Steel-Maitland papers, GD 193/339: Steel-Maitland to Marlowe, 14 Oct. 1924.

175 Lloyd George papers, G/17/1/19: Rothermere to Lloyd George, 22 June 1927; *ibid.*, G/17/1/28: Ward Price, *Daily Mail*, to Lloyd George, 17 Mar. 1928.

176 *Daily Mail*, 3 Oct. 1924.

177 *The Times*, 16, 17 and 18 Oct. 1924.

178 Speeches by Churchill and Birkenhead in *The Times*, 27 Oct. 1924.

effect the letter might have on the election. In the absence of any clarification from the Prime Minister Labour candidates added to the confusion by making contradictory statements.[179]

It is therefore not surprising that the Central Office of the Conservative Party paid the then enormous sum of £5,000 to obtain the letter from C. D. im Thurn, an ex-Intelligence officer, who had been entrusted with it.[180] The immediate reaction of Labour ministers after the elections was to blame their defeat on the 'Zinoviev letter' affair. A careful study of the election results, however, suggests that the Liberal decline rather than the 'Zinoviev letter' was responsible for the Conservative victory, though the affair probably made the majority an overwhelming one.[181]

Although the letter apparently influenced the results of the election only marginally, it remained a controversial issue between the two parties. Clynes, presenting the Labour case in Parliament, was one of the few to draw attention to the real effect of the letter on Anglo-Soviet relations: 'This document must materially affect our general future relations with Russia, just as it so materially scared and affected the minds of many thousands of honest electors.'[182]

The letter of protest to the Soviet Government with a copy of the 'Zinoviev letter' was simultaneously handed to Rakovsky and issued to the Press on the afternoon of 24 October. The Note

179 Snowden, Vol. 2, *An Autobiography*, pp. 710–15; J. H. Thomas, *My Story* (London, 1937), p. 78; J. R. Clynes, *Memoirs* (London, 1937), pp. 63–64.

180 Chester *et al.*, *The Zinoviev Letter*, pp. 65–69. Im Thurn was introduced to the Central Office of the Conservative Party by Guy Kindersley, who belonged to the diehard section of the Party. The correspondence between the two is in *ibid.*, pp. 204–206; a copy of Im Thurn's diary is in *ibid.*, pp. 197–200. An exchange of letters between Davidson, a leading Conservative, and Ball, who was the head of the central office in 1924, in R. R. James, *Memoirs of a Conservative* (London, 1969), pp. 194–204 and 271–72, confirms that the few members of the central office who were involved in the affair sincerely believed that the letter was authentic.

181 Graubard, *British Labour*, pp. 283–88. According to K. E. Miller, *Socialism and Foreign Policy* (The Hague, 1967), pp. 131–32, despite the loss of 42 seats Labour's popular vote had risen from 30.7% in 1923 to 33.7% in the 1924 elections.

182 *Parl. Deb. H.C.*, Vol. 179, col. 198, 10 Dec. 1924.

held the Soviet Government responsible for the activities of Comintern, condemned the 'Zinoviev letter' as a 'direct interference from outside in British domestic affairs', and demanded an explanation from the Russians. Rakovsky hastened to send the Note and letter to Moscow but did not wait for his Government's reply before taking action.[183] On the morning of 25 October, he sent a Note on his own initiative to the Foreign Office, dismissing the 'Zinoviev letter' as a forgery and offering internal evidence to that effect. Rakovsky described the forgery as an 'audacious attempt to prevent the development of friendly relations' between the two countries; he also protested against the wide publicity given to the letter before the Soviet Government had been able to make any observations.[184] On the instructions of the Soviet Government, Rakovsky addressed a second Note to the Foreign Office on 27 October, reiterating that the letter was 'an impudent forgery aiming to wreck the Anglo-Soviet Treaties and to ruin friendly relations between the Soviet Union and Great Britain'. It also repeated Zinoviev's proposals to the TUC that the question of authenticity be submitted to impartial arbitration. This letter, however, contained a demand for the punishment of 'both the private and official persons involved in the forgery'.[185]

While the exchange of Notes was taking place, MacDonald was spending the last few days before the election in his Welsh constituency. Crowe, aware that MacDonald had not intended to send the draft Note, anxiously sent Gregory and Strang to Aberavon for the week-end to explain the Foreign Office's action to the Prime Minister. MacDonald, however, did not see them until 28 October, when he instructed Gregory to return the Soviet Note without delay to Rakovsky as an 'inadmissible interference' in British domestic affairs. On his return to London that afternoon, Gregory found Rakovsky 'unable or unwilling' to come over to the Office; he had no intention of accepting the

183 Baldwin's account in *Parl. Deb. H.C.*, Vol. 215, col. 62, 19 Mar. 1928; F.O. 371 10478 N8105/108/38: Gregory to Rakovsky, 24 Oct. 1924.

184 F.O. 371 10478 N8121/108/38: Rakovsky to Gregory, 25 Oct. 1924. To the embarrassment of Rakovsky, the Soviet reply had found its way to the *Daily Herald*, 27 Oct. 1924, before it was delivered to the Foreign Office, as a result of confusion in Moscow; see F.O. 371 10479 N8472/10/38, 27 Oct. 1924.

185 F.O. 371 10478 N8271/108/38: Rakovsky to MacDonald, 27 Oct. 1924.

returned Note. This became apparent in the evening when Gregory called at Rakovsky's home. After the verbal struggle which ensued, Gregory managed to leave the Note behind.[186] The Russian Note awaited Gregory in the Office the next morning. Attached to it was a covering letter suggesting that Gregory had left the Note with Rakovsky by mistake.[187] However, in a second letter addressed to MacDonald, Rakovsky opened the door for an agreement by which the withdrawal of the original Note, which had provoked the Russian Notes, might be followed by a similar Russian move. This proposal followed a hint dropped by Gregory during the conversation of the previous night to the effect that MacDonald intended to reconsider the correspondence between the two countries upon his return from Wales.[188] Once more the Note was returned to Rakovsky with an intimation that it was the paragraph accusing the Foreign Office officials which the Government found unacceptable.[189]

On 31 October, the Cabinet, unable to offer its resignation because of the King's absence from London, proceeded to deal with the question of the 'Zinoviev letter'. MacDonald came under strong criticism for his handling of the affair. A group of ministers including Parmoor, Charles Trevelyan, Josiah Wedgwood, Haldane and Snowden demanded a Committee of Inquiry which would 'table all the available evidence' and 'expose' the secret service, and report before the Government left office.[190]

The Cabinet decision reassured Rakovsky that MacDonald hoped to reverse the decision taken by the Foreign Office. Sending the Soviet Note back to the Foreign Office for the third time, Rakovsky explained that it had been the subject of a misunderstanding. The aim of the Russian Note was a recourse to arbitra-

186 F.O. 371 10479 N8473/108/38: minute by Gregory, 2 Nov. 1924. See also Strang, *Home and Abroad*, p. 57, and Middlemas, *Thomas Jones*, Vol. 1, p. 300. A rather detailed and entertaining version of Gregory's meeting with Rakovsky, the 'catch-as-catch-can, or its equivalent in the exchange of notes', is in Gregory, *On the Edge of Diplomacy*, pp. 224–27.

187 F.O. 371 10479 N8475/108/38: Rakovsky to Gregory, 29 Oct. 1924.

188 F.O. 371 10479 N8824/108/38: 29 Oct. 1924.

189 F.O. 371 10479 N8475/108/38: Gregory to Rakovsky, 31 Oct. 1924.

190 Cab. 23/48, 57(24)2, 31 Oct. 1924; Middlemas, *Thomas Jones*, Vol. 1, pp. 298–301.

tion. The meeting which took place between MacDonald and Rakovsky on 2 November shows that both sides were anxious to reach an agreement without admitting defeat. MacDonald, who did most of the talking, went as far as to admit that the protest Note had been sent by the Foreign Office against his will, but was insistent that the Soviet reply should be withdrawn before any further steps were taken. He concluded with the veiled threat that the matter, if left open, would have to be settled by his successor.

MacDonald departed in the belief that Rakovsky was ready to withdraw the Russian Note, while in fact Rakovsky remained firm that this would be conditional on the withdrawal of the British Note. After his meeting with Rakovsky, MacDonald instructed Gregory to return the Russian Note, and inform Rakovsky that the Prime Minister understood that he acquiesced in the view that it could not be accepted by the British Government.[191] On the same day, the Cabinet adopted the conclusions of the Committee of Inquiry that it was 'impossible on the evidence before them to come to a positive conclusion on the subject'. They did establish, however, that no department had seen the original letter.[192] When no answer arrived from Rakovsky, MacDonald made an unexpected attempt to patch up relations with the Russians. On 6 November, he surprisingly instructed that the original protest letter of 25 October to the Soviet Government be withdrawn: 'The dispatch sent to him [Rakovsky] was prepared on the assumption of the authenticity of the Z. letter and this Cabinet do not accept that view. The dispatch shd be withdrawn (provided no agreement is reached with Mr. Rakovsky) and that carries with it the Rakovsky reply.'[193] Had it been withdrawn the Conservative Government would have been placed in a delicate situation as far as policy towards the Soviet Union was concerned. However, on the same afternoon MacDonald relinquished office, and the Department delayed any

191 F.O. 371 10478 N8272/108/38: Rakovsky to Gregory, 1 Nov. 1924; minute by MacDonald, 3 Nov. 1924; Gregory to Rakovsky, 4 Nov. 1924; *Dok. Vne. Pol.*, Vol. VII, p. 530: Rakovsky to Chicherin on conversation with MacDonald, 3 Nov. 1924.

192 Cab. 23/48 57(24)2, 4 Nov. 1924. See also Parmoor, *A Retrospect*, p. 211.

193 F.O. 371 10478 N8272/108/38.

action until the new Foreign Secretary took charge. Two days later Rakovsky replied, returning to his previous demand for arbitration and claiming that MacDonald had mistaken his attitude.[194]

[194] F.O. 371 10479 N8412/108/38: Rakovsky to Gregory, 8 Nov. 1924.

2

The Policy of Doing Nothing

The formulation of a Conservative policy towards Russia

While MacDonald was throwing all his resources into a last attempt to recover his damaged reputation as well as to soothe the strained Anglo-Soviet relations, Stanley Baldwin was engaged in the difficult task of forming a Cabinet. He was 'surprised and excited' at the result of the elections and the preceding campaign centred on the 'Red menace'. On 4 November he told Thomas Jones, the deputy secretary of the Cabinet, that he was satisfied with the new composition of the House of Commons in which there were to be only two major political parties, one on the left and one on the right. The disappearance of the Liberals as a major party was the first step in this direction, which would be followed by the 'elimination of the Communists by Labour'.[1]

Baldwin entrusted the direction of the Foreign Office to Sir Austen Chamberlain, an experienced politician and former leader of the Conservative Party and of the House. Chamberlain, a capable administrator though with a somewhat narrow and conventional outlook on diplomacy, and 'rather wooden in his outlook on domestic problems', was to run the Office with little interference from Baldwin, who willingly admitted that he knew 'less than nothing' about foreign affairs.[2] At the time, however, Chamberlain's sharp criticism of Baldwin's inclusion of Churchill in the Cabinet and the refusal of Cabinet posts to Sir Robert Horne and G. T. Locker-Lampson[3] cast a momentary doubt

1 Middlemas, *Thomas Jones*, Vol. 1, p. 301.

2 For an appraisal of Chamberlain see *The Times*, 7 Nov. 1924. On relations between Chamberlain and Baldwin see Chamberlain papers, 4/1/1964: Chamberlain to his wife, 20 Sept. 1925. See also K. Middlemas and J. Barnes, *Baldwin* (London, 1969), pp. 342–47.

3 Locker-Lampson was subsequently appointed by Chamberlain as Parliamentary Under-Secretary for Foreign Affairs.

in Baldwin's mind about the wisdom of appointing Chamberlain as Foreign Secretary.[4]

The pressing issue facing Chamberlain on taking office was the formulation of a policy towards Russia. The Foreign Office's resentment of Labour and embitterment over the accusation of civil servants in the 'Zinoviev letter' affair were relieved by the advent of the Conservative Party to power. In a personal letter to Chamberlain, Crowe gave vent to his feelings: 'Need I say that the prospect of having you as our chief fills not only myself but this whole office with the utmost satisfaction and delight.'[5] Notwithstanding these sentiments the Northern Department's recommendation was to refrain from drastic action against Russia. Gregory proposed that 'the result of the elections remain the real answer to Rakovsky' while O'Malley added that public opinion was ready 'for some other form of entertainment'. Chamberlain resented, however, the 'very unsatisfactory condition' in which the outgoing Government had left the 'Zinoviev letter' affair by avoiding decision on its authenticity. The Labour Government had made a grave charge, then considered the grounds for making it, and finally announced its failure to reach a decision.[6]

A Foreign Office memorandum concerning Anglo-Soviet relations was submitted to the Cabinet when it met on 12 November. The memorandum distinguished between two questions: the immediate one of whether a reply or replies should be sent to Rakovsky's Notes of 25 October and 8 November; and the substantial one of the adoption of a general policy towards Russia. The three courses open to the Government appeared to be, in order of severity: to protest and bring about a rupture; merely to protest; or to disengage itself from the controversy altogether and 'ignore the Soviet Government as much and as long' as was

[4] Chamberlain papers, 35/5/3–4: Chamberlain to Baldwin, 31 Oct. and 6 Nov. 1924; Middlemas, *Thomas Jones*, p. 303.

[5] Chamberlain papers, 35/6/18: Crowe to Chamberlain, 6 Nov. 1924. See also Gregory, *On the Edge of Diplomacy*, pp. 30–31, and D. G. Bishop, *The Administration of British Foreign Relations* (Syracuse, 1961), pp. 215–16, for the inherent Conservatism of the Office.

[6] F.O. 371 10479 N8473/108/38: minutes by Gregory and O'Malley, 7 Nov. 1924, and Chamberlain, 8 Nov. 1924. See also Chamberlain in *Parl. Deb. H.C.*, Vol. 179, col. 673, 15 Dec. 1924.

tenable. The memorandum put forward numerous objections to a rupture and strongly advocated the third proposal.[7]

Although the Conservative Government had in common sentiments concerning Russia, it was far from united on the policy to be adopted. The focus of the discussion on policy towards Russia was the affair of the 'Zinoviev letter'. It was decided, therefore, that a special committee be set up to examine the question of authenticity in the light of the fresh evidence.[8]

The recommended lenient course towards Russia was the subject of political moves behind the scenes in the week which elapsed before the next Cabinet meeting. Churchill addressed letters to Baldwin and Chamberlain in which he argued that the Government had failed to 'respond to the mandate given them by the Electors'. He warned that no action short of revoking the recognition of the Soviet Government would be satisfactory and that he intended to press this point further in the forthcoming Cabinet meeting. A similar letter was sent by Joynson-Hicks to Chamberlain.[9] In the Cabinet meeting of 19 November Chamberlain encountered resistance to proposals for a moderate policy which was to become all too familiar. Although the Committee of Inquiry expressed the unanimous opinion that the letter was genuine, the Cabinet failed to reach agreement on the proposed policy or on the draft replies to Rakovsky. More discussions followed the next day when it was finally resolved to send three Notes to the Soviet Government but to leave open the question of general policy.[10]

Despite the failure of the Government to make a clear declaration of intent, the three Notes transmitted to the Soviet Government marked a rapid deterioration in Anglo-Soviet relations. The first undid at a stroke most of the achievements of Soviet foreign policy under the previous administration, stating that the Government was 'unable to recommend the Treaties for the consideration of Parliament' or to submit them to the King for ratification. The second, a reply to Rakovsky's Note of 25 October, maintained the tension by making clear that the

7 F.O. 371 10479 N8467/108/38: F.O. memorandum, 11 Nov. 1924.

8 Cab. 23/49 59(24)1, 12 Nov. 1924. See also pp. 38–39.

9 Baldwin papers, 114 FA/B: Churchill to Baldwin, 14 Nov. 1924; H.O. 45/14654 455518/28: Joynson-Hicks to Chamberlain, 14 Nov. 1924.

10 Cab. 23/49 60(24)9, 19 Nov. 1924; 61(24)3, 20 Nov. 1924.

information in the possession of the Government left 'no doubt whatsoever' of the authenticity of the 'Zinoviev letter'. A third letter from Gregory referred to Rakovsky's Note of 27 October and explained that it had not been found by the Secretary of State in the records left by the previous Government.[11] The Notes were correctly interpreted by a leader in *The Times* on 22 November as a warning to the Russians that they were 'on probation' and that they would not be allowed to 'repeat the experiment of combining political and commercial negotiations with revolutionary propaganda'.

A week later the Foreign Office received two replies from Rakovsky. The first, expressing regret that relations were placed 'on a very precarious foundation', reiterated the Soviet Government's belief that the letter was a forgery. In the second Rakovsky regretted the rejection of the treaty and absolved the Soviet Government from any responsibility for the 'feeling of discontent which the decision of the British Government will cause in both countries'. This sentence infuriated Chamberlain, who thought it 'an impertinence if not merely an ineptitude'. He consequently decided to terminate the correspondence with Rakovsky.[12]

The next month was devoted to elaborating different lines of policy towards Russia. Gregory expressed his anti-Soviet feelings, suggesting that the position of Bolshevik Russians in Britain was most unsatisfactory: 'We neither know how many there are nor when they come in or go out.' He proposed the setting up of machinery to follow and observe Soviet citizens residing in Britain as 'every one of them must be assumed to be engaged in propaganda in some form or another'.[13] This advice would be taken up by the Home Office in the course of 1925. In the meantime, considering the heated sentiments involved in the issue, Chamberlain decided to delay any major decision on Anglo-Russian relations.

The Speech from the Throne on 19 December, while rejecting the draft treaty, nevertheless expressed the desire that 'normal intercourse' between the two countries should not be interrupted so long as the Russians strictly fulfilled the conditions placed

[11] F.O. 371 10501 N8664/7016/38: 21 Nov. 1924.

[12] F.O. 371 10501 N8809/7016/38 and 10479 N8810/108/38: Soviet Notes, 28 Nov. 1924; minute by Chamberlain, 10 Dec. 1924.

[13] F.O. 371 10500 N8905/6863/38: minute by Gregory, 5 Dec. 1924.

before them and accepted by them in the trade agreement of 1921.[14] Despite the moderate tone of the speech, there could be no doubt that relations were in decline. In the ensuing debate on the address, Joynson-Hicks, taking advantage of MacDonald's confused handling of the letter, was able to present the Government's policy as a continuation of its predecessor's. It was after all MacDonald who had not been satisfied with the conduct of the Russians and had dispatched the Note of protest. Chamberlain, however, was determined to accept the course of policy recommended in the Foreign Office memorandum of 11 November. Although sharing the view that the Soviet system was cracking and could not 'fit into the system prevailing over the whole of the rest of the world', he thought that the best course of policy would be to 'wait and watch before deciding on any fresh action in either direction'.[15]

The return to power of a Conservative Government and the rejection of the treaty were received in Moscow with anxiety. In a survey of international affairs published under a pseudonym, Chicherin pessimistically remarked: 'The New Year in international politics is not like the last. Then the sky seemed to have a soft caressing radiance. Now the sky seems to be hidden by dark threatening clouds.'[16] Nevertheless, he must have been relieved to learn from Krasin in Paris that discussions with British politicians had convinced him that a severance of relations was unlikely, as nobody wished to put an end to trade with Russia.[17]

In an attempt to forestall the deterioration of relations with England which they feared would be the result of the Conservative victory, the Russians directed their efforts towards regulating

[14] *Parl. Deb. H.C.*, Vol. 179, cols. 47–48, 9 Dec. 1924.

[15] *ibid.*: Joynson-Hicks, cols. 312–15; Chamberlain, cols. 673–79. Chamberlain was unjustifiably presented by the Russians as their worst enemy. This view was subsequently revised by Soviet historiography; see Rakovsky, 'Moi Besedy s Chemberlenom', *Molodaya Gvardiya* (Nov. 1927), p. 205; Ya. Viktorov, 'Tri Chemberlena', *Bol'shevik* (1940), No. 8, pp. 83–84; I. M. Maisky, *Vospominaniya Sovetskogo Diplomata* (Moscow, 1971), p. 27.

[16] Chicherin under pseudonym of M. Sharonov in *Izvestiya*, 30 Dec. 1924; for Zinoviev's similar observation see p. 100. See also F.O. 371 10491 N9200/1185/38: Peters, First Secretary in the Moscow Embassy, on conversation with Litvinov, 5 Dec. 1924.

[17] *Dok. Vne. Pol.*, Vol. VIII, pp. 19–20: Krasin to Chicherin on conversation with Kenworthy, 7 Jan. 1925.

questions outstanding between the two countries. Early in January 1925 Litvinov instructed Rakovsky 'to bring about the resumption of talks' with the Conservative Government.[18] To facilitate the work of the Soviet representative in London, Chicherin once more denied emphatically the authenticity of the 'Zinoviev letter' and rejected accusations that Soviet agents were engaged in subversive activities throughout the British Empire.[19]

The first meeting between Chamberlain and Rakovsky took place on 6 January. It was during this meeting that the future pattern of relations between the two countries was set. Rakovsky tried to break through the isolation forced on his Government and to bring about the revival of the negotiations. He was aware that Chamberlain's comments in Parliament on Anglo-Soviet relations meant either the preservation of the *status quo* or, even worse, a deterioration of these relations. Therefore, instead of assuming a defensive position over the 'Zinoviev letter' affair, he directed Chamberlain's attention to acts which he thought indicated the formation of an anti-Soviet bloc by the British Government. Chamberlain, while insisting that there was no foundation to this accusation, asserted that normal relations between the two countries were quite impossible so long as one of them interfered in the domestic affairs of the other. Rakovsky, wishing to avoid the insoluble controversy over 'Narkomindel versus Comintern' relations, dismissed as 'absurd' the suggestion that the Soviet Union was only interested in spreading revolution all over the world. The Russian intention in improving relations with Britain, Rakovsky emphasized, was to promote trade between the two countries and to revive the Soviet economy. Unimpressed by Rakovsky's arguments, Chamberlain made clear the Government's refusal to consider the grant of a loan to Russia. However, to alleviate Rakovsky's fear and suspicion that a hostile policy towards Russia was being contemplated by the British Government, he expressed his willingness 'to consider fresh proposals' when Rakovsky had any to make to him.[20]

[18] *ibid.*, pp. 11–12: 3 Jan. 1925.

[19] *Izvestiya*, 4 Jan. 1925.

[20] F.O. 371 11015 N102/102/38: Chamberlain on conversation with Rakovsky; *Dok. Vne. Pol.*, Vol. VIII, pp. 33–38: Rakovsky to Litinov on conversation with Chamberlain, 10 Jan. 1925.

After his meeting with Chamberlain, Rakovsky left for Russia to attend the meeting of the central committee of the CPSU. During the stay in Moscow, Rakovsky did little to allay Russian fears. In a speech delivered to the All-Union congress of teachers he accused Chamberlain of fomenting an anti-Soviet bloc. Although the Soviet Government was not yet explicitly referring to the threat of a new war, Rakovsky warned that the international scene resembled Europe in 1914. In another speech delivered in Leningrad, Rakovsky emphasized that, although Anglo-Soviet relations had improved in 1924, they were 'not so far from conflicts and the possibility of a new war'.[21] Rakovsky's utterances were not taken by the Foreign Office to represent the Soviet Government's policy. His association with Trotsky, who by that time was coming under criticism in the CPSU, strengthened the feeling that Rakovsky could not be fully trusted because 'he was appointed to London to get him out of the way'.[22] This was indeed the case; however, the idea that he was for that reason unreliable was introduced by the Foreign Office to excuse their conduct towards him. The course of events would probably have been much the same had Russia been represented by a Stalinist *chargé d'affaires* in 1925.

Meanwhile the British Government's irresolute attitude towards Russia, combined with the hostile utterances of the Press and the apprehensions expressed in Moscow, gave a new lease of life to the White Russians. Grand Duke Kiril, one of the most prominent leaders of this group, submitted concrete plans for a new intervention for the consideration of the Foreign and War Offices.[23] Chamberlain positively ruled out contact with these elements, which could provide the Russians with an excuse to justify their propaganda and subversive activities within the British Empire. However, these deliberations were also based on previous experience; the divided Whites could not be relied upon to present a serious challenge to the Soviet regime.[24] Despite

21 Rakovsky's speeches are in *Izvestiya*, 27 Jan. 1925 (inaccurately reported in *The Times*, 30 Jan. 1925) and 24 Feb. 1925.

22 F.O. 371 11017 N712/114/38: Peters to Chamberlain, 30 Jan. 1925.

23 F.O. 371 11021 N596 and N1054/596/38: reports from Muller, British Ambassador in Warsaw, 27 Jan. and 20 Feb. 1925.

24 F.O. 11015 N145 and N1410/75/38: minutes by Chamberlain, 12 Jan. and 12 Mar. 1925.

British denials, the Soviet Press continued to level accusations of Britain's involvement in alleged anti-Soviet intrigues in the Balkans and the Baltic States.[25]

In Rakovsky's absence from London his deputy, Berzin, an old Bolshevik who had been involved in the formation of Comintern and was the first Soviet representative in Switzerland, sought an interview with O'Malley. O'Malley took advantage of the occasion and declared once more that Britain did not have any intention of forming a continental bloc against Russia. Pressed on this point, Berzin admitted that the fears in Moscow were a result of uncertainty about British intentions.[26] When Hodgson met Chicherin in Moscow in mid-February, he found that the Russians had not shaken off the idea that Britain was organizing a European coalition against them. Hodgson, always a protagonist of moderation, emphasized that such steps were not being contemplated. He pointed out that during his previous meeting with Chamberlain in London he had been assured that the Cabinet wished to maintain good relations with the Soviet Union.[27] Shortly after his meeting with Chicherin, Hodgson denied in the Soviet Press the prevailing rumours of a *volte-face* in Britain's attitude towards Russia.[28] Chamberlain was highly disturbed by Hodgson's independent actions in Moscow. The Government's policy, he minuted, was punctilious in that it did not encourage any anti-Soviet confrontation, yet its attitude should not be 'more than correct'. He instructed that a dispatch should be sent to Hodgson to ensure that he was well informed of this policy.[29] Hodgson's reassurances did little to subdue the suspicious attitude of the Soviet Press, which now maintained that the Conservative Government was organizing financial blocs against Russia as a preliminary move towards launching 'an active

[25] Typical leaders are in *Izvestiya*, 15 Feb. and 27 Mar. 1925.

[26] F.O. 371 11016 N1112/1/38: minute by O'Malley, 2 Feb. 1925.

[27] *Dok. Vne. Pol.*, Vol. VIII, pp. 137–40: memorandum by Chicherin on the meeting, 12 Feb. 1925; F.O. 371 11015 N1314/102/38: Hodgson to Chamberlain on conversation with Chicherin, 14 Feb. 1925.

[28] *Pravda*, 17 Feb. 1925.

[29] F.O. 371 11015 N1314/102/38: minute and letter to Hodgson by Chamberlain, 18 and 30 Mar. 1925. Chamberlain's first draft was harsh: 'All this is for your guidance if Chicherin holds similar language in future, otherwise, say nothing.' The final draft was slightly modified.

attack on the Fatherland'. This campaign was believed by the Foreign Office to be intended for home consumption.[30]

The Russians had not abandoned their hopes of a reversal of the British policy. Upon his return from Moscow, Rakovsky sought an interview with Chamberlain in which he referred to a speech delivered by Chicherin at Tiflis at the beginning of March. Chicherin had expressed the desire for an understanding with England that would foster friendly relations and encourage the development of commerce.[31] The Government, informed of this overture, had made clear in Parliament its willingness to examine carefully proposals put forward by the Soviet Government. The initiative, it was stressed, should however come from the Soviet Government. During his interview with Chamberlain, it became obvious that Rakovsky was not equipped with new directives from his Government. Moreover, Chamberlain had been briefed before the meeting on hostile Soviet operations against Britain which suggested that the attitude of the Soviet Union was 'less than correct' and that propaganda and Comintern subversion remained the 'stumbling block' to the development of Anglo-Soviet relations.[32] Basing his arguments on this information, Chamberlain ruled out fresh negotiations so long as the Soviet Government did not abide by the political clauses of the 1921 trade treaty, and so long as it refused to admit responsibility for the activities of Comintern. Rakovsky, for his part, rejected these arguments and pointed out that neither Russia nor Britain could expect the other party to change its principles. However, to encourage further communication he explained that the Soviet Government had previously been insecure and had encouraged revolutionary activities abroad but that now they had 'other means of defence', such propaganda was no longer necessary to them.[33] Thus the meeting ended with an impasse: Chamberlain holding fast to the policy of *status quo*,

[30] Steklov, editor of *Izvestiya*, 27 Mar. 1925; F.O. 371 11015 N2177/75/38: minute by Rayner, Northern Department, 24 Apr. 1925.

[31] F.O. 371 11015 N1852/102/38: Chamberlain to Hodgson on conversation with Rakovsky, 1 Apr. 1925.

[32] *Parl. Deb. H.C.*, Vol. 181, cols. 1315–18, 11 Mar. 1925; F.O. 371 11015 N1782/102/38: minute by Maxse, 1 Apr. 1925.

[33] F.O. 371 N1852/102/38; *Dok. Vne. Pol.*, Vol. VIII, pp. 207–210: Rakovsky to Chicherin on conversation with Chamberlain, 5 Apr. 1925.

and Rakovsky unwilling to put forward proposals which would impose new obligations on the Soviet Government.

Within the Conservative Party there was strong indignation at the state of affairs. The diehards succeeded in moving a motion in Parliament, following a debate on Anglo-Soviet relations, which strongly condemned revolutionary propaganda in Britain and encouraged the Government to carry out 'any action necessary to suppress it'.[34] However, although the existence of subversive propaganda was taken for granted, Chamberlain was unable to produce clear-cut evidence to that effect. On occasions, when the Government was pressed to bring into the open proof for the existence of propaganda, the absence of any such evidence forced Chamberlain to act evasively.[35]

Meanwhile differences of opinion in Cabinet over Russia were coming to the fore. The anti-Soviet campaign, which gathered momentum in May 1925, seems to have been aimed at creating an atmosphere of 'Red menace' which would enable the diehards to push through a tougher policy towards the communists and the Russians when Parliament met after the recess. The campaign, with Joynson-Hicks emerging as its principal figure, represented Russia as a threat to the social structure 'which had been laboriously built up in the country through many centuries'.[36] It was continuously stressed that propaganda was a new and effective weapon employed by the Russians to undermine Britain's constitutional Government at home as well as throughout the Empire.

Confrontation within Cabinet over Russia first emerged around questions of departmental responsibilities. Joynson-Hicks' constant insistence that it was his duty as Home Secretary to guard the country from 'evil, from communism and from Bolshevism'[37] rendered a clash with Chamberlain inevitable. Chamberlain,

[34] *Parl. Deb. H.C.*, Vol. 181, cols. 353–98, 3 Mar. 1925.

[35] F.O. 371 11011 N29/29/38: 30 Mar. 1925; *Parl. Deb. H.C.*, Vol. 182, cols. 926–27, 30 Mar. 1925. A leader in *Izvestiya*, 4 Apr. 1925, pointing out the 'deliberately ambiguous' policy of the Conservatives, suggested that Chamberlain actually 'wished proofs of propaganda were in his hands'.

[36] Joynson-Hicks launched his campaign in a speech delivered on 3 Mar. reported in *The Times*, 25 Mar. 1925; Horne in *ibid.*, 25 Mar. 1925.

[37] *The Times*, 1 and 16 May 1925; see also a speech by Birkenhead in *ibid.*, 20 July 1925. For the diehards' position see Earl of Birken-

however, was eager to minimize friction in his relations with colleagues in the other departments, especially over a topic like Russia, which after all was of secondary importance. Indeed, measures taken by the Home Office to curtail the number of visas to Soviet citizens seeking residence in Britain met with the approval of the Foreign Office.[38] Russian complaints on this subject remained unanswered, and the Foreign Office upheld the policy of the Home Office.[39]

Throughout the early months of 1925 the Home Office continued to provide the Foreign Office with evidence of Soviet propaganda in Britain. This evidence, however, was taken *cum grano salis* after the experience of the 'Zinoviev letter' affair.[40] The feeling in the Foreign Office was that the divergence of opinion with the Home Office was of no significance. The prevailing opinion was: 'The Unionist Headquarters are rather tired of this alien bogey; so perhaps we may hear less of it in the future.'[41] However, this problem of departmental responsibilities was only a prelude to the constant pressure brought by Joynson-Hicks on Chamberlain to change the policy towards Russia.

Chamberlain was also not impressed by Joynson-Hicks' unrestrained anti-Soviet campaign at the beginning of May. He had not revised his opinion that suspicion should not be the foundation of a rupture of relations with Russia. He maintained that this was one of those cases 'where the man who loses his head loses his ship and the man who keeps his nerve wins.' He intended, therefore, to keep Rakovsky at 'arm's length', but to resist an open breach as long as there was no real cause. When, however, such a cause occurred he assured Joynson-Hicks that the Government would 'strike, and strike hard'.[42]

head, *F.E.: The Life of F. E. Smith, First Earl of Birkenhead* (London, 1959), pp. 525–27.

38 F.O. 371 11016 N695/1/38: minutes of inter-departmental meeting, 30 Jan. 1925. See also H.O. 45/10465 4555/18/28: Joynson-Hicks to Chamberlain, 20 Nov. 1924.

39 F.O. 371 11016 N1112/1/38: Gregory to Joynson-Hicks, 12 Mar. 1925.

40 See for example F.O. 371 11019 N1180 and 2559/289/38: Joynson-Hicks to Chamberlain, 2 Mar. and 5 May 1925.

41 F.O. 371 11010 N2980/29/38: minute by Maxse, 25 May 1925.

42 F.O. 371 11010 N2298/29/38: Chamberlain to Joynson-Hicks, 5 May 1925.

Before long, however, it became obvious that Joynson-Hicks' utterances were not an isolated phenomenon but indicated a definite Home Office policy. In answer to an inquiry by the Foreign Office regarding the extension of a visa for a certain Russian citizen, the Home Office made the point that granting visas was under the sole jurisdiction of that Office.[43] Later in June, in connection with events in China,[44] and the revival of hostility towards Russia in June, Joynson-Hicks demanded from Chamberlain that the Home Office should be given sole authority to deal with propaganda.[45] This time Chamberlain sought an inter-departmental conference to establish patterns of conduct and responsibilities regarding the Russian issue. The meeting revealed Chamberlain's readiness to compromise and surrender to pressure put on him by fellow Ministers, a weakness which was critical in the deterioration of Anglo-Soviet relations between 1925 and 1927. Joynson-Hicks easily induced Chamberlain to admit that the prevailing feeling in the Conservative Party was for firm handling of Bolshevik propaganda and that this could be efficiently executed by the Home Office. It was promptly arranged that in further communications with Soviet representatives the Foreign Office should 'place the onus upon the shoulders of the Home Secretary'. Warnings by the Northern Department that the arrangement threatened future relations with Russia could not shake Chamberlain's resolve to end the friction between the Offices at all costs.[46]

The speeches of the Home Secretary provided the Russians with a sound basis for pursuing matters with Chamberlain. Until then their evidence of a hostile British attitude was based on the foreign and the British Press. Rakovsky wasted no time in complaining to Sir William Tyrrell, Crowe's successor as Permanent Under-Secretary, that the speeches contradicted the attitude hitherto adopted by the Prime Minister and the Foreign Sec-

[43] F.O. 371 11016 N2088/1/38: Joynson-Hicks to Chamberlain, 22 Apr. 1925.

[44] See below, pp. 67–68.

[45] F.O. 371 11017 N3807/1/38: Joynson-Hicks to Chamberlain, 26 June 1925.

[46] F.O. 371 11017 N4380/1/38: record by Joynson-Hicks of conversation with Chamberlain, 29 July 1925; minutes by O'Malley and Gregory, 31 July, and by Chamberlain, 4 Aug. 1925.

retary, which 'had been in every respect correct'. Tyrrell promised that he would submit these observations to Chamberlain but emphasized that the speeches were confined to propaganda and subversive activities which justified measures of self-defence on the part of the countries affected.[47] However, in spite of the pressure brought on the Foreign Office, it maintained that the Government had 'most to gain' by maintaining its attitude of 'correct aloofness' and refusing either to renew negotiations or to break off relations. Any external pressure, it was argued, would only 'produce a reconciliation between the Russian Government and international communism'.[48]

The third congress of the Soviets, which met in May, heard a general report on foreign policy by Chicherin, in which Britain occupied the most prominent place. 'When we ask ourselves what part can this or that country play', he stated, 'we must first of all consider the position of England.' Chicherin was alarmed by Britain's intention to restore the balance of power system in Europe through the conclusion of new alliances, which in turn might serve as the springboard for offensive activities. Although evidence of such a policy was not yet available, it was possible to discern 'general tendencies, which float in the air, are written about in the Press, and spoken by politicians'. Chicherin finally argued that the refusal of the British Government to 'abandon the point of view that the Communist Party should cease to be a Communist Party' hampered the sincere efforts of Soviet diplomacy to reach a *modus vivendi* in Anglo-Soviet relations.[49] While Chicherin only referred to diplomatic alliances and the potential danger of war, the resolution passed by the congress stressed the existence of combinations and agreements which took the 'form of an entire series of military conferences'. This resolution, which called upon the Russians to close ranks and guard themselves against external dangers, had a sequel in the Press. Radek warned that the forthcoming session

[47] F.O. 371 11016 N2600/102/38: Tyrrell on conversation with Rakovsky, 6 May 1925. Tyrrell was regarded by the Russians as Chamberlain's right-hand man in the formation of anti-Soviet blocs; *Mir. Khz. i Mir. Pol.* (1928), No. 3, pp. 10–11.

[48] F.O. 371 11016 N2735/102/38: minute by Maxse, 5 May 1925.

[49] G. V. Chicherin, *Stat'i i Rechi po Voprosam Mezhdunarodnoi Politiki* (Moscow, 1961), pp. 372–79.

of the League of Nations was a link in 'lengthy military preparations on the part of the capitalist world against the USSR'.[50]

In order to provide Chamberlain with a better insight into the proceedings of the congress, William Peters[51] described a conversation he had had with Chicherin at a reception given by Litvinov's wife two days before the opening of the congress. Chicherin, according to Peters, 'desired to utilise the friendly atmosphere associated with caviare and champagne cup to lend support to action taken in London in more official surroundings'. In contrast to the report delivered to the congress, Chicherin conveyed his willingness to undertake 'not to engage in or facilitate' propaganda against Great Britain if this could lead to an agreement.

The essence of the dispatch, however, which affirmed the Russians' eagerness to regulate relations, was overlooked by the Foreign Office, while close attention was given to Peters' concluding observations. These were to provide the basis for the long-sought definition of the state of relations with Russia. Peters' impression was that the Russians' attempt to come to terms with England stemmed from their failure to expand trade with the industrialized countries. There was a growing opinion among foreign business circles that the advantages which Russia offered as a trading partner had 'in the past been exaggerated'. He believed therefore that the Soviet Government was in desperate need of normal communications with Europe. Chamberlain registered complete agreement with him: 'Mr. Peters hits the nail on the head when he observes that the Soviet Government above all things cannot bear to be ignored.' Chamberlain went on to minute, not without satisfaction, the Russian apprehensions which ensued from the fact that Britain was now leaving Russia out of its consideration. He wished that 'everyone at home understood the value of the reserve which foreigners believe to be our national characteristic'. By 'everyone' he specifically meant his fellow Ministers and above all Joynson-Hicks.[52] Hodgson's

[50] *Dok. Vne. Pol.*, Vol. VIII, pp. 307–309, 16 May 1925; *Pravda*, 23 May 1925.

[51] Peters had served as Assistant Agent to the British Commercial Mission in Moscow since 1921. After recognition, he acted as First Secretary at the Moscow Embassy.

[52] F.O. 371 11016 N3153/102/38: Peters to Chamberlain, 22 May 1925;

vigorous arguments, against the prevailing opinion in the Office, that ignoring Russia would encourage its internal conflicting forces were given little attention.[53]

Chamberlain, however, was now finding it increasingly difficult to hold back the diehards and to 'kill this canard' of forthcoming action against Russia. In Parliament he again denied rumours that Britain was approaching other Governments with a view to pursuing an anti-Soviet policy. He was prepared to consider any proposals by the Soviet Government but had no intention of initiating them.[54]

Rakovsky's further protests against the stream of violent speeches by Joynson-Hicks evoked little response. Chamberlain had previously expressed dissatisfaction with Joynson-Hicks' speeches. Yet in order to preserve the appearance of Government unity, he maintained that the speeches were not different in character from corresponding anti-British utterances of Soviet leaders.[55] Besides, Chamberlain was finding general consent in Geneva for his policy of aloofness. Peters' single sentence had become a policy, although it had not been formally sanctioned by the Government. From the League of Nations Chamberlain informed Tyrrell that he was more than ever convinced that it would be very inexpedient to provoke a controversy with the Soviet Government and that the less attention was paid to it the more anxious the Russians would be to come to terms.[56]

The reluctant approval of Chamberlain's policy

The tension between the two countries reached a new level at the end of May and beginning of June as a result of upheavals in the far East. These started with a strike in the textile mills of Shanghai, which was motivated by both patriotic passion and

minute by Chamberlain, 9 June 1925. At first Chamberlain wrote 'everyone at the Home Office . . .' but then crossed out 'the Home Office' and substituted 'at home'.

[53] F.O. 371 11018 N2988/265/38: minute by Maxse, 25 May 1925; N3971/265/38: Hodgson to Chamberlain, 3 July 1925.

[54] F.O. 371 11015 N2872/102/38: minute by Maxse, 18 May 1925; *Parl. Deb. H.C.*, Vol. 184, cols. 398 and 1361–62, 20 and 27 May 1925.

[55] F.O. 371 11016 N3089/102/38: exchange of letters between Rakovsky and Chamberlain, 27 May and 5 June 1925.

[56] F.O. 371 11016 N3432/102/38: Chamberlain to Tyrrell, 10 June 1925.

a demand for higher wages. On 24 May a rally of workers and students took place in memory of a student who had been shot dead by the police. Arrests followed, and another protest march was organized for 30 May. This time the British police opened fire and shot dead several of the protesters. This sequence of events was the first in which a Leninist programme was apparent in terms of organization and exploitation of upheavals for political ends. Evidence of collaboration between Moscow and the Chinese Communist Party was difficult to find since the two parties differed from each other in many respects.

Stalin was hesitant and inconsistent in his attitude to the events in China. As long as the strike lasted he expressed confidence in its success and gave his full support to the strikers. Yet once the upsurge of 30 May was over, the Russians realized that the foreign powers had held their ground, and returned to national united front tactics.[57] The commentary of the Soviet Press reflected the lack of unanimity with respect to developments in China. One tendency was to dissociate Russia from the upheavals in China and to emphasize the 'national liberation' character of the movement, thereby removing the grounds for a British retaliation against Russia.[58] The other conflicting tendency was clearly to underline the importance of the first step which had been taken towards a successful Marxist revolution. In one of Zinoviev's analyses of the international situation, he forthrightly declared: 'Bolshevization – this is the order of the day in China.'[59] The prevailing tendency, however, was the former. Rakovsky was informed with no delay, by Narkomindel, that although the Russian experience might have influenced the course of events in China, the Soviet Government had neither initiated nor controlled the strike in Shanghai.[60]

Information about the events was slow to reach London. By the time the situation was grasped, the disturbance was practically over and Russia was once again conducting a moderate

57 Carr, *Socialism in One Country*, Vol. 3, pt. 1, pp. 719–32; C. Brandt, *Stalin's Failure in China 1924–1927* (Harvard, 1958), pp. 50–51 and 63–69.

58 Leaders by 'Asiatikus' in *Izvestiya*, 4, 6 and 18 June 1925.

59 *ibid.*, 2 June 1925.

60 *Dok. Vne. Pol.*, Vol. VIII, pp. 360–61: Rothstein to Rakovsky, 10 June 1925.

policy. While Baldwin and Chamberlain wished to minimize the incident, the diehards saw in the developments a confirmation of their evaluation of Soviet subversive intentions and propaganda and tried to use the affair to change the policy towards Russia. After a short incident-free period in Anglo-Soviet relations, Birkenhead, the Secretary of State for India until 1928 and an ardent anti-Bolshevik, delivered a speech in which he explicitly expressed the view that Britain would have to use different methods to deal with the Russians, who had embarked on 'subterranean activities seeking no other purpose than the destruction of the British Empire'.[61]

The Russians watched these developments with anxiety. Berzin informed Chicherin that on a few occasions Chamberlain had held the Russians responsible for the events in China. He also quoted parts of Birkenhead's speech, but conveyed the impression prevailing in Labour circles that the anti-Soviet campaign was intended above all for domestic consumption and that there was no immediate threat of severance of relations.[62] Armed with this information, Chicherin called a Press conference to try to end the deterioration of Anglo-Soviet relations. In the course of his statement, Chicherin did not attempt to play down the whole affair; on the contrary, he called attention to the impediments to improvement of relations between the two countries. He warned that the speeches contained a demand for extremely hostile measures against Russia 'beyond which there is only war'. With business and Labour circles in mind, he dwelt on unemployment in Britain and promised that Soviet industry would place orders in Britain if the appropriate credits were allocated.[63] Chicherin's statement seemed to confirm the Foreign Office's assumption that the Soviet Union was desperate to break out of isolation; the question was whether it would modify its policy and beg to be re-admitted to the European community or alienate itself even further.[64]

Meanwhile a proposal by the Far Eastern Department for an ultimatum leading to the severance of relations with Russia was rejected by Gregory. The only prospect of successful challenge

61 *The Times*, 29 June 1925.
62 *Dok. Vne. Pol.*, Vol. VIII, p. 402: 30 June 1925.
63 Chicherin, *Stat'i*, pp. 395–406.
64 F.O. 371 11016 N3810/102/38: minute by Mounsey, 4 July 1925.

to Russia lay in a joint action in the East with the other powers involved, particularly the USA, and with the firm support of Poland and Rumania. Both Chamberlain and Tyrrell, though not opposed to the principle, agreed that such measures were premature at that stage.[65]

The Foreign Office's final memorandum endorsed by the Cabinet explained that the Bolshevik influence in China, although clearly evident, played only a minor role compared with the main reasons, which were the ever-present xenophobia, the growth of student movements, and nationalism.[66] Berzin apprised Chicherin of the solution of the crisis on 3 July, at the same time informing Narkomindel of further hostile steps taken by the Government towards Russia. He had learnt that Baldwin had advised business circles to postpone contracts with the Russians because the Government was about to make decisions concerning relations between the two countries.[67]

Parliament met on 6 July to discuss the latest developments in China, although the Cabinet had not yet decided upon policy. Chamberlain told the House that the Government did not contemplate making representations to Russia but reserved 'full liberty to take what ever action they may think required'. He insisted that the Government should remain free to act as was necessary to protect British interests. At the same time Chamberlain pleaded with the diehards to refrain from speeches which might be a source of embarrassment to the Cabinet. Under pressure he admitted that the Government was not considering the severance of relations but could not pledge that the policy would remain unaltered if the situation changed.[68] Berzin hastened to send Chicherin another telegram informing him of the removal of the immediate danger of rupture. He believed that the pressure exerted on the Government by the trade unions, as well as the tension between the USA and Britain over interests in China, were responsible for the Government's decision.[69]

Berzin certainly overestimated the influence of the trade unions. The General Council of the TUC had sent to the Prime Minister

[65] F.O. 371 10943 F2579/194/10: minutes, 6 June 1925.
[66] F.O. 371 10943 F2589/194/10: 29 June 1925.
[67] *Dok. Vne. Pol.*, Vol. VIII, p. 408.
[68] *Parl. Deb. H.C.*, Vol. 186, cols. 20–21, and Vol. 187, cols. 386–88.
[69] *Dok. Vne. Pol.*, Vol. VIII, p. 419: 8 July 1925.

a resolution calling upon the Government to extend 'complete recognition to the Soviet Government' on 7 July. It also urged the Government to avoid any action in China which was 'likely to provoke a breakdown in diplomatic relations at the present time'. The resolution, however, reached Baldwin only on 9 July, a day after the Cabinet had discussed the events in China.[70]

In the Cabinet meeting of 8 July, relations with Russia were thoroughly examined for the first time since the Conservative Government came to power. In the course of the meeting Chamberlain outlined the assumption on which the Foreign Office had been acting: as the Soviet Union was dependent in essence 'on its extensions to other countries', the Russians' greatest source of concern was to be treated 'as though they did not exist'. It was advisable, therefore, to keep formal relations 'as distant as possible'. To mollify the diehards, Chamberlain agreed to take any necessary action 'when evidence of Soviet misdeeds was forthcoming'. At the same time he was critical of the anti-Soviet utterances of the diehards. The resolution reflected a compromise: Chamberlain's policy was endorsed, while it was agreed that it was difficult to avoid references in public speeches to the Soviet Government 'and more particularly to the failure of their economic system in their own country'.[71]

After Rakovsky had learnt more or less what had transpired in the Cabinet meeting, he met Chamberlain on 13 July. Rakovsky not only demanded further assurances that the Government would not nullify the 1921 trade treaty but once more proposed the re-opening of negotiations. Chamberlain adhered to his previous position, which in his view was given an added justification by the Chinese affair. He could not see any advantages in beginning negotiations so long as there were 'fundamental differences of principles' between the two Governments.[72] Rakovsky emerged from the meeting convinced that the crisis in Anglo-Soviet relations would remain chronic so long as Cabinet Ministers used every incident, 'real or artificial', to bring about a severance of relations with Russia.[73]

70 F.O. 371 11016 N3904/102/38.

71 Cab. 23/50 36(25)3.

72 F.O. 371 11016 N4201/102/38: minutes by Chamberlain on conversation with Rakovsky; Rakovsky's version in *Dok. Vne. Pol.*, Vol. VIII, pp. 432–33.

73 Press statement by Rakovsky in *The Times*, 15 July 1925.

The end of June and beginning of July witnessed the outbreak of yet another Soviet Press campaign describing Britain's intrigues in organizing the anti-Soviet bloc. This impression was reinforced by events in neighbouring countries and in particular the visit of a British squadron to Baltic ports, which was described by Chicherin as 'sinister machinations destined to convert the Baltic Sea into a British lake'.[74]

Hodgson at first interpreted the renewed Soviet campaign as a sign that Russia was either suffering from a peculiar form of 'persecution mania' or following a deliberate policy intended to persuade public opinion that the sole aim of Britain was 'to accomplish the destruction of the Soviet Union'. The persistence of the campaign even after Chamberlain's assurances in Parliament that relations with Russia would not be broken off convinced Hodgson that the intention was to 'instil into the mind of the Russian people' the belief that Great Britain was determined by hook or by crook to crush the Soviet Union while there was still time.[75] Since it seemed to him that the scare was assuming alarming proportions, he sent a telegram to Chamberlain conveying his impression that Chicherin sincerely believed that most of the anti-Soviet material in the British Press was communicated to it by the Government. Moreover, the continual reiteration of these stories was 'having an inevitable effect upon a population which has little reasoning powers and only sees the side of things which the government wishes it to see'. He therefore proposed the handing of a *démenti* to Narkomindel. This would be on record and 'would do something to allay the increasingly unpleasant situation'.

Chamberlain, faithful to his 'reserved' policy, strongly opposed this proposal, which he thought would only 'give importance to the rumours and the discussion to which they give rise' and which he hoped to avoid. Once more he criticized Hodgson for not being *au courant* with Government policy. Such a move, he

74 *Izvestiya*, 29 July 1925. See also leaders in *ibid.*, 17 and 18 June 1925.

75 F.O. 371 11016 N4270/102/38 and 11024 N3969/1317/38: Hodgson to Chamberlain, 2 and 17 July 1925. The scare was initiated by a leader in *Pravda*, 5 July 1925, accusing Chamberlain of 'creating a united front against communism at home and in the sphere of international relations against the USSR'; see also *Pravda*, 7 July 1925.

reiterated in a letter to the British Ambassador in Warsaw, 'would be a mistake. Qui s'excuse s'accuse.'[76]

Meanwhile the pattern of the Government's relations towards Russia was becoming clear. Repeated statements were made in Parliament that the failure of the Russians to observe the propaganda clause of the 1921 agreement excluded the possibility of improving relations. Chamberlain declined, however, to specify cases of infringement, arguing that the facts were 'always notorious' and that in his view no useful purpose could be achieved by a 'constant stream of detailed complaints'.[77] A Cabinet meeting on 5 August resulted, even more than previous meetings, in a compromise between Chamberlain and the die-hards. The basic conclusion was that there was 'no occasion at the present moment for the Government to change its policy towards Russia'. At the same time it was agreed that a Cabinet committee formed to assist Chamberlain in certain questions of foreign affairs should reconvene to review the situation in the light of any fresh developments, and that in any case it should meet after the recess.[78] The propaganda issue, however, subsided somewhat after the events in China, while the Locarno conference became the main issue in Anglo-Soviet relations.

Locarno: the ostracism of Russia

The Soviet Government had devoted the first half of 1924 to the improvement of relations with Britain to the detriment of relations with Germany.[79] The developments in England in the autumn of 1924 apparently did not inflict an immediate setback on the Soviet Union. The Conservative victory coincided with the

[76] F.O. 371 11016 N4519/102/38: Hodgson to Chamberlain, 7 July 1925; minute by Chamberlain, 12 Aug. 1925. F.O. 371 11016 N5059/102/38: Chamberlain to Ambassador in Warsaw, 12 Aug. 1925.

[77] *Parl. Deb. H.C.*, Vol. 186, col. 1812, and Vol. 187, cols. 13–15, 20 and 27 July 1925. See also Vol. 187, cols. 1809–39: debate on Chamberlain's statement on foreign policy, 7 Aug. 1925.

[78] Cab. 23/50 43(25)1. The committee was appointed in a previous Cabinet meeting, 41(25)3. Among its members were Baldwin, Birkenhead and Joynson-Hicks.

[79] Soviet-German relations were also strained by the police raid on the premises of the Soviet delegation in Berlin in May 1924; see *Izvestiya*, 17 May 1924.

French recognition of the Soviet Union, a fact which was exploited by the Russians in their relations with both Britain and Germany.[80] The Russians expected the conclusion of a treaty with France which would compensate for the rejection of the treaty in England. Their expectations were at first fully encouraged by Herriot, who appreciated the importance of the Russian market for French products.[81] However, soon after coming into office Chamberlain paid a visit to Herriot and discussed *inter alia* Russian-French relations. Herriot explained that *rapprochement* with Russia was a move designed to prevent an alliance between Germany and Russia. He agreed to an exchange of opinions on any further negotiations with the Russians. Before long the progress of the negotiations was halted when a deadlock occurred on the issues of private debts and the monopoly of trade.[82]

Whereas from the beginning of 1925 onwards German foreign policy acquired a measure of flexibility, the Russians grew increasingly dependent on the Germans. In order to revive the Rapallo spirit, they pressed the Germans in early December to conclude a commercial treaty. They in turn suggested a treaty defining the two countries' attitude to Poland.[83] However, the occupation of the Ruhr in January 1923 and the communist rising in Germany in October 1923 had reinforced Germany's cautious policy towards both Britain and Russia. Gustave Stresemann, Chancellor and Foreign Minister since 1923, preferred to remain aloof. He was aware that the new French Government headed by Herriot, unlike its predecessor, was ready to cooperate with Britain in a reconciliation with Germany. Association with the West seemed to hold better hopes for a political revision of the Versailles Treaty than commitment to the Soviet Union.[84] Yet in order to keep equilibrium in relations

[80] F.O. 371 10471 N8864/44/38: observations by Peters.

[81] F.O. 371 10471 N8650/44/38: Crewe, Ambassador in Paris, to Chamberlain, 20 Nov. 1924.

[82] F.O. 371 10471 N9223/44/38: Chamberlain on conversation with Herriot, 5 Dec. 1924; N9354/44/38: Crewe to Chamberlain.

[83] Z. J. Gasiorowski, 'The Russion Overture to Germany of December 1924', *Journal of Modern History* (1958), No. 2, pp. 101–105.

[84] Z. J. Gasiorowski, 'Stresemann and Poland before Locarno', *Journal of Central European Affairs* (1958–59), Vol. XVIII, No. 1, p. 29. See also J. Korbel, *Poland between East and West* (Princeton, 1963), pp. 153–54.

between East and West, Stresemann instructed the German Ambassador in Moscow to open limited negotiations with the Russians on the two countries' attitude towards Poland. He was taken by surprise when on 20 December Chicherin made clear to him that agreement on Poland was an issue secondary to that of Germany's entry into the League of Nations. Chicherin suggested that the German and Russian Governments should 'commit each other not to enter into any political or economical alliance or understanding with a third party which was directed against the other'. At the end of December Chicherin proposed to the German Ambassador: 'We shall do nothing with Herbette [the French Ambassador to Moscow] if you do nothing with Chamberlain.'[85] This was followed by the fanciful hope that Germany would join France and Russia in a 'continental bloc' intended to contain the British hegemony in Europe.[86] The new proposals were generated by Russia's isolation consequent on the Anglo-French understanding and the fear that the next stage would be the inclusion of Germany in an anti-Soviet bloc which, Russia insisted, was crystallizing in Europe around Britain.

The German-Soviet negotiations dragged out between 1924 and 1925. The Germans carefully observed the outcome of the Anglo-Soviet crisis. They also preferred not to bind themselves by treaties before a reply was received to their memorandum to the French Government of February 1925, which proposed an arrangement for security in Europe. In addition the slow progress of the negotiations reflected a divergence of opinion within the German Government as to the economic advantages to be gained from the proposed German-Soviet commercial treaty.[87]

The Russians were deeply disturbed when they learnt in early March that talks on a security pact had started. Radek commented that Russian diplomacy did not function in a vacuum and that any change in the position of Germany in Europe would

[85] Korbel, *Poland between East and West*, pp. 157–58.

[86] H. L. Dyck, 'German Soviet Relations and the Anglo-Soviet Break, 1927', *Slavonic Review* (Mar. 1966), No. 1, p. 69.

[87] Carr, *Socialism in One Country*, Vol. 3, pt. 1, pp. 257–67. See also K. Rosenbaum, *Community of Fate: German-Soviet Diplomatic Relations 1922–1928* (Syracuse, 1965), pp. 149–56, and R. P. Morgan, 'The Political Significance of the German-Soviet Trade Negotiations 1922–25', *The Historical Journal* (1963), No. VI, pp. 253–71.

have direct effects on Soviet policy.[88] However, Schubert, the German Secretary of State for Foreign Affairs, had no intention of antagonizing the Russians. He communicated to Moscow that the British Government had been told that Germany would not sacrifice its relations with Russia by joining the League. However, the Russians were not reassured when they learnt from Stresemann that if the negotiations on the security pact led to an arbitration treaty with Poland it would only be a façade to reassure France. Germany would not use force against Poland but would stay neutral in the case of a Russian initiative.[89]

Germany had become the 'battle-field' between Soviet and British diplomacy, and the proposed Locarno Pact was viewed by the Russians as a new constellation in which the British were to occupy a prominent position and from which the Russians were excluded. This appeared to the Russians as yet another proof that the reserved policy of the Conservative Government was now being applied successfully to the international arena.[90] In these circumstances, accord with Germany and the perpetuation of the Rapallo spirit became the main criterion for the success of Soviet diplomacy in 1925. Although the emphasis on different aspects of the 'anti-Soviet treaty' kept shifting throughout 1925, the only consistent anxiety concerned Germany's *volte-face*. The Locarno Treaty, although not necessarily a rejection of the Rapallo Treaty, was a path on which it would 'scarcely be possible to continue the policy of Rapallo'.[91] Germany's *rapprochement* towards Britain was explained as stemming from the inflation of the mark, and the growing dependence on credit granted through Britain from the USA. Thus the Dawes plan was considered to be 'the economic platform for the launching of the political plan of the Security Pact'.[92] Although the Russians generally assigned economic motivations to Germany's

88 *Izvestiya*, 15 Mar. 1925.

89 Gasiorowski, 'The Russian Overture to Germany of December, 1924', p. 109; Rosenbaum, *Community of Fate*, p. 192.

90 *Izvestiya*, 24 May 1925.

91 *Pravda*, 18 Oct. 1925.

92 *ibid.*, 5 Nov. 1925; later repeated by Stalin in *XIV S'ezd Vseoyuznoi Kommunisticheskoi Partii* (*B*). *Stenograficheskii Otchet* (Moscow, 1926), p. 13 (hereafter referred to as *XIV S'ezd VKP*), and in the resolution on the report of the central committee, *XIV S'ezd VKP*, p. 514.

move, there were some pragmatists who accused Germany of voluntarily capitulating to Britain.[93]

A textual analysis of the Locarno Treaty could have given the Russians no grounds for suspecting that it was an expression of an anti-Soviet policy. In the protocol signed on 16 October 1925, the signatories declared their intention of 'preserving their respective nations from the scourge of war' and 'providing for the peaceful settlement of disputes of every nature which might eventually arise between them'. The central part of the protocol was a treaty of mutual guarantee between Germany, Belgium, France and Italy.[94]

However, when the wider implications of the international alignment established by the treaty are considered, the Soviet allegations cannot easily be dismissed.[95] The embryo of an anti-Soviet bloc was inherent in the treaty. The Russians emphasized the anti-Soviet character of the treaty and played down its declared intentions. Rakovsky, although admitting that 'Russia was not even mentioned there', claimed that the regrouping of interests and countries posed a new threat to Russia.[96] The Russians did not ignore the apparent contradiction but explained that the treaty was a mask behind which all their 'notorious' enemies were hiding.[97]

The basic assumption underlying the Soviet view was that the treaty was aimed at solving the crisis of the capitalist system. The capitalist countries had reached a critical stage as a result of their inability to export their expanding surplus production.

93 *Pravda*, 18 Oct. 1925; see also Rakovsky in *Mirovoe Khozyaistvo i Mirovaya Politika* (1926), No. 1, p. 39. Radek was one of the first to suggest, in *Izvestiya*, 24 May 1925, that Germany was becoming a 'pawn in the hands of Entente diplomacy'.

94 A. G. Grün, 'Locarno: Idea and Reality', *International Affairs* (1955), Vol. XXXI, p. 478.

95 See for instance Klyuchnikov, Soviet expert on international law, in *Mezhn. Let.* (1925), Nos. 10–11, p. 63.

96 *Mir. Khz. i Mir. Pol.* (1926), No. 1, p. 44. The same views are expressed by Rakovsky in *Liga Natsii i SSSR* (Moscow, 1926), p. 52.

97 *Izvestiya*, 22 Nov. 1925. *ibid.*, 11 Nov. 1925, declared: 'In order to prepare the encirclement of the USSR it is not at all obligatory to call things by their proper names.' See also *Pravda*, 18 Oct. 1925. A more balanced evaluation appears in V. M. Turok, 'Anglo-Frantsuzskie Peregovory o "Zapadnom Bloke"', *Seriya Istorii i Filosofii* (1948), No. 4, pp. 337–54.

Both Stalin and Zinoviev maintained that Locarno was an attempt to close the ranks of the capitalist countries and overcome their problems by waging wars which would open up new markets, in particular the Russian market. The method of achieving this consisted of bringing Germany under their influence.[98] The ultimate aim of such declarations was apparently not only to minimize the failure of Soviet diplomacy but to encourage the negotiations with France on a common anti-British line[99] and cause the Germans to reconsider their Russian policy. Since the Russians believed the economic issue to be the dominant factor in Locarno, they dismissed as myth Chamberlain's reputation as the architect of peace in Europe. Radek explained that more attention should be paid to the role of the Americans as the initiators of the treaty. 'Locarno', he wrote, 'can be considered at once an English and American victory.'[100]

In addition to their apprehension of the potential dangers in the treaty, the Russians had good reason to fear its practical consequences. They pointed out that, although Britain expressed its desire to guarantee the security of Europe, it was not inclined to guarantee Germany's Eastern frontiers; in the event of conflict in the area Britain could take advantage of the situation to launch an attack against the Soviet Union. They predicted that, despite French opposition, Germany would eventually be allowed to re-arm, and that in return for joining the entente it would be rewarded at Poland's expense.[101] However, these fears were unfounded. From Locarno, Chamberlain conveyed to Tyrrell his impression that the Germans had not relinquished their desire to change their Eastern frontier; yet he thought such a move very unlikely as they had 'neither the power nor the will to seek a solution to the problem by force'. However, although a motion to secure an agreement regarding the Eastern frontier was tabled, Chamberlain wrote to Tyrrell that he would not be 'in the first instance at any rate, and may not be at any time, an actual participant' in the negotiations regarding this frontier.[102]

98 *XIV S'ezd VKP*: Stalin, pp. 18–19; Zinoviev, p. 652. See the same views in an earlier leader in *Ekonomicheskaya Zhizn'*, 20 Oct. 1925.

99 S. Schram, 'Christian Rakovskij et le Premier Rapprochement Franco-Soviétique', *Cahiers du Monde Russe et Soviètique*' (1960), No. 4, p. 584.

100 *Izvestiya*, 8 Dec. 1925.

101 Leaders in *ibid.*, 30 June and 18 Oct. 1925.

102 F.O. 371 10741 C12491/459/18: Chamberlain to Tyrrell, 2 Oct. 1925.

The Russians interpreted Britain's virtual disregard of Germany's Eastern frontier as part of the Locarno conspiracy. They believed this policy to be a consequence of the failure of the intervention. According to this interpretation, the British had realized that in order to secure a better performance in the future, troops would have to be transferred to the Russian front via Germany.[103] To ensure Germany's approval for such a move it would be allowed to expand into Polish territory. This menace, the Russians claimed, would materialize once Germany was accepted into the League and bound by its Covenant. These assumptions were also groundless. During the discussions in Locarno on its admittance to the League, Germany resisted all attempts to make it subscribe to article 16 of the League's Covenant. A letter modifying the article was therefore added to the pact.[104] Soviet historians still maintain that Locarno was a pillar in British foreign policy, the first step towards Munich, where Britain again proved ready to isolate Russia by guaranteeing the integrity of some countries at the expense of others.[105]

However, it was Poland which was the immediate victim of the failure to reach an arrangement on the Eastern frontier.[106] Before the negotiations in Locarno, Poland played an important role in the context of Anglo-Soviet relations. By spreading rumours that Locarno was above all the nucleus of an anti-Soviet bloc, Poland expected the Russians to put pressure on Germany not to sign the treaty and join the League of Nations. Count Skrzynski, Poland's Foreign Minister, 'found it hard to believe' that Britain did not realize that it was in its interests to 'detach Germany from Russia', Although Chamberlain

[103] Zinoviev, *XIV S'ezd VKP*, p. 652; Rakovsky, *Mir. Khz. i Mir. Pol.* (1926), No. 1, p. 36.

[104] This is even accepted by the Russian official publication of documents dealing with Locarno, Narkomindel, *Lokarnskaya Konferentsiya 1925g.* (Moscow, 1959), pp. 13–16. On the German position see E. Sutton (ed.), *Gustave Stresemann, His Diaries, Letters, and Papers* (London, 1937), Vol. II, pp. 476–77.

[105] *Lokarnskaya Konferentsiya 1925g.*, p. 19; L. Karoi, *Velikobritaniya i Lokarno* (Moscow, 1961), p. 27; S. B. Nikonova, *Antisovetskaya Vneshnyaya Politika Angliiskikh Konservatorov, 1924–1927* (Moscow, 1963), p. 86.

[106] The natural move for Poland would have been to seek a *détente* with Russia, but memories of the war, fears of Bolshevism and the endemic anti-Russian feelings militated against this.

instructed the Ambassador in Warsaw to deny the existence of such plans, Skrzynski retained his opinion and informed the British Ambassador in Warsaw, after his meeting with Chicherin, of the terror which British policy inspired in Moscow and which he thought was 'not a bad thing'.[107] Once in Locarno, Skrzynski rejected Chamberlain's denial that England was contemplating an anti-Soviet bloc. He insisted that it was Chicherin's profound fear of Britain which had prompted him to approach Poland.[108]

The Soviet interpretation erred by grossly exaggerating the anti-Soviet intentions of Chamberlain. Chamberlain never contemplated a conflict involving armed intervention. He thought in terms of re-organizing Europe in a manner favourable to Britain, one result of which would be the containment of a strong Russia in the future. As early as February, Chamberlain expressed the view that in the not too distant future Russia would re-emerge as a great power in Europe. His aim was to link Germany with the Western countries and prevent it from joining Russia in an anti-entente bloc. However, these were considerations of secondary importance; Chamberlain believed that the less they 'spoke about it in public the better it would be'.[109] Indeed, throughout the discussion on Germany's entrance to the League and on the future of the Eastern frontiers, Chamberlain tried to refute the concept of Britain as leader and initiator of an anti-Soviet bloc. He welcomed the improvement of relations between the signatories and Russia, and emphasized that British policy aimed at securing the peace of Europe and that 'any *rapprochement* between the Soviet Government and the European powers could only assist towards this end'.[110]

The Foreign Office was nevertheless aware of the anti-Soviet implications of the treaty. Peters drew the attention of Chamberlain to the fact that the settlement would draw Europe together and thus prevent the Russians from 'playing one power off

107 F.O. 371 11016 N5059 and N5491/102/38: Muller on conversations with Skrzynski, 7 and 28 Sept. 1925.

108 F.O. 371 10742 C12818/459/18: Chamberlain to Tyrrell, 9 Oct. 1925.

109 D. Johnstone, 'Austen Chamberlain and the Locarno Agreement', *University of Birmingham Historical Journal* (1961), Vol. VIII, No. 1, p. 78; F.O. 371 10734 C1895/459/18: Chamberlain to Tyrrell, 12 June 1925.

110 F.O. 371 10742 C12822/459/18: Chamberlain to Tyrrell, 8 Oct. 1925; also F.O. 371 11016 N5812/102/38: 13 Oct. 1925.

against another'. It would also make the Soviet Union 'approximate more and more in its foreign policy to an ordinary state' by forcing it to abandon propaganda and relax the monopoly of trade.[111] Tyrrell, in correspondence with Chamberlain in Geneva, referred to the Soviet Union by pointing out that the effort Chicherin was making to undo Chamberlain's work was an 'eloquent argument on the wholesomeness' of Chamberlain's policy and of the 'disastrous character of the policy represented by Prinkipo and Genoa'.[112]

The Locarno Treaty and its implications for Anglo-Soviet relations were discussed in the Cabinet on 25 October. Chamberlain informed the Cabinet that during the negotiations in Locarno, the French and German representatives had expressed anxiety about the British attitude to Russia. He also repeated Peters' information that Chicherin was alarmed at the failure of his policy and said that he hoped that the need for credits would compel the Soviet Government to approach the Western European countries before long. Chamberlain proposed that in the light of the treaty the Cabinet should reconsider its policy towards Russia.[113]

It appeared as if moderation were winning the upper hand. Gregory was instructed to prepare a memorandum on a possible solution of differences with the Soviet Union. The basic assumption of the memorandum was that a peaceful settlement in Europe could not be effective without Russia's participation. At the same time the hostile attitude towards Russia could be detected from Gregory's opinion on the advantages to be gained by reaching such an agreement. These were basically the control of Russia once it became a member of the League, and the undoing of Russian communism by accepting it into the Concert of Europe, and thus the aggravation of the conflict between Comintern and the Soviet Government.[114]

However it became evident that the speculations about Russia's

[111] F.O. 371 11021 N5875 and N5876/710/38: Peters to Chamberlain, 9 Oct. 1925.

[112] Chamberlain papers, 37/154: Tyrrell to Chamberlain.

[113] Cab. 23/51 50(25)4, 25 Oct. 1925.

[114] This was the main reason for Rakovsky's fierce objections to the League, *Mezhdn. Let.* (1925), No. 12. See also similar views by Chicherin in *Stat'i*, p. 375.

change of policy on the lines suggested during the Cabinet meeting and in Gregory's memorandum would not be justified. The Foreign Office was taken by surprise when news reached London of the conclusion of the German-Soviet Treaty of 12 October 1925.[115] The treaty, which was signed out of purely political considerations in spite of its economic content, stemmed from Germany's wish to balance its position between East and West. It also demonstrated Russia's ability to extricate itself from the isolation imposed on it by Locarno.[116] A resolution of the central committee of the CPSU in early October re-affirmed that the monopoly of trade was an effective means of repulsing the economic pressures of the capitalist countries.[117]

In mid-November Rakovsky was assigned to the post of Ambassador in Paris to help in the negotiation of a treaty to which the Russians attached great importance. He was to be replaced in London by Krasin, who, however, did not arrive in London until autumn 1926. Before leaving London, Rakovsky had a last interview with Chamberlain. This meeting was more frank and straightforward than previous ones. Chamberlain categorically refuted the Russian accusations that Locarno was a prelude for an anti-Soviet move. Rakovsky did not contradict this statement but expressed doubts as to whether Chamberlain's colleagues really allowed him 'to give full effect' to his policy. Chamberlain denied the existence of any divergence of views in the Cabinet. He admitted, however, that the breaking off of relations had been contemplated and discussed in Cabinet. He then retaliated by expressing his doubts 'whether the Soviet Government was indeed the Government of Russia or only the instrument of another body', namely Comintern and the CPSU.[118] Perhaps the most important feature of the talk was Rakovsky's request to Chamberlain to prevail upon the Cabinet to change its policy as far as credits and loans to Russia were concerned. This was a clear

115 F.O. 371 11018 N7151/265/38: Board of Trade's memorandum, 30 Dec. 1925. Hodgson had reported in July that a deadlock in the negotiations had occurred, F.O. 371 11018 N3971/265/38. On the conclusion of the treaty see also Sutton, *Gustave Stresemann*, Vol. II, pp. 478–86.

116 E. H. Carr, *Socialism in One Country*, Vol. 3, pt. 1, p. 278. See leader in *Ekon. Zhzn.*, 13 Oct. 1925.

117 *Dok. Vne. Pol.*, Vol. VIII, pp. 564–71.

118 F.O. 371 11016 N6213/102/38: Chamberlain to Hodgson, 5 Nov. 1925.

hint that Krasin would concentrate on attracting capital in the City if the Russians failed to receive direct loans from the Government.

While in Moscow Rakovsky described the *status quo* in Anglo-Soviet relations, specifically commenting on the unwillingness of British financial circles to grant credit to Russia.[119] Throughout 1925 the Russians maintained pressure on the British Government to reconsider the question of credit. The provision of Russian industry with modern equipment was still hindered by the scarceness of capital and the reluctance of European countries to grant credits. In July G. Sokolnikov, the Russian Commissar of Finance, appealed to Britain to advance credits to Russia which, he believed, would ease unemployment in Britain by opening the vast Russian markets for British products. Frumkin, in charge of foreign trade in the Commissariat, warned that if the financial blockade continued Russia would have to 'turn to the Soviet Union's population for achieving domestic credit' and become self-sufficient.[120] Krasin echoed these views at the end of September when he stressed that credits were the 'essential condition and prerequisite' for the development of Russia's trade.[121] His views found full expression in a resolution passed by the congress of the CPSU in December which emphasized that peaceful co-existence with the capitalist countries was 'vital' in order to facilitate the implementation of a socialist structure in Russia.[122] However, Chamberlain saw in Rakovsky's request and the Russians' appeal a sign that the policy of aloofness had 'succeeded very well', and a justification of the policy he had proposed in the Cabinet meeting. He suggested to Churchill that in order to pursue this policy, Churchill should advise the City to present a united front to Krasin, who should not be allowed 'to conquer it bit by bit'.[123]

Attempts to bring about Anglo-Russian understanding in the economic sphere were followed by similar moves in the diplomatic field. During a reception held at the Soviet Embassy in Berlin to mark the eighth anniversary of the Russian revolution,

119 Rakovsky interviewed in *Izvestiya*, 10 Oct. 1925.
120 *Ekon. Zhzn.*, 7 July 1925.
121 *ibid.*, 22 Sept. 1925.
122 *XIV S'ezd VKP*, p. 513.
123 Chamberlain papers, 52/171: Chamberlain to Churchill, 5 Nov. 1925.

Chicherin approached Lord D'Abernon, the British Ambassador there. Chicherin was anxious to discuss with him the differences between the two countries. Since the British Government insisted on starting negotiations with an authoritative figure, such a move should have been appreciated in London. D'Abernon, who was as usual reluctant to reach any kind of understanding with the Bolsheviks, was evasive and told Chicherin that he was not acquainted with the Government's attitude towards solving the outstanding problems. D'Abernon was well-informed of the Government's policy but pursued the attitude of 'great reserve' as practised by the Office. Both Chamberlain and Maxse agreed that the longer they remained 'steadily elusive' the more the Soviet Government would have to 'precise its ideas for a development of more normal relations'.[124]

The most curious attempt to relax the tension in Anglo-Soviet relations took place in London. It was conceived by Hodgson, who was on leave in London at the end of 1925. Hodgson had advised the Foreign Office to embark upon negotiations with the Russians but had been discouraged by Chamberlain. This time, however, Hodgson's stay in London coincided with Chamberlain's departure for Geneva and for a holiday in Italy; Hodgson, therefore, felt free to pursue his own line. Rosengoltz and Maisky, whom Hodgson met on a friendly visit to the Soviet Mission, complained that they were 'kept at a distance and practically ignored by the British Government'. According to Hodgson, Rosengoltz proposed informal talks in the Foreign Office at which Hodgson would be present.

Hodgson pressed Mounsey in the Office to respond favourably to the Russian move, which he believed was a result of the Locarno arrangement and which might bring advantages to Britain before the Franco-Soviet talks came to a successful conclusion. Familiar with Chamberlain's views on this matter, Mounsey tried to dampen Hodgson's enthusiasm and prevent any impetuous action, suggesting that it would be preferable to watch the progress made in the Franco-Soviet negotiations. Gregory was even more definite in refusing to embark on negotia-

[124] F.O. 371 11016 N6274/102/38: D'Abernon to Chamberlain on his meeting with Chicherin, 8 Nov. 1925; *Dok. Vne. Pol.*, Vol. VIII, pp. 657–60: Chicherin to CC of the CPSU on conversation with D'Abernon, 8 Nov. 1925.

tions: 'Set an inconvenient ball of this sort prematurely rolling and we never know when it is going to stop.' However, so as not to miss a possible drastic change in the Russian position, nor to provide the Opposition with ammunition to claim that the Government was determined to undermine Russian efforts to reach an agreement, Tyrrell suggested that Mounsey should tactfully explain to the Russians that the question would have to be raised again upon Chamberlain's return.

When this meeting took place, Mounsey must have been surprised to learn from Rosengoltz that the proposal to start informal talks had originated with Hodgson and not with himself. Mounsey, however, managed to bring back the talks to their more 'traditional' pattern, explaining to Rosengoltz that negotiations were unlikely to occur as long as the two Governments avoided facing questions which involved differences of principles. Rosengoltz exploited the evident differences between Hodgson and the Foreign Office. He concluded the meeting, and with it this abortive attempt to bring about a change in Anglo-Soviet relations, by saying that he had not come to see Mounsey with the object of passing on Hodgson's tentative proposals but in order to ascertain the Government's view. Both Gregory and Tyrrell were critical of the steps taken by Hodgson but in the absence of Chamberlain the incident was quickly forgotten.[125]

125 F.O. 371 N6928/102/38: minute by Mounsey on conversation with Hodgson, 13 Dec. 1925; minutes by Gregory and Tyrrell, 14 Dec. 1925.

3

The Anglo-Soviet Trade Union Alliance: An Uneasy Partnership

From recognition to a united front

The momentary enthusiasm and optimism prompted by the 'historic step' of recognition stemmed from awareness of alarming setbacks in the revolutionary situation. However, the swift disenchantment with the Labour Government, now labelled as 'a third bourgeois party', meant a return to a more gloomy outlook.[1] Zinoviev's powerful oratory during the fifth congress of Comintern in June 1924, desperately endeavouring to prove that revolutionary conditions were still building up though at a slower pace, was indicative of these reversals.[2] The situation was defined as an 'era of stabilization of capitalism', characterized by a regrouping of the capitalist forces, which required a re-orientation in the activities of the communist parties and the front organizations in defence of the Soviet Union. It also paved the way for alliances with left-wing movements.[3] In addition to the new concept of stabilization, another was introduced, that of Bolshevization, which severely limited the independent development of the different parties.[4] They were called upon to follow the example set by the CPSU and safeguard the existence of the 'only party to have carried out a successful revolution'.[5]

1 *Pyatyi Vsemirnyi Kongress*, Vol. I, p. 60.

2 *ibid.*, pp. 441–42; resolution on 'two perspectives' of stabilization in Vol. II, p. 47. Zinoviev's severe obsession about the revolutionary drive is explained in V. Serge, *Memoirs of a Revolutionary, 1901–1941* (Oxford, 1963), p. 177, as a result of his opposition to the rising of 1917.

3 *Pyatyi Vsemirnyi Kongress*, Vol. II, pp. 33–34.

4 See for example the CPGB's complaint that the proposed policy towards Labour meant 'self-liquidation' in *ibid.*, Vol. I, pp. 123–24 and 265, and in *Kommunisticheskii Internatsional* (1924), No. 9, p. 57.

5 A. Tivel' and M. Kheimo, *10 Let Kominterna* (Moscow–Leningrad, 1929), pp. 104–105. A. Balabanoff, *My Life as a Rebel* (London, 1938), p. 247, describes Bolshevization as a process which made foreign parties'

The identification of the interests of the Soviet state with those of the Party and the gradual emergence of the CPSU as the *primus inter pares* weakened Narkomindel's assertion of complete detachment from Comintern. However, the point of convergence between Comintern's policy and Soviet diplomacy concerning relations with Britain had been reached during the thirteenth congress of the Party earlier in May. Zinoviev, despite his position as the president of Comintern, was chosen to deliver the report of the Party's central committee on the international situation of the Soviet Union. His speech, which displayed an unusual restraint and lack of revolutionary fervour, expressed a 'resolute will' to improve relations with Britain. The report revealed no trace of tension between Narkomindel and Comintern; on the contrary, Zinoviev urged the Party to pay more attention to problems of foreign policy and expected Narkomindel to become 'one of the most popular commissariats in the country'.[6]

The prominence given to Britain was also a result of a fast-growing left wing in the trade unions, the potential of which was recognized by both Comintern and Narkomindel. The emergence of this left wing at first passed unnoticed, but when perceived it provoked a heated debate in Moscow, the outcome of which was that trade union relations between the two countries became a cornerstone in Soviet diplomacy[7] and the focus of Comintern's aspirations in Britain.

The sudden *volte-face* in Anglo-Soviet trade union relations was totally unforeseen. The year 1923 witnessed escalating rivalry between Profintern, whose strongest support came from the Soviet trade unions, and the IFTU, whose most numerous and influential members were the English unions.[8] The Plymouth TUC, which met in September 1923, refused to establish

members move in the 'reflected glory of the October revolution'. See also K. McKenzie, *Comintern and World Revolution, 1928–1943* (Columbia, 1964), pp. 51–57.

[6] *Trinadtsatyi S'ezd* (*B*), pp. 48 and 54.

[7] Rakovsky included these relations 'among the gains of Soviet foreign policy': interview in *Pravda*, 25 Jan. 1925.

[8] J. Braunthal, *History of the International, 1914–1943* (London, 1967), Vol. 2, p. 319. The membership of the Socialist International was 6,637,622, out of which 3,388,286 were English: Comintern numbered 1,707,769 out of which the Russians were 1,210,954 (in 1928). See also A. Pankratova in *Bol'shevik* (June 1925), Nos. 9–10, p. 39.

communication with Profintern and defeated all resolutions put forward by members of the British bureau of that organization.[9]

The TUC's position, however, changed considerably as a result of the election of the Labour Government and the subsequent recognition of Russia. The immediate and perhaps decisive factor was the election of Purcell, Swales and Hicks to the General Council of the TUC to replace the more conservative Thomas, Gosling, Bondfield and Clynes, who now took government posts.[10] Of the new General Council, Purcell, who was elected chairman of the Council as well as president of the executive committee of the IFTU in 1924, was mainly responsible for the change. Although he had refused to join the CPGB, Purcell was closely associated with the Party at its foundation. Later, as an active member of the Labour delegation to Russia in summer 1920 and the leading spirit in the 'Hands off Russia' campaign to end intervention, he became outspoken in his pro-Soviet sentiments.[11] The new direction in the TUC was reinforced by the desire to safeguard its own identity and secure its interests against the Labour Government. In addition the reorganization of the General Council for the first time concentrated power to implement policy on a national level.[12] The economic argument for full friendly relations with Russia was widespread in the unions; it was taken for granted that this would lead to the re-opening of Russia for British goods and consequently ease economic hardship and the severe unemployment.[13]

The Anglo-Soviet Conference, which lasted from April to

[9] *Report of Proceedings at the 55th Annual Trades Union Congress* (London, 1923), pp. 298 and 343–50.

[10] A. Bullock, *The Life and Times of Ernest Bevin* (London, 1960), Vol. 1, p. 261; J. T. Murphy, *Preparing for Power* (London, 1934), p. 227.

[11] TUC archives, CTP, biographical notes. See also *Trud*, 11 Nov. 1924, and J. Klugmann, *A History of the Communist Party of Great Britain* (London, 1968), Vol. 1, pp. 83–84 and 214.

[12] *Report of Proceedings at the 56th Annual Trades Union Congress* (London, 1924), p. 81 (hereafter referred to as *Report of 56th TUC*); on reorganization see A. D. Flanders, *Trade Unions* (London, 1952), pp. 60–67 and 137. The divergence of interests became acute during the transport workers' strike, in which the Labour Government contemplated invoking the Emergency Powers Act; see R. Miliband, *Parliamentary Socialism* (London, 1964), p. 110.

[13] *Report of 56th TUC*, pp. 436–37.

August, provided the occasion for trade union leaders of both countries to become acquainted. The inclusion of Tomsky, the president of the AUCCTU, as well as the disproportionately high number of trade unionists in the eleven-member Soviet delegation, was initially calculated to demonstrate its proletarian character. It appears that the composition was a reaction to the Labour Government's decision not to allow representatives of the TUC to sit in the conference.[14] The CPGB indeed used to the full the composition of the delegation for propaganda purposes, describing it as 'the first occasion in the history of any diplomatic negotiations when the trade unions had a direct representative participating on their behalf'.[15] The other purpose was to show the degree of integration of the trade unions in the process of the economic recovery of Russia. The trade unionists were not chosen at random but represented those branches of industry which the Russians seriously hoped to reconstruct by placing orders in Britain.[16]

The statement issued by Purcell and others deploring the Bankers' Memorandum gave birth to the idea that support could be recruited from the trade unions, bearing in mind their defence of the Soviet Union during the intervention. This idea was seized upon and embodied in the AUCCTU's declaration protesting against the bankers' action on one hand and calling on the British to revive the 'Hands off Russia' movement on the other.[17] A major step in this direction was a reception hastily arranged on 14 May in honour of the Russian delegation to the Anglo-Soviet Conference by the General Council on the initiative of A. Purcell and Fred Bramley, the creator of the General

[14] A. Lozovsky, *Za Edinstvo Mezhdunarodnogo Profdvizheniya* (Moscow, 1925), p. 17. See also *supra*, p. 17.

[15] Pollitt in foreword to A. Lozovsky, *British and Russian Workers* (London, 1927), p. 9; see also Kalnin of the AUCCTU in *Trud*, 17 Apr. 1924.

[16] Tomsky, *Getting Together*, pp. 20–21. Discussions on the adoption of the 'productionist' line by the Russian trade unions are in I. Deutscher, *Soviet Trade Unions* (London, 1950), pp. 62–70, and in D. V. Antoshkin, *Kratkii Ocherk Professional'nogo Dvizheniya v Rossii* (Moscow, 1928), p. 128.

[17] *Trud*, 20 Apr. 1924, and leader in *Trud*, 24 Apr. 1924. Similar resolutions of the seventh congresses of the Soviet Railwaymen and Miners in *Trud*, 22 Apr. 1924.

Council in 1921 and its powerful general secretary.[18] The reception turned into a miniature conference in which 'a very cordial and frank exchange of opinions occurred'; all present realized 'the necessity of direct contact between the two movements' but no concrete proposals were made in that direction.[19] However, the favourable impression gained by the General Council from the encounters with their Russian counterparts and their receptiveness to 'everything which emanated from Russian official sources' facilitated further *rapprochement*.[20] Tomsky, overwhelmed by the 'most hearty comradely reception' he had received, as well as by the General Council's pledge to stand by Russia, returned home to participate in the forthcoming congresses of Comintern and Profintern as an ardent advocate of trade union unity.[21]

Tomsky's case was further justified by the conduct of the General Council's delegation to the IFTU congress in Vienna which met on 2–6 June 1924. There the issue at hand was a proposal to bring to an end communication with Moscow. The attempts of the Russian trade unions to approach the IFTU dated back to 1922, when Comintern had launched a campaign for the creation of a united front against capitalism. After two years of polemics, the Russians were informed in December 1923 that further contact was possible only on the basis of acceptance of the rules and general policy of the IFTU.[22] In the Vienna congress, the TUC delegation led by Bramley emphasized that the British Government's recognition of and negotiations with the Soviet Government necessitated a change of attitude toward the trade unions. 'It would be a very serious anomaly', said Bramley, 'if at the very moment when our nation was endeavouring to establish friendly relations with the Russians, we should refuse to continue negotiations and consultations with the Trade Union movement in the same country.' Despite fierce opposition

18 TUC archives, *Minutes of the General Council, 1923–24*, p. 97, 28 May 1924.

19 *Report of 56th TUC*, p. 244.

20 W. Citrine, *Men and Work* (London, 1964), p. 88. See also Cramp in *Report of 56th TUC*, p. 317. The Russians were described as 'men of high character and broad outlook' in *Report of 56th TUC*, p. 315.

21 Reported in *Trud*, 28 May 1924.

22 *The Activities of the International Federation of Trade Unions, 1922–1924* (Amsterdam, 1924), pp. 87–93; *Report on Activities during the Years 1924, 1925 and 1926* (Amsterdam, 1927), p. 47.

to the new British standpoint, the commission which had produced the report was directed to alter it.[23] A final compromise version regretted the 'continued absence' of the Russian trade unions from the IFTU but blamed this on the refusal of the Russians to accept the rules and constitution of the Federation.[24]

The tactical victory of the British in Vienna combined with the prospects of collaboration with the TUC strengthened the hand of the champions of united front tactics in the Soviet trade unions, a bone of contention in the impending congresses of Comintern and Profintern. It also opened new dimensions for Soviet diplomacy. In the fifth congress of Comintern, Zinoviev restated the strategy of the united front within the trade unions as a means of fulfilling revolutionary aspirations as well as of manoeuvring against the capitalist offensive. As had already been intimated before the congress, Zinoviev introduced the Lilliputian CPGB as 'the most important section of the Communist International' precisely because of its deep roots in the trade unions.[25] The sharp turn to the left and the growing wave of sympathy towards Russia in the British trade unions were described as the high watermark in the world revolution.[26] In view of the reemergence of Britain as the most important imperialist power, the parties were instructed to support the CPGB in fulfilling its 'historic role'; this referred to activities on two fronts. On the domestic front, the CPGB was to seek the support of the masses in the trade unions and the left wing of the Labour movement in exposing MacDonald's anti-socialist policy. On the international front, to counteract the formation of a capitalist offensive, the Party was called upon to exert pressure on the Labour Government to change its foreign policy on a variety of questions: disarmament, the Dawes plan, colonial policy and relations with Russia.[27]

[23] *The Activities of the International Federation of Trade Unions, 1922–1924*, pp. 231 and 227–32, and *Report of 56th TUC*, p. 246.

[24] *The Activities of the IFTU*, p. 260.

[25] *Pyatyi Vsemirnyi Kongress*, Vol. I, pp. 59–81. A study of the emergence of the united front tactics is in J. Degras, 'United Front Tactics in the Comintern 1921–1928', *International Communism*, St. Antony's Papers, No. 9 (ed. D. Footman) (London, 1960).

[26] *Pyatyi Vsemirnyi Kongress*, Vol. II, p. 66.

[27] *ibid.*, pp. 48–49: resolution on the tasks of the CPGB; pp. 119–20: resolution on the Labour Government.

In the course of the previous year the CPGB had been a subject of continuous and severe criticism for its shortcomings both in organization and in interpretation of Comintern's policy.[28] As recently as the CPSU congress in May, the Party had been described as 'nothing more than a small propagandist group' and accused of adopting 'an unnecessary attitude of respect' towards the Labour Government.[29] The sudden elevation of the CPGB to the position of model party and Zinoviev's thesis on the united front therefore resulted in a long debate in which constant hints were dropped regarding the CPSU's opportunism. The fiercest attacks on the CPGB came from Ruth Fischer, representing the left wing of the KPD, who mercilessly exposed rightist tendencies in the Party and expressed doubts about its experience and its competence to combat reformism in the Labour movement. Comintern, she concluded, could not be satisfied with the mild attitude of the Party towards the Government, which amounted to approaching MacDonald and telling him: 'Dearest Mr. MacDonald, please conduct a little bit of socialist policy.'[30] This brought J. T. Murphy to the rostrum. Referring to Lenin's thesis on the 'infantile disease of leftism in communism', which had been presented to the second congress of Comintern and introduced united front tactics, he restated that the future of the Party was within the framework of both the Labour Party and the trade unions.[31]

In spite of attempts by the presidium of the congress to remove the question of trade union unity from the agenda, this was duly dealt with in the last session of the congress. It was immediately apparent that the Russian leadership had not as yet defined its attitude. In May, when unity had been used merely as a propaganda device, A. Lozovsky, Profintern's general secretary, had appeared as the partisan of that slogan, although most of the

[28] *Speeches and Documents of the Sixth Conference of the Communist Party of Great Britain* (London, n.d.), pp. 50–51 (hereafter referred to as *Sixth Conference CPGB*); *International Press Correspondence*, 21 Feb. and 27 Feb. 1924.

[29] *Trinadtsatyi S'ezd (B)*: Radek, p. 341; Bukharin, pp. 326–27. See also Radek in *Komm. Int.* (1924), No. 2, pp. 51–67.

[30] *Pyatyi Vsemirnyi Kongress*, Vol. 1, p. 191.

[31] *ibid.*, pp. 265–67; see also MacManus in *ibid.*, pp. 350–57. Murphy was for extended periods the CPGB's resident representative in Moscow.

European unions were controlled by reformists.[32] However, the unexpected outcome of the Vienna congress and the invitation to the Russian trade unions to join the IFTU, seriously considered by the AUCCTU, caused Lozovsky concern about the future of Profintern. He hastened to warn the AUCCTU, which was in session at the time, that the price of accepting the proposal was too high; it meant abandoning the revolutionary groups and becoming a minority.[33]

In the few days before the Comintern congress, Lozovsky was desperately trying to minimize the achievements of the emerging left flank of the English TUC. The left leadership of the TUC, he argued, was no match for the German Social Democrats, the real force behind the Amsterdam International.[34] However, Tomsky's recent involvement in the international trade union movement, hitherto the undisputed domain of Lozovsky, and the contacts already established with the TUC forced Lozovsky to redesign his policy. Tomsky's long-standing rivalry with Lozovsky, in whom he saw an opportunist who threatened his own authority in the trade unions, also gave greater vehemence to his arguments.[35] Lozovsky's half-hearted appeal to Comintern to achieve unity at the international level through negotiations with the Amsterdam leadership met with fierce opposition from the KPD delegates and Amadeo Bordiga, the founder of the Italian Communist Party, for the Italian CP.[36] Lozovsky's reply once

[32] *Komm. Int.* (1924), No. 3, pp. 71–78. Lozovsky, a former Menshevik, had joined Zinoviev in opposing the uprising of 1917. However, his ambition soon led him to the Bolshevik Party where he played an active role in the organization of the Soviet trade unions. A skilful tactitian, he survived the upheavals of the 20s and 30s and retained prominent roles in the trade union movement and the Soviet Foreign Ministry until he perished ironically in the last purge of 1952. His most important achievement was the foundation and control of Profintern through which he exercised great influence on the development of Comintern.

[33] *Trud*, 3 June 1924.

[34] *Trud*, 10 June 1924.

[35] Speech by Tomsky on involvement in *Trud*, 28 May 1924. On Lozovsky's relations with Tomsky see J. T. Murphy, *New Horizons* (London, 1941), pp. 160–61; this was confirmed in a conversation with Berger Barzilai (Joseph Berger), one of the few prominent members of Profintern to survive Stalin's labour camps.

[36] *Pyatyi Vsemirnyi Kongress*: Lozovsky, pp. 819–30; KPD, pp. 831–42; Bordiga, pp. 890–91.

again revealed scepticism about Profintern's expectations of the emerging British left. He placated the opposition by stating that he himself was the last person to contemplate the liquidation of Profintern. His defence of the integrity of Profintern was not confined to the congress but found expression in extensive publications.[37]

The discussion was carried on in the fourth plenum of IKKI which met on 12 and 13 July, at the end of which disagreements were, according to Zinoviev, 'more or less liquidated'. Nevertheless, the third congress of Profintern, which had been in session since 8 July, displayed differences of opinion, although it finally adopted Comintern's resolutions. This was a result of Comintern's instructions to the parties to form united fronts from below, but which left the door open for negotiations with reformist leaders in countries where they were still 'powerful and influential'. In the fourth plenum of IKKI, Zinoviev had drawn up the outline of a plan by which the two Internationals would be merged after the convening of a 'world congress of trade unions based on proportional representation'.[38] He nevertheless envisaged negotiations with Amsterdam which would involve the Russian trade unions alone.[39]

The main point at issue in the third congress of Profintern was the attitude to be adopted towards the left wing of the General Council of the TUC. A. Dogadov, the secretary of the AUCCTU, had made clear the Russian trade unions' point of view a few days before the congress, when he expressed his opinion that the change in Amsterdam was controlled from beginning to end by the British, 'who should be the object of further approaches'.[40] However, in the opening speech to the Profintern congress, Lozovsky resolved that 'neither liquidation, self-liquidation Japanese-style, or entry to Amsterdam of the Russian unions' was contemplated. This was a repetition of his standpoint in the Comintern congress, when he had stated that the support of the

[37] *ibid.*, p. 908. See for example *Bol'shevik* (20 June 1924), Nos. 5–6, p. 28: 'The days are not far away when Profintern will remain the sole organization in the world trade union movement.'

[38] This was first proposed by Lozovsky in *Trud*, 7 June 1924.

[39] Zinoviev's speech is in *Pyatyi Vsemirnyi Kongress*, Vol. II, pp. 10–11; endorsed by Profintern, *Desyat' Let Profinterna v Rezolyutsiyakh*, p. 128.

[40] *Trud*, 4 July 1924.

left wing was by no means 'the sole task of our life and existence'. Lozovsky explained the proposed unity as a manoeuvre to turn the Amsterdam organization on its head, expel its leadership and revolutionize the rest.[41] The representatives of the British bureau of Profintern sided with Lozovsky without reservations. G. Hardy warned 'in a most determined way' that little should be expected from the left wing of the British trade unions, whose activities in Vienna were calculated to 'catch the eye of the progressive world proletariat' in order to secure its own position.[42]

It was however at this stage that the Russian predominance in the congress became conspicuous. Russian delegates expounded the view that unity with the IFTU was not only a propaganda device but also a policy which could be followed without abandoning revolutionary principles. However, A. Kalnin, representing the AUCCTU, justified the future alliance on grounds of pure national interests as a bulwark against the approaching capitalist offensive.[43] Yet it was Tomsky who tipped the scale by re-affirming the correctness of Comintern's thesis on the slowing down of the revolutionary pace which imposed a struggle on the economic front. He had adopted this course during his negotiations in England with Purcell and Cook, whom he esteemed highly. Tomsky ended by warning that although the Russian trade unions obediently sought the consent of Profintern for their policy they could not let the chance of negotiations with Amsterdam and the British left wing there slip out of their hands. However, as a result of unyielding opposition to an independent Russian move, the thesis on international unity, based on Tomsky's speech, had to be referred to a special committee, which adopted it with minor alterations only after prolonged discussion.[44]

The popularity which Tomsky's point of view enjoyed in the AUCCTU was shown by demands to Profintern outside the congress hall to seize the opportunity of establishing connections

41 *Pyatyi Vsemirnyi Kongress*, p. 812; *III Kongress Krasnogo Internatsionala Profsoyuzov. Stenograficheskii Otchet* (Moscow, 1924), pp. 106 and 109 (hereafter referred to as *III Kongress Profinterna*).

42 *III Kongress Profinterna*, pp. 161–62 and 192. Mann had earlier divulged the view of the British delegates, *ibid.*, pp. 64–66. See also MacManus, *ibid.*, pp. 198–99.

43 *ibid.*: Yuzefovich and Krol′, pp. 163–65; Kalnin, pp. 180–87.

44 *ibid.*, pp. 274–82 and 284–86.

with the left wing of Amsterdam.[45] Lozovsky, always a turncoat, finally capitulated. However, to remove the threat to Profintern's existence, his earlier assertion that the left wing was only a result of pressure exerted on the formal leadership by the rank and file from below was embodied in another resolution. In this the left wing was described as a 'barometer' indicating the dissatisfaction of the workers with their reformist leadership.[46] This evidently did not prove a deterrent strong enough to prevent the Russians from continuing to cultivate their relations with that leadership.

Significantly, the transformation of the British bureau of Profintern into a National Minority Movement, which had been contemplated for some time, took place concurrently with the development of Anglo-Soviet trade union relations.[47] This movement was accepted as the appropriate means of implementing united front tactics from below by recruiting support among dissidents in the unions without displaying an obvious communist programme. The NMM's façade of an appeal for struggle on economic issues did little, however, to hide its underlying political character. The congress of Profintern perspicaciously stated that political demands should be integrated with the economic programme of the movement.[48] However, the political programme of the NMM ambivalently reflected the revolutionary and diplomatic fundamentals of the Russian policy.[49] The inaugural conference of the NMM, which met on 23 and 24 August, indeed defined its ultimate aim as the organization of the workers to overthrow capitalism and to establish the 'Socialist Commonwealth'.[50] However, a no less important objective was

[45] Liss, a Russian member of Profintern's executive bureau, in *Trud*, 3 July 1924.

[46] Lozovsky in *III Kongress Profinterna*, pp. 195–96 and p. 321; resolution on the left wing in *Desyat' Let Profinterna*, p. 132.

[47] The inauguration was at first scheduled for May but was postponed, apparently until after the debate in the Profintern congress: *All Power* (May 1924), No. 28, and *ibid.* (June 1924), No. 29.

[48] *III Kongress Profinterna*, p. 369: resolution on the tasks of the CPGB. On the industrial aspects of the NMM's activities see R. Martin, *Communism and the British Trade Unions, 1924–1933* (Oxford, 1969), pp. 55ff.

[49] *Sixth Conference CPGB*, p. 75; Bela Kun in *Inprecorr*, 25 Jan. 1925.

[50] *Report of the National Minority Conference Held on August 23rd and 24th 1924* (London, 1924), p. 20.

the formation of blocs on the international as well as national scales to anticipate the capitalist offensives.[51]

Notwithstanding the large number of adherents to the movement, doubts were cast from the outset on its ability to fulfil these tasks. In the CPGB, which was entrusted with the guidance of the NMM, objections were raised to the formation of a movement which was largely composed of deserters from the Party. The NMM also posed a threat of elimination to the Party by duplicating its roles.[52] The purity of the political line of the NMM was even further diluted by the scarceness of Party leadership at local union level.[53] There was even less enthusiasm from the General Council, which constantly refused invitations to appear on the same platform as the NMM and prohibited NMM members from affiliation to the TUC.[54] Once more it was the overwhelming majority of the Russians in Profintern which decided the issue. Kalnin rather offhandedly expressed his conviction in the third Profintern congress that the CPGB was powerful enough to control the movement and that in the light of the stabilization of capitalism it was imperative to establish 'tight friendly mutual relations between the British and Soviet workers'.[55]

Launching the Anglo-Russian Joint Advisory Council

Steps had in fact been taken by the British and Russian trade unions even before the closing of the congress to consolidate their mutual relations. During the first meeting of the General Council's recently elected International Committee, with Purcell in the chair, a resolution was moved advising the General Council to invite a Russian fraternal delegate to attend the TUC Hull congress.[56] This recommendation coincided with a pressing

51 Pollitt in *ibid.*, p. 19, and manifesto of NMM to TUC in *ibid.*, pp. 4–6.

52 On the threat see Gallacher in *Sixth Conference CPGB*, p. 12, and Bell, p. 27; MacManus in *III Kongress Profinterna*, p. 138, and Mann, p. 177.

53 Report of meeting of Orgburo of IKKI on 15 Dec. 1924 in *Inprecorr*, 5 Feb. 1925. On the strong syndicalist tendencies in the movement and rejection of the CPGB see G. Hardy, *Those Stormy Years* (London, 1956), pp. 171–73; he was the NMM's organizational secretary.

54 See for example TUC archives, *Minutes of GC, 1923–24*, p. 135, 29 Aug. 1924, and *Minutes of GC, 1924–25*, p. 40, 29 Dec. 1924.

55 *III Kongress Profinterna*, pp. 188–89.

56 TUC archives, *Minutes of International Committee, 1923–4*, meeting No. 5, 17 July 1924. Profintern's congress closed on 20 July 1924.

invitation to the General Council by the AUCCTU to send a delegation to Russia to 'establish regular connections'.[57] The General Council endorsed the International Committee's proposal but, because of strong suspicions among its members with regard to the Russian aims, refrained for a time from responding to the Russian invitation.[58] The Russians were not discouraged by the reserved attitude of the General Council. Their expectations were further encouraged by what they believed was the vital contribution of the left wing to the successful conclusion of the Anglo-Soviet negotiations. An unexpectedly large five-man delegation, fully backed by the CPSU, left for Britain at the end of August with, however, only a vague concept of how to realize the collaboration between the two movements.[59]

The TUC's growing involvement in foreign affairs during 1924 was manifested at Hull by Purcell's thorough defence of trade union unity and the effusive welcome of the Russian delegation. This, however, did not conceal a deep-rooted opposition to alliance with the Russians for varied reasons. Some speakers interpreted 'unity' as absorption by Profintern, while others outlined the different ideological backgrounds of the two movements and predicted a paternalistic and inegalitarian approach on the part of the Russian communist unions because of the 'dramatic happenings in their country'.[60] Tomsky, who opened his speech by rejecting the title 'diplomat' which he had been given in connection with the Anglo-Soviet Conference, succeeded in mollifying the worriers by insisting that the Russians were determined to discuss the prospects of unity on an 'equal footing' and with no preliminary conditions.[61] However, the congress moved no resolution recommending further collaboration with the Russian trade unions, while the outgoing General Council referred to

57 TUC archives, B 38/947: Dogadov to Citrine, 20 July 1924.

58 TUC archives, *Minutes of GC, 1923–4*, p. 117, 23 July 1924. For the CPGB's backing of these developments see *Workers' Weekly*, 1 Aug. 1924.

59 On the resolution of the plenum of the central committee of the CPSU see *KPSS v Rezolyutsiyakh i Resheniyakh* (Moscow, 1970), Vol. 3, pp. 130–31. See also Dogadov's interview on the eve of his departure in *Trud*, 22 Aug. 1924, and Citrine, *Men and Work*, p. 89.

60 *Report of 56th TUC*, pp. 72 and 315–18.

61 *ibid.*, pp. 315–18.

its successor the Russians' standing invitation to a fraternal delegation.[62]

Immediately after the congress dispersed, a meeting between the Russian representatives and the new General Council was hastily arranged, in which Tomsky was challenged to specify the aims of the proposed tour. Tomsky tactfully suggested that the delegation would confine its work to obtaining knowledge of conditions in Russia, which had been 'grossly misrepresented' in the British Press. The frequent interruptions prove that the General Council was not at one; nevertheless, it was finally agreed to accept the invitation 'for the express purpose of considering the conditions' in Russia and submitting a report.[63]

The CPGB's repeated warnings to the Russians of the 'suicidal' nature of the alliance with the unreliable General Council were overruled.[64] Tomsky was aware of the failings of the General Council, but his *modus operandi* was based on a pragmatic and administrative outlook; new dimensions were opened merely by the formation of a bloc with six million organized workers previously loyal to Amsterdam.[65] The parliamentary crisis in Britain justified the pessimistic forecasts of Comintern and made Tomsky's position easier. He now held fast to the idea of unity with the TUC, even if this did not lead directly to Amsterdam, as the only way to confront the capitalist offensive.[66]

The visit of the British delegation was gaining momentum. The Russians proposed to postpone the opening of the trade unions' congress to enable the British delegates, delayed by the elections, to attend it.[67] The delegation finally reached Russia on 10 November and received a tremendous reception, with pictures of the delegates and interviews making front page news in the Press. It was immediately discernible that the Russians

62 TUC archives, *Minutes of GC, 1923–4*, p. 117: special meeting of GC at Hull, 4 Sept. 1924.

63 *ibid.*, 5 Sept. 1924.

64 Campbell in *Comm. Rev.* (Oct. 1924), p. 287; Murphy in *ibid.* (Sept. 1924), p. 230, and in *Trud*, 11 Sept. 1924; MacManus in *Trud*, 13 Sept. 1924.

65 Opening and concluding speeches to fourth congress of Metal Workers of Moscow District in *Trud*, 26 Oct. and 4 Nov. 1924.

66 Speech to Moscow conference of Factory Committees in *Trud*, 5 Nov. 1924.

67 TUC archives, *Minutes of GC, 1924–5*, p. 14, 16 Oct. 1924.

expected not only the publication of a favourable report but the acceptance of a common political platform.[68] Interviews with the members of the delegation revealed a spectrum of political views but on the whole were confined to the declared aims of the visit. However, Purcell, the dominating figure in the delegation, showed from the beginning that he was in full accord with the Russians: 'We wish to learn what the Russian workers' movement has done for the consolidation of the international solidarity of the working class and the creation of a united anti-capitalist front.'[69]

The delegation was rushed to Moscow in time to hear Zinoviev's survey of the discouraging international situation. He saw an improvement in the situation not so much in the 'art of the Red diplomats' or the strength of the Red Army but in the increasing industrial productivity. To revive the Russian economy it was necessary to recruit the support of the world proletariat through unity, based on the elementary fundamentals of combating reaction and capitalism.[70] Purcell and the other delegates received a tumultuous ovation when they rose to speak. Purcell, carried away by the reception, launched into an oration heavily loaded with revolutionary idiom. Clearly the most significant part of it was a pledge on behalf of the General Council to bring about unity with the Russians if Amsterdam failed to do so.[71] In his main address, Tomsky seized on Purcell's declaration. Sceptical about the prospect of entering Amsterdam, correspondence from which read like 'a bad cheap novel in letters', he praised

68 See *Pravda*, *Izvestiya* and *Trud*, 11 Nov. 1924. On the organization behind the scenes of such receptions see Balabanoff, *My Life as a Rebel*, pp. 282–85, who was in charge of the first Labour delegation. See also *The Official Report of the British Trades Union Delegation to Russia* (London, 1924), pp. XIII–XVII.

69 *Pravda*, 11 Nov. 1924. Bramley like Purcell recognized the urgency of establishing unity, *Trud*, 12 Nov. 1924. Peters correctly observed that Purcell was the only member 'interested in policy qua policy', F.O. 371 10478 N8665/530/38: Peters to Chamberlain, 21 Nov. 1924.

70 *VI S'ezd Prof. Soyuzov*, pp. 17–37.

71 *ibid.*, pp. 49–51. Purcell's declaration in *Trud*, 12 Nov. 1924, that the USSR was 'the first stage towards the creation of a revolutionary working class in the united states of Europe' shocked the IFTU, which expressed doubts about its authenticity. This was confirmed by Purcell in *Pravda*, 16 Nov. 1924.

the British attitude, which guaranteed 'mutual understanding and solidarity'.[72]

The congress then proceeded to discuss the other business on its agenda while the presidium of the congress carried on an improvised conference with the British delegates, which resulted in an agreement in principle by the delegation on the necessity of forming an Anglo-Russian Committee of Unity. The climate for such an understanding had been created in Hull during informal talks between Tomsky and some members of the General Council.[73] Lozovsky's revelation of this, made during Profintern's report to the last session of the congress, took the wind out of Tomsky's sails; he was to make the formal announcement later in the day. Lozovsky tried to minimize the achievement by pointing out that it was only a 'small step forward' and made with a clear understanding of the differences between the movements. He also reminded the congress that the proposal had still to be ratified by the General Council.[74]

In the ensuing debate one of the speakers asked for guarantees that the agreement would not end as 'a scrap of paper'. There was also a considerable opposition to condoning reformism by means of dissolving Profintern. As a rule the opposition was directed against an independent move by the AUCCTU to join Amsterdam but favoured *rapprochement* with the TUC.[75] The far-sighted Lozovsky rounded off the discussion by siding with Tomsky; there was no reason to doubt the sincere will of the delegation to form the committee. The congress then moved a resolution empowering the AUCCTU to continue negotiations with the General Council with a view to forming the proposed committee.[76]

In spite of a consensus among the Russians on the desirability of collaborating with the TUC, there was a wide range of opinions on the character and aim of such a move. Zinoviev at first sided with Tomsky, providing him with a theoretical justification for closing ranks with the TUC. Soon afterwards, however, Zinoviev

[72] *VI S'ezd Prof. Soyuzov*, pp. 56–57 and 74–78.

[73] Tomsky in *Trud*, 5 Nov. 1924. Account of the improvised conference in *Report of Fifty-Seventh Annual Trades Union Congress* (London, 1925), pp. 295–96 (hereafter referred to as *Report of 57th TUC*).

[74] *VI S'ezd Prof. Soyuzov*, pp. 386–89.

[75] *ibid.*, pp. 391–96 and 398.

[76] *ibid.*, pp. 410 and 440–41.

took up a non-committal position, entertaining hopes that the visit of the delegation, some members of which had been hostile to the Soviet Union, might strengthen the forthcoming unity.[77] Zinoviev's memory of the four-hour cordial meeting with the delegation must have been spoiled by the visitors' naïve demand that Zinoviev should leave the trade unions' transactions to their accredited leaders.[78]

Tomsky enjoyed majority support in the Politburo for the formation of the trade union committee to serve as a bulwark against the still extant danger of war.[79] Tomsky's policy was fully backed by Stalin, who believed that the support of the European workers was a prerequisite for the success of constructing socialism in Russia: 'No one denies that common endeavours of the proletariats of several countries are necessary in the interest of the complete safeguarding of the revolution from the restoration of the old order.'[80]

Prevailing opinion in Comintern, however, emphasized the revolutionary principles underlying the formation of the committee; under certain circumstances it might be a turning-point in the international labour movement.[81] It found its expression in Lozovsky, who advocated the establishment of the committee against the background of class struggle and expected *rapprochement* to facilitate the task of the NMM in winning over the masses and replacing the reformist leadership.[82] Trotsky voiced the main opposition in his publication 'The Lessons of October', which *inter alia* ruled out the possibility of achieving communism through the trade unions unless these were under a decisive communist influence. He enjoyed the support of the Leningrad trade union organization, which greeted the British delegates with a resolution permitting the collaboration only on the basis of a communist programme and restating the loyalty of the Russian trade unions to the flag of Profintern.[83]

The attitude of the delegation in Moscow was by no means

[77] *Trud*, 2 Dec. 1924.
[78] Bramley in *The Times* and *Manchester Guardian*, 9 Feb. 1925.
[79] *Pravda*, 19 Nov. 1924.
[80] *Inprecorr*, 23 Jan. and 11 Feb. 1925.
[81] See Manuilsky in *Inprecorr*, 4 Dec. 1924.
[82] *Trud*, 2 Dec. 1924, and *Krasnyi Internatsional Profsoyuzov* (1925), Nos. 2–3, p. 9.
[83] Quoted in L. Trotsky, *The Third International After Lenin* (New York,

shared by the General Council of the TUC, which passed a resolution prohibiting members of the delegation from making any public statement without the authorization of the General Council.[84] This, however, was ignored by Purcell and Bramley, who upon the return of the delegation undertook to produce a report which would 'remove many misunderstandings with regard to Russian affairs' and 'justify the Trade Union and Labour Policy supporting the full diplomatic and economic recognition of Russia'.[85] Discipline in the General Council was soon restored, and the embargo on further speeches enforced, though not before the agreement with the AUCCTU, reached in the impromptu conference in Moscow, was endorsed.[86]

The acceptance of this resolution could not, however, cover up the conflicting views apparent not only in the General Council but also among the members of the delegation. Any hopes that as a result of the visit the General Council would embark on a revolutionary path were dismissed by Bramley himself, who stated that he returned from Moscow 'more opposed to Communism as understood by the Communist Party' than he had been before. Ben Turner, the veteran textile trade union leader, went so far as to describe the proletarian character of the Soviet Union as 'inverted snobbishness'.[87]

Awareness of the General Council's vacillating position induced the Russians to call a special conference of the NMM to promote international unity. The NMM was created to ensure that the General Council held a correct line; it was anticipated that a demonstration of rank-and-file feelings in the trade unions would secure the General Council's support of the Russian point of view in the scheduled meeting of the General Council of the IFTU.[88] This proved, however, to be a miscalculation and should

1970), p. 124; for views of the Leningrad organization see *VI S'ezd Prof. Soyuzov*, pp. 122–25, and *Trud*, 13 Dec. 1924.

84 TUC archives, *Minutes of GC, 1924–5*, pp. 31–32, 17 Dec. 1924.

85 *The Shop Assistant*, 27 Dec. 1924. For Bramley's strong position in the newly-organized GC see V. L. Allen, 'The Re-organization of the Trades Union Congress, 1918–1927', *British Journal of Sociology* (1960), Vol. 11, p. 37.

86 TUC archives, *Minutes of GC, 1924–5*, p. 40, 29 Dec. 1924.

87 *The Shop Assistant*, 10 Jan. 1925.

88 *Pravda*, 28 Jan. 1925. See also Nin in *Kras. Int. Prof.* (1925), No. 1, pp. 5–7, and in *Inprecorr*, 11 Feb. 1925.

have warned Tomsky that revolutionary and diplomatic objectives could not be so blatantly combined. The purpose of the conference antagonized the majority of the General Council, which not only boycotted it but also informed Tomsky that the attendance of a Russian delegate was 'inadvisable' and would 'militate against the success of the unity programme'.[89] The priority given to diplomatic considerations was demonstrated when Tomsky immediately withdrew his participation, which provoked a complaint from Pollitt that the campaign for unity was becoming a 'subject for diplomatic negotiations between trade union officials'.[90] The campaign in support of the conference now excluded extreme militant overtones and mainly advocated the formation of a 'united front against fascism and reaction'.[91]

The high attendance at the conference could not disguise its reduced significance in the absence of representatives of both the General Council and the Russian trade unions. The proceedings mirrored the ambivalent Russian attitude to unity. Profintern's demand for a world trade union conference based on proportional representation was adopted, although it was *ab initio* unacceptable to the IFTU.[92] By the same token the General Council's overtures to the IFTU, favouring the affiliation of the Russian unions to this organization, were encouraged.[93]

Reactions in Moscow to the conference were subdued. It appeared wise to observe attentively the procedure adopted by the General Council in the impending IFTU meeting before taking sides. Expectations from the General Council were particularly high since the AUCCTU had been notified of the General Council's decision to enact the agreement reached in Moscow if the IFTU failed to respond to the British initiative.

89 TUC archives, *Minutes of GC, 1924–5*, pp. 40–41; B 113 18/2/51: report of GC's delegation to IFTU.

90 *Workers' Weekly*, 2 Jan. 1925.

91 Melnichansky in *Trud*, 11 Jan. 1925. See also Palme Dutt in *Labour Monthly* (Feb. 1925), pp. 79–93.

92 The IFTU had only recently condemned the British delegation for its failure to recognize the 'Potemkin villages' presented to it by the Russians; *Report on Activities during the Years 1924, 1925 and 1926*, pp. 47–48.

93 *Report of the Special Unity Conference Held on 25 January, 1925* (London, 1925).

It seemed inconceivable that the IFTU would adopt a Russian proposal which diverged from the British by demanding not only the calling of an unconditional conference but the formation of an International which would provide the framework for the fusion of Amsterdam and Profintern.[94] Indeed, in the meeting of the General Council of the IFTU on 5–7 February, the majority, alert to the substantial differences between the two proposals, postponed any further parley with the Russians until they had declared their willingness to enter Amsterdam. All attempts by the General Council to move an amendment to the resolution were resisted. The IFTU had in fact regained the diehard position it had held in early 1924.[95]

The Russians regarded the meeting as an abortive but inevitable step on the way to Anglo-Soviet trade union unity inasmuch as it exposed the IFTU's rejection of the Soviet trade unions. In fact while the General Council of the IFTU was in session, the Russians had sent a Soviet delegation headed by V. Shmidt, the Commissar of Labour, to carry out secret negotiations with the British delegates. Shmidt had no difficulty in convincing Bramley and Purcell that the IFTU's resolution would amount to the capitulation of the General Council. There and then he presented a four-point plan which detailed concrete steps to promote unity through the formation of a permanent Anglo-Soviet Committee.

On their return to London Bramley and Purcell once again found themselves ahead of the General Council when it met to hear a report on the Amsterdam meetings. Shmidt's proposals were corroborated by a letter from Tomsky to the General Council rejecting the IFTU's resolution as 'humiliating conditions' for the Russians. After sharp criticism of the secret negotiations, a majority of seventeen to five voted down the Russians' substantial proposals, leaving intact only the first point, which called for a meeting of representatives from both countries' unions for the purpose of 'discussing steps to be taken arising out of the Amsterdam decision'. The Russians, moreover, were

94 See for example *Kras. Int. Prof.* (1925), Nos. 2–3, pp. 99–103, and A. Lozovsky, *The World's Trade Union Movement* (London, 1925), pp. 223–25; TUC archives, B 113 18/2/51: British proposals to IFTU, 31 Jan. 1925.

95 TUC archives, B 113 18/2/51: report of GC's delegation to IFTU.

informed through Shmidt that they would be expected to justify their objections to the IFTU's resolution.[96] These developments further displayed the hesitancy with which the General Council was approaching the Soviet trade unions. However, the immense importance attached in Moscow to the collaboration was evident from the enthusiasm with which the agreement simply to meet the Russian trade unionists was accepted.[97]

The last preparations for the convening of the Anglo-Soviet trade union conference coincided with the sitting in Moscow of the fifth plenum of IKKI from 21 March to 6 April, in which diplomatic considerations and revolutionary aspirations were blended in an unprecedented partnership. The importance given in the plenum to the implementation of socialism in Russia, in contrast to the dominance of reaction elsewhere, forced the issue of international trade union unity to the foreground.

Zinoviev's opening speech harnessed together the questions of stabilization of capitalism and Bolshevization which had been introduced by Comintern's fifth congress. He now admitted that the abrupt termination of the democratic pacific era, marked by the defeat of Labour, afforded 'breathing space to the bourgeoisie'. The failure of the revolution to materialize dictated a retreat to defensive positions and Bolshevization as the appropriate means of containing counter-revolutionary forces provoked by the growing strength of the Soviet state. The world proletariat was therefore allotted the task of standing firmly by the Soviet Union, as long as its existence was threatened.[98]

From here the short step of recognizing the prominence of the Soviet Union in Comintern and the undisputed authority of that body was taken by the CPGB's congress in May: 'The Soviet Union is growing in its power of attraction to the masses of the Social-Democratic workers who begin to feel that they have been misled and that the real building of Socialism has begun in

[96] TUC archives, *Minutes of GC, 1924–5*, pp. 59–60, 25 Feb. 1925; *Minutes of IC, 1924–5*, Meeting 3, 12 Mar. 1925, and Meeting 4, 31 Mar. 1925. For Tomsky's letter see *Report of 57th TUC*, p. 297.

[97] *Pravda*, 28 Feb. 1925. For the CPGB's similar attitude see Campbell in *Workers' Weekly*, 3 Apr. 1925.

[98] *Rasshirennyi Plenum Ispolkoma Kommunisticheskogo Internatsionala Stenograficheskii Otchet* (Moscow, 1925), pp. 6–8, 36–39 and 45–46 (hereafter referred to as *V Plenum IKKI*).

the Soviet Union . . . All sections of the International now look to the International Executive as its leader.'[99]

The uncontested support for the British left wing in the IKKI plenum had however been subject to reservations on the eve of the meeting. These were not restricted to criticism of the official left wing in the TUC but extended to include more revolutionary groups. The CPGB had continuously expressed the fear that the NMM might 'take the place of the Revolutionary Communist Party'.[100] A meeting of the Orgburo of IKKI, preceding the plenum, heard complaints from British delegates about the multiple loyalties imposed on Party members, to the Labour Party, the trade unions, and the NMM; these impaired the activities of the CPGB.[101] Even Gallacher, the CPGB's main representative at the plenum, had denounced the left wing of the trade unions as 'uncoordinated, lacking any organizational basis and unwilling to condemn the right wing before the masses'.[102]

The plenum, however, showed no sympathy towards these misgivings; the correctness of united front tactics, particularly in the trade unions, was impregnably established in view of the success achieved by the visit of the British delegation to Russia and the impending London conference between the trade union leaders of the two countries. Even Lozovsky, doubtful about the Russians' expectations from the collaboration, had conveyed to the British trade unionists 'the warmest wholehearted support of their work to establish trade union unity'.[103] However, in his long speech on this subject to the plenum, Lozovsky extracted the utmost propaganda value from the projected alliance and especially from the blow which it struck at the IFTU. He followed Zinoviev's two-edged praise of the proposed Anglo-Russian Committee for its revolutionary and practical qualities, elaborating on the temporary character of capitalist stabilization together with the revolutionary import of the support given to the Russian workers by the formation of the committee; this opened 'a wider

99 *Report of the Seventh Congress of the Communist Party of Great Britain* (London, 1925), p. 181.

100 Campbell in *Workers' Weekly*, 30 Jan. and 6 Feb. 1925.

101 *Inprecorr*, 31 Mar. 1925.

102 *Pravda*, 22 Mar. 1925.

103 *Kras. Int. Prof.* (1925), Nos. 2–3, pp. 7–9 and 21.

scope for exclusively communist activities'.[104] Lozovsky, who rather effectively credited Profintern with the achievement of the foundation of the committee, failed however to outline its most urgent tasks.[105]

Only when winding up the discussion did Lozovsky lay aside his militant outlook in a more realistic description of developments. After making a bold statement admitting a setback on the revolutionary front, he accepted the ARJAC as an appropriate means of defence so long as it was not a device to introduce the Russian trade unions into the IFTU. This he strongly condemned on the grounds that the two organizations held 'opposing and uncompromising ideological ideas'.[106] This hostility to the IFTU, in fact, encouraged a divisive policy by making the formation of the committee conditional on the termination of the TUC coalition with Amsterdam. The leaders of the left wing, argued Lozovsky, had to make up their mind 'either with the left wing of the working class, or with the left wing of the bourgeoisie'.[107]

In the plenum itself, however, no serious attempt was made to challenge the correctness of the alliance with the TUC, which had been so heatedly debated the year before. The London trade union conference received a strong mandate from the plenum's resolution on Bolshevization in Britain, stressing the priority of the Party's work in the trade unions. A clear distinction was made between the TUC and the Labour Party, thereby legitimizing trade union unity. The working class all over the world was called upon 'to grant resolute and energetic support to the Anglo-Soviet trade union collaboration'.[108]

The disagreement between Tomsky and Lozovsky over the issue of the committee was less fierce than it seemed. The points of divergence were the means and the urgency with which the committee was to be formed. Lozovsky's antagonism to the

104 *V Plenum IKKI*, pp. 59–60; Lozovsky in *Za Edinstvo Mezhdunarodnogo Profdvizheniya*, pp. 5–13. See also Bukharin in *Inprecorr*, 2 July 1925.

105 See for example Lozovsky's review of the debate in *Kras. Int. Prof.* (1925), No. 5, p. 66, and in *Mezhdunarodnoe Rabochee Dvizhenie*, No. 1, 26 Mar. 1925.

106 *V Plenum IKKI*, pp. 298–302.

107 *Kras. Int. Prof.* (1925), No. 4, pp. 29–32.

108 *V Plenum IKKI*, pp. 517 and 545.

IFTU, and association of the NMM with the committee, were calculated to prevent Tomsky from sacrificing Profintern in order to establish the committee. However Tomsky, aware of the General Council's rejection of Shmidt's proposal for a permanent committee yet eager to strengthen further the fraternal ties, was disinclined to limit his freedom of action. His cautious and moderate approach to the London conference was displayed when he told the crowds who came to see him off at the station in Moscow that the AUCCTU 'could not accept or refuse the Amsterdam International's proposals without preliminary agreement on this question with the fraternal British unions'.[109]

This attitude proved to be productive from the opening session of the conference on 6 April; A. Swales in the chair declared the intention of the General Council to get down to 'real business' rather than allow the conference to sink into propaganda exchanges. Tomsky, on whose shoulders fell the burden of explaining the Russian refusal to accept the IFTU's resolution, argued that it repeated in different words earlier demands that the Russians accept unconditionally the statutes and rules of Amsterdam. His appeal to the General Council to give the alliance with the Russians a permanent character to forestall the organized offensive of capitalism had strong diplomatic overtones.

Tomsky's proposal was next discussed by the International Committee of the General Council, which was prepared to accept the Russian objections to the IFTU's resolution; however, it clearly showed that the General Council hung back from full collaboration with the Russians unless all attempts to approach Amsterdam proved abortive. Conscious of the feelings in the General Council, Tomsky agreed to continue negotiations with the IFTU while pressing for a concrete form for Anglo-Soviet collaboration.

The last and most vital stage of the conference was the meeting of a sub-committee, whose two British members, Swales and Bramley, were partisans of close relations with the Russians, to draft a concluding statement. This reflected a compromise: the underlying assumptions, not inconsistent with the principles of Soviet diplomacy, recognized that the serious threat of new wars necessitated the promotion of 'international good-will amongst the workers as means of more adequately safeguarding the

[109] Reported in *Trud*, 28 Mar. 1925.

interests of international peace'. However it provided for the establishment only of a joint advisory council to 'weld closer the friendly relations' between the trade unions of the two countries. Moreover, the provisions to set up the advisory council were most unsatisfactorily defined from the Russian point of view. The Council was to promote cooperation between the two nations' trade unions as 'advisable', to initiate discussions as 'necessary . . . from time to time', and to extend joint contacts to develop mutual aid 'as opportunities were provided'.

The failure of the conference to reach any practical solution escaped attention mainly because of the cordial atmosphere in which negotiations were carried out. This was particularly noticeable in Purcell's concluding speech, which hailed the conjunction of the two workers' movements, 'one in possession and the other waiting to leap to get possession', as the most important page in the history of the working class; the names of those involved would 'shine on the brightest pages of that history'.[110]

However, the amicable atmosphere surrounding the London conference could not conceal the Russians' feelings of disappointment. Upon Tomsky's arrival in the border town of Sebej, he excused himself from the now customary interviews on grounds of poor health, making only a short statement to the effect that the London conference had further strengthened the relations established earlier in Hull. This and excerpts from the London statement appeared in the Press, accompanied by non-committal commentaries describing the agreement as 'a firm step on the way to international trade union unity'.[111]

Reports from London that the conference had instituted adequate machinery to pursue the political struggle against capitalism were dismissed by Lozovsky, who detected only 'a trifling change' in the British position. He was most perturbed by the concluding statement of the conference, which 'did not embody what we had expected'; the formation of a permanent committee might have decreased the probability of the Russians' entry to the IFTU.[112] Indeed the executive bureau of Profintern

110 TUC archives, B 114 9/8/7: typed record of inaugural meeting of ARJAC, 6–8 Apr. 1925.

111 *Trud*, 15 Apr. 1925. and *Pravda*, 16 Apr. 1925.

112 Murphy from London in *Pravda*, 24 Apr. 1925, and Lozovsky in *ibid.*, 28 Apr. 1925.

immediately delivered its verdict on the conference, hailing the formation of the advisory council provided it was capable of fusing Amsterdam and Profintern. The resolution expressed unwillingness to dismantle Profintern before this was achieved.[113] The hesitance of the reformist leaders to follow the Russian proposals was accepted *cum grano salis* in *Pravda*, which described the alienation of the workers from their leaders and prophesied the emergence of a new leadership based on a sectional trade union organization under Communist and NMM control.[114]

The final assessment of the London conference by the AUCCTU was put off until after the fourteenth conference of the CPSU, which met on 27 April. The conference, like the preceding IKKI plenum, inspired little discussion on the topic, but Zinoviev disclosed that the central committee had thoroughly discussed it before the conference met.[115] The announcement of 'socialism in one country' in the conference and awareness of the rapidly deteriorating relations with Britain provided Tomsky with support for the continuation of the collaboration policy. His policy also received an impetus when the already intertwined diplomatic and revolutionary aspects were further combined in the conference.[116] In a moment of frankness, Zinoviev admitted that Comintern, which had been born and developed in the 'course of the victory of the first revolution in the USSR', was carrying out a policy strikingly coordinated with 'the general political situation in our own country'. Turning the doctrine of 'permanent revolution' on its head, it was now accepted that the establishment of socialism in Russia with the support of the world proletariat would eventually help Russia to foment revolutions in other countries. However, in the present situation of stabilization of two increasingly hostile systems, it was important initially to secure the bastion of the revolution in Russia; this fully justified collaboration with the British trade unions in view of their 'significant move to the left'.[117] The identification of international revolutionary efforts with the safeguarding of Russia

113 *Mezh. Rabo. Dviz.*, No. 4, 8 Apr. 1925.

114 *Pravda*, 11 Apr. 1925.

115 *Chetyrnadtsataya Konferentsiya Rossiiskoi Kommunisticheskoi Partii. Stenograficheskii Otchet* (Moscow, 1925), p. 243.

116 Resolution on socialism in one country in *ibid.*, p. 311.

117 *ibid.*, 28 Apr. 1925.

indicated the reconciliation of revolutionary and diplomatic expectations from the alliance but ignored the acute divergence of views between Profintern and the Russian trade unions.[118]

On the day after the conference ended, a special session of the AUCCTU was called to review the results of the London conference.[119] This session followed immediately upon a meeting of the General Council in which, with little publicity, the agreement was ratified.[120] Tomsky justified his policy of containing the threat of new wars which faced Russia. He believed that the memory of the 'Hands off Russia' movement would force both the Conservative Government and Amsterdam to give serious consideration to a bloc of 13 million organized workers. Tomsky then proceeded to enumerate the economic advantages which collaboration would entail in view of the soaring unemployment figures and the possibilities opened by expanding trade with Britain; these, however, were only a minor facet of his arguments.[121]

In the two weeks before the session, strenuous attempts had been made by Tomsky to conciliate Lozovsky. In two meetings of the executive bureau of Profintern, Melnichansky had effectively defended the position taken by the delegation; he had managed to pass a resolution supporting the advisory council yet forecasting unity only on the basis of the formation of a 'militant international trade union'.[122] This accounted for Lozovsky's delicate handling of the advisory council; however, he spared no effort in repudiating the indecisive activities of the General Council, which he feared would lead to the formation of a new International to which the Russians might adhere and which would not be based on revolutionary foundations. A militant speech by Mary Quaile, a member of the TUC women's delegation visiting Russia,[123] did nothing to dissuade the rest of the

118 *ibid.*, p. 314. Zinoviev pursued the same line in *Izvestiya*, 8 June 1925.

119 Discussion of session based on records in *Trud*, 1 May 1925; a censored version, smoothing over disagreements, appeared in *Inprecorr*, 14 and 28 May 1925.

120 TUC archives, *Minutes of GC, 1924–5*, p. 82, 28 Apr. 1926.

121 On acute problem of unemployment in Russia see Nove, *An Economic History*, p. 115. On economic advantages involved in formation of committee see *Ekon. Zhzn.*, 7 May 1925.

122 *Mezh. Rabo. Dviz.*, Nos. 5–6, 30 Apr. 1925.

123 On visit see Volkov, *Anglo-Sovetskie Otnosheniya*, p. 146.

speakers from treading in the steps of Lozovsky. All expressed indignation at the idea of an independent Russian move to join the IFTU and at the General Council's unity policy.

The resolution, which had been endorsed by the Party before the meeting,[124] did not entirely reflect the proceedings of the session when it expressed 'satisfaction at the establishment and strengthening of the fraternal ties between the Soviet and British trade unions which undoubtedly reflect the victory of the cause of unity'. After the resolution was moved, an international committee of the AUCCTU, including prominent Profintern figures like Lozovsky, Glebov-Avilov and Mikhailov, was formed; significantly, however, none of these was among the delegates chosen to represent the Russian unions in ARJAC. This task was allocated to M. Tomsky and A. Andreev – in strong positions in the Party organizations – and A. Dogadov, G. Melnichansky and I. Lepse, straightforward trade unionists.

Immediately after the session of the AUCCTU, Lozovsky embarked upon an outspoken campaign to reinstate Profintern as 'the only guarantee for unity'. It was prompted by apprehensions that under certain circumstances Tomsky might succumb to pressures, exerted by the General Council, to join Amsterdam.[125] The appearance of complete confrontation between Tomsky and Lozovsky was deceptive and their points of friction concerned mainly questions of tactics. Tomsky primarily envisaged the General Council as a 'potential counter-weight to Chamberlain's England'. To animate the collaboration he was prepared to endorse the slow course, suggested by the General Council, of repeated approaches to Amsterdam. However, like Lozovsky he was not eager to see the Russian trade unions join the IFTU, but believed that the discrediting of the IFTU by its refusal to admit the Russian unions would foster Anglo-Soviet trade union relations.[126] In order to unmask the IFTU, Tomsky approached it in accordance with the resolutions of the London conference, proposing an unconditional preliminary conference to discuss

[124] Interview with Melnichansky in *Trud*, 30 Apr. 1925.

[125] *Kras. Int. Prof.* (1925), No. 5, pp. 19 and 29, and *ibid.* (1925), No. 6, p. 58. Nin followed suit in *Inprecorr*, 25 June 1925. See also A. Lozovsky, *Anglo-Sovetskaya Konferentsiya Professional'nykh Soyuzov* (Moscow, 1925), pp. 50–51, 62–63 and 94–97.

[126] *Trud*, 9 May and 22 May 1925.

the creation of an International based on 'class struggle and the final emancipation of the working class from the oppression of capitalism'. Tomsky made the fullest concessions in indicating that this International was not expected to 'differ vitally' from the present organization.[127]

The Russians, however, clearly had too high hopes from the still incipient committee. In a letter to the General Council soon afterwards, Tomsky expressed little hope of receiving a positive response from the IFTU. He therefore pressed the General Council to invigorate the collaboration by convening ARJAC to 'draft a formal constitution of the Anglo-Russian Committee' and declare 'its immediate tasks'.[128]

The revolutionary expectations from ARJAC were fortified when immediately after the London conference the last strongholds of the CPGB's resistance to the collaboration were surrendered. The Party, which controlled only a hundred factory groups, most of which were 'weakly connected with the Party' and with unmistakably 'clear trade union orientation', admitted its failure to become a mass party.[129] Neither the remodelling of the CPGB nor the Bolshevization policy allowed the Party to continue its existence as a political sect, in spite of its manifest wish to do so.[130] Of the two channels open to the Party for activities in the trade unions, the NMM was clearly more attractive than the official left wing, although the fear remained that the NMM might emerge as an 'alternative to the Party'.[131]

The attitude of the CPGB to ARJAC resembled the equivocal posture of the Russians: it sought the formation of a permanent committee on one hand but continued to expose the reformist policy of its leaders on the other. The Party congress which met in Glasgow between 30 May and 1 June was significantly pre-

127 TUC archives, B 113 18/2/42: AUCCTU to GC and enclosed copy of letter to IFTU, 20 May 1925.

128 TUC archives, B 114 T65: AUCCTU to GC, 6 June 1925.

129 Murphy in *Pravda*, 13 June 1925. See also *Otchet Ispolkoma Kominterna (Aprel' 1925-Yanvar' 1926)* (Moscow–Leningrad, 1926), pp. 22–23, and *Komm. Int.* (1925), No. 6, p. 50.

130 Rothstein in *Report of the Seventh Congress of the Communist Party of Great Britain*, pp. 109–10. On changes in the CPGB see L. J. Macfarlane, *The British Communist Party* (London, 1966), pp. 133ff.

131 *Report of the Seventh Congress of the Communist Party of Great Britain*: Murphy, p. 61; resolution, pp. 184–85.

sided over by Harry Pollitt, the secretary of the NMM. In his main address Pollitt emphasized the revolutionary potential embodied in the committee, which he considered to be the 'storm centre of the struggles'.[132] The CPGB's attunement to Profintern was embodied in warnings that it was not enough to achieve an Anglo-Russian agreement; a 'committee of action' which would emancipate the workers from their leaders was necessary.[133]

Stalemate in the collaboration

The General Council's initial boldness in launching the committee was gradually fading as suspicion grew regarding the Russians' real aims in view of the increasingly organized activities of the CPGB in the unions and Lozovsky's militancy. This was clearly demonstrated in the pages of the new journal to promote unity issued by Purcell under the auspices of the General Council. Purcell's appeal for unity as a means of acquiring 'POWER to make an end of capitalism' was eagerly taken up by Lozovsky, who called on the revolutionary trade unions to support the alliance and give it the right character.[134] Tomsky gave it a cool reception. He modestly outlined the aims of unity as overcoming 'economic difficulties' and 'reducing the menace of war'. This was echoed by Pugh, gradually emerging as a leading figure in the General Council, who deplored any revolutionary ideology behind the committee and justified its activities only if 'outside the political arena' and confined to an 'economic and industrial basis'.[135]

It was this central bloc of the General Council which took the lead when Tomsky's proposal to convene ARJAC was discussed. The tentative arrangements which had already been made for a meeting of the committee in July were cancelled, and it was agreed that it 'should not be held'.[136] In effect the General

132 *ibid.*, pp. 7–12; for resolution see p. 190. See also Campbell in *Comm. Rev.* (May 1925), pp. 31–34.

133 Brown in *Kras. Int. Prof.* (1925), No. 6, pp. 27–36; Radek endorsed this position in *Komm. Int.* (1925), No. 6, pp. 95–107.

134 *Trade Union Unity* (Apr. 1925), No. 1, and *ibid.* (June 1925), No. 3.

135 Tomsky in *ibid.* (May 1925), No. 2, and Arthur Pugh, Secretary of the Iron and Steel Trades Confederation who in 1926 served as the chairman of the General Council, in *ibid.* (July 1925), No. 4.

136 TUC archives, *Minutes of GC, 1924–5*, p. 118, 23 June 1925.

Council retained its mediatory function and sought unity within the framework of the IFTU. This only confirmed Lozovsky's critical attitude towards the General Council. He now reiterated that unity could only be secured by Profintern, 'the weapon of the Socialist revolution', and through the NMM and the CPGB.[137]

The Russians, however, were not despondent about the General Council's refusal to call ARJAC; the General Council had acceded to Russian requests to be present in the forthcoming TUC. The General Council's active support of the Soviet Union through representations made to Baldwin during the events in China in May[138] was seized on with relief by Tomsky to prove that the English proletariat could be counted upon to stand by Russia when required.[139] The initiative taken by the General Council in July during the dispute in the mining industry, which later had a tremendous effect on the course of Anglo-Soviet relations, was reassuring.

The proposed wages agreement between the miners and owners meant a deterioration in wages and conditions. The miners, led by Cook and Herbert Smith, both closely connected with the NMM and the CPGB, rebuffed the proposals and approached the General Council. An agreement with the Railway Workers' Union and the General Workers' Union to put an embargo on coal movements forced Baldwin to intervene. On 31 July, triumphantly named 'Red Friday' in contrast with the defeat inflicted on the miners on 'Black Friday' in 1921, the Government agreed to grant a subsidy of £20 million to maintain wages at their present level, while a commission headed by Herbert Samuel was set up to inquire into the state of the industry.[140]

The restrained Russian reaction to the event, which was perhaps the most significant achievement of the centralized General Council, seems surprising; yet from their point of view the issue fell outside the scope of their immediate interests. The attack on the miners was presented in Moscow as a complementary step

[137] *Mezh. Rabo. Diviz.*, No. 17, 14 July 1925.
[138] See above, pp. 70–71.
[139] *Trud*, 9 July 1925.
[140] *Report of 57th TUC*, pp. 173–83. See also Bullock, *Ernest Bevin*, Vol. 1, pp. 272–78, and a Russian version in V. G. Trukhanovskii, *Noveishaya Istoriya Anglii* (Moscow, 1958), pp. 126–29.

in the anti-Soviet policy: this was the offensive of capitalism on the domestic front. The swift and by no means anticipated success gave rise to fear that the General Council might be overwhelmed by the event, which would then lead to complacency. Zinoviev warned that in spite of the success of Red Friday it was unwise to underrate the forces of stabilization. United front tactics remained the key to success and the only possible means of penetrating the rigid façade of stabilization.[141]

Dangerous symptoms of disparagement of the growing anti-labour forces were diagnosed by the second NMM conference, which preceded by a week the annual TUC congress. The conference, representing an impressive number of trade unionists,[142] aimed 'to give a lead' to the TUC, which may account for the strongly pro-Russian sentiments of the congress. The success of the international unity campaign and the formation of ARJAC, which clearly dominated the conference, were attributed to the political agitation of the NMM no less than to the voluntary activities of the General Council. The resolutions endorsed Russian demands to form a permanent committee and convene an international conference of organizations adhering to the IFTU on one hand and to Profintern on the other.[143] Overtones of support for Russian diplomacy were discernible in the resolution, which condemned the Locarno Treaty as aiming primarily at 'smashing the First Workers' Socialist Republic, Soviet Russia', and declared solid unity with the Russian workers and readiness 'to prevent at all costs any intervention against them'.[144]

The militant tenor of the TUC congress and the success of the NMM with regard to Red Friday raised the reputation of the left wing to new heights. Ominous signs that the congress was a turning-point rather than a landmark in the struggle for unity

141 See Radek in *Pravda*, 22 Aug. 1925; see also *Kras. Int. Prof.* (1925), Nos. 7–8, pp. 47–52. Zinoviev is in *Inprecorr*, 17 Sept. 1925.

142 *Mezh. Rabo. Dviz.*, Nos. 25–26, 17 Sept. 1925: 683 delegates represented 750,000 workers compared with 271 delegates representing 200,000 workers in Aug. 1924 and 614 delegates representing 600,000 workers in Jan. 1925.

143 NMM, *Report of Second Annual Conference of the N.M.M.* (London, 1925): MacManus, pp. 7–12 and 14; resolution, pp. 18–19.

144 *Report of Second Annual Conference*, p. 30. For a first-hand description of the events of summer 1925 see H. Pollitt, *Serving My Time* (London, 1940), pp. 203–208.

were disregarded. Earlier warnings by G. Allison, later to become the NMM secretary, that most of the trade union leaders had already 'hit the road further than they actually wished' also passed unnoticed.[145] Swales' opening speech of the congress on 7 September in Scarborough was outstanding in its nonconformist style and concurrence with the political line of the NMM. However, the essence of this speech did not seriously diverge from opinions held by the majority of the General Council. His appeal for the improvement of relations with Russia and the Soviet trade unions also occupied a substantial position in the report of the General Council. This appeal dwelt primarily on the economic advantages involved in expanding trade with Russia, which it was feared would otherwise be diverted to other countries. Swales' view of ARJAC was lacking in concrete shape; unity was anticipated on the rather vague basis of 'toleration, mutual understanding and unity of purpose'.[146]

Tomsky's report as a fraternal delegate displayed unanimity among the Russians and betrayed no sign of his confrontation with Lozovsky. Tomsky had earlier made no secret of his intention to secure during his visit to Britain the establishment of a permanent body, 'the nucleus of a new International to which unions of other countries could adhere'.[147] Aware of the criticism which he had received after the London conference, Tomsky now denied the possibility of the Russian unions' acceptance of IFTU membership or abandonment of revolutionary principles. However, in order to reassure those TUC members who feared that a new International would fall under Russian domination, Tomsky emphasized the democratic foundations of the proposed organization.[148]

The strongest and most impressive oration in support of the committee, displaying great admiration of the achievements of the Russian revolution, came from Bramley in a speech which was to be his political testament. Bramley stood fast behind Tomsky's proposal to form an all-inclusive federation of trade

145 *Kras. Int. Prof.* (1925), No. 9, pp. 82–86.
146 *Report of 57th TUC*, pp. 67–72 and 154–71.
147 *Trud*, 1 Sept. 1925; the CPGB's call upon the GC to 'lay the foundations of the new Trade Union International' is in *Comm. Rev.*, 6 Sept. 1925, pp. 197–202.
148 *Report of 57th TUC*, pp. 474–77.

unions with a flexible constitution, but reflected the prevalent anxiety in insisting that each country should be allowed 'to deal with its own domestic policy in its own domestic way'.[149] These speeches, however, did nothing to define a pattern for the amorphous ARJAC. A resolution was moved simply repeating the General Council's earlier elusive promises to do its utmost 'towards securing world-wide unity of the Trade Union movement through an all-inclusive International Federation of Trade Unions'.[150]

Tomsky, desperate not to return to Russia with empty hands again, was determined to complete the task that he had undertaken in April. His entreaties finally brought about an extraordinary meeting of the joint council, attended by a depleted Russian delegation, immediately after the conclusion of the congress.[151] Throughout the meeting, Tomsky tried to test the feelings of the British delegation on the possibility of setting up a definite basis for the committee. However, the General Council, although represented for the last time by its more militant members with Purcell in the chair, saw in the committee only a vehicle for the encounter between the Russian trade unions and Amsterdam. Tomsky managed however to secure a breathing space by reaching an agreement which left the door open, though not for long, for a reconsideration of the decisions taken by the committee. A resolution originated by Tomsky gave the General Council's secretary the same function in the committee. This move secured the post for Bramley but his early replacement by Citrine turned the gain into a disadvantage.[152]

The pattern of future Anglo-Soviet trade union relations was set not so much by ARJAC's resolutions as by the crushing victory of the right-wing and moderate leaders in the elections to the General Council. From the Russian point of view, the election of Thomas was the most alarming; he had deplored the activities of the left wing throughout 1925 and had undertaken in the Railway Workers' conference in July to 'fight to the death' Moscow's methods. Margaret Bondfield and Clynes were also

[149] *ibid.*, pp. 483–84. See also Murphy, *New Horizons*, p. 206.

[150] *Report of 57th TUC*, p. 487.

[151] TUC archives, *Minutes of GC, 1924–5*, p. 164: Citrine's report on conversation with Tomsky, 11 Sept. 1925.

[152] TUC archives, *Minutes of GC, 1925–6*, p. 2, 23 Sept. 1925.

returned, while Ernest Bevin, creator and general secretary of the Transport and General Workers' Union, was elected for the first time.[153] These changes in personnel had an immediate effect on the composition of the British delegation to ARJAC. Pugh, clearly to the right of the TUC and apathetic towards international politics, now headed the delegation, while Bramley, who died within the month following the congress, was succeeded by Citrine.[154] Although Purcell, Hicks and Swales remained in the General Council, their freedom of action and influence were considerably reduced.

The Russians and the CPGB, misled by the enthusiasm with which their representatives had been greeted, were slow to forecast the gathering storm. Pollitt, dizzy with his own success in the congress, held the opinion that the conversion of the reformist central wing to the cause would open the door for more spectacular developments.[155] The CPGB appraised the achievements of the congress as the proof of its own influence in the trade unions on one hand and antagonism between Labour and the TUC on the other hand.[156] Scepticism, however, crept in steadily after the congress; Palme Dutt protested against the calmness with which this antagonism, most ill-timed in view of the intensity of the capitalist offensive, was accepted. Faithful to the CPGB's long-standing though suppressed belief, he repeated his conviction that Labour was fertile soil for the Party's activities.[157]

153 Quoted in G. Blaxland, *J. H. Thomas* (London, 1964), pp. 181–83. Bevin was counted among the supporters of ARJAC, despite his explicit wish to see the AUCCTU affiliated to Amsterdam, because of his association with the 'Hands off Russia' movement in 1920. He soon emerged, however, as an opponent of the collaboration. See Murphy, *New Horizons*, pp. 170–71 and 203, and *Labour's Big Three*, p. 129.

154 Bullock, *Ernest Bevin*, Vol. 1, p. 283. Biographical information on Pugh is in the TUC Library, Box CT/P. On the increasing importance of the trio Pugh, Bevin and Citrine in the GC see Allen, 'The Re-organization of the Trades Union Congress', p. 32 and fn. 39.

155 *Kras. Int. Prof.* (1925), No. 9, pp. 82–86; *Labour Monthly* (Oct. 1925), pp. 601–5.

156 *Workers' Weekly*, 25 Sept. 1925.

157 *Labour Monthly* (Oct. 1925), pp. 577–89; the same views are expressed in *Komm. Int.* (1925), No. 6, pp. 48–64, and *Workers' Weekly*, 7 Aug. 1925. Palme Dutt held no post in the CPGB at that time for reasons of ill health; see Macfarlane, *The British Communist Party*, p. 136.

Moreover, no less an authority than Purcell warned that the successes in the congress would not be complete until the actual implementation of the resolutions moved.[158]

The Russians, though hailing the congress as 'yet another step forward', displayed confusion with regard to the perfunctory attitude of the General Council in forming the alliance with the Soviet trade unions.[159] Radek's analysis of the congress, however, stressed the Russians' overall satisfaction with the success of the left nucleus in restraining British imperialism from pursuing its anti-Soviet course. In this respect the preservation of ARJAC and the encouragement of the unity policy were of major importance, despite the success admittedly scored by the right wing in other spheres.[160] Lozovsky did not restrain his gratification at the prominence of the unity issue and the victory of the left at Scarborough. He cited these as arguments against allying with the IFTU, the backbone of which was a 'hot-bed of the anti-Soviet and anti-communist bloc'.[161]

The Labour Party conference, which met in Liverpool on 29 September, was a complete antidote to Scarborough and a severe blow to Russian hopes that the trade unionists would take the lead in challenging the political programme of the Labour Party. With the exception of Pollitt, who strongly defended the course taken in Scarborough, the majority of the union leaders stood aside while a resolution was moved prohibiting the affiliation of communists to the Labour Party even as representatives of their unions. In addition the trade union faction clearly kept in step with its newly-elected leadership, led by Bevin, in defending the 'evolutionary democracy' represented by Labour.[162] The conference did not in fact pose a direct threat to the future of Anglo-Soviet trade union relations as even the new centre leadership had not as yet turned its energies against ARJAC. It did, however, shake the foundations of the alliance with the left-wing

[158] *Trud*, 27 Sept. 1925.

[159] *Pravda*, 12 Sept. and 15 Sept. 1925; Melnichansky in *Trud*, 13 Sept. 1925.

[160] *Pravda*, 12 Sept. and 27 Sept. 1925. See also the satisfaction expressed by Dogadov and Tomsky, interviewed in *ibid.*, 24 Sept. 1925.

[161] *Mezh. Rabo. Dviz.*, No. 27, 24 Sept. 1925; also similar views in *Kras. Int. Prof.* (1925), No. 10, pp. 5–25.

[162] *Report of the Twenty-Fifth Annual Conference of the Labour Party. Liverpool, 1925*, pp. 38 and 352.

unionists, who showed themselves to be fundamentally social democrats in that their willingness to embark on a class struggle was fading; a re-evaluation of the communist attitude towards them was inevitable.

The Russian reaction to the inconsistent performance of the left wing in the two conferences threw fresh light on their opportunist motives for preserving unity. In the intensive soul-searching which followed, aimed at justifying the alliance, they deliberately ignored the fact that the militancy at Scarborough primarily reflected the conflict in the coal industry and the events of Red Friday.[163] Profintern's views, also propagated by the CPGB, which outrightly disputed the significance of the TUC congress as compared with the 'well lubricated' machine in Liverpool, enjoyed little support in Russia.[164] In view of the Locarno Treaty, the Conservatives' stringency with the Communist Party and the struggle for power in the CPSU, the time was ripe neither for jeopardizing ARJAC nor for challenging Tomsky, whose sympathies still lay with the General Council.[165]

Theoretical juggling was therefore necessary to solve the problem of the contradictory conferences and restore credit to the General Council without leaving the impression that this was done for reasons of expediency. The most striking example of this was Palme Dutt's complete *volte-face*, ruling out any political alliance with Labour. In comparing the two conferences, he chose to stress the alienation of the trade unions from the Labour Party, which he believed heralded 'the emergence of the idea of class war in England'.[166] By and large, however, the tendency was to minimize the significance of Liverpool in which, it was suggested, the workers' mood had found no expression. Scarborough, on the other hand, was hailed as the real victory for the workers by virtue of its system of representation. Liverpool

[163] This interpretation of the Scarborough congress is in H. Pelling, *The British Communist Party* (London, 1958), p. 34.

[164] *Kras. Int. Prof.* (1925), No. 11, p. 19. Pollitt reviewed the bankruptcy of the left wing with relief in a meeting of the executive committee of the CPGB, while Campbell advocated thwarting the capitalist offensive 'by means of class struggle' and 'outside Parliament'; see *Inprecorr*, 15 Oct. 1925, and *Workers' Weekly*, 9 and 16 Oct. 1925.

[165] *KPSS v Rezolyutsiyakh i Resheniyakh*, Vol. 3, pp. 223 and 235–38.

[166] *Komm. Int.* (1925), No. 10, pp. 97–110.

was dismissed, therefore, as the 'occasion, seized by the right wing, to take revenge for Scarborough'.[167]

The final touches to the official interpretation were added by Petrovsky, Comintern's representative in Britain. In a long and detailed account of the events, he pointed out the substantial differences between Labour and the TUC, which came to a head in Liverpool and caused an irremediable split. The trade unions were to be trusted because of their close contact with the masses; Labour, however, was responsible to the masses only during elections, while in intermediate periods, like the rest of the bourgeois parties, it served varying interests.[168] This explanation was taken up by Zinoviev in his report to the CPSU's congress, later in December, to demonstrate the CPGB's influence in the trade unions and inject new life into united front tactics.[169]

Tomsky was unable to hide his perplexity over the results of the Liverpool conference and the anomaly of the Scarborough congress, where militant resolutions were moved simultaneously with the return of a right-wing leadership to the Council. However, despite these alarming signs he retained his belief in the General Council's unanimous support of ARJAC, and was confident that the committee would soon be 'launched in the international arena'.[170] This faith in the General Council was erroneously strengthened by the visit of Citrine and Hicks to Russia. Soon after his return Citrine was to become with Bevin the leading exponent of the crystallizing opposition to the committee. However, still under the influence of the militancy at Scarborough, he spared no praise for the Soviet Union. Tomsky must have been delighted to hear Citrine launching into one of his most militant speeches ever during the session of the Moscow trade union organization, in which he stated: 'Our task is to exhaust all means at our disposal to create such an International of trade unions which will embrace the trade unions of the entire world and which will provide the proper means for the abolition

167 *Pravda*, 1 Oct. 1925. See also Murphy in *Comm. Rev.* (Nov. 1925), p. 303.

168 *Komm. Int.* (1925), No. 10, pp. 97–110. In retrospect Petrovsky admitted that Scarborough was the turning-point in Anglo-Soviet trade union relations; see *ibid.* (1927), No. 24, p. 30.

169 *XIV S'ezd VKP*, pp. 653–56.

170 *Trud*, 16 Oct. 1925.

of Capitalism; such an International would be capable of building on the foundations laid down by your October revolution.'[171]

Yet Tomsky's fervent though futile endeavours to activate ARJAC best illustrate the gap between theories elaborated in Moscow and reality as reflected in the Liverpool conference. *The Times* observed correctly that as a result of changes in the General Council the 'passion for unity with the Russians at all costs' had 'considerably abated'.[172]

The long-expected meeting of the General Council of the IFTU to discuss the Russian letter of May was preceded by a meeting of its executive bureau with the General Council of the TUC in London in early December. Indeed, the cordial atmosphere between the two organizations was immediately restored in the opening session when the British delegation, now led by Bondfield and Pugh, made the following conciliatory statement: 'The General Council deprecates any attempt to represent its action as being hostile to the International Federation of the Trade Unions.' Even more significant was the General Council's unequivocal declaration of its wish to see the Russian unions affiliated to Amsterdam, though this was accompanied by approval of the Russian demand for a preliminary unconditional conference. This clearly implied that the General Council regarded ARJAC only as a temporary body with a merely advisory function.

A few days later in Amsterdam, on the basis of the apparent understanding reached in London, Hicks attempted to push through a resolution calling upon the IFTU to meet Russian representatives to discuss 'the possibilities of the affiliation of the Russian Trade Union movement'. However, the strongly prevailing anti-Russian sentiments were manifested when a proposal by Stenhuis, a prominent Dutch Socialist and member of the IFTU secretariat, rendering 'any new decisions unnecessary' superseded Hicks' resolution by an overwhelming majority.[173]

[171] *Trud*, 16 Oct. 1925. Citrine's detailed recollections of the trip in *Men and Work*, pp. 95–122, only prove that the Soviet political scene remained incomprehensible to him.

[172] *The Times*, 30 Nov. 1925.

[173] TUC archives, B 113 18/2/54: records of the IFTU executive bureau's meeting; *Report on Activities during the Years 1924, 1925 and 1926*, pp. 50–51.

The obviously placatory attitude of the TUC towards the IFTU and its opposition to the creation of a rival international organization by far exceeded the Russians' apprehensions. In addition, when ARJAC met in Berlin on 8–9 December, the Russians had to face for the first time the new British delegation headed by Pugh and Citrine, in which Purcell, who was present only as an observer, was the sole unreserved supporter of the Russian position.[174] The first day was devoted to reports of the earlier meeting of the General Council with the IFTU while the repercussions of these meetings were thoroughly discussed in the subsequent meeting of the committee. Tomsky's familiarity with the mood of the British delegation compelled him to modify his original proposal to establish forthwith a permanent committee. Instead he urged the TUC to fulfil its obligation by using its 'mediatory influence' between the IFTU and the AUCCTU to 'convene a conference which would endeavour to promote international trade union unity'. In view of this the Finnish and Norwegian requests to join ARJAC were once more turned down, not to be raised again until February 1928 when Profintern was seeking a substitute for the alliance with the British, which had just broken down.[175] The abortive meeting culminated in a small compensation for the Russians when as a result of their insistence a protest was registered against attempts by the Amsterdam leadership to misrepresent the aims of the *rapprochement*.[176]

A review of the AUCCTU's policies in the light of the ARJAC meeting was left over for the impending fourteenth Party congress. Meanwhile a non-committal commentary described ARJAC as potentially capable of 'securing peace' and preventing the splitting policy of Amsterdam. The Russian delegates closed their eyes to what had transpired in Berlin and remained confident that the committee would be established on a permanent basis.[177] The CPSU congress, however, dominated by the internal crisis in the Party as a result of the appearance of the Leningrad bloc as an organized open opposition, proved to

174 *Trade Union Unity* (1925), No. 1.

175 G. M. Adibekov, 'K 50-Letiyu Profinterna', *Novaya i Noveishaya Istoriya* (1971), No. 4, p. 25.

176 TUC archives, B 114 T65: report of the Berlin meeting.

177 *Pravda*, 11 Dec. 1925; interviews with Tomsky, Dogadov and Melnichansky in *ibid.*, and *Trud*, 15 Dec. 1925.

be an unsuitable forum for judging ARJAC on its own merits regardless of party politics. The inner Party debate was a godsend for Tomsky. His key position in the Politburo in support of the right wing and staunch defence of Stalin against Kamenev's severe attack in the congress temporarily immunized him against any serious challenge. This impeded the solution of the problem but could not prevent the increasing dissatisfaction with his policy in the Party.[178]

Tomsky's secure position was immediately evident in view of Stalin's measured report on the international situation which accommodated national interests with Comintern's aspirations; Stalin emphatically established that the stabilization of capitalism removed from the agenda of Europe 'the seizure of power by the proletariat from one day to another'. In his opinion this fully justified rallying behind the workers' movement in the West, the 'barrier against each and every possibility of intervention'. The diplomatic considerations gained the upper hand when Stalin launched a peace offensive, urging the cultivation of normal relations with the European countries. The revolutionary task of encouraging the formation of mass parties was subordinated to the first aim of providing a shield for the Soviet Union.[179] Strong advocacy of socialism on the national level and diminishing expectations of world revolution were embodied in the resolution drafted on the basis of Molotov's and Stalin's reports, which provoked no objections.[180]

Zinoviev found the best outlet for his views on the international situation and the trade union policy in his report on the activities of the Russian delegation to Comintern. However, his speech was designed to harmonize with Stalin's report and avoid any major collision which might endanger his position in Comintern, which was left intact for the time being. Indeed, in his concluding words Zinoviev expressed relief that no differences of opinion on the 'principal substance' of his report could be traced in the debate.[181] However, clearly discernible between the lines is Zinoviev's desperate attempt to upset Stalin's order of priorities by emphasizing the temporary character of the stabilization and

[178] Tomsky's defence of Stalin in *XIV S'ezd VKP*, pp. 291–92.
[179] *ibid.*, pp. 8–11, 21 and 25–26.
[180] *ibid.*, p. 513.
[181] *ibid.*, p. 706.

reviving revolutionary fervour. Zinoviev believed that his optimism was vindicated by the intensifying revolutionary situation in Britain. This was a remarkable departure from his previous views as a member of the triumvirate; they had been epitomized in October: 'The fight against the dangers of new wars must become the Alpha and Omega of the work of the Communist International.'[182] Zinoviev's report to the CPSU paid lip-service to the correctness of his former line but warned against overestimating the significance of the left wing. He recognized the Communist Party and the minority in the trade unions as 'the essence of our foundations in England'. Zinoviev also made some passing observations about ARJAC in which he sided with Lozovsky. He did not contest the importance attached to the committee in terms of winning over the masses and uniting the left wing under a communist programme, but deliberately belittled its diplomatic achievements. Zinoviev was concerned that the glorification of these achievements might give rise to accusations that the Russian initiative was motivated by opportunist calculations.[183] While Lozovsky was prevented from elaborating his views at this stage, Shmidt, the Commissar of Labour, who had been actively involved in the formation of the committee, reasserted its significance.[184]

The major debate on trade union policy was put off until the last days of the congress. By this time the congress had reached its climax, with the regrouping of forces in Stalin's favour completed. When Tomsky rose to make the report of the AUCCTU, his position next to Stalin ensured its acceptability. Before Scarborough Tomsky had wavered between two different attitudes towards the committee: between wishing to see the Russian trade unions in the IFTU and accepting nothing short of a conference between the IFTU and Profintern. However, even then it was clear that Tomsky was primarily attracted by the political

[182] *Inprecorr*, 28 Oct. 1925. On Zinoviev's change of line see W. Korey, 'Zinoviev on the Problem of World Revolution' (Columbia Univ. Ph.D. thesis, 1961), pp. 270–71. Zinoviev was accused by other members of the CPSU's delegation to Comintern of using it as a forum for deviationist views. This served as an excuse for tightening the CPSU's majority control over Comintern; see *XIV S'ezd VKP*, pp. 685, 689–94, and 698–700.

[183] *XIV S'ezd VKP*, pp. 639–50, 657 and 657–78.

[184] *ibid.*, pp. 702 and 703–706.

advantages embodied in a bloc with the TUC, even one not professing communist ideology.[185] The Party congress now revealed that the gap between Tomsky's and Lozovsky's expectations was becoming unbridgeable. Tomsky, no longer satisfied with the alignment as an 'agitation manoeuvre', was justifiably accused by Ryazanov of practising 'opportunist policies in the international trade union movement'. Tomsky denied such accusations but admitted that there was much to be desired from the alliance from the communist point of view. Moreover, in his concluding speech Tomsky freely admitted his belief that Bolsheviks were obliged to 'stick to the devil's horns, approach the Pope in Rome, go anywhere if the interests of the working class or workers' revolution dictated it'.[186]

Tomsky had no difficulty in defending the course taken by ARJAC in its Berlin meeting, although he neither passed over the unsatisfactory state of affairs nor underestimated the obstacles ahead. He still contended that fostering the alliance with the TUC would be a gain for Russia even if it demanded long and patient preparatory work. The controversial part of his report was an intimation that to maintain ARJAC the Soviet trade unions were even willing to consider joining the IFTU; however, to avoid laying too much stress on this proposal he expressed the hope that unity could be achieved 'over the head of Amsterdam'.[187]

Tomsky had already taken practical steps in this direction before the congress met. The statutes of the major unions had been discreetly altered, without consultations in the Party, to facilitate their adherence to a 'United International Trade Union Organization' instead of to Profintern. This position, thoroughly antagonistic to the spirit of the declared intentions of Comintern, was scrupulously maintained after the congress as long as the purges against the Leningrad opposition were in full swing.[188]

Lozovsky's reply to Tomsky was postponed while congratulations were conveyed to the winning faction, with greetings from

185 Speech to enlarged presidium of AUCCTU in *Trud*, 21 Aug. 1925.

186 *XIV S'ezd VKP*: Ryazanov, p. 784; Tomsky, p. 803.

187 *ibid.*, pp. 743–47.

188 Trotsky revealed this in the Politburo meeting in July 1926: Trotsky archives, T-881. Andreev echoed Tomsky in a meeting of the Leningrad trade union organization, advocating a 'realistic policy' which would be characterized by leaving themselves a 'free hand' in relations with Amsterdam; reported in *Trud*, 13 Jan. 1926.

factory and Party cells. When Lozovsky finally got a chance to challenge Tomsky, he found himself in an uncomfortable situation, for his opinions could easily pass for those of the Leningrad opposition. Whatever the difference of opinion between Tomsky and Lozovsky, they both worked within the Party line, and neither would have gone outside it. Indeed Lozovsky was immediately attacked by Melnichansky for delivering a minority report (*sodoklad*) which bore a suspicious resemblance to Zinoviev's earlier report of the minority in the central committee.[189] It was doubly difficult to assail Tomsky because he had brilliantly avoided giving an explicit declaration of intent to enter Amsterdam, yet had left the door open for such a move. However, well aware of Tomsky's determination to cultivate the committee at all cost, Lozovsky emphatically demanded that the Russian unions should not be allowed to join Amsterdam. Drawing parallels between Amsterdam and the League of Nations, he insisted that the attempt to capture the Russian trade unions was part of the plot against the Soviet Union, connected with the Locarno Treaty and aimed at sowing confusion in the revolutionary unions.[190] Winding up the discussion, Tomsky left no room for doubt that Lozovsky and the opposition were of one mind and compared their activities to an opera performance: 'Running about, running about, in fact staying on the stage and only singing one aria in the course of an hour: "Unity of the trade unions, unity of the trade unions". But everything stays in the same place and moves neither forward nor backward.' However, after this crushing indictment he felt able to excuse Lozovsky for his defence of Profintern on the grounds of his personal ambition as president of that body.[191]

Tomsky's overbearing behaviour in the course of the debate by no means reflected feelings in the Politburo. Of the forty-three clauses of the resolution adopted by the congress on the activities of the Russian trade unions, only the last mentioned ARJAC. It

[189] *XIV S'ezd VKP*, p. 792. Lozovsky's position was made even more disagreeable when Glebov-Avilov, the most distinguished trade unionist among the opposition, supported his views on ARJAC; see *ibid.*, pp. 788 and 792.

[190] *ibid.*, pp. 747–78. Lozovsky's inference that ARJAC should be broadened to include more organizations drew comment from Melnichansky: 'A new International?'

[191] *ibid.*, pp. 800–804.

hailed it as 'the first practical step on the way to establishing international trade union unity' but provided no clues about its operational character.[192] It appears that the majority of the Politburo was in fact disinclined to allow the development of ARJAC at any cost. The policy, clearly and consistently executed until the general strike, was to limit their involvement in ARJAC and keep it in a dormant state. Indeed between the congress and the strike the intense campaign for the strengthening of the committee was allowed to lapse; it was in fact confined to a minute anniversary editorial in *Trud* characterized by its critical tone.[193]

Scarcely had the congress ended when the future of ARJAC took a dramatic and decisive turn, though accomplished discreetly behind the scenes. A well-defined directive on the attitude to be adopted towards the committee was urgently required in view of the IFTU's decision, communicated to Moscow, to invite the affiliation of the Soviet trade unions. A special meeting of the central committee of the CPSU took place early in January as the purges of Zinoviev's supporters in the Leningrad organizations were approaching their completion. It categorically repudiated 'all the counter-revolutionary talking with regard to the alleged intended affiliation of the Russian trade unions to Amsterdam'.[194]

The AUCCTU duly informed Amsterdam on 6 January that it could 'add nothing new to the proposals made heretofore'. This coincided with a letter from the General Council which pleaded with the IFTU to reconsider its resolution. However, the executive of the IFTU was adamant in its refusal to modify its decision, and the issue was deferred to the next meeting of the IFTU's General Council, which was expected to take place in January 1927; by this time, however, the question had lost its relevance.[195] Yet, while the Party had unequivocally defined its attitude towards the question of affiliation, it refrained from passing judgement on the organizational form of the alliance

192 *ibid.*, pp. 987–88.

193 *Trud*, 6 Apr. 1926.

194 Open letter from central committee of CPSU to all sections of Comintern in *Inprecorr*, 21 Jan. 1926; *VI Rasshirennyi Plenum Ispolkoma Kominterna, Tezisy i Rezolyutsii . . .* (Moscow, 1926), p. 29 (hereafter referred to as *VI Plenum IKKI: Rezolyutsii*).

195 *Report on Activities during the Years 1924, 1925 and 1926*, pp. 51–52; thorough coverage in *The Times*, 22 Feb. 1926.

with the British trade unions. This remained a point of controversy between Lozovsky and Tomsky, to be interrupted only by the general strike.

The Russians' swift disengagement from their previously frequent approaches to the British General Council was demonstrated during the sixth IKKI plenum, which met from 17 February to 15 March 1926, and the fourth session of Profintern, which sat at the same time; in these the question of ARJAC was only casually referred to. Despite Zinoviev's insecure position his assertion that the question of whether the Russian unions should enter Amsterdam could be solved only on an international basis, and never 'on the national level only', encountered little opposition. Lozovsky dismissed as 'legends' suggestions that a unilateral move by the Russian unions was contemplated; in the words of the central committee's resolution, he affirmed: 'The Soviet trade unions did not, do not and cannot conduct any policy other than that of Profintern and Comintern.'[196] Zinoviev, like Lozovsky, maintained the undisputed line that the united front tactics had to be interpreted in terms of the 'restoration of workers' unity on the basis of the revolutionary struggle against the bourgeoisie'.[197] The emphasis laid for the first time on the prospects of revolutionary developments in the East was also not conducive to a coalition within the framework of Amsterdam. The entrance of the Russian unions, it was argued, might have an effect on the European scene but would be felt only marginally in the entire world.[198]

Once the question of the attitude towards Amsterdam had been settled, Lozovsky anxiously sought a *modus vivendi* with Tomsky. He readily admitted that although the left wing of the General Council was not yet politically or ideologically conscious, it was a suitable candidate for an alliance because of its alertness to the worsening economic situation. It was wrong, he argued, 'to treat these groups with hostility or antagonize

196 *Shestoi Rasshirennyi Plenum Ispolkoma Kominterna. Stenograficheskii Otchet* (Moscow–Leningrad, 1927), pp. 292–93 and 303 (hereafter referred to as *VI Plenum IKKI*). For the CPGB see also Ferguson in *ibid.*, pp. 267–69.

197 *ibid.*, pp. 42–43; *VI Plenum IKKI: Rezolyutsii*, pp. 21–22 and 44–45.

198 Lozovsky in *Chetvertaya Sessiya Tsentral'nogo Soveta Krasnogo Internatsionala Profsoyuzov, Otchet* (Moscow–Leningrad, 1927), p. 31 (hereafter referred to as *IV Sessiya Profinterna*).

them'.[199] These observations were overtly based on the expectation of different contributions from the communists and the minority movement among the rank and file on one hand and from the left wing on the other. This move towards appeasement held little appeal for Tomsky, whose close connection with the British trade unionists made him view with suspicion any attempt to idealize the masses. In fact he was skating on thin ice in approving united front tactics from above, claiming that only the General Council, 'leading the trade unions, conducting its activities', could be trusted as an ally.

A long and acrimonious debate took place in the special committee formed to draft IKKI's resolution on the activities of the trade unions. The outcome was an uneasy compromise between the two points of view, clearly favourable to Profintern yet failing to supply any new directives to ARJAC.[200] It once more welcomed the *rapprochement* between the trade unions of the two countries and called upon Comintern 'to help the Anglo-Russian Committee in fulfilling the tasks set by itself'. At the same time it expressed strong scepticism about the success of such a policy, insisting that unity would be accomplished even if the committee should 'fail for one reason or another to expand its activity'.[201] In the session of Profintern, from which Tomsky was conspicuously absent, emphasis was put on the 'state of insufficient development' in which the left wing found itself. Andrés Nin, Lozovsky's deputy, in one of his rare appearances, bombarded the meeting with objections to full collaboration with the formal left wing. He warned that overestimating the strength of this wing was equivalent to underestimating the power and strength of the Soviet Union as represented by Profintern. He also attributed the achievements of ARJAC to the activities of the CPGB and the NMM in the trade unions.[202]

The General Council was either slow or unwilling to appreciate the fast-changing attitude of the Russians to the committee. They were still eager to bring the Russian and IFTU representatives together, thereby avoiding any crisis with either. To encourage such a contact the Russians were invited to send representatives

199 *VI Plenum IKKI*, pp. 282–84.
200 *ibid.*, pp. 318 and 484.
201 *ibid.*, p. 46; *VI Plenum IKKI: Rezolyutsii*, p. 30.
202 *IV Sessiya Profinterna*: Lozovsky, p. 18; Nin, pp. 7–12.

to an ARJAC meeting in mid-May which was to coincide with an international migration conference attended by IFTU representatives.[203] For the first time the Russians turned down, politely but firmly, the English initiative, pointing out 'the inconvenience and the great awkwardness' which such a meeting would cause. The Russians were now determined to embark on the next stage, in which it was the task of ARJAC to convene an International Conference of Unity.[204]

203 TUC archives, *Minutes of IC, 1925–6*, 13 Apr. 1926; B 113 18/2/42: Citrine to Dogadov, 14 Apr. 1926.

204 TUC archives, B 113 18/2/42: Dogadov to Citrine, 30 Apr. 1926. This crossed a second invitation by Citrine to Dogadov during the general strike, *ibid.*, 5 May 1926.

4

Russia and the General Strike

Signs of a thaw in the British policy

At the beginning of 1926 it looked as if Anglo-Soviet relations had deteriorated beyond recovery. Chamberlain had been under constant pressure from the obdurate diehards to sever relations with Russia, while Chicherin manifested increasing animosity towards Britain. However, Chamberlain, aware of a move towards moderation in Moscow, refused to act hastily. Moreover, he realized that any hostile activity towards Russia would be interpreted in Germany as an attempt to drive a wedge between these countries; this might compromise Germany's entry to the League, which was vital for the pacification of Europe. Thus, although he did not ostensibly share Germany's contention that 'Russia must be friends with somebody',[1] he had taken cautious steps to establish a more normal pattern of relations with Russia. These efforts were promptly frustrated by the outbreak of the general strike.

Ever since Locarno, the Russians had been obsessed by the idea that Chamberlain was contemplating the transformation of the treaty into an alliance against Russia. Typical of this obsession was their attribution of anti-Soviet articles written under the pseudonym of 'Augur' by Poliakov, a White Russian, to none other than Chamberlain himself.[2] Consequently they abandoned for a time their hopes of resuming negotiations in Britain. The only activities towards this end were pursued by Citrine on behalf of the General Council of the TUC. At the beginning of February he described to Chamberlain the economic advantages which he believed lay in trade with Russia. In spite of this

[1] D'Abernon, *Diary*, Vol. III, p. 249.

[2] See 'Moskvich' in *Izvestiya*, 14 Feb. 1926. A representative leader is 'Podgotovka Novykh Voin', *Ekon. Zhzn.*, 16 Jan. 1926.

Chicherin did not for a moment believe that Chamberlain would be prepared to accept the 1924 agreement as a starting point in further negotiations; for the Russians this was the fixed condition for a *pourparler*. Chicherin acted on the assumption that Chamberlain hoped to draw Russia out 'by looking the other way, by affecting to ignore her'. He had even withdrawn the suggestion, conveyed by Briand, that he and Chamberlain should meet, because he believed that Chamberlain was determined to force Russia to come to agreement on Britain's terms. Litvinov, who apparently held similar views, decided to delay Krasin's departure for London because the moment was 'not ripe for reopening negotiations'.[3]

The Russians planned to extricate themselves from imposed isolation by exploiting, to the utmost, clashes of interests between England and the rest of the signatories of the Locarno Treaty. They were particularly encouraged by the economic advantages to be expected from the commercial treaty with Germany of October 1925 and the favourable prospects of following it up with a political one.[4] It was also foretold in Moscow that France, dissatisfied with the role of supreme arbiter taken by Britain in Locarno, would be eager to conclude an agreement with the Russians. Attention was therefore turned to strengthening Russia's bargaining position through the improvement of relations with Germany and France. 'The route to London', suggested Rakovsky, now led 'through Paris'.[5]

At the beginning of February, the Cabinet discussed Chicherin's mistrust of the Locarno Treaty and its implications for Anglo-Soviet relations. On Chamberlain's advice, it was agreed after little discussion that 'no action' was necessary. In Parliament a day later Locker-Lampson, the Under-Secretary of State, restated the familiar attitude of the Government: although

[3] F.O. 371 11786 N387/387/38: Peters to Mounsey on conversation with Chicherin, 14 Jan. 1926. On correspondence between Citrine and Chicherin see *Dok. Vne. Pol.*, Vol. IX, pp. 142–44. For Litvinov's position see *Dok. Vne. Pol.*, Vol. IX, pp. 24–25: Litvinov to Rosengoltz, 13 Jan. 1926, and F.O. 371 11778 N317/23/38: Peters to Chamberlain, 13 Jan. 1926.

[4] Chicherin interviewed in *Manchester Guardian*, 19 Feb. 1926.

[5] Interview with Rakovsky in *Izvestiya*, 14 Jan. 1926, and a speech delivered on 30 Jan. to the Institute of Foreign Affairs in Moscow in *Mir. Khz. i Mir. Pol.* (1926), No. 2, pp. 14–15.

they were fully aware of Russian propaganda they did not contemplate the abrogation of the 1921 treaty.[6]

Meanwhile, however, a new chapter in Anglo-Soviet relations was in the making. Misgivings about the policy of disregard were mostly a result of economic calculations; they were, however, intensified by a changing outlook on the political situation within the Soviet Union. The Foreign Office welcomed the emergence of the 'strong, stern, silent' Stalin as the 'indisputable' leader of the Party; it was a sign that Soviet foreign policy would employ 'nationalist rather than internationalist weapons'. This argument was buttressed by a further report on the measures taken in Leningrad against the 'honest fanatic' Zinoviev.[7] Reports confirming these earlier observations came in throughout February. By the end of the month Peters submitted a detailed memorandum underlining the indubitably steady progress of the Soviet economy. He therefore saw no objection to granting Russia the credits on which the pace of industrialization depended, as there was a 'reasonable prospect' of their being promptly repaid.[8]

The Franco-Soviet negotiations provided the occasion for making adjustments in the policy towards Russia; this took place only a week after the Cabinet meeting which re-affirmed the *status quo* in Anglo-Soviet relations. The French, aware of the pre-eminence which the Russians gave to an agreement with Britain, were probably convinced about the possibility of a sudden change in the British position once tangible progress had been made in the negotiations.[9] Herriot, therefore, tried to impress on Chamberlain that the negotiations were pursued 'simply as a fulfilment of an engagement to the Russians'. Yet the suspicions of the Office were alerted by the fact that the French refused either to cooperate with or inform the British on the course of

[6] Cab. 23/52 23(26)2, 3 Feb. 1926; *Parl. Deb. H.C.*, Vol. 191, col. 340, 4 Feb. 1926.

[7] F.O. 371 11779 N120/53/38: Peters to Chamberlain, 1 Jan. 1926; F.O. 371 11779 N560/53/38: Peters to Chamberlain (dispatch from Preston in Leningrad), 18 Jan. 1926, and minute by Maxse, 11 Feb. 1926; F.O. 371 11779 N319/53/38: minute by Maxse, 27 Jan. 1926.

[8] F.O. 371 11793 N1070/1070/38: Hodgson to Chamberlain (memorandum by Peters), 24 Feb. 1926. Similar views are expressed in F.O. 371 11793 N1335/1070/38: Hodgson to Chamberlain, 8 Mar. 1926.

[9] On the significance of the negotiations see Fischer, *The Soviets in World Affairs*, Vol. 2, p. 617, and Schram, 'Christian Rakovskij', pt. 2, p. 584.

the negotiations.[10] In view of this Chamberlain rejected the Foreign Office's draft reply to a Parliamentary question which conditioned the renewal of Anglo-Soviet relations on Russian admittance of their obligations. He suggested instead that 'a hint of the glad eye might be useful at home & abroad'. Chamberlain promptly declared in Parliament that the Paris negotiations might 'facilitate the renewal of negotiations with Britain'.[11]

In the meantime a Foreign Office memorandum to the Cabinet observed the rise of nationalist and more traditional characteristics in Soviet foreign policy and suggested that this implied an aspiration by the Soviet Union to establish normal relations with the capitalist world. Chamberlain admitted that the policy of reserve nourished Soviet obsessions, leading to dangerous consequences, but did not propose any practical measures for the improvement of relations. He simply concluded that it was a mistake to represent the British as 'irreconcilable enemies of the Soviet Union, unwilling to listen to any overtures if such were made'.[12]

A contributory factor in Chamberlain's reluctance to take positive steps towards the resumption of negotiations was opposition in the Government's economic departments. The strongest resistance came from the Board of Trade, which dismissed Chamberlain's political as well as economic arguments for departing from the agreed policy and sought a European 'common or co-ordinated economic policy in dealing with Russia'. Chamberlain, still vacillating about *rapprochement*, welcomed the idea in principle despite warnings from the Northern Department that this was a 'departure from the policy of "doing nothing"'. However, he realized that the suggestion was impracticable because of Germany's 'puzzling decision to be tangled by credits'.[13] Even when the plan had to be completely abandoned in April following the conclusion of the German-Soviet Treaty, the Board

10 F.O. 371 11787 N1460/418/38: memorandum by Gregory on conversation with Fleuriau of the French Embassy, 27 Mar. 1926.

11 F.O. 371 11786 N644/387/38: minute by Chamberlain, 6 Feb. 1926; *Parl. Deb. H.C.*, Vol. 191, col. 1017, 10 Feb. 1926.

12 F.O. 371 11789 N640/640/38: Foreign Office memorandum, 10 Feb. 1926.

13 F.O. 371 11776 N1377/7/38: Chapman, BOT, to Tyrrell, 24 Mar. 1926; minutes by Orde and Chamberlain, 27 Mar. 1926.

of Trade persisted in its opposition to a change in the policy. It was dubious about Peters' 'prosperous picture' of the Soviet economic recovery, convinced that this was not inconsistent with the 'ultimate breakdown of Soviet finance'. It therefore seemed wise to maintain the '"very nuffin" public policy about Russian trade'.[14]

The Treasury's immediate reaction to Chamberlain's memorandum was also negative. They restated their categorical rejection of any negotiations which entailed a Government loan. The Foreign Office's attention was drawn to Churchill's advice to the City to adopt an unfavourable attitude towards countries which had not reached agreement on war debts with Britain. In addition the Treasury, convinced of the City's hostility to Russia, could 'not see on the horizon any possibility whatever of a Russian market loan'.[15] However, in the course of March, Churchill seems to have absorbed Peters' reports on the changing conditions in Russia. He told Parliament that if the Russians initiated discussions on a loan they would not be treated 'with less consideration' than other debtors. This, as was recognized in the Northern Department, indicated that the Government was becoming less 'stiff-necked' in its attitude towards Russia.[16]

Stresemann's determination not to sacrifice his ally in the East to gain a new one in the West also contributed to the thaw in Anglo-Soviet relations. Stresemann had embarked on negotiations with the Russians shortly after the signing of the Locarno Treaty. However, it was not until 24 April 1926 that a treaty of neutrality and friendship was signed. The Treaty of Berlin was preceded by a preamble safeguarding the friendly relations between the two countries on the lines of the Rapallo Treaty and granting both countries most favoured nation status.[17]

At the end of March, when the initial difficulties had been overcome, Stresemann decided to inform the major powers of the

[14] F.O. 371 11794 N2072/1070/38: minute by Samuel, BOT, transmitted to Foreign Office, 17 Apr. 1926.

[15] F.O. 371 11776 N744/7/38: Niemeyer, Treasury, to Gregory, 16 Feb. 1926; F.O. 371 11776 N964/7/38: Niemeyer to Wellesley, 27 Feb. 1926.

[16] *Parl. Deb. H.C.*, Vol. 193, col. 1251, 24 Mar. 1926; F.O. 371 11788 N1406/519/38: minute by Maxse, 30 Mar. 1926.

[17] Rosenbaum, *Community of Fate*, pp. 183 ff., and Korbel, *Poland between East and West*, pp. 191 and 194–95.

general content of the treaty to protect Germany 'against any misinterpretation'.[18] He emphasized that the cornerstone of German diplomacy was the elimination of the menace which Russia presented if left 'at a loose end'. However, the conclusion of the treaty was propelled by considerations beyond the mere protection of the German rear. Stresemann regarded it as a splendid opportunity to soothe Russian apprehensions of the anti-Soviet bloc crystallizing around the League and to discourage Britain from embarking on such a policy. He also seems to have taken full advantage of Chamberlain's total commitment to the reconciliation of Europe and his eagerness to introduce Germany into the League of Nations. Stresemann, therefore, impressed on Chamberlain that the treaty was not only 'compatible' with the Covenant of the League and with the German obligations undertaken in Locarno, but also a 'completion of Locarno'. Believing that it was wrong to leave Russia outside the European constellation, he presented the Treaty of Berlin as 'the least dangerous of available bridges'.[19]

One of the reasons for Chamberlain's restrained attitude to the treaty was his emergence after Locarno, very much to his satisfaction, as the leading arbitrator in European affairs. On this occasion Germany consulted him on the substance of the treaty while Poland, France and Czechoslovakia all addressed their protests to the British Foreign Office. The Poles, who were the severest critics of Germany's move in consequence of their claim on the seat in the Council now offered to Germany, drew Chamberlain's attention to parallels between the present treaty and that of Rapallo with its secret clauses. They also played on Britain's animosity towards Russia, warning Chamberlain that under the new treaty Germany could 'certainly refuse to take part in any execution of orders' by the League against Russia and would interpret Article 16 of the League 'as they thought it best'.[20] Skrzynski, the Polish Foreign Minister, hastened to Prague to consult Beneš about the grave situation. He remained highly agitated even after the British Ambassador to Prague had

[18] Sutton, *Gustave Stresemann*, Vol. II, p. 462.

[19] F.O. 371 11791 N1489, 1555, 1593/718/38: D'Abernon to Chamberlain on conversations with Stresemann, 1, 6 and 9 Apr. 1926.

[20] F.O. 371 11991 N1600/718/38: Muller, Ambassador in Warsaw, to Chamberlain, 11 Apr. 1926.

conveyed to him Germany's assurance to Britain that its policy would not contradict the principles of the League.[21]

The French, siding with the Poles over the dispute in the Council, were disturbed by the conclusion of the treaty; they may also have felt the chance of a favourable Franco-Soviet treaty slipping out of their hands.[22] However, they regarded the treaty as essentially anti-British and did not press the British Government to take any measures against it. P. Berthelot, the Political Director of the Quai d'Orsay, went so far as to suggest that the urgency with which the Russians sought to conclude the treaty was the outcome of Britain's rigid attitude towards them. Aristide Briand, the French Foreign Minister, repeated the same opinion when consulted by Chamberlain and agreed that any pressure exerted on Germany would drive it towards the East, thereby endangering the policy of pacification.[23]

In spite of the Northern Department's suggestion that the Germans were trying to exert pressure on Britain to review its policy towards Russia, Chamberlain's only concern was the effect of the treaty on Poland and France in connection with the League. Just as he had washed his hands of arrangements in Eastern Europe during the Locarno negotiations, he now ignored this aspect of the Treaty of Berlin. Siding with Tyrrell, he was more inclined to assume Germany's good faith and accept the treaty at its face value.[24] His failure to appreciate the motives behind Germany's move, which he thought was both 'unfortunate and unnecessary', was due to his refusal to recognize Russia as an emerging major power. Yet his final verdict to Cabinet was a vindication of the German policy, which was 'innocuous' and 'in conformity with the Locarno Model'.[25]

21 F.O. 371 11791 N1675/718/38: Clerk, Ambassador in Prague, to Chamberlain, 14 Apr. 1926; F.O. 371 11791 N1762/718/38: Chamberlain to Clerk, 21 Apr. 1926.

22 Schram, 'Christian Rakovskij', pt. 2, p. 589.

23 F.O. 371 11791 N1585/718/38: Crewe to Chamberlain on conversation with Berthelot, 9 Apr. 1926, and Chamberlain to Crewe on conversation between Gregory and Cambon of the French Embassy; F.O. 371 11791 N1641/718/38: Crewe to Chamberlain on conversation with Briand, 13 Apr. 1926.

24 F.O. 371 11791 N1489/718/38: minutes by Maxse, Gregory and Tyrrell, 5 Apr. 1926, and Chamberlain to D'Abernon, 7 Apr. 1926.

25 F.O. 371 11791 N1600/718/38: Chamberlain to Muller, 11 Apr. 1926; Cab. 23/52 15(26)1, 14 Apr. 1926.

Throughout the period following the disclosure of the Treaty of Berlin, Stresemann's communications to London showed no signs of remorse. On the contrary, he made repeated efforts to persuade Chamberlain of the unwisdom of Britain's aloof attitude towards Russia. Stresemann's censure was provoked by Locker-Lampson's remark to the German Ambassador in London that 'those who sup with the Devil should be furnished with a very long spoon'.[26] Stresemann was further aggrieved at Chamberlain's unwelcoming attitude to the treaty; Chamberlain was reported to have complained that Germany tended 'to run with the hare and hunt with the hounds'. Scrupulous examination of the treaty in the Office, however, had revealed only slight variations from Germany's affirmations.[27]

Stresemann took the matter up with D'Abernon and thoroughly reviewed British policies. He rejected Chamberlain's belief that the old order would be restored in Russia simply by allowing the communist system to collapse; this was only likely to 'aggravate the present evils'. He further drew D'Abernon's attention to the recent swift changes in Soviet foreign policy, pointing out Chicherin's eagerness to accept a draft Russo-German treaty which had been the subject of his ridicule only a year before. In a second meeting with D'Abernon after the conclusion of the treaty, Stresemann emphasized that he had been 'not less concerned with Locarno or less responsible' for it than Chamberlain. Yet he concluded that the isolation of Russia would be, at least for Germany, 'practically equivalent to suicide'. D'Abernon, who had always been an avowed enemy of communism, supplemented his report with a private letter to Chamberlain in which he described the unanimity with which Stresemann's policy of the 'bridge to Europe' was accepted in Germany. He himself, though sceptical, could not completely discard the possibility of moderate Russian foreign policy.[28]

[26] F.O. 371 11791 N1873/718/38: memorandum by Locker-Lampson, 21 Apr. 1926.

[27] F.O. 371 11792 N1954/718/38: Chamberlain to D'Abernon on conversation between Locker-Lampson and the German Ambassador in London, 28 Apr. 1926.

[28] F.O. 371 11792 N1892/718/38 and F.O. 371 11323 C5237/5139/18: D'Abernon to Chamberlain on meetings with Stresemann, 25 Apr. and 30 Apr. 1926; Chamberlain papers, 53/229: D'Abernon to Chamberlain, 29 Apr. 1926.

Stresemann's detailed statement to the Press on the treaty left no doubt that it was an insurance against the possibility of Germany being recruited to any anti-Soviet bloc. Analysing it from a purely political point of view, he stated: 'The Treaty of Rapallo, which provided for the relations between Germany and Russia, had now been adjusted to the conditions created by Locarno and the Rhineland Pact.'[29]

Beside the obvious advantages which the Russians gained by concluding the treaty, they saw in it a good opening to emerge from the isolation which they were convinced had been devised by Britain. Radek laid emphasis on the political significance of the German pledge 'taken openly before the whole world' not to become 'a weapon in the war against the Soviet Union'.[30] However, Chicherin remained convinced that England, despite signs of temperance in its attitude, was involved in a 'complicated game aimed at isolating the USSR and unifying in one form or another all the leading governments' against that country.[31] It is not surprising, therefore, that even after the treaty had been signed, with no opposition from Britain, it was still believed that Chamberlain would try to prevent Germany from ratifying it.[32]

Notwithstanding the general suspicion of British motives, however, it was increasingly believed that the treaty might hasten the thaw in Anglo-Soviet relations characterized by the 'substantial move forward' in the position of Chamberlain and Churchill, who were 'responsible for the direction of British foreign policy'. Clear hints were made about Russia's readiness to resume negotiations while regret was expressed that it had been 'prevented from doing so'.[33] A journal published under the auspices of Narkomindel compared the treaty to the Russo-German Treaty of 1887. The article expressed hopes that, as in the eighties, the treaty would encourage Britain to re-assess its policies and cultivate more friendly relations with Russia.[34]

29 Sutton, *Gustave Stresemann*, Vol. II, pp. 455–56.

30 *Pravda*, 27 Apr. 1926.

31 *Dok. Vne. Pol.*, Vol. IX, pp. 198–205, 5 Apr. 1926. A leader of *Ekon. Zhzn.*, 17 Apr. and *Izvestiya*, 22 Apr. 1926, followed the same lines.

32 *Ekon. Zhzn.*, 27 Apr. 1926.

33 *Izvestiya*, 9 Apr. 1926. 'Pervoe dvizhenie l'da' in *ibid.*, 14 Apr. 1926, characterized the cautious optimism: 'Now the situation is beginning (*only beginning*!) to change in our favour.'

34 *Mir. Khz. i Mir. Pol.* (1926), No. 3, pp. 3–9.

Numerous suggestions were now made that mutual commercial interests might create a firm basis for lasting accord with Britain.[35]

Litvinov, however, was the most optimistic in his evaluation of the effect of the treaty on Anglo-Soviet relations. Speaking to a session of the central committee of the Soviets on the day of the signing of the treaty he marked 'a certain trend favourable to Russia' in Britain. Hoping to encourage this trend, he announced Russia's willingness to resume negotiations without delay 'in a businesslike manner and carry them through to a favourable end' without allowing formalities to interfere.[36]

Chamberlain could not much longer ignore the persistent Russian attempts to achieve accommodation. The news of the impending treaty had already broken when he received information through an intermediary that Chicherin was now prepared to confer with him. In contrast to similar occasions in the past, Chamberlain did not reject out of hand the proposal or the suggestion to resume negotiations. However, he insisted that these should be made through official channels as other methods were 'certain to lead to misunderstanding and therefore to be avoided'.[37] Chamberlain treated warily Hodgson's telegram communicating the salient point of Litvinov's speech. He agreed with Hodgson that the treaty had taken 'some of the anti-Soviet sting from Locarno', but thought that the Russians were 'really suffering from swollen head' if they seriously believed that British foreign policy was 'dictated by thought of them'. Once again he expressed willingness to examine any serious proposals for negotiations, provided these were made 'in good faith'. At the same time he instructed the enthusiastic Hodgson not to initiate any talks himself.[38]

Chamberlain's attitude changed considerably as a result of further confrontations with Stresemann and with Hodgson, and pressure exerted by a group of Conservative MPs who returned

35 Sorokin, a director of Arcos (All-Russian Co-operative Society Limited), in *The Soviet Union Monthly* (Apr. 1926), pp. 53–54; Wise in *ibid.*, pp. 55–56; J. M. Kenworthy, MP, a staunch protagonist of trade with Russia, in *ibid.* (May 1926), p. 77.

36 Speech reported in *Izvestiya*, 25 and 26 Apr. 1926.

37 F.O. 371 11784 N1834/245/38: memorandum by Gregory on conversation with Mackie, a Canadian colonel stationed in Moscow, 17 Apr. 1926, and minute by Chamberlain, 20 Apr. 1926.

38 F.O. 371 11792 N1906/718/38: Chamberlain to Hodgson, 26 Apr. 1926.

from a visit to Russia convinced of the importance of trade with that country.[39] At the beginning of May, Hodgson boldly challenged Chamberlain 'to examine the merits of a more constructive policy'. In his opinion the policy towards Russia was based on an invalidated concept; the Soviet Union, far from 'tottering towards its fall', was 'gaining ground, winning through to solidity'. Hodgson, putting forward arguments identical to those of Stresemann, believed that leaving Russia out of the arrangements for the pacification of Europe only reinforced traditional animosity towards England and encouraged new alliances in Europe, undesirable from the British point of view. In conclusion he fully agreed with Peters' earlier recommendations to resume negotiations and extend the credit scheme to Russia with no delay. Hodgson won over, by force of argument, the Northern Department, whose fervent anti-Bolshevik sentiments were on the decline. Gregory agreed with C. W. Orde, a senior official in the Department, that it was difficult to be 'altogether happy about the policy of reserve'. He regretfully admitted that as a result of the Soviet-German Treaty Russia was clearly no longer isolated and was unlikely to 'surrender to an ultimatum' from Britain if they decided to issue one.

Chamberlain was now willing to consider Hodgson's suggestion; indeed, he instructed the Department to prepare a memorandum on the modifications to the 1924 draft treaty, which would serve as the basis for renewed negotiations. However, in view of the recent Russian involvement in the general strike, he agreed with Gregory that it would be wise not to allow Hodgson to make any overtures so long as the present conflict was not resolved.[40] In fact the Russians, by throwing their weight

[39] F.O. 371 11798 N2147/2147/38: minute by Locker-Lampson on meeting between members of the Conservative delegation to Russia and Chamberlain, 11 and 17 May 1926. The delegation published a favourable report on the Russian economy in *Manchester Guardian*, 1 June 1926. R. J. Boothby, who headed the delegation, gives a most favourable impression of the trip in *I Fight to Live* (London, 1947), pp. 74–86. He believes it was 'a tragedy' that because of circumstances prevailing in London during the strike the report 'got an extremely cold reception'.

[40] F.O. 371 11786 N2241/387/38: Hodgson to Chamberlain, 6 May 1926, minutes by Orde and Gregory, 20 and 24 May 1926, and Chamberlain to Hodgson, 29 May 1926.

behind the miners, had missed a golden opportunity to establish a more normal pattern of relations with Britain. Chamberlain soon brought to an end the preparations for the opening of negotiations. In July he minuted that 'conditions had altered so much (to the worse)' that there was 'no good purpose' in responding to Hodgson's dispatch.[41]

The unforeseen general strike

Russia's intensive search for accommodation with Britain on the diplomatic front coincided with a loss of interest in the activities of ARJAC in the field of world trade union unity. The Russians, thoroughly disillusioned with the General Council's lack of militancy, retained only those functions of the committee which promised to facilitate trade between the two countries and secure a loan for Russia. These aims, which involved the participation of Soviet diplomats and which both sides were eager to pursue, caused the Russians to disregard the developing conflict in the mining industry. It was only after the strike had occurred that they made a full turn, claiming to have diligently prepared for it.[42]

The arrest of the entire CPGB leadership in October 1925 and the repeated failure of the Party to overcome its major weaknesses reinforced the Russians' pessimistic assessment of the strength of the British working-class movement after the Liverpool Labour conference. Only a negligible number of new members was temporarily enrolled in the Party during a special recruiting week, while the new factory committees, through which it was hoped to exert pressure in the unions, fell short of expectations. The character of these committees was described in IKKI as not dissimilar to the 'tradition of the old propagandist sect'.[43] Still less

[41] F.O. 371 11786 N3139/387/38: minute by Chamberlain, 20 July 1926.

[42] I. M. Maisky, 'Iz Londonskikh Vospominanii', *Novyi Mir* (1968), No. 4, pt. 1, pp. 212–16. In the winter of 1925–26 Maisky was in charge of liaison between the trade unions and the Soviet Embassy. On the General Council's appeals to Baldwin and contacts with McKenna of the Midland Bank see TUC archives, *Minutes of IC, 1925–6*, Meeting No. 2, 25 Jan. 1926, and Meeting No. 3, 13 Apr. 1926.

[43] CPGB's report to Orgburo of IKKI in *Inprecorr*, 13 Jan. 1926. Proceedings of meeting of IKKI on 20 Jan. 1926 in *Otchet Ispolkoma Kominterna* (*Aprel' 1925-Yanvar' 1926*), pp. 6 and 141–43.

promising were the reports from NMM leaders who had escaped imprisonment on the consolidation of the 'strong and well organized' right wing of Labour in the unions in contrast with the scattered and 'difficult to identify' left-wing movement.[44]

The only encouraging news from Britain in January was that of the radicalization of the ILP. It had condemned Labour for its 'gradualism' and had appealed to the Second International 'to renew its efforts to create an all-inclusive International'. However, the prospects of creating a successful left-wing movement, even with the support of the ILP, seemed meagre owing to the 'active and unscrupulous' attitude of the right wing.[45] Although the ILP's transformation had little direct effect, its propaganda value was not missed by Lozovsky, who utilized it in his tireless paper war with Amsterdam to prove the 'weakness of international reformism'. The 'swing' towards Russia was bound to 'lend force to the whole revolutionary trade union movement, and thus to Profintern'.[46]

Lozovsky's rosy prognosis met a poor reception at the sixth plenum of IKKI, which was in session from 17 February to 15 March 1926, and in the fourth session of Profintern which kept in step with IKKI, meeting from 9 to 15 March. The proceedings of the two meetings interrupted the inner party struggle. Zinoviev seems to have been glad of the temporary truce after the heavy defeat inflicted on him in his Leningrad stronghold. The result was the avoidance of thorough discussion of contentious topics. The leading theme in the IKKI plenum was the contrast between the dismal reports on the strength of reaction in the capitalist countries and the fortification of the revolutionary basis in Russia. The implementation of socialism in Russia was held to be the reason for its growing popularity among the world's workers, and the communist parties were therefore instructed to defend it.[47]

44 Allison in *Kras. Int. Prof.* (1926), No. 1, pp. 101–105, and No. 2, pp. 150–55.

45 On the ILP's moves see C. Brand, *The British Labour Party* (Stanford, 1965), pp. 117–18. Palme Dutt's scepticism in *Inprecorr*, 4 Feb. and 4 Mar. 1926.

46 *Komm. Int.* (1926), No. 1, pp. 84–92; *Kras. Int. Prof.*, No. 2, 29 Jan. 1926, pp. 142–43.

47 *10 Let Kominterna*, p. 221; *VI Plenum IKKI: Rezolyutsii*, pp. 19–20. For Lozovsky see *VI Plenum IKKI*, p. 284. On measures against

The tendency to belittle the importance of the approaching dispute in the British mining industry contributed much to the conduct of the CPGB during the general strike. Zinoviev's eagerness to animate the proceedings by emphasizing the uneven stabilization and the overall deterioration of world capitalism was checked by his own cautious estimate that even if the revolution followed the quickest route it was expected only within '3–4–5 years'. Moreover, in his subsequent survey of the plenum, Zinoviev revealed his concern about the strengthening position of the right in Labour and in Amsterdam.[48] Bukharin's complementary report dampened the sparse optimism in Zinoviev's speech. He assured the plenum that the revolution was close to the heart of all present but insisted that it was a mistake to ignore the objective situation, which appeared to be unrevolutionary. Profintern's session was conducted in the same spirit. Lozovsky presented restrained slogans calling for 'a more practical, concrete approach to the masses, and the implementation of united-front tactics'.[49]

The blind eye turned to the approaching major conflict in Britain was also a result of a persistent wave of depressing news from Britain. Early unfounded descriptions by Comintern of the preparations taken by the British workers in anticipation of the capitalist offensive were soon discounted.[50] The executive committee of the CPGB in its meeting of 9 and 10 January had admitted that the party stood only a slim chance of winning the race against time to bring the working class to 'revolutionary aims and objectives' before the capitalists prevented it.[51]

By the time the IKKI plenum met, the Russians had realized that the fate of the left wing in the trade unions, 'only a few of which were "real left wingers"', was determined. Rather than intervening more actively in the conflict, the Russians allowed the hopeless outlook to dictate a fatalist policy of 'letting the

Zinoviev see R. V. Daniels, *The Conscience of the Revolution* (Harvard, 1960), pp. 269–72.

48 *VI Plenum IKKI*, pp. 6, 11 and 22–23; *Komm. Int.*, No. 3, 15 Mar. 1926, p. 3.

49 *VI Plenum IKKI*, pp. 201–202; *IV Sessiya Profinterna*, pp. 3 and 33.

50 *Komm. Int.* (1926), No. 1, pp. 23–26. On the changing outlook see leader in *Pravda*, 29 Jan. 1926; Petrovsky and diplomatic correspondent in *Pravda*, 7 Feb. 1926.

51 *Workers' Weekly*, 15 Jan. 1926.

events show the results'.[52] The British delegation to the plenum, composed of second-rank personnel because of the imprisonment of the leaders, continued to soft-pedal the gravity of the crisis looming over the coal industry. It clearly preferred to avoid the confrontation which the Government seemed anxious to provoke and which was likely to be 'more acute, brutal and bloody' than any of the previous struggles.[53] The same views prevailed in Profintern's session. Nin's report for the central council, which, out of habit one must suppose, praised the 'enormous achievements' in Britain, brought a violent reaction from the British delegation. A warning was issued that while the Government was 'not sitting with folded arms' the workers had 'no fortified movement, no means for struggle with the ruling class'.[54]

On the whole, the miners' battle was treated as an industrial dispute. Except for passing references to the necessity of popularizing the slogan of a general strike, it was clearly understood that the conflict would not develop into 'terror or civil war'. Although Zinoviev expressed regret, in closing the IKKI plenum, that not enough time had been devoted to discussion of the British question, his outlook on the impending events remained cautious. The struggle was likely to 'conceal in itself only the embryo of the approaching colossal social struggle' which was 'inevitable' in England.[55]

Urgent appeals from the CPGB for practical directives during Profintern's session elicited no response. The only relevant resolution simply radiated confidence in the ability of Profintern's adherents in Britain to take a lead in the hope that the General Council would follow suit.[56] At the same time severe shortcomings in coordination within the NMM rendered dubious the capacity

[52] Yoffe in *Mir. Khz. i Mir. Pol.* (1926), No. 3, pp. 121–22.

[53] *VI Plenum IKKI*, pp. 88–91 and 258–59. The speeches were later issued by the CPGB in a pamphlet, *Orders from Moscow?* (London, Aug. 1926), curiously intended to prove that the party was not under the spell of 'a dark and sinister power in Moscow'.

[54] *IV Sessiya Profinterna*, pp. 12 and 60–61.

[55] *VI Plenum IKKI: Rezolyutsii*, pp. 116–17 and 121; Zinoviev in *VI Plenum IKKI*, pp. 426–63 and 598.

[56] *IV Sessiya Profinterna*, p. 148. W. H. Crook, *Communism and the General Strike* (Connecticut, 1960), pp. 88–89 and 97, believes that the session was indeed responsible for the stiffening attitude of the miners towards the General Council.

of the movement to deal effectively with the complicated situation. The outline of a plan for re-organization was drawn up but was not expected to come into effect until June, after the date on which the miners' agreement with the owners was due to expire. For the time being a message was dispatched to an extraordinary conference convened by the NMM to deal with the situation; however, it also lacked any operative instructions. The leaders of the NMM themselves had become convinced that the General Council would avoid the struggle by hook or by crook.[57]

Once the probability of coordinated activity by the major trade unions had receded, a local conflict in the mining industry represented the limit of expectations. When the NMM conference met on 21 March, it was therefore mounted primarily as a demonstration of Profintern's solidarity with the miners and as a warning against severe reaction. This was reflected in Tom Mann's[58] address, which defined the conference as a condemnation of the capitalist offensive and an expression of solidarity with 'those rotting in capitalist prisons'. Although he recognized the complacency of the General Council, Mann was unable to suggest concrete defensive measures or an effective new leadership to replace the absent communist one.[59]

Neither Comintern nor the Soviet trade unions followed up these preliminary steps with further preparations. The Soviet Government, in the midst of a diplomatic *rapprochement*, was not inclined to associate itself with the turbulent situation in Britain. The conduct of these affairs passed, therefore, into the hands of Lozovsky, whose ultimate concern was to prove the bankruptcy of the reformist organization in dealing with the predicament. He hailed the success of the NMM conference but warned that if the crisis came to a head the powerful right-wing

[57] *IV Sessiya Profinterna*, pp. 80 and 124–27; Hardy, succeeding Pollitt as the effective leader of the NMM after the latter's arrest, in *VI Plenum IKKI*, pp. 329–30.

[58] Mann, a founder member of the CPGB in 1920, served as the chairman of the NMM throughout its existence.

[59] NMM, *Report of the Special National Conference of Action, March 21st 1926* (London, 1926), pp. 3–8, and review of the conference in *Inprecorr*, 8 Apr. 1926. Hardy, *Those Stormy Years*, pp. 183–89, gives an account of the 'intensive preparation' made after the conference. This is contradicted by his admittance that the strike threw the movement into great confusion.

leaders would 'seize the faintest opportunity to start negotiations with the capitalists and sell out the workers'.[60]

Profintern's evaluation of the situation was for the most part based on information from affiliated organizations in Britain, where the mood was rather despondent. Much of the news pouring in from the unions reflected a state of unpreparedness and apathy among the workers which reduced to a bare possibility any explosive development. Thomas had replaced Purcell in the negotiation committee of the General Council at the beginning of April and with other leaders was anxiously seeking to avoid the strike by a compromise between the miners and the owners.[61] The discouraging impression was strengthened by noncommittal replies to approaches by the CPGB and the NMM to all labour forces to join hands and embark on 'positive measures to alleviate the miners' difficulties'.[62]

Profintern's overtures in the same vein to the IFTU and the General Council were made with few hopes and with the purpose of proving that the General Council 'had started the sabotage even before the strike'. The CPGB had already passed its verdict on the 'hopeless reactionaries' of the General Council in mid-April, placing the blame of the failure of the struggle 'on the heads of the degenerate "leaders"'.[63] Lozovsky, posing the question of 'struggle or submission', accepted at its face value the CPGB's prediction that the miners were already doomed because of the 'reactionary and unclear position of the General Council'. As the day set for the strike approached, he became even more convinced that the miners were heading for defeat, not so much because of the Government's threatening preparations, but because of the demoralizing behaviour of the Labour leaders, who were already acting the role of 'traitors and strike-breakers'.[64]

60 *Kras. Int. Prof.* (1926), No. 4, pp. 467–71.

61 On the search for compromise see G. D. H. Cole, *British Trade Unionism To-Day* (London, 1945), pp. 73–75, and Thomas, *My Story*, pp. 96–102. On compliancy in the unions see for example editorial notes in *A.E.U. Monthly Journal* (May 1926), No. 70, p. 51, and in *A.E.U. Monthly Journal* (June 1926), No. 71, p. 46.

62 *Workers' Weekly*, 19 Mar. 1926; *Izvestiya*, 9 Apr. 1926.

63 *Comm. Rev.* (Apr. 1926), pp. 533–37. See also Lozovsky in *Sedmoi S'ezd Professional'nykh Soyuzov SSSR. Stenograficheskii Otchet* (Moscow, 1927), p. 324 (hereafter referred to as *VII S'ezd Prof. Soyuzov*).

64 Lozovsky in *Kras. Int. Prof.*, No. 4, 5 Apr. 1926, p. 460; also in *Mezh. Rabo. Dviz.*, No. 15, 15 Apr. 1926, and in *Pravda*, 16 and 24 Apr. 1926.

The Russians showed not the least intention of embarking on a political struggle in spite of their claims to that effect after the strike.[65] However, they were committed to stand fast by the miners, among whom were the strongholds of both the CPGB and the NMM. The Russians, well aware that neither movement was in a position to lead the struggle, called upon the miners to abandon their role of opposition within the Miners' Federation and withdraw their campaign for better wages. They proposed instead a defensive line whereby the miners were to align themselves behind the policy of the Federation, which notwithstanding the communist influence was collaborating fully with the General Council.[66]

With the deadline now only a week ahead, a letter from Mann, the president of the NMM, which confirmed the worst fears was read to the executive of Profintern. There was no mention of a general strike, while the success of a miners' strike seemed remote unless 'utmost support on the international level were forthcoming'. The information was immediately incorporated in a campaign to prove the supremacy of Profintern as the only international organization prepared to hasten to the aid of the miners. Profintern published a manifesto condemning the 'dreams of peace and tranquillity' indulged in by the international miners' organization.[67]

Mann himself arrived in Moscow just before the strike and attended the meeting of the executive bureau of Profintern. This time, probably because of the belated steps taken by the General Council to support the miners, he withdrew the contents of his letter, trying to convince Lozovsky that a militant mood was fast spreading among the workers. However, he found it impossible to

[65] Boothby, *I Fight to Live*, p. 81, testifies that Radek, who regarded the strike as a 'simple wage dispute', instructed the Soviet Press 'to keep calm'.

[66] M. G. Woodhouse, 'Rank and File Movements among the Miners of South Wales, 1910–1926' (Oxford Univ. D.Phil. thesis, 1969), pp. 310–318 and 343. On the influence of the CPGB see *Inprecorr*, 31 Jan. 1926: of 27 new factory committees created during the recruiting week, 16 were in Wales, and all but 2 in other mining districts.

[67] *Mezh. Rabo. Dviz.*, Nos. 18–19: meeting of executive bureau of Profintern, 22 Apr. 1926; manifesto published in *Trud*, 25 Apr. 1926. See also Lozovsky's speech to the central council of the Ukrainian trade unions, reported in *Trud*, 27 Apr. 1926.

dissuade Lozovsky from his conviction that because of the 'inevitably treacherous role' taken by the General Council the miners would be isolated in their struggle.[68] Indeed the prospects of a prolonged struggle seemed so unreal that in Russia itself no consultations were made with trade union leaders, not even with miners' leaders, to plan assistance to the British miners.[69]

The Russian forecast was to be completely discredited by the succeeding events. On 1 May, as a result of the termination of the agreement with the Government and the refusal of the owners and the miners to step back from their demands, the miners found themselves locked out. A special conference of trade union executives which was already in session placed the authority for conducting a national stoppage in the hands of the General Council. The date was set for 3 May, to allow for hasty preparations but also to enable the General Council, averse to taking such a course, to find a way out through negotiations with the Government. This, however, proved to be unexpectedly difficult because of the Cabinet's confidence in its ability to handle the situation with the help of the adequate strike-breaking machinery meticulously prepared by Joynson-Hicks. In view of the General Council's reluctance, it is significant that the strike started as a result of two incidents which were entirely out of its control. The first of these was that the compositors of the *Daily Mail* refused to set the paper for 3 May because of a Government appeal for anti-strike volunteers on one of its pages; the second was that Baldwin, either because of impatience with the negotiations or because of a misunderstanding, retired to bed on the night of 2 May without waiting to hear the miners' final proposals.[70] In view of the breakdown of negotiations, the planned national strike came into effect.

68 *Mezh. Rabo. Dviz.*, Nos. 18–19: meeting of executive bureau of Profintern, 29 Apr. 1926.

69 Lozovsky admitted this in sharp exchanges with Akulov, leader of the Ukrainian miners, in *VII S'ezd Prof. Soyuzov*, p. 324.

70 Accounts of the events in J. Seymons, *The General Strike* (London, 1957), pp. 28–47, and MFGB, *Annual Volume of Proceedings for the Year 1926* (London 1927), pp. 204–206. A. J. P. Taylor, *English History 1914–1945* (Oxford, 1965), pp. 245–47, suggests that the Government was only too eager to enter the conflict; Bullock, *Ernest Bevin*, Vol. 1, pp. 320–23, believes that the Government 'precipitated the strike' much against the will of the General Council.

The General Council's declaration on 1 May of a general strike had thrown the Russians into a state of perplexity. No commentary was issued while the unprecedented step was taken of withholding publication of all major dailies so long as negotiations were in progress and the occurrence of a strike remained uncertain. In the meantime feverish activity took place behind the scenes in an attempt to establish a unanimous attitude towards the strike. This was particularly difficult as the Russians could neither 'unreservedly approve' the policy of the General Council, which had been a target for continuous abuse, nor remain 'mere onlookers, mere observers of the greatest historical events'.[71] Yet by the time the strike entered its first day hardly any signs of hesitancy could be detected. A special meeting of the executive bureau of Profintern which was convened on 4 May spent only a little time on self-incrimination. Lozovsky managed to cover the confusion by depicting the event as a victory for Profintern; he simply admitted that he had underestimated to what extent the British masses had shed their illusions and prejudices.

Only meagre excuses for Russia's unpreparedness were made the next day when the papers reappeared. These either followed Lozovsky's example, implying that the Labour leadership was being unwillingly dragged to a revolutionary position, or simply explained the outbreak of the strike as a result of the 'provocative position of the British Government'.[72] In general, crude attempts were made to conceal the Russians' embarrassment and create the impression that these revolutionary events were inevitable. This campaign was so successfully executed that only a month later Stalin, turning a blind eye to a similar Russian failing, made an uncontested accusation that the General Council had been 'taken by complete surprise' by the strike.[73]

The demonstration of a united façade and the support for the

[71] A. Andreev, *Anglo-Russkii Komitet* (Moscow–Leningrad, 1927), p. 21. On the CPGB's unawareness of the imminence of the general strike see CPGB, *The Eighth Congress of the Communist Party of Great Britain: Papers, Theses, and Resolutions, 1926* (London, 1927), pp. 8, 10 and 63; Campbell's speech to the congress is reported in *Workers' Weekly*, 22 Oct. 1926.

[72] *Mezh. Rabo. Dviz.*, Nos. 18–19: meeting of executive bureau of Profintern, 13 May 1926; leaders in *Trud* and *Pravda*, 5 May 1926.

[73] Stalin, *Sochineniya*, Vol. 8, p. 160. L. Trotsky, *My Life* (London, 1930), p. 450, was enraged by the 'cynical distortion of fact' in the Press.

miners led observers to dramatize the spontaneous enthusiasm of the Russians, who 'hung on the telegraph wire waiting with tense impatience for every tiny item of news'.[74] However, it was not until 6 May that all the central executive committees of the Soviets passed resolutions in support of the strike, following the lead given by the Government.[75] Heart-felt jubilation was mostly manifested in lower echelons, where party members were not up to date with the animosity which had penetrated the relations of the Russian trade unions with their British counterparts.[76]

Despite their conversion the Russians remained highly doubtful about the outcome of the strike so long as the General Council remained in control. Even Zinoviev's exhilaration about the arrival of a 'new era in the English and world workers' movement' was diluted with awareness of the 'acute danger from the right leaders of both the trade union movement and Labour'. His doubts were reflected in his observation in the Press that it was too early to predict the victory of the proletariat, which was 'still occupying defensive positions'. Zinoviev went so far as to suggest that the two prerequisites for success, the transfer of the strike to the political arena and the support of the entire world proletariat, were not present. On the contrary, the strike was proceeding on 'purely economic' lines and 'in defiance of a Government ultimatum'.[77] A Comintern manifesto composed on the second day of the strike deduced from the long history of class conflict in Britain that the present clash was led by a few treacherous leaders, 'placing themselves at the head of a Labour movement in order to betray it at the first opportunity'.[78]

Lozovsky, who was quickly emerging as the authoritative commentator on the strike, accepted with reservations the first communications from London on the enthusiastic response of the workers to the strike. He told an extraordinary meeting of the Moscow trade union council on 6 May that the British workers

74 Fischer, *The Soviets in World Affairs*, Vol. II, p. 626.

75 *Kras. Int. Prof.* (1926), No. 7, p. 19.

76 For instance, the Leningrad trade union organization still praised the General Council for its 'high level organization and leadership' after the Russian aid had been rejected: TUC archives, B 132 13/7/23: letter to Citrine, 11 May 1926.

77 Zinoviev, 'Velikie Sobytiya v Anglii', *Pravda*, 5 May 1926.

78 *Inprecorr*, 13 May 1926.

still displayed 'strong feelings of conservatism'. His impression, like Zinoviev's, was that most of the Labour leaders were horrified by the developments and were oscillating between the two camps, searching for a face-saving formula to enable them to call off the strike.[79] It became clear that the Russians did not anticipate a full-scale revolution. Lozovsky preferred to compare the strike to the Russian 1905 revolution: a general rehearsal for the real revolution. At present he considered 'securing the formation of a true workers' government in England' as a considerable achievement.[80]

The Russians could not turn their backs on a class struggle of such magnitude even if their expectations of it were limited. They also had to take account of the critical presence of the opposition. However, utmost precautions were taken to disclaim direct interference by the Soviet Government in the conflict; this would be more than likely to strain Anglo-Soviet relations. Support of the strike was therefore initially explained as discharging the debt of the Russian proletariat to the British workers for their help during the intervention when the capitalist world was conspiring against Russia.[81] At the same time the Russians were careful to present their assistance as part of the international support for the miners, assigning the task to Profintern. Lozovsky had a particularly free hand now that Zinoviev was in disgrace and Tomsky's authority in international trade union policy severely restricted. He capitalized on this by using the relief to the miners as a demonstration of Profintern's supremacy over Amsterdam.

The sincerity behind Lozovsky's appeal to the IFTU to 'bury all differences of opinion' and collaborate is to be doubted; in the same breath he was unveiling the betrayal of the strike by that organization, condemning it for its 'verbal assistance'.[82] Perhaps even more significant is the fact that Lozovsky, who drew the first lessons from the strike, hailed it as the harbinger of a new era in Comintern. The epithet for the new period was

79 A. Lozovsky, *Klass Protiv Klassa* (Moscow–Leningrad, 1926), pp. 18–20. See also Lozovsky in *Pravda*, 7 May 1926, and in *Mezh. Rabo. Dviz.*, Nos. 18–19: speech to executive bureau of Profintern, 13 May 1926.

80 Lozovsky, *Klass Protiv Klassa*, pp. 26–27, and 'Bor'ba Idet' in *Pravda*, 7 May 1926.

81 Leaders in *Ekon. Zhzn.*, and *Pravda*, 5 May 1926.

82 Lozovsky in *Trud*, 6 May 1926, and in *Izvestiya*, 8 May 1926.

suggested by Lozovsky at the very start of the strike: 'the tremendous conflict between Labour and Capital sets class against class'. IKKI's open letter to the CPGB plainly repeated that the sharpening of class confrontation in Britain would inevitably transform the conservative trade unions there into 'newly born and fortified patterns for the workers' movement – new forms of class struggle'. It was an unretraceable step towards disengagement from the policy of collaboration with the reformist unions and a challenge to united front tactics.[83] However, in view of the diplomatic advantages of the collaboration and the controversy with the inner party opposition, it took some time until the new line was implemented as the formal policy of Comintern.[84]

From Lozovsky's point of view the rejection of Russian assistance by the General Council could not have occurred at a better moment. It shook the foundations of the collaboration with the British trade unionists and entrenched Profintern's influence in the conduct of the AUCCTU's international policy.

To forestall any suggestion of Government interference, and maintain the strict observance of trade unionist procedure, the organization of the contribution was entrusted to Profintern. A committee for that purpose was formed in the meeting of the executive bureau of Profintern on 4 May, consisting of Dogadov, for the AUCCTU, Gorbachev, representing the Russian miners, and Lozovsky. Two days later it transmitted to Citrine a first instalment of £26,427, the initial response to 'an appeal by the Red International of Labour Unions and International Workers' Aid'.[85]

The General Council discussed the contribution on 8 May. For the first five days of the strike it had been desperately trying to counter the Conservatives' 'powerful chorus of Establishmentarians';[86] this depicted the strike as a 'challenge to Parliament' and a 'road to anarchy and ruin'.[87] On no account was the General Council prepared to admit that the strike was more

83 *Izvestiya*, 8 May 1926. IKKI's letter is in *Pravda*, 8 May 1926.

84 See below p. 205, fn. 115.

85 TUC archives, B 132 13/7/27: committee to Citrine, 6 May 1926.

86 Miliband, *Parliamentary Socialism*, pp. 138–42. On the legal aspects of the strike see W. H. Crook, *The General Strike* (Univ. of North Carolina, 1931), pp. 469–77.

87 See Baldwin in *British Gazette*, 6 May 1926. See also *ibid.*, 7 May 1926.

than 'an industrial dispute'.[88] In this context, the acceptance of the 'Red Gold' would have been interpreted by the diehards as *ipso facto* proof of the subversive nature of the strike. In addition, the General Council was acting on the assumption that the strike would be short enough for the unions 'to be able to get along with their own funds'. It was unanimously resolved, therefore, to return the Russian aid on the grounds that it would be 'wilfully misrepresented and acceptance would be misunderstood'.[89] The action was agreed upon without much discussion, and there is little evidence to confirm Russian suggestions that the rejection was deliberately contemplated as 'a gesture towards the bourgeoisie or a demonstration of loyalty to the Government'.[90] The decision, however, was applied only to the first contribution, as a second instalment of £100,000, part of a levy of a quarter of a day's wages imposed by the AUCCTU on its members, was blocked on the Government's instructions under the terms of emergency regulations introduced by Parliament on 9 May.[91]

The rejection of the money was by no means foreseen and caused much indignation in Moscow. There were still those who hoped that the General Council would reverse its decision during the course of the strike.[92] The overwhelming opinion, however, was that by rejecting the assistance the General Council had finally betrayed all expectations. Leader-writers, pledging themselves not to 'hush up the false steps of the General Council', accused it of 'vacillation and half-heartedness' in the conduct of the strike. Simultaneously, open statements were made on the inevitability of the collapse of the strike due to the sabotage and 'anti-class nationalist' position of the trade union movement.[93]

88 *British Worker*, 5 May 1926: 'Our Reply to "Jix"', *ibid.*, 6 May 1926.

89 No minutes of the General Council's meetings were taken during the strike. Accounts of the meeting are in TUC archives, B 125 13/6/25: Decision No. 247, and B 132 13/7/23: Citrine to Dogadov, 8 May 1926; description by Hicks, *Paris and Berlin Meetings of the Anglo-Russian Advisory Council. Stenographic Record* (typescript copy), p. 15 (hereafter refered to as *Paris-Berlin Meetings*).

90 *Bol'shevik*, No. 11, 15 June 1926, p. 41; P. V. Gurovich, *Vseobshchaya Stachka v Anglii 1926 g.* (Moscow, 1959), p. 119.

91 TUC archives, B 132 13/7/32: Lloyds Bank to Citrine, 11 May 1926.

92 Dogadov and leader in *Trud*, 11 May 1926.

93 Leaders in *Pravda* and *Ekon. Zhzn.*, 11 May 1926, and in *Trud* and *Izvestiya*, 12 May 1926.

As soon as the news had reached Moscow of the unconditional surrender of the strike, Lozovsky, who had most consistently objected to the entanglement with the General Council, formed a committee to draw the lessons from the strike. In the meantime he spared no criticism of the General Council's 'disastrous and treacherous' conduct of the strike, as contrasted with the masses, who showed 'an example of how to lead such a gigantic strike'.[94]

The crucial departure from earlier criticism, however, was the onslaught on the left wing. In doing so, Lozovsky attacked the pillars of Anglo-Soviet trade union collaboration in an attempt finally to remove the threat to the survival of Profintern. This fitted in well with his earlier observations on the sharpening conflict within the working class in Britain as a result of the strike. The first suggestion of disowning the militants in the General Council was made by Lozovsky in a meeting of the executive bureau of Profintern on 15 May, when he complained that during the struggle the left wing had vanished; its leadership 'could not be seen anywhere'.[95] A major article by Lozovsky, which appeared a day after the meeting, opened a copious Press campaign.[96]

With Lozovsky in full control, the diplomatic considerations behind the collaboration policy seem to have fallen into temporary decline, particularly because of the massive support to the miners, which introduced further tensions into Anglo-Soviet relations. However, there had always been great doubt about the miners' ability to carry out a successful strike without the active support of the rest of the unions. It was also realized that because of the permanent depression in the mining industry in Britain the owners were not in a position to respond to the miners' demands.[97]

In fact the decision to transfer to the British miners the funds refused by the General Council was taken by the AUCCTU

[94] *Mezh. Rabo. Dviz.*, No. 20: meeting of executive bureau of Profintern, 13 May 1926; see also savage attack on the GC by Radek, 'Tragediya Mass i Fars Pravykh Vozhdei', *Pravda*, 13 May 1926.

[95] *Mezh. Rabo. Dviz.*, No. 20, 20 May 1926.

[96] 'Kapitulatsiya General'nogo Sovieta i Perspektivy Dal'neishei Bor'by', *Pravda* and *Izvestiya*, 16, 18 and 19 May 1926. See also Dogadov in *Trud*, 18 May 1926.

[97] Lozovsky, *Klass Protiv Klassa*, p. 14; *Mir. Khz. i Mir. Pol.*, Nos. 5–6, 18 May 1926, pp. 3–5.

when the strike was still at its height. When the Soviet miners' congress endorsed the decision on 15 May, it did so mainly in appreciation of the 'courageous step' taken by the British miners but with little expectancy of a prolonged struggle. No measures were taken to advise and assist the miners with the practical organization of the strike.[98] The propaganda value of the strike and the Russian assistance was, however, exploited to the utmost to expose the strike-breaking activities of the General Council and the IFTU.[99] It was not until well into June that Comintern became aware of the real determination of the miners and suggested that the defeat of the miners would be 'a great blow for the entire revolutionary working-class movement'.[100] By then, however, Russian policy had passed into a new dimension with the active interference of the opposition and the threat of a severance of Anglo-Soviet relations.

The opposition's challenge to ARJAC

The opposition seized upon the general strike to cement their new alliance. At the theoretical level, they saw it as proof of the instability of capitalism and therefore a contradiction of Stalin's thesis of socialism in one country. At the practical level they regarded the strike as a sign of the failure of united front manoeuvres with non-communist organizations – and particularly of ARJAC, the symbol of this policy. However, the majority was able to fall back on the mere fact that the attitude of the General Council had been viewed with reservations even before the strike. The opposition also played into the hands of the majority by their political ineptitude.[101] The collision, however, left its mark on the collaboration policy in so far as it pressed the Russian leadership to defend and, on the whole, overstate its revolutionary character. In doing so they seriously compromised ARJAC and strained relations with British trade union

[98] Leader in *Trud*, 18 May 1926. A. Horner, a Welsh communist leader, who was Cook's closest friend, mentions in *Incorrigible Rebel* (London, 1960), pp. 93–94, that the Russians made no attempt to influence the course of the miners' strike.

[99] *Pravda*, 22 May 1926.

[100] Comintern's thesis of 8 June in *Comm. Rev.* (July 1926), pp. 121–23.

[101] For an excellent survey of the rise and fall of the 'united opposition' see Daniels, *The Conscience of the Revolution*, Chap. 12.

officials. This occurred at the peak of the crisis in Anglo-Soviet relations when fraternal relations were of greater value than ever before.

Of all the members of the opposition Trotsky was the most justified in initiating the attack on the Politburo regarding its trade union policy. His publication of *Where is Britain Going?* was a forceful challenge to the attempt to introduce communism via the trade unions at a time when Anglo-Soviet trade union collaboration was at its apex. In this work Trotsky saw in the CPGB the only legitimate successor of the revolutionary tradition established by the Cromwellian and Chartist movements; he distinguished it from the rest of the Labour and trade union movement, which conformed with the old Fabian school of 'gradualism'.[102] This analysis sparked off a protracted debate between Trotsky and left-wing British intellectuals, but he did not follow it up with any political activities in Russia, even when the issue became a subject for heated debate in the fourteenth Party congress.[103]

The new opposition, the result of the reconciliation of Zinoviev and Kamenev with Trotsky, was set up on frail foundations in the course of the meeting of the central committee of the CPSU in April 1926. The opposition's platform at this initial stage did not include criticism of Comintern's trade union policy or more specifically of ARJAC.[104]

The outbreak of the general strike found the unsuspecting Trotsky convalescing in Berlin after a minor operation. Like his opponents in Moscow, he had only recently expressed the opinion that revolutionary events in Britain were 'still far away'.[105] However, Trotsky's high hopes from the new alliance seem to have roused him from inactivity. While still in Berlin, he launched a barrage of attacks on the General Council. He urged the CPGB to engage in 'the systematic unmasking of the muddle-heads of the left' and replace the irresolute leadership in the trade unions,

102 L. Trotsky, *Where is Britain Going?* (London, 1926).

103 On the polemics see I. Deutscher, *The Prophet Unarmed* (Oxford, 1970), pp. 221–23.

104 *XV Konferentsiya Vsesoyuznoi Kommunisticheskoi Partii (B). Stenograficheskii Otchet* (Moscow–Leningrad, 1927), pp. 128 and 441–42 (hereafter referred to as *XV Konferentsiya VKP*).

105 *Inprecorr*, 11 Mar. 1926; Trotsky, *My Life*, pp. 445–49.

which, he suspected, would do anything 'towards paralysing the general strike'.[106] In addition Trotsky self-righteously published fragments of notes and essays, written in the course of the previous year, in which he had recognized the CPGB as the only potential leader of the British workers' movement.[107]

Trotsky gradually focused his attacks upon the Russian leadership, pinning the blame for the failure of the strike on the opportunist motives guiding the Politburo's policies in Britain. He strongly opposed the present course, in which the activities of the different communist parties were attuned to the 'fulfilment of the interests of the Soviet state'. Trotsky argued in support of the independence of the communist parties, which unlike the General Council should be 'patriots of the working class, of the toiling masses and of the international proletariat'.[108]

It should also be emphasized in this connection that despite the integrity of Trotsky's arguments his initial criticism concentrated on Stalin's attitude to the General Council and the CPGB, rather than on ARJAC – the formation of which, he admitted even after the strike, was an 'indisputably correct element in the politics of the united front'. It was incorrect, however, for the Russians not to have used their right of 'complete, free and revolutionary criticism' of the British delegates in ARJAC; they had adopted an 'administrative, diplomatic, reactionary' attitude to the General Council. The diplomatic considerations, argued Trotsky, were responsible for the neglect of the CPGB and its failure to develop beyond a 'propagandist group on the fringe of the left wing'; eventually it was not powerful enough to extract the utmost political significance from the strike.[109]

The strike also revitalized Zinoviev, who may have regarded it as an opportunity to maintain his precarious position at the head of Comintern. He immediately claimed that the strike proved

[106] Preface to German edition of *Where is Britain Going?* written on 6 May and reproduced in *Inprecorr*, 10 June 1926.

[107] *Komm. Int.*, Nos. 5–6, 19 May 1926, pp. 58–75.

[108] *Inprecorr*, 3 June 1926, and a speech reported in *Trud*, 29 May 1926.

[109] Trotsky, archives, T–2985: 'Vseobshchaya Stachka, General'nyi Sovet i Nasha Politika', 18 May 1926. Trotsky, *The Third International After Lenin*, p. 128, recognized the fault in the unity policy in the moment when ARJAC was 'transformed from an episodic alliance into an inviolable principle standing above the real class struggle'.

the correctness of his observation that the stabilization of capitalism was 'very ephemeral, fragile, already tottering'.[110] Yet, unlike Trotsky, Zinoviev as a former member of the triumvirate was directly associated with the activities of ARJAC. There was an 'inevitable vacillation' before he took the step of siding with Trotsky.[111]

Zinoviev's *volte-face* was apologetic and cautious; he excused his early support of the General Council's policy on the grounds that it 'seemed at first to be progressive'. He did not, however, launch a frontal attack on ARJAC, and so found himself close to the new official line, which had been initiated with much publicity by Lozovsky.[112] In this context, Zinoviev's utterances appeared so orthodox that they received wide publication without fear that they would be interpreted as dissident.[113] It was not until June, after Zinoviev had established that the General Council was infested with the 'Judas spirit' of leaders like Thomas, that the question of the alliance cropped up. Zinoviev then laid bare the incompetence of ARJAC to provide any defence for Russia. It seemed to him more likely that at a critical moment the committee would 'turn out to be behind the bourgeoisie and serve the beliefs and rights of the capitalists of its own country'.[114]

The new opposition was nevertheless lagging behind the Politburo in the race for disengagement from full alliance with the leaders of the British trade unions. Stalin did not allow the opposition enough time to transform the Politburo into a hotbed of discussion. Trotsky had hardly returned from Germany when

[110] *Pravda*, 5 May 1926.

[111] Trotsky, *My Life*, p. 450. Mikoyan in *XV Konferentsiya VKP*, p. 683, claimed that Trotsky and Zinoviev voted for the creation of the committee although Trotsky was opposed to the overtures made to the IFTU.

[112] For a laboured theory on Zinoviev's central role in the attack on ARJAC and uniformly negative attitude towards the committee from Dec. 1925 onwards see W. Korey, 'Zinoviev's Critique of Stalin's Theory of Socialism in One Country, December 1925–December 1926', *The American Slavic and East European Review* (Dec. 1950), pp. 255–67.

[113] Zinoviev, 'Vseobshchaya Zabastovka v Anglii i Ee Mirovoe Znachenie', in *Pravda* and *Izvestiya*, 3, 4 and 5 June; also in *Inprecorr*, 17 and 24 June 1926.

[114] *Komm. Int.* (1926), Nos. 5–6, pp. 27–38.

Stalin provoked the opposition into a confrontation. In the Politburo meeting of 3 June, he distorted Trotsky's references to the CPGB, suggesting that he regarded the party as 'a reactionary organization, an impediment in the path of the working class'. The misrepresentation of his views enraged Trotsky; it triggered off a prematurely direct attack on the 'dictatorship of the party apparatus' with regard to criticism of the collaboration with non-communist allies.[115]

Stalin, however, had anticipated the opposition's criticism of the opportunist motives behind the collaboration and of the AUCCTU's independent policy of affiliation to Amsterdam. All he needed to do was to give official *cachet* to Lozovsky's recent prolific publications as well as to the critical attitude towards the General Council which had been gaining momentum since long before the outbreak of the strike. Stalin, Rykov and Lozovsky ostentatiously attended the congress of food industry workers which was in session at the time of the dispute. They heard a report by Tomsky pledging complete allegiance to Profintern's international policy and condemning the policy of the General Council during the strike. On the other hand the opposition's persistent attacks on ARJAC paradoxically forced the majority to adhere to it. It now received a new lease of life under the pretext that it was the best channel through which to arrange aid to the miners.[116] Tomsky, therefore, concluded his speech by calling upon the leadership not to submit to the opposition. The failure of the strike, he argued, should 'in no way affect our attitude to the Anglo-Soviet Committee'.[117]

Tomsky reintroduced the subject two days later in a report on the general strike delivered to a session of the AUCCTU plenum. Lozovsky must have been pleased with Tomsky's irrevocable criticism of the General Council, including its left wing, for

[115] Trotsky archives (microfilm in the possession of Dr J. M. Macfarlane): declaration to Politburo meeting, 3 June 1926; Trotsky archives, T–2986: declaration to Politburo meeting, 6 June 1926.

[116] First mention of this by Lozovsky in *Pravda*, 18 May 1926.

[117] Report of the congress in *Trud*, 6 June 1926; Tomsky's speech in *Trud*, 7 June 1926. There is no evidence whatever to confirm Fischer, *Stalin and German Communism*, p. 561, in her suggestion that Tomsky and Petrovsky 'endorsed the strike breaking policy' of the General Council to save ARJAC. See also a similar suggestion in B. Souvarine, *Stalin* (London, 1939), p. 428.

'dragging their feet' at the height of the struggle.[118] At the end of the meeting a declaration in the same vein 'to the entire international proletariat' was issued; it received wide dissemination and later became the immediate cause for the deterioration of relations with the British trade unions. However, the resolution repeated that the Russians had no intention of sacrificing ARJAC, which was not an alliance of leaderships but 'an expression of solidarity between the masses of both countries'.[119]

Very shortly afterwards a Politburo meeting took place in which the opposition was forestalled by the majority's declaration that the left wing of the General Council was 'as much responsible' as the right wing for the 'shameful collapse' of the strike. The opposition, anxious to evolve an independent line, now unequivocally demanded the withdrawal of the Russians from ARJAC. Stalin was on solid ground in resisting this, quoting Lenin's arguments in support of the seizure of power through the trade unions. Bukharin invoked the old precept that because of capitalism's threat to Russia it was 'imperative to approach the workers in the West'. The only concession made to the opposition was the admission that the incompetence of the General Council required the replacement of the British trade union leadership to ensure the future of the collaboration policy.[120] Stalin defended the CPGB from Trotsky's wrath by claiming that its failure to do so during the strike was due to its 'numerical weakness'.[121]

The lessons IKKI drew from the strike, thoroughly exposing the betrayal by the left wing, frustrated any opposition hopes to loosen Stalin's stranglehold by transferring the controversy to the international arena. Hardy, a prominent figure in the NMM who was in Moscow during the strike, had launched a devastating attack on 'Purcell and Co.', who were 'soft as putty' and had capitulated to the right wing 'without a murmur'. The lessons, however, stressed that while ARJAC was not to be preserved

118 *Kras. Int. Prof.* (1926), No. 7, pp. 26–28 (one of the rare occasions when a speech by Tomsky was quoted in full by Profintern).

119 *Trud*, 8 June 1926; endorsed by the CPSU in *Pravda*, 8 June 1926.

120 For the call to change the leadership see also *Komm. Int.* (1926), No. 55, pp. 183–89; Levin in *Mezh. Rabo. Dviz.*, No. 20, 10 June 1926, and in *Kras. Int. Prof.* (1926), No. 6, pp. 803–804.

121 Account of meeting in Bukharin's speech to party activists in Moscow on 8 June 1926 reported in *Pravda* and *Izvestiya*, 26 June 1926. For Stalin's views see *Sochineniya*, Vol. 8, pp. 163–67.

out of 'national-State considerations' its dissolution would be a '"heroic" but politically childish and ill-advised gesture'. It was once again justified by its transient role in the organization of support to the miners.[122] The preparations for the clash ahead were completed by administrative measures against the opposition following the discovery of clandestine activities.[123]

The major appearance of the new opposition was signalled by a minority report during the meeting of the central committee of the CPSU, which met for ten days on 14 July. It discussed a wide range of subjects, although in essence it was a straightforward struggle for power. Among the vital topics dealt with, and perhaps the most important after that of differentiation between industry and agriculture, was the question of the international situation, with pointed reference to recent events in Britain and Poland.[124] The opposition's proposed resolution stated that from a Marxist point of view it was incorrect to 'by-pass' the CPGB, which was the real 'historic organization of the proletariat', and to put in its place ARJAC, which had been created to cope with 'specific circumstances'. Moreover, it was 'a serious offence in relation to the peoples of the Soviet Union and in relation to the world proletariat' to cultivate illusions that the General Council was in a position to thwart an imperialist war. The majority was criticized for not ending the alliance at the moment of the 'malicious termination' of the strike, when the reputation of the General Council with the British masses was at its lowest level ever. As the intention of the General Council was to convene the committee to 'gain time' and evade discussion of its conduct of the strike, perhaps even to rehabilitate itself, the Politburo was called upon to dissolve the committee without delay.

During the central committee meeting it was also suggested by Zinoviev that Comintern had become a tool in the hands of opportunists of the Amsterdam type.[125] A letter from the leaders

[122] IKKI thesis in *Comm. Rev.* (July 1926), pp. 113–32; Hardy's speech to executive bureau of Profintern on 17 June 1926 in *Mezh. Rabo. Dviz.* (1926), No. 24.

[123] E. H. Carr, *Foundations of a Planned Economy 1926–1929* (London, 1971), Vol. II, pt. I, pp. 4–5.

[124] *ibid.*, pp. 5–12; the only records of the meeting are quoted in B. A. Abramov, 'Razgrom Trotskistsko-Zinov′evskogo Antipartiinogo Bloka', *Voprosy Istorii KPSS* (1959), No. 6, pp. 30–35.

[125] Trotsky archives, T–881: 'Rezoliutsiya Predlozhennaya Iyul′skomu

of the opposition to the Russian delegation to IKKI claimed that 'a bureaucratic regime' had been established in Comintern and was manifested by the 'appointment from above of leading elements in the different communist parties', a 'retreat from their own revolutionary position to the position of assisting the Soviet state'.[126]

By now Stalin had proved to be immune from these attacks and could afford a return to the offensive. The appeals through Comintern, moreover, met with little success. The KPD, in which the opposition found its strongest support, soon came out with a condemnation of the opposition's wish to 'dismantle the massive alliance'; by so doing they would enlist 'in the service of the imperialist interventionists against the country of the proletariat dictatorship'.[127] The central committee did not devote its entire energies to a theoretical debate with the opposition, whose forces had seriously dwindled before the meeting. In view of the setbacks caused by the strike to relations with Britain, great efforts were made to restore the respectability of ARJAC. Lozovsky's constant attacks on the General Council, particularly his scepticism about the efficiency of the General Council's 'verbal defence of the Soviet Union from Conservative attacks', no longer enjoyed the unequivocal support of the Politburo.[128]

The lessons of the strike published in the party's theoretical journal on the eve of the meeting dismissed the opposition's call for the abandonment of the committee as 'superficial' and based on a 'primitive and formalist' understanding of the concept of class struggle. The miners' strike, always described as being in its 'acute stage', was produced once more to justify the preservation of the committee as the 'best channel for the organization of relief'.[129]

Plenomu Oppozitsiei o General'noi Stachke v Anglii'. In *XV Konferentsiya VKP*, p. 508, Trotsky described the period of collaboration in ARJAC as 'perselevshchina', characterized by reformism and reaction.

126 On Zinoviev's criticism of Comintern see Abramov, 'Razgrom Trotskistsko-Zinov'eskogo', p. 34; Trotsky archives, T-2988: letter to IKKI, July 1926.

127 Resolution passed on 5 Aug. 1926 reproduced in *Pravda*, 16 Aug. 1926.

128 *Mezh. Rabo. Dviz.*, No. 26, 1 July 1926.

129 'Uroki i "Uroki" Angliiskogo Maya', *Bol'shevik*, No. 12, 30 June 1926, pp. 3–19.

Still more striking was the reintroduction of diplomatic reasoning in support of ARJAC. In publications issued in Moscow before the meeting of the central committee, it was openly stated that ARJAC could be counted upon to play a 'momentous role in the struggle against all attempts at intervention directed against the USSR'.[130] Tomsky and Shmidt, the targets of the opposition during the meeting, were held responsible for the opportunist policy; however, they were only temporarily removed from the scene, and were soon rehabilitated and presented as the 'symbols of the workers, the pride of the party'.[131]

Stalin's speech to the meeting was certainly the most important indication of the return to the original aims of the committee. After embarrassing Zinoviev by confronting him with some of his earlier statements in support of ARJAC, he defended it as an instrument to win over the masses but also as an appropriate means of preventing 'intervention in our country on the part of the mightiest of the imperialist powers of Europe'. These expectations, he added, were absolutely legitimate so long as the Soviet Union was the 'bulwark and basis of the international revolution'. However, he made an important reservation in suggesting that the Soviet Union retain the right to criticize its allies when it deemed this necessary. The resolution followed these lines, objecting to the dissolution of the committee on the grounds that such a move would be 'of service to the belligerent British bourgeoisie and the treacherous leaders of the General Council and of Amsterdam'.[132]

Although Stalin had succeeded in removing the threat to the existence of ARJAC at home, he found himself at a loss in trying to restore the confidence of his British allies and halting the deterioration of the collaboration. Stalin, who was now committed to a critical view of the General Council's domestic politics, could not avoid repeated confrontation with the British

130 Quoted by Vuiović in *Puti Mirovoi Revolyutsii. Sed'moi Rasshirennyi Plenum Isponitel'nogo Komiteta Kommunisticheskogo Internatsionala* (Moscow–Leningrad, 1927), Vol. II, p. 182 (hereafter referred to as *Puti Mirovoi Revolyutsii*); see also Trotsky, *The Third International after Lenin*, p. 134.

131 Molotov in *XV Konferentsiya VKP*, p. 669.

132 Stalin, *Sochineniya*, Vol. 8, pp. 176–90; *KPSS v Rezolyutsiyakh i Resheniyakh*, Vol. 3, p. 332.

delegates to ARJAC at a time when the collaboration seemed to be of unprecedented value.

The general strike: setbacks to rapprochement

The Foreign Office, which was in the process of revising its Russian policy, was slow to appreciate the tremendous impact of the general strike on Anglo-Soviet relations. However, soon after the strike had been crushed, the diehards of the Cabinet concentrated their efforts on loosening what they believed was Russia's firm grasp on the trade unions, which had precipitated the strike in the first place. Chamberlain, backed by Baldwin, opposed any action which threatened his carefully thought-out plan to pacify Europe. However, to mollify the strong anti-Russian lobby in the Party and the diehard wing in Cabinet, who were disturbed by the Russians' massive support of the miners, he registered a mild protest. This step proved to be a fatal blow to the hard-won improvement in Anglo-Soviet relations and marked the beginning of a steady deterioration towards a rupture.

As early as April the Foreign Office had discussed possible Russian interference in the mining dispute. This was prompted by a description of the Soviet Government's thorough preparations for the conflict.[133] Chamberlain found it difficult to 'stomach this stuff' but refrained, on Gregory's advice, from making any remonstrations to Moscow.[134] Indeed, consultations with Hodgson convinced the Department that the solidarity campaign was primarily inspired by Lozovsky and did not go much further than May Day slogans. Although the Soviet Government was held responsible in principle for the activities of Comintern, in practice Chamberlain reacted only to activities which indisputably reflected the Government's complicity. It was agreed therefore that the solidarity campaign should not be a subject for diplomatic action, as any reference to Russia's internal matters was only likely to be 'taken up with howls of delight' in Moscow.[135]

The outbreak of the strike and the Russians' financial offer

133 *The Times*, 13 Apr. 1926.

134 F.O. 371 11794 N1687/1687/38: minutes by Gregory and Chamberlain, 14 Apr. 1926.

135 F.O. 371 11794 N1700/1687/38: Hodgson to Chamberlain, 16 Apr. 1926; F.O. 371 11794 N1715/1687/38: minute by Orde, 23 Apr. 1926.

to the General Council did not provoke a revision of the earlier decision. The first involvement of the Office in the strike was a result of information from the British Consul in Constantinople on a boycott imposed by the Russians on British ships loading cargoes in Black Sea ports. This cable, which reached the Office on the last day of the strike, was laid aside; it was minuted, rather prematurely, that 'protests no longer need consideration'.[136] A telegram from Hodgson informing London of the Soviet trade unions' decision to contribute to the strikers' fund was also passed over. It was a subject for the cynical remark that the Russians must have been feeling 'pretty sore at their money being taken for a lost cause', but no thought was devoted to the repercussions of this move.[137]

The discussion of the events in Cabinet on 19 May also failed to predict any extraordinary developments. The Treaty of Berlin, rather than the recent general strike, was the focus for animated debate. The question of foreign financial aid to the strikers was raised by Joynson-Hicks, who only sought the Cabinet's approval for maintaining the ban on such aid now that emergency regulations had lapsed. However, no decision was reached on this subject.[138] When Kindersley, a confirmed anti-communist, raised the matter in Parliament on the same day as the Cabinet meeting, Chamberlain was determined to prevent a full-scale discussion from developing. He preferred to employ delaying tactics, suggesting that he could not furnish any information before he received a review of the situation from the Embassy in Moscow.[139]

Hodgson's dispatch, which arrived the next week, lent little force to allegations of the Soviet Government's complicity with the solidarity movement. The two points which Hodgson believed transgressed international law were: the appeal of the Moscow Soviet to subordinate organizations to give moral and material support to the strike; and the transfer of funds to Britain, for which special Government authorization must have been given.

136 F.O. 371 11794 N2148/1687/38: British Consul in Constantinople to Chamberlain, 11 May 1926, and minute by Orde, 12 May 1926.

137 F.O. 371 11794 N2260/1687/38: Hodgson to Chamberlain, 8 May 1926, and minute by Gascoigne, 18 May 1926.

138 Cab. 23/53 33(26)3 and 15.

139 *Parl. Deb. H.C.*, Vol. 196, cols. 263–64, 19 May 1926; F.O. 371 11794 N2317/1687/38: minute by Chamberlain, 18 May 1926.

The Office remained faithful to the policy it had suggested the previous month. It preferred not to hold the Soviet Government responsible for activities on the home front, while recognizing that the British Government would have been fully justified in doing so.

To convey to the Russians this policy, as well as to placate those who wished the Government to take a harder line, Chamberlain accepted Gregory's proposal that a memorandum should be sent to Narkomindel. This memorandum was expected to be a limited protest against the action of Narkomfin in granting special permission for the transfer of funds. Chamberlain, however, vetoed a draft protest which suggested that the Russian contribution was calculated to succour those elements in Britain committed to the 'overthrow of the established institutions of Great Britain'.[140]

In the immediate aftermath of the strike, the Russians, still sanguine about the recent *rapprochement*, believed that they had managed to avert a major diplomatic embroilment by maintaining a clear-cut distinction between the activities of the Government and those of the trade unions. Hodgson, familiar with the views of the Foreign Office yet remote from the growing pressures and anti-communist sentiments at home, encouraged this outlook. He had made inquiries to Narkomindel on two occasions about the refusal of the dockers in Batum to load British ships, but did not reveal any intention of proceeding beyond this point. After a meeting with Hodgson on 5 June, Chicherin was left with the impression that Britain did not wish to dispute the right of the trade unions to express their solidarity.[141]

Narkomindel, however, in spite of its assumption that the trade unions' contribution gave no foundation for representations, remained alert to the 'class struggle' nature of the conflict, which evoked fierce emotions in Britain. Alarm was expressed that relations towards Russia would be determined by the 'inner struggle in the ruling party in Britain'. At present Narkomindel distinguished between two balanced tendencies: that of the business-

[140] F.O. 371 11794 N2367/1687/38: Hodgson to Chamberlain, 19 May 1926, and minutes by Gregory and Chamberlain, 31 May 1926.

[141] *Dok. Vne. Pol.*, Vol. IX, pp. 297–98 and 304: Chicherin to Rosengoltz, 4 and 11 June 1926.

like moderates, who recognized the economic advantages of trading with Russia; and that of the diehards, who acted upon prejudice.[142] Concern was expressed, however, that the bankers, who were believed to have the upper hand over the industrialists, would undermine the common commercial interests of the two countries.[143] Complaints by the diehards against Russian involvement in the strike, and particularly suggestions made by Tweed[144] that the contribution to the strikers emanated directly from the Soviet Government's treasury and possibly from confiscated property, were immediately rebutted. Dogadov received prominent space in the Press to give a detailed account of the collection of donations and of the financial situation of the trade unions. To emphasize the spontaneous and enthusiastic nature of the contribution, he added that it had been necessary 'to restrain trade union members' who wished to give a full day's wage.[145]

Dogadov's announcement, however, could hardly satisfy the diehards, who followed up Tweed's article with a sharp attack on the 'Russian Gold'. The memorandum to Narkomindel, which had been prepared for dispatch, had to be postponed until the Cabinet had met to discuss the situation on 9 June. In this meeting Joynson-Hicks mounted the heaviest attack yet on the Government's policy towards Russia; according to his biographer he was convinced not only of the Russian Government's connivance at the financial support, but also of their participation in the strike itself and even in the plans to call it.[146] Joynson-Hicks was strongly supported by Churchill, who had conveyed to Chamberlain a day earlier the 'deep and widespread' feeling in the Party in support of positive action to counter 'Bolshevik intrigues against the country'. This was rejected by Chamberlain;

142 *Mir. Khz. i Mir. Pol.* (1926), Nos. 5–6, pp. 119–21. Thorough discussion on the split in the Cabinet in *Izvestiya*, 25 June 1926. On balance between economic considerations and pressure of diehards see leaders in *Izvestiya*, 25 June 1926, and *Ekon. Zhzn.*, 4 June 1926.

143 I. Taigin (pseudonym of Maisky), *Angliya i SSSR* (Leningrad, 1926), pp. 89–90.

144 Chairman of the Association of British Creditors in *The Times*, 22 May 1926.

145 *Trade Union Bulletin*, Nos. 5–6, 12 June 1926. Dogadov's reply was also published in *Workers' Weekly*, 28 May 1926, in *Pravda*, 29 May 1926, and in *Izvestiya* and *Ekon. Zhzn.*, 1 June 1926.

146 H. A. Taylor, *Jix – Viscount Brentford* (London, 1933), p. 195.

although he was prepared to discuss the problem 'without any prejudice', he preferred at present not to seize the opportunity to expel the Russian diplomats from Britain.[147] The meeting ended indecisively in the absence of Baldwin, whose resolute handling of the general strike had won for him the respect of his ministers and the position of final arbiter in Cabinet.[148]

Joynson-Hicks was absolutely determined to use the occasion to substantiate the connection between communist activities in Britain and the Soviet Government. On the day of the Cabinet meeting he submitted, for the Foreign Office's comments, a memorandum consisting of a selection of utterances by Soviet leaders before and during the strike which he thought left no doubt of the complicity of the Soviet Government in the events.[149] In December 1925, Joynson-Hicks had indicated in Parliament his intention of publishing papers seized in the raid on the CPGB headquarters, which would conclusively prove the involvement of the Soviet Government.[150] No measures had been taken since. However, on 10 June these documents were suddenly produced for Foreign Office examination pending their publication as a White Paper. No forceful objections were put forward against this. Gregory realized that it would 'intensify the outcry of the unappeasable diehards' but held that it was 'hardly likely to unsteady' those who saw the wisdom of maintaining relations.[151] Nobody in the Office paid any attention to the timing of the publication and its conceivable effect in Russia.

The worst, however, was still to come. On 10 June Joynson-Hicks revealed in the House 'intimations' from the Foreign Office that it possessed sufficient evidence to prove the Russian Government's direct participation in the organization and transfer of funds to Britain.[152] His speech, which was apparently based on a verbal misunderstanding, tied the hands of the Foreign Office. Gregory complained that the statement was not 'suscep-

[147] Churchill papers, 22/84: exchange of notes between Churchill and Chamberlain.

[148] Cab. 23/53 37(26)5, 9 June 1926. On Baldwin's position see Chamberlain papers, 53/122: Chamberlain to Lord Robert Cecil, 15 June 1926.

[149] F.O. 371 11795 N2753/1687/38: memorandum by the Home Office, 9 June 1926.

[150] *Parl. Deb. H.C.*, Vol. 188, col. 2093, 1 Dec. 1925.

[151] F.O. 371 11799 N2745/2745/38: minute by Gregory, 18 June 1926.

[152] *Parl. Deb. H.C.*, Vol. 196, cols. 1673–76.

tible of proof' and was inconsistent with the line hitherto held by the Office. This policy was to charge the Soviet Government only with violating their embargo on the export of capital. Gregory proposed to adopt two courses to reconcile the contradiction between the Home Secretary's statement and the memorandum. The first was to 'slur over the difference' between the two by informing the House of the content of the memorandum submitted to Moscow with the hope that it would 'not press the distinction'. The second was to prepare another memorandum for the next Cabinet meeting elucidating the Foreign Office's opposition to a rupture on the grounds that there was 'nothing to be gained by violent action'.[153]

In the meantime to deflect any further pressure, as well as to avert Russian remonstrations regarding the Home Secretary's speech, Chamberlain dispatched the memorandum to Hodgson on 11 June, before the Cabinet had reached any conclusion on Russian interference. The memorandum, which was handed to Chicherin on 12 June, was considered by the Department to be the mildest course of action in the circumstances and did not constitute a representation.[154] Chamberlain followed Gregory's advice and informed Parliament on 14 June of the protest made to Moscow. In order to neutralize the diehards, he expressed the opinion that the memorandum would be 'a deterrent in further improvement of relations'. He refused, however, to comment on a possible severance of relations before the Cabinet had met to discuss the question.[155]

The memorandum was received in Moscow as an ominous sign of the 'renewed assault' on the Soviet Union. The mild form of the protest was regarded as deceptive; it was the 'forerunner of a violent attack, possibly an ultimatum'.[156] The Russians had of course no information on the reasoning behind the memorandum. They viewed it as a sequel to Joynson-Hicks' speech to Parliament, which was taken to be the official policy. The

153 F.O. 371 11795 N2868/1687/38: memorandum by Gregory, 11 June 1926.

154 F.O. 371 11786 N2784/387/38: minute by Orde, 14 June 1926.

155 *Parl. Deb. H.C.*, Vol. 196, cols. 1960–61.

156 *Izvestiya* and *Trud*, 13 June 1926, and *Pravda*, 15 June 1926. Similar observations were made in Moscow by P. Scheffer, *Seven Years in Soviet Russia* (London, 1931), p. 231.

memorandum was regarded, therefore, as a sign of the much-feared victory of the diehard wing; if the British still wished to maintain normal relations, they were advised to 'call to order Birkenhead and Jix'.[157]

Soviet diplomacy now directed its efforts towards repairing the damage inflicted on Anglo-Soviet relations by the dispatch of the memorandum. The first official Russian reaction was a complaint about Joynson-Hicks' speech to Parliament sent to Chamberlain on 14 June by Rosengoltz, the acting Chargé d'Affaires. Although Rosengoltz denied that the English trade unions had accepted any money during the strike, he defended the right of the Soviet unions to dispose of the funds belonging to them in any way they saw fit.[158] Two days later Chicherin handed Hodgson a note which dismissed the charges of the British memorandum; the Soviet Government could lift restrictions and issue permits as it chose. Since the Government represented the 'will of the workers and peasants' of the Soviet Union, it could not be expected to forbid the transfer of contributions by the trade unions to their British counterparts.[159] As if to illustrate this last point, a large demonstration of workers took place in Moscow on 17 June in protest at the efforts of British diplomacy 'to interfere in the domestic affairs of the Soviet trade unions'.[160]

Another reproof about the British memorandum came from the General Council, which despite its direct involvement in the affair received scant attention in the Foreign Office. Citrine, who surmised that the Russian aid was being used as a 'strong attempt to break off relations', consulted Pugh, the chairman of the British delegation to ARJAC, and decided to approach Baldwin. In his letter Citrine not only denied receiving the contribution but also insisted that he had not come across 'the slightest vestige of evidence' to support the allegation that the money was raised 'directly or indirectly from the resources of the Government of the USSR'. Chamberlain, who was consulted on the matter, had no intention of taking into account the General Council's view.

[157] *Pravda*, 16 June 1926.

[158] F.O. 371 11795 N2721/1687/38: Rosengoltz to Chamberlain. Rosengoltz expressed similar views in *Manchester Guardian*, 17 June 1926.

[159] F.O. 371 11795 N2800/1687/38: Hodgson to Chamberlain, 16 June 1926.

[160] *Pravda*, 18 June 1926.

He simply acknowledged receipt of the letter and suggested that the General Council should in future follow the Government's policy through statements made in Parliament.[161]

Litvinov used the good offices of R. J. Boothby, who had headed the recent Conservative delegation to Russia, to restate his desire to open negotiations while complaining that no response was forthcoming from the British Government. The Russian Press followed the same course, suggesting that the memorandum's only effect was to leave a bad taste; the outstanding problems between the two countries could be solved only by way of an agreement 'advantageous to both sides'.[162]

The Russian moves, however, proved to be abortive. The Cabinet meeting of 16 June was an irrevocable step towards a severance of Anglo-Soviet relations. Chamberlain's hopes that thorough debate could be avoided did not materialize, while he seriously misjudged the strength of the diehards' feelings on the Russian question. He succeeded, however, in preventing, at least temporarily, a complete breakdown of relations.

In the meeting Joynson-Hicks led the main attack on Chamberlain's Russian policy. He was not dissuaded from pressing for a rupture of relations by a private message from the King which requested forbearance on the subject of Russian aid to the miners and expressed anxiety about the remonstrations made to Russia.[163] In a memorandum submitted by the Home Secretary to the Cabinet before the meeting, he demanded that the Government act on the Foreign Office's conviction that the Soviet Government, undifferentiated from the CPSU, was responsible for the activities of Comintern. The memorandum dwelt at length on the subversive activities of the Russians in the British trade unions and suggested that the help to the miners had not been a '*bona fide* charity'. It admonished Chamberlain for

[161] TUC archives, B 132 13/7/32: exchange of telegrams between Pugh and Citrine, 12 June 1926; Baldwin papers, Vol. 12, 6a: Citrine's letter to Baldwin and reply, 12 and 22 June 1926; F.O. 371 11795 2746/1687/38: minute by Chamberlain, 16 June 1926.

[162] F.O. 371 11786 N2675/387/38: Boothby to Chamberlain (communication from Litvinov), 11 June 1926; leaders in *Ekon. Zhzn.* and *Izvestiya*, 15 June 1926.

[163] Quoted in Nicolson, *King George the Fifth*, p. 421: letter from Stamfordham, private secretary to the King, to Joynson-Hicks, 14 June 1926.

continuing to deal with Russia at a purely conventional diplomatic level and called for the immediate expulsion of the Soviet Embassy and the Trade Delegation from Britain.[164] During the meeting Chamberlain also came under fire from Churchill, who complained that the memorandum to Russia presented the Cabinet with a *fait accompli.*[165] It was evident from the Foreign Office's memorandum, also laid before Cabinet, that Chamberlain did not wish to exonerate the Russians from the charges. It emphasized the tight control exercised by the Politburo on the activities of the Soviet Government as well as those of Comintern. Chamberlain had earlier commented that it was 'a mere quibble' to say that the Soviet trade unions did 'not form part of the Government of the country'.[166] In his memorandum he readily admitted that the Russian trade unions were in fact 'Government institutions or party institutions – the two being in essence the same thing'. However, he maintained that any measure in addition to the protest Note would be superfluous. Extreme action was likely to jeopardize the increasing volume of trade between the two countries and lead to an 'intensification of propaganda'.[167]

The Cabinet unanimously agreed that the Russians' 'malignant hostility to the British Empire' fully justified severance of relations. However, a majority still accepted Chamberlain's arguments that the moment was 'not opportune' for a rupture. But under the pressure of the diehards it was agreed that the door should be left open for review of the policy when necessary, and that the 'menacing character' of the Soviet Government's policy towards England should be revealed to the public.[168]

The diehards indeed made full use of this last provision. Churchill, in a speech on 19 June, described 'the great deal of satisfaction' which would ensue from the expulsion of the Bolsheviks. He proceeded to warn traders with Russia not to lend money to that country as the Cabinet retained a free hand to take 'any action it may think in public interest' and could accept

164 Cab. 24/180 C.P. 236.
165 Baldwin papers, Vol. 12, 8a: Cecil to Baldwin, 16 June 1926.
166 F.O. 371 11795 N2719/1687/38: Hodgson to Chamberlain, 3 June 1926, and minute by Chamberlain, 17 June 1926.
167 Cab. 24/180 C.P. 250.
168 Cab. 23/53 39(26)7.

no responsibility for investments in these circumstances. Birkenhead displayed similar views on the same day, expressing doubts on the desirability of association with a state whose purpose in every part of the world was to undermine 'the historical greatness of this country'.[169] Such utterances caused much dismay both to the Russians and to Chamberlain, who was placed in an awkward position as the speeches were taken to represent the Government's views. His complaints to the Prime Minister remained unanswered; the pressure exerted on him to change the policy was beginning to bear fruit.[170]

The Russians had cherished hopes that Churchill as Chancellor of the Exchequer would give more weight to economic considerations than to emotional preconceptions. They immediately devoted much space in the Press to prove, with the help of statistics, the increasing significance of trade between the two countries. In England they found their best spokesman in E. F. Wise, an enthusiastic advocate of trade with Russia who as an official of the Food Ministry had played an important role in the conclusion of the 1921 trade agreement and was now serving as an advisor to Arcos. He warned that if Churchill's advice was accepted it might be 'disastrous to many British interests'; it would close the door to 'Russia's vast markets and deprive England of essential raw materials'.[171]

These voices, however, could not compete effectively with the anti-Russian campaign which followed the publication of the White Paper by the Home Office on 24 June and the subsequent Commons debate. A group of Conservatives put forward a resolution calling for the cancellation of the 1921 trade agreement. Although the motion was eventually lost, the debate displayed a wide range of opinions on relations with Russia and the increasing vulnerability of the Government to the diehards' lobby. Locker-Lampson, introducing the resolution, bluntly described the Russians as an enemy which 'under the cloak of

169 *The Times*, 21 June 1926.

170 F.O. 371 11786 N3098/387/38: Chamberlain to Baldwin, 30 June 1926.

171 Leader in *Ekon. Zhzn.*, 24 June 1926; Wise in *Manchester Guardian*, 22 June 1926; Sorokin in supplement of *The Soviet Union Monthly* (July 1926), p. 9. On Wise see Ullman, *The Anglo-Soviet Accord*, pp. 15–19 and 440–44.

friendship' was replacing the old weapons of steel by 'gold and propaganda'. The CPGB, he believed, would not have existed had it not 'suckled upon Soviet shekels'.[172] Joynson-Hicks and Knox elaborated on the domestic situation in Britain. Knox described the 1921 agreement as 'immoral' and suggested to Chamberlain that his achievements in Locarno would be complete only after he had eradicated the 'Soviet sore'.[173]

Ponsonby, for the Opposition, appealed for moderation. He deplored the attitude adopted by the diehards who, in a 'perfect state of frenzy', were speaking 'from the gutter'. Moreover, he deprecated Joynson-Hicks' use of the issue for domestic political purposes and pointed out the danger posed to the conciliation of Europe by leaving a vast country 'out in the cold'.[174] Further arguments against the resolution were brought forward by Lloyd George, defending the 'interests of industry', while MacDonald expressed his doubts whether the proposed abrogation of the agreement would root out propaganda.[175] Chamberlain, winding up the debate, reproached the Russians for their policy, which was neither 'cordial and friendly' nor 'cordial and correct'. He nevertheless reiterated that a break would be most inconvenient at that time, as it would introduce 'a new and disturbing issue into European politics'. By the same token he ruled out the possibility of 'any new fresh agreement'.[176]

The Russians were now fully aware that as a result of the general strike, relations with Britain had reached a critical stage. Although they were relieved to find out that a rupture was not imminent, they still feared that Chamberlain's gradual capitulation to the diehards would have grave consequences for Anglo-Soviet relations.[177] Soon after the debate in Parliament and the publication of the White Paper, Litvinov delivered a speech in which he emphatically denied the association of Soviet diplomatic missions with the activities of local communist parties and dismissed accusations of 'interference in the domestic political

[172] *Parl. Deb. H.C.*, Vol. 197, cols. 702–707.

[173] *ibid.*, cols. 718–20. Joynson-Hicks delivered an even more powerful anti-Soviet speech a few days later; see *The Times*, 29 June 1926.

[174] *Parl. Deb. H.C.*, Vol. 197, cols. 712–15.

[175] *ibid.*: Lloyd George, cols. 723–24, and MacDonald, cols. 766–67.

[176] *ibid.*, cols. 769–77.

[177] *Pravda*'s diplomatic correspondent, 20 June 1926.

life' of any country where they functioned.[178] This was to be followed by desperate attempts to patch up the growing estrangement between the two countries.

[178] See also *Pravda*, 27 June 1926. On the campaign repudiating allegations made in the White Paper see Nikonova, *Antisovetskaya Vneshnyaya Politika*, pp. 44–47.

5

Attempts to Heal the Breach

Krasin's mission to Britain

The Russians, increasingly aware of the strain which the general strike had contributed to the deterioration of Anglo-Soviet relations, resorted to two major strategies in pursuing their policy of conciliation. In order to stabilize relations they concentrated their efforts on winning over the City and commercial circles, thereby exerting considerable pressure on the British Government to resist the emotional calls of the diehards to sever relations. Simultaneously, steps were taken to restore the solidarity movement between the trade unions of the two countries to thwart possible aggression by the British Government. The emphasis initially laid on formal diplomatic efforts was gradually transferred to the defensive measures when it was realized that the general strike had inflicted irreparable damage on Anglo-Soviet relations. The diplomatic nature of the trade union alliance was particularly evident in view of the radicalization of Comintern's politics in Britain after the strike and the subsequent distinction between the tasks assigned to the trade unions and those of the communist organs.

When Chamberlain met Rosengoltz on 13 July, he left the Russians very little room for interpretation of the future British policy towards Russia. He certainly gave them no grounds for illusions of an improvement in relations. Chamberlain faithfully reflected the feeling in Cabinet when he told Rosengoltz that the 'gulf of principles' separating the two countries was 'unbridgeable'. The conditions he laid down for renewed negotiations were clearly calculated to forestall any positive move by the Russians: they were called upon to comply with their undertaking to refrain from propaganda, to fully compensate former private owners of business in Russia, and to pay their war debts.[1] It

[1] F.O. 371 11786 N3278/387/38: minute by Chamberlain on conversation with Rosengoltz, 13 July 1926; Cab. 23/53 46(26)4, 14 July 1926.

soon became clear to the Russians that the interview was by no means an isolated event but a landmark in the course of Anglo-Soviet relations. When Litvinov approached Hodgson in August in an attempt to erase the memory of the strike and resume negotiations, he was informed that the actions of the Soviet Government 'were not such as to lead to an improvement of relations'.[2]

The tenor of the conversation with Litvinov did not, however, correspond to Hodgson's own convictions. He was still attempting to impress on Chamberlain the fundamental shifts within the Soviet leadership which made it 'more of a Russian government and less of an international conspiracy organization'. This time, however, his recommendations fell on deaf ears: they went no further than a junior official who evaluated the struggle for power as a trivial '*scène de famille*'.[3] The persistent Hodgson nevertheless continued to call upon the Office to consider the favourable implications of the struggle on relations between the two countries. This was dismissed out of hand by Gregory: 'They are all Bolsheviks.' The dissensions within the leadership were viewed as a permanent feature of Soviet life and did not, therefore, constitute a reason for changing the policy towards Russia.[4]

The Russians' prospects of regaining the ground they had won before the strike seemed very dim. The Cabinet's decision to maintain relations did not deter the diehards from assiduously working to reverse it. An upsurge of the traditional rivalry in Central Asia and clashes with Russian interests in China offered them fresh ammunition, while the Committee of Imperial Defence provided the forum for a new attack.[5] During a meeting of the committee in July, Tyrrell, representing the Foreign Office,

[2] F.O. 371 11787 N4062/387/38 and 11796 N4058/1687/38: Hodgson to Chamberlain on conversation with Litvinov, 24 Aug. 1926.

[3] F.O. 371 11779 N3549/53/38: Hodgson to Chamberlain, 29 July 1926; F.O. 371 11779 N3688/53/38: Hodgson to Chamberlain, 30 July 1926, and minute by Gascoigne, 8 Aug. 1926.

[4] F.O. 371 11779 N4648/53/38: Hodgson to Chamberlain, 7 Oct. 1926, and minute by Gregory, 17 Oct. 1926; F.O. 371 11780 N4885/53/38: Hodgson to Chamberlain, 22 Oct. 1926, and minute by Orde, 2 Nov. 1926.

[5] On Britain's clash with Russia's growing influence in China see M. S. Kapitsa, *Sovetsko-Kitaiskie Otnosheniya* (Moscow, 1958), pp. 160–68. On the confrontation over India see Z. Imam, 'Soviet Russia's Policy towards India and its Effect on Anglo-Soviet Relations, 1917–1928' (London Univ. Ph.D. thesis, 1964), pp. 267–79.

acquiesced in Churchill's proposal to form a world-wide common front against Russia. He was referring, however, to diplomatic rather than military activities. The revival of the Anglo-Japanese alliance and the economic penetration of China was regarded as an adequate bulwark against Russian aspirations in the Far East. As for Europe, Tyrrell expressed the opinion that by 'giving effect' to the Locarno Treaty Britain would provide itself 'with the best and most effective protection against the common Russian danger'.[6]

Such a deviation from the declared 'stationary' position in Anglo-Soviet relations was not embarked upon without the consent of Chamberlain, who was steadily succumbing to pressure and losing his moderating influence. In a speech delivered to the Imperial Conference, which met in October, Chamberlain stepped into Curzon's shoes, referring to the 'traditional expansive instinct of Russia' as the main hindrance to a 'return to friendly relations'.[7] In a further meeting of the CID in November, Chamberlain confirmed that Tyrrell's views 'coincided with his convictions'; Russia, which encouraged 'constant anti-British feelings', represented the greatest danger to the British Empire.[8]

Considerable pressure was brought to bear on the Government through demonstrations and 'Clear out the Reds' campaigns. A large meeting in the Albert Hall, which included eighty MPs, called upon the Prime Minister to deal with the 'menace to our freedom and stability'.[9] Even more significant was a recommendation by the annual conference of the Conservative Party that the Government should terminate the 1921 agreement and close down 'all official Russian Soviet Agencies' in Britain.[10]

The reversion of British diplomacy to an inimical attitude towards Russia immediately revived dormant apprehensions of Britain's bellicose designs. Litvinov's denunciation of anti-Soviet intrigues in countries adjacent to Russia seems to have been pro-

[6] F.O. 371 11787 N3539/387/38: memorandum by Tyrrell, 29 July 1926.

[7] Chamberlain papers, 50/249: statement to the Imperial Conference.

[8] Cab. 2/4: minutes of the 218th meeting of the CID, 25 Nov. 1926.

[9] F.O. 371 11787 N3832/387/38: resolution presented to Baldwin, 16 Aug. 1926. Joynson-Hicks' pledge to counteract Soviet activities in Britain and 'destroy their ideals' is in *The Times*, 17 Aug. 1926.

[10] F.O. 371 11787 N4708/387/38: Conservative Central Office to Selby, 18 Oct. 1926. For a detailed description of the 'Clear out the Reds' campaign see Coates, *A History of Anglo-Soviet Relations*, pp. 235–38.

voked by the *coup d'état* on 19 May by Marshal Pilsudski, who hitherto was considered to hold socialist views, and his unexpected persecution of local communists.[11] Despite this move, Pilsudski was quick to assure the Russians of his intentions of preserving the continuity of Polish foreign policy, particularly towards Russia.[12] The Soviet Press admitted, indeed, that it possessed no 'clear-cut evidence' that the British were behind the coup, while Stalin in a major speech on the subject avoided any such suggestions.[13] Nevertheless, groundless allegations of Britain's complicity persisted. They were designed to counterbalance the accusations of Russian interference in the general strike as well as to prevent Pilsudski from becoming in the future a 'weapon in the hands of British policy in Eastern Europe'.[14] Muller, the British Ambassador in Warsaw, complained to Chamberlain that although he had not actually 'set eyes' on Pilsudski since 1923, the 'ridiculous story' initiated by Moscow that he had masterminded the coup was rampant.[15]

Accusations that Britain was striving to create a 'political, military, diplomatic' encirclement of the Soviet Union received new impetus when it became clear that the British Government had no intention of restoring normal relations.[16] Litvinov shared these views. In a letter to Krasin he expanded on his mistrust of Pilsudski and revealed fears that the slightest encouragement of his 'maniacal bellicose intentions' might end in adventures against the Soviet Union.[17]

[11] *Dok. Vne. Pol.*, Vol. IX, pp. 397–99: memorandum by Litvinov on conversation with Hodgson, 24 Aug. 1926; Korbel, *Poland between East and West*, pp. 203–204.

[12] *Dok. Vne. Pol.*, Vol. IX, p. 275: Stomonyakov, Narkomindel, to Voikov, Soviet Ambassador in Warsaw, 16 May 1926.

[13] *Pravda*, 23 May 1926; Stalin, *Sochineniya*, Vol. 8, pp. 168–72.

[14] Leaders in *Pravda* and *Izvestiya*, 15 May 1926; *Izvestiya*, 21 May 1926, and *Ekon. Zhzn.*, 14 July 1926.

[15] F.O. 371 11763 N2549 and N2743/41/55: Muller to Gregory, 23 May and 7 June 1926.

[16] *Pravda*, 18 July 1926. K. Voroshilov, the Commissar of War, warned of the danger of war in *ibid.*, 21 Sept. 1926; this was elaborated on by Bukharin in *Puti Mirovoi Revolyutsii*, Vol. I, pp. 22–23 and 56–65. Apprehensions of war continued until the end of the year; see *Pravda*, 29 Dec. 1926.

[17] *Dok. Vne. Pol.*, Vol. IX, p. 479, 4 Oct. 1926; interview with Litvinov in *Daily Herald*, 8 Oct. 1926.

From its earliest days Soviet diplomacy, cognizant of the reluctance of the capitalist world to embark on friendly political relations with Russia, had made increasing use of economic inducements to compensate for lack of goodwill. This incentive was offered after the general strike in a desperate attempt to forestall a débâcle in Anglo-Soviet relations and was vital in view of the recognition that a certain balance had been reached between the socialist state and the capitalist 'encirclement' dominated by Britain.[18] The emergence of Litvinov, a proponent of accommodation and expansion of trade with the capitalist world, as the strong man in Narkomindel intensified this tendency. Chicherin's ill-health necessitated his absence from Russia for long periods at the end of 1926.[19]

The Russians had embarked on a campaign to demonstrate the benefits of trade with Russia soon after Churchill had advised traders with Russia to curtail their activities.[20] Dzherzhinsky, the president of the Supreme Council of National Economy, emphasized the significance of the British market to Soviet industry. While in 1913 only 5% of total Russian imports originated in Britain, the figures for 1925–26 had risen to 25%. However, in a subsequent interview it was intimated that the prerequisite for the continuation of the trend was that the bodies concerned should 'sweep aside the unfriendly, even unfair' attitude of the Conservative Government.[21]

A memorandum on these lines was published by the Russians and extensively distributed in Parliamentary and business circles. It confirmed a steady increase of Anglo-Soviet trade since 1921. British exports to Russia had risen by 13% while imports had reached 67.5% of the pre-war total. Britain's negative balance of trade with Russia was attributed to the nature of the imports, essentially food products and raw materials indispensable to Britain. It was also stressed that the figures did not include significant British revenues derived from re-exports, storage, ship-

18 Bukharin in *XV Konferentsiya VKP*, p. 19; review of the conference in *Pravda*, 26 Oct. 1926.

19 L. Fischer, *Men and Politics* (New York, 1966), pp. 127–28; R. Hodgson, obituary of Chicherin, *The Slavonic Review* (1937), Vol. xv, p. 700. On Chicherin's decline see also Chamberlain papers, 50/268: memorandum by Chamberlain, 6 Dec. 1926.

20 See above, pp. 176–77.

21 *Ekon. Zhzn.*, 2 and 4 July 1926.

ping and insurance services. The negative balance of trade was thus transformed into a positive one. The upward trend of the volume of trade was attributed to the political normalization of relations, marked by the 1921 agreement and recognition in 1924, while the low figures of 1923 were ascribed to the Curzon ultimatum.

The obvious conclusion was that the deterioration of political relations was bound to cause a parallel decline in trade.[22] Both Hodgson and Peters supported the Russian arguments. Hodgson believed that as the allocation of orders was clearly bound up with political considerations it was advisable to regulate relations. Peters further pointed out the alarming fact that as a result of the present political constellation Soviet buyers were becoming 'accustomed to German-made machinery'.[23]

When it was realized that the British Government was ignoring the Russian overtures, Krasin was rushed to his post in London as a last resort. The Politburo had appointed Krasin as Chargé d'Affaires, apparently without consulting him, as early as 3 November 1925, in response to Chicherin's paranoiac fear of an imminent rupture of Anglo-Soviet relations after Locarno. It was anticipated that Krasin, the architect of the 1921 agreement, would be capable of prevailing on business circles, whose respect he widely enjoyed, 'to exert pressure on the Government to make a careful study of the situation'.[24] This was indeed to be the pattern of Krasin's diplomatic activities in London. For the moment, however, his failing health delayed his departure. Still more important, Krasin apparently had serious reservations about the conduct of Anglo-Soviet relations. In a memorandum

[22] *Dok. Vne. Pol.*, Vol. IX, pp. 352–63, and note 75, p. 731. The same conclusions appear in the supplement to *The Soviet Union Monthly* (July 1926), pp. 5–6. British imports from Russia for the years 1920–1925 amounted to £64,609,071. Original exports amounted to only £21,339,285; but re-exports and services were estimated at £48,815,093, giving an export total of £70,154,378.

[23] F.O. 371 11777 N4450/7/38: Hodgson to Chamberlain, 24 Sept. 1926; F.O. 371 11777 N4882/7/38: Hodgson to Chamberlain (memorandum by Peters), 22 Oct. 1926.

[24] R. F. Karpova, *L. B. Krasin* (Moscow, 1962), pp. 191–92. On expectations from Krasin see also *Dok. Vne. Pol.*, Vol. IX, p. 489: Chicherin to Krasin, 8 Oct. 1926, and Maisky, 'Iz Londonskikh Vospominaniya', pt. 2, p. 155.

submitted to the Politburo at the beginning of 1926, he stated that the only chance of improving political relations lay in abandoning the demand that Britain accept the 1924 draft treaty as a basis for renewed negotiations.[25]

In the summer of 1926, when relations were rapidly deteriorating, Krasin's terms seem to have been met. His first impression upon arrival in Britain on 28 September was that with the exception of the 'horribly aggressive position of the diehards' the British were not opposed to 'embarking upon negotiations'.[26] Meanwhile, in the absence of Chamberlain from London, he devoted his energies to restoring confidence by publicizing Russia's efforts for peace on the international front and economic growth at home.[27] In doing so he received full support from Moscow, where strong emphasis was laid on the achievement of a positive balance of trade through the expansion of commerce with the capitalist world. In a key interview with the Press on the eve of Krasin's arrival in London, Mikoyan demonstrated with facts and figures the soundness of the Russian economy and its ability to establish satisfactory trade and financial relations with countries and firms which showed willingness to do so.[28] Yet another proof of Russia's economic offensive was the appointment of L. M. Khinchuk[29] as head of the Trade Delegation in London to assist Krasin in his work. He immediately announced that Russia intended to place numerous orders in Britain.[30]

Krasin did not expect to bring about a swift change in relations but was prepared for strenuous work. He believed that the 'route to success' lay not through the Foreign Office but through the City. His main efforts were, therefore, directed to converting the economic milieu.[31] Making the acquaintance of

25 Karpova, *L. B. Krasin*, pp. 193–94; L. Krassin, *Leonid Krassin* (London, 1929), p. 258.

26 *Dok. Vne. Pol.*, Vol. IX, pp. 492–94; Krasin to Litvinov, 9 Oct. 1926.

27 *Manchester Guardian*, 2 Oct. 1926. See also reports in *The Times*, 24 Sept. and 7 Oct. 1926.

28 Mikoyan in *Izvestiya*, 25 Sept. 1926. See also 'Voprosy Vneshnei Torgovli', *Pravda*, 14 Oct. 1926, and Rykov in *XV Konferentsiya VKP*, p. 134.

29 President of Tsentrosoyuz (the All-Union Central Union of Consumers' Societies).

30 *Izvestiya*, 26 Oct. 1926.

31 'Sdvig v Positsii Delovykh Krugov?', *Pravda*, 31 Oct. 1926.

Chamberlain, whom he considered to be a toy in the hands of Gregory, did little to alter his conviction. In fact he was somewhat disappointed that in real life the Foreign Secretary bore no resemblance to a lion or a crocodile, which was how he was frequently portrayed in Soviet caricatures. In comparison to Curzon, remarked Krasin, Chamberlain appeared 'little more than a clerk'.[32] Chamberlain, in turn, neither perceived the qualities of Krasin nor appreciated his authority. He received the false impression that Krasin had been sent to Britain merely as a restraining influence and without powers to formulate fresh proposals. This misconception was due to Krasin's energetic search for assurances that relations would not be severed, probably to allow himself time to sound the feelings in the City.[33]

Meanwhile Krasin was encouraged by his meetings with Montagu Norman, the Governor of the Bank of England, and Reginald MacKenna of the Midland Bank. Norman in particular exercised his charm on Krasin, agreeing with him that Russia's participation was essential to the restoration of the European economy. However, he expressed a 'categorical negation' to Krasin's inquiries about the prospects of long-term credits and loans. Krasin attributed this to the miners' strike; so long as it continued there was no chance even of 'semi-official' negotiations.[34] In two further meetings with Gregory and Tyrrell, Krasin mistook their courtesy for a sign of a thaw in Anglo-Soviet relations.[35] In fact the Office retained its non-committal position. Chamberlain had made up his mind to refrain from taking a new direction until he had tested Krasin's 'skill as a fisherman in the City'.[36]

Before Chamberlain could pass his verdict, however, Krasin's vigorous activities came to an unexpected halt. Succumbing to

[32] *Dok. Vne. Pol.*, Vol. IX, pp. 499–506: Krasin to Chicherin on meeting with Chamberlain, 14 Oct. 1926.

[33] F.O. 371 11787 N4571/387/38: memorandum by Chamberlain on conversation with Krasin, 11 Oct. 1926.

[34] *Dok. Vne. Pol.*, Vol. IX, pp. 512–22: Krasin to Narkomindel, 23 Oct. 1926.

[35] *ibid.*, pp. 526–27: memorandum by Krasin on conversation with Gregory, 29 Oct. 1926; F.O. 371 11787 N4717 and N4818/387/38: minutes by Tyrrell and Gregory on conversations with Krasin, 15 and 24 Oct. 1926.

[36] F.O. 371 11787 N4818/387/38: minute by Chamberlain, 25 Oct. 1926.

his illness in the second half of October, he was obliged to abstain from major undertakings and delegate much of his work. On his death-bed he still expressed unfounded optimism that Britain would respond to Russia's offers to discuss all 'outstanding questions which had not been solved before'.[37]

British policy, however, was moving towards a different solution. Soon after Krasin's death, Locker-Lampson, the Parliamentary Under-Secretary for Foreign Affairs, minuted that agitation to expel the Russians was growing 'well-nigh irresistible'. He accordingly assigned Gregory to revise a departmental memorandum on the pros and cons of a severance of relations; this memorandum had only recently advised against harsh measures. Gregory, assuming a rancorous attitude reminiscent of the Curzon era, arrived at the conclusion that arguments were 'evenly balanced'. Although the ejection of the Russians would be 'a thoroughly pleasurable proceeding', it was unlikely to yield any positive results so long as the Government was unable to follow up such a move by 'dealing the Russians a damaging blow'. Gregory, fully aware of the weight of domestic considerations in the issue, was forced to admit in conclusion that a rupture would be 'the satisfaction of an emotion rather than an act of useful diplomacy'.[38] In addition Gregory revealed to Rosengoltz that relations with Russia no longer rested entirely with the Foreign Office but depended to a large extent 'on the inner party situation'.[39]

This was reflected in Parliament, where demands were made for the declining of any Russian proposal until after the Russians had undertaken to abstain from anti-British propaganda and had fulfilled all their financial obligations.[40] A Conservative deputation which besieged Baldwin with similar propositions was sympathetically received, although the Prime Minister still

[37] *Izvestiya*, 7 Nov. 1926. On Krasin's last days in London see S. V. Zarnitskii and L. M. Trofimova, *Krasin, Sovetskoi Strany Diplomat* (Moscow, 1968), pp. 247–58.

[38] F.O. 371 11787 N5452/387/38: memorandum by Hamilton-Gordon, 7 Dec. 1926; F.O. 371 11787 N5670/387/38: memorandum by Gregory, 10 Dec. 1926.

[39] *Dok. Vne. Pol.*, Vol. IX, pp. 574–77: Rosengoltz to Narkomindel on conversation with Gregory, 19 Nov. 1926.

[40] *Parl. Deb. H.C.*, Vol. 200, cols. 2082–83.

appeared to be in favour of 'the waiting game'.[41] The hardening attitude was displayed in the Cabinet meeting of 15 December when the distinction between communist activities in Britain and Soviet diplomacy, which had been *de facto* recognized, was abandoned. It was agreed to oppose the appointment of a successor to Krasin because of hostile Soviet activities in Britain,[42] and to reconsider the future of Anglo-Soviet relations after the Christmas recess.

The Russians helplessly watched the speedy deterioration. They seem to have lost confidence in their ability to manipulate the Foreign Office through pressure in the City. Their only hope was that the 'sober-minded in business circles' in Britain, who realized that it was 'essential to improve relations with Russia', would secure a normal flow of trade.[43] The frustration found full expression in Chicherin's review of Soviet foreign policy in 1926. With regard to Britain he acknowledged that the efforts to reach direct understanding had failed. Russia had 'stretched out a hand for peace', he concluded, but this hand 'remains in the air'.[44]

The disappointing response from ARJAC

The general strike was certainly ill-timed from the point of view of Russian diplomacy. Simultaneously with intensive diplomatic activities to forestall reprisals, the Russians retreated from their involuntary commitment to a revolutionary posture, hoping to secure massive support from British trade unions in defence of Soviet Russia.[45] The strike, however, had seriously impaired the effectiveness of the alliance. There was little likelihood that the General Council, closely associated with alleged Russian plots to overthrow the British Government, weakened by its defeat in the strike and a target for abuse from the Russians themselves, would wholeheartedly stand by the Soviet Union in an hour of need. Moreover, any move towards reactivating ARJAC as a diplomatic weapon had to be made obliquely in view of the opposition's denunciation of the Politburo's opportunist use of

[41] *The Times*, 15 Dec. 1926.
[42] Cab. 23/53 65(26)3.
[43] Leaders in *Izvestiya*, 7 and 12 Dec. 1926.
[44] Chicherin, *Stat'i*, pp. 487–90, 8 Dec. 1926.
[45] See for example leader in *Pravda*, 29 June 1926, and Gurovich, *Vseobshchaya Stachka*, pp. 177–80.

the committee. The future activities of ARJAC were therefore impeded by the emphasis which the Russians had to lay, at least outwardly, on the revolutionary character of the collaboration.

An opening to revive the committee presented itself at the end of June, when a conference of the executives of unions affiliated to the TUC effected a reconciliation with the miners and promised to assist them in the continuation of their struggle.[46] The Russians, who had consistently championed the miners, seized the moment to seek an urgent meeting of ARJAC 'in view of the exacerbation of the struggle of the Bourgeois forces against the strike'.[47] This call, unlike earlier assistance to the miners, was not motivated exclusively by fraternal concern for the miners' sufferings. It was to a considerable degree a response to national interests.

Before ARJAC had even met, serious doubts were expressed about its capacity to inject new life into the strike.[48] Yet no suggestions were made that the proposed meeting could be utilized to expose the weaknesses of the General Council and press for the dissolution of the committee. The meeting was justified on the grounds that the measures taken by the Conservative Government against the miners were 'strongly linked with the anti-Soviet campaign' and part of a comprehensive capitalist assault. Lozovsky himself, who had not let slip a single chance to admonish the General Council, agreed that even if the committee failed to fulfil its immediate expectations it would still remain 'a symbol of friendship and fraternity between the British and Soviet proletariats'.[49]

The General Council, which had understandably failed to grasp the intricacy of Soviet politics, was perplexed by the AUCCTU's ambiguous attitude, preferring to adopt delaying tactics.[50] Citrine, therefore, responded to the AUCCTU's in-

[46] MFGB, *Annual Volume of Proceedings for the Year 1926*, pp. 1247–70.

[47] TUC archives, B 113/134: Dogadov to Citrine, 28 June 1926.

[48] See leaders by Pepper, member of presidium of IKKI, in *Pravda*, 30 June 1926, and by Lozovsky in *ibid.*, 3 July 1926.

[49] Leader in *Trud*, 30 June 1926; Lozovsky in *Kras. Int. Prof.*, No. 7, 6 July 1926, pp. 7–9.

[50] TUC archives, *Minutes of Financial and General Purposes Committee, 1925–6*, Meeting 13, 25 June 1926. Citrine complained to the AUCCTU on 16 June about Tomsky's 'misleading and innaccurate' representation of the strike: TUC archives, B 132 13/7/23.

itiative with a non-committal promise that the request would be dealt with 'as soon as possible'.[51] Citrine's reply alarmed the Russians; vulnerable to opposition at home and embroiled in a diplomatic crisis, they could not permit another blow from the General Council. Strenuous efforts were now made to secure a meeting of ARJAC by emphasizing the fact that the miners' strike was in its 'crucial stage'.[52] The NMM, assuming the mantle of the discarded left wing of the TUC,[53] addressed the Miners' Federation with a request to exert pressure on the General Council to convene ARJAC. This was followed by a second telegram from Dogadov to Citrine on 3 July demanding in strong terms the 'acceleration' of the General Council's decision.[54]

In the meantime the Russians had begun to look for a 'supplementary stronghold'[55] in the British trade union movement to deter the General Council from terminating the collaboration. On 7 July representatives of the Russian miners met James Cook, Secretary of the Miners' Federation, and W. Richardson, its Treasurer, in Berlin and laid the foundation for an Anglo-Russian Miners' Committee. Several resolutions were moved on the organization of international assistance to the miners, but most significant for the Russians was an urgent call for the immediate convening of ARJAC.[56] This move, however, was superfluous as the General Council had meanwhile 'carefully discussed' Dogadov's telegrams and had agreed on a meeting of ARJAC. Nevertheless another anxious week passed before the Russians were informed of the General Council's willingness to meet them in Paris at the end of July.[57]

The Russians proposed to put on the agenda of the meeting

[51] TUC archives, B 113/134: Citrine to Dogadov, 29 June 1926.

[52] A leader in *Pravda*, 4 July 1926, commented: 'The issue of saving the miners is now entirely in the hands of the international proletariat.'

[53] Nin in *Kras. Int. Prof.* (1926), No. 8, pp. 131–32.

[54] *Pravda*, 29 June 1926: reproduction of NMM's letter; TUC archives, B 113/134: Dogadov to Citrine.

[55] Bukharin in *XV Konferentsiya VKP*, p. 95.

[56] F.O. 371 11328 C7660 and C7836/7660/18: Addison, Berlin Embassy, to Chamberlain on miners' meeting, 8 and 10 July 1926. See also *Mezh. Rabo. Dviz.*, No. 28, 15 July 1926.

[57] TUC archives, *Minutes of Financial and General Purposes Committee, 1925–6*, Meeting 14, 6 July 1926; TUC archives, B 113 18/2/42: Citrine to members of the International Committee of the GC, 7 July 1926.

the issue of aid to the miners in order to guarantee a 'common language' and avoid mutual recriminations on the conduct of the strike.[58] Indeed, Tomsky, who as a signatory of the AUCCTU's condemnation of the General Council was a victim of circumstances, was prevented from participating in the delegation on dubious grounds of ill-health. Moreover, a letter addressed by him to the meeting made no secret that Russia's prime objective was to ensure that the General Council would 'stand unswervingly at the advanced post of the struggle against imperialist wars'. He not only avoided repetition of the accusations made in the June declaration but urged the continuation of the collaboration, 'disregarding the differences' between the two movements.[59]

These aspirations suffered a grave reversal at the outset of the meeting in Paris on 30 July. The Russians were informed that the General Council was doubtful whether it 'ought to continue participating in this Council'. Pugh followed this up by accusing Russia of interference in the TUC's domestic policies and misrepresenting the original aims of ARJAC. He ended with the ultimatum that future contacts would depend on Tomsky's repudiation of all his 'charges and insults'.[60]

The General Council's implacable position confused Andreev, who seems to have been uncertain whether to enter into polemics with the British on their conduct during the strike or to concentrate on the immediate Russian objections. As a result he delivered a somewhat schizophrenic speech in which Lozovsky's revolutionary outbursts and Tomsky's diplomatic overtures were discernible in turn. Yet it was crystal clear which was the predominant component. His appeal to adopt a 'class policy of proletarian defence' was avowedly based on the conviction that the defeat of the miners would 'signal the offensive of capitalism in all countries'. Russia was particularly susceptible as the British Government wished to vent on it 'all their malice' for the assistance granted to the strikers.[61] Dogadov, conscious of the hostility of the British delegates, assured them that there would be 'no control, no dictation, no interference in the affairs of the

[58] Andreev, *Anglo-Russkii Komitet*, p. 17.

[59] TUC archives, B 113: handwritten note by Tomsky to Andreev and enclosed letter to ARJAC, 21 July 1926.

[60] *Paris–Berlin Meetings*, pp. 2–5.

[61] *ibid.*, pp. 3–8; Andreev, *Anglo-Russkii Komitet*, pp. 10–11.

British trade unions'; the Russians wished only to pursue the activities of ARJAC 'along the lines laid down originally'.[62]

A long day of futile debate ended with the British delegates insisting that discussion of the aid to the miners would do 'more harm than good'. Even long-standing allies like Purcell, who had maintained before the meeting that it would be 'the gravest historical mistake' to jeopardize the existence of the committee, now followed the majority in refusing further collaboration until the issue of a *démenti* by the AUCCTU. However, as both sides wished to reach some sort of conclusion it was agreed to adjourn for the night to enable Andreev to consult Moscow by cable; it was also hoped that the two delegations would redraft their statements to ensure the issue of a joint declaration at the end of the meeting.[63]

The result of the consultations was the relegation of the miners' issue to an even less prominent position. The Russians called upon the British delegation to take heed of the Conservative Government's intentions 'to revenge themselves on the workers of the Soviet Republics' and condemn any moves directed towards 'new wars and new attacks on the USSR'.[64] The British delegation, however, distrustful of the Russians' conciliatory mood, apparently chose this occasion to demonstrate that they were not so easily manipulated. They reiterated that a repudiation of the AUCCTU'S declaration was a *sine qua non* for the preservation of ARJAC.

The Russians' dejection at their failure to restore cordial relations with the General Council was evident in the suppression of all reports on the meeting until the AUCCTU had reviewed it. Their only comfort was that before the adjournment of the meeting for a month, to allow the two sides to reconsider their position, Purcell had assured them that the danger to the existence of ARJAC had receded.[65]

Oddly enough, the CPGB also joined in the protest against

[62] *Paris–Berlin Meetings*, pp. 11–16. His speech was drastically condensed in the General Council's version circulated to the unions; see *Russia and International Unity*, pp. 9–10.

[63] *Trade Union Unity* (Aug. 1926), No. 6, p. 81; *Paris–Berlin Meetings*, pp. 16–17 and 26–27.

[64] *Paris–Berlin Meetings*, pp. 27 and 29–30.

[65] *ibid.*, pp. 30–31.

the AUCCTU's declaration.[66] This demonstrated, however, that united-front tactics had finally struck root in the Party's political programme and were closely associated with the defence of Russian interests. The report submitted to the CPGB's congress in October maintained that the Party had unhesitatingly exposed the betrayal of the left wing of the General Council during the general strike. However, the Party's lessons of the strike, issued at the end of May, while adopting in general terms IKKI's theses, displayed a lenient attitude towards the left wing.[67] On the eve of the Paris meeting, when the political fate of former allies like Purcell and Hicks had been determined by the Russians, the CPGB still left them the option of winning back 'the honourable title of "left wingers"'.[68] The CPGB was left in the dark about both the events leading up to the AUCCTU's declaration and the precautions taken by the Russians to prevent the dissolution of the committee. As a result, in a debate on the collaboration policy in the presidium of IKKI on 7 August, Murphy ironically found himself passionately defending ARJAC against Stalin on the grounds that it 'might prove useful in the campaign against the Government's policy of breaking off relations with Russia'.[69] Murphy also argued that for tactical reasons Comintern and Profintern should have served as the channels for criticism of the General Council rather than the AUCCTU, which was associated with the Soviet Government.

The clash with Murphy suggests that Stalin chose this moment to immunize the Politburo against the opposition's accusations of opportunism and their criticism of the proceedings in Paris. Stalin could afford a revolutionary posture as a result of the assurances he had received in Paris that there was no immediate threat to the committee. In fact, Stalin attributed this undertaking to pressure exerted by the AUCCTU on the General

66 Stalin, *Sochineniya*, Vol. 8, p. 194, mentions a letter from the CPGB to the central committee of the CPSU after the Paris meeting.

67 CPGB, *The Eighth Congress of the Communist Party of Great Britain*, p. 9; the lessons of the strike, adopted by the CPGB's executive committee on 31 May, are in *Workers' Weekly*, 4 June 1926. See also Palme Dutt in *Inprecorr*, 20 May 1926.

68 *Workers' Weekly*, 11 June 1926. See also *ibid.*, 18 June 1926, and Campbell in *Comm. Rev.* (July 1926), p. 112.

69 Murphy, *New Horizons*, pp. 226–29.

Council through its 'most active support of the miners'.[70] Even after the confrontation, the CPGB was slow to fall into line; for a while it retained an ill-defined attitude towards the left wing. The door was left open for Purcell and Hicks to make 'a clear break with the past in both words and deeds'[71] in the forthcoming Berlin meeting.

An extraordinary session of the AUCCTU was convened shortly after the meeting of the IKKI presidium and heard an unusually detailed report by Andreev on the proceedings in Paris. These revelations were made, without the consent of the British delegates,[72] on the assumption that the Russians' massive assistance to the miners would deter the General Council from drastically altering the nature of the alliance.[73] The principal object of Andreev's speech, therefore, was to prevent the suppression of the proposals to step up the relief for the miners introducd by the Russians in Paris.[74] The representatives of the major unions unanimously urged the preservation of the committee even 'against the will' of its British members, in view of the 'capitalist offensive, gaining momentum from day to day'. At the same time they unrepentantly reiterated the charges against the General Council, which according to one of the speakers 'deserved a beating and not a declaration'.[75]

The AUCCTU's session coincided with a period of increasing friction on the diplomatic front. Full use was made of the 'punitive steps' taken by the British Government in reprisal for the Russian assistance to the miners in order to entreat the General Council not to 'weaken the workers' resistance to capitalist attempts to wage war against the Soviet Union'.[76] Yet another demonstration of support for the committee was a special

[70] Stalin, *Sochineniya*, Vol. 8, pp. 194–99.

[71] *Workers' Weekly*, 20 and 27 Aug. 1926.

[72] *Paris–Berlin Meetings*, p. 31.

[73] Leader in *Pravda*, 18 Aug. 1926; similar views are reflected in *Workers' Weekly*, 27 Aug. 1926.

[74] Andreev, *Anglo-Russkii Komitet*, pp. 8–9 and 23–26; resolution of session in *Pravda*, 13 Aug. 1926.

[75] Full report of the debate in *Trud*, 13 and 14 Aug. 1926.

[76] Leader in *Pravda*, 12 Aug. 1926; fears that the General Council might 'loosen the ties of friendship between the Russians and the British' in the Berlin meeting are also expressed in a leader in *ibid.*, 18 Aug. 1926.

meeting of the Moscow trade union organization, in which repeated references were made to the 'danger of wars'.[77]

Meanwhile final arrangements were under way for resumption of the ARJAC meeting. The Russians explicitly renewed their demand that the miners' strike should head the agenda. They had ostentatiously forwarded a further twenty thousand pounds to the strike fund, while the executive bureau of Profintern condemned Amsterdam for its failure to raise similar assistance.[78]

The reconvening of ARJAC on 23 August in Berlin was overclouded from the start by the General Council's rage at the Russians' revelation and interpretation of the proceedings of the previous meeting. The General Council, refusing to be side-tracked, accused the Russians of attempting to distort the scope of the committee; they demanded a review of the whole constitution of ARJAC. The Russians refused to comply, having received 'definite instructions to discuss the aid to the miners first'.

After a long hard day of bitter exchanges, Pugh yielded to the Russians to avert deadlock.[79] Andreev then produced a fourteen-point plan for intensifying the miners' struggle which involved the prevention of blacklegging of coal shipments to Britain, appeals to different international trade union organizations and drastic methods of organizing financial support. Innocuous though this seems, it was correctly recognized by Pugh as an indirect attack on the General Council for having 'no idea of what was going on in Great Britain' and for taking 'no steps whatsoever, not even to discuss any measures'. He categorically refused to accept this programme, which he believed had 'nothing new to offer'.[80] Andreev's long 'frank' speech, which even Swales could only describe as rude, now suggested that the General Council's delegates had prevented ARJAC from taking 'any decision which would lead to an extension and increase of the aid' to the striking miners.[81]

77 *Trud*, 18 Aug. 1926.

78 *Pravda*, 17 Aug. 1926.

79 *Paris–Berlin Meetings*, pp. 33–40 and 44–46.

80 *ibid.*, pp. 46–48 and 51–54. Ugarov, a member of the Russian delegation, openly made such accusations in an interview in *Pravda*, 31 Aug. 1926.

81 *Paris–Berlin Meetings*, pp. 54–57.

Although Andreev's speech caused much resentment among the British delegates, it did not lead to a breakdown in the negotiations. With the TUC congress only a fortnight ahead the British delegation seemed determined to avoid adding a 'Russian issue' to the already controversial question of the general strike. In order to straighten matters out, Citrine somewhat ingenuously proposed that the issue of the help to the miners could be solved if the Russians, in return for an expression of gratitude for their assistance, would endorse the General Council's statement that they were doing their utmost in support of the miners. However, a subsequent speech by Pugh, though sharing Melnichansky's 'disappointment at the way that Amsterdam acted', sought to reconcile the AUCCTU with the IFTU.[82]

In the evening of the last session the Russians responded with harsh criticism of the attitude of the British delegates to ARJAC and demanded the recording of 'the patent unwillingness of the British delegates that ARJAC should pass resolutions intended to strengthen the aid for the miners'. However, at the eleventh hour the Russians were forced to relax their constant pressure when A. Findlay,[83] who had up to now refrained from participating in the discussion, diverted it to a new path. He stated that he believed Russian tactics consisted of heaping pressure on the General Council through the miners and, as they hoped, the whole of the rank and file of the TUC. Findlay warned that these tactics, of which the Russians had grossly inflated expectations, 'gravely prejudiced' the existence of ARJAC.[84]

The Russians, aware that these allegations struck a responsive chord in the British delegates, moderated their reproaches and brought the meeting to an inconclusive end by declaring that ARJAC's popularity in Russia guaranteed the continuation of the collaboration policy. In order to deprive the General Council of grounds for dissolving the committee, they endorsed without a murmur a resolution put forward by the British which called for a conference between Amsterdam and the AUCCTU rather

[82] *ibid.*, pp. 57–59, 62–64 and 79–81.

[83] TUC library, CT/P: Findlay, a member of the 1924 delegation to Russia, had become disenchanted with Russia and sided with Citrine and Bevin in curtailing Soviet influence in the TUC.

[84] *Paris–Berlin Meetings*, pp. 83 and 85–86.

than Profintern; Russian policy had previously insisted on the latter.[85]

The Paris-Berlin meetings marked the termination of the friendly relationship between the British and Soviet trade union representatives, although for a while neither side was inclined to dismantle the framework of the collaboration. In view of the impending TUC and NMM annual congresses, Andreev hastened to report to the plenum of the AUCCTU. The bulk of his speech was taken up by a denunciation of the attitude of the British delegation to Berlin, which 'wholly and fully confirmed the correctness of the criticism' which the Russians had levelled against the General Council after the strike. However, although Andreev complained that ARJAC had deteriorated into a 'talking-shop', the plenum resolution vigorously advocated the preservation of the committee on the grounds of its powers to 'struggle against the offensive of capitalism, win over the workers, achieve international trade union unity' and last but not least 'oppose the preparation of new imperialist wars'.[86]

Once again Andreev's report received wide publication in Britain to prevent the General Council from suppressing the Berlin proceedings.[87] The task of castigating the General Council was, however, transferred to Profintern, which described the British delegates in Berlin as defenders of the mine owners, 'behaving not as representatives of the toilers but as those of the bourgeoisie'. In order to contrast the General Council's erratic support of the miners with the Russians' devotion to their cause, Profintern adopted some of the measures proposed by the AUCCTU in Berlin: it imposed a levy of 1% of the wages of its affiliated members for the miners' fund, and called for further assistance.[88]

85 *ibid.*, pp. 86–93; Andreev, *Anglo-Russkii Komitet*, pp. 48–49.

86 *Anglo-Russkii Komitet*, pp. 50–52; resolution in *Trud*, 1 Sept. 1926. The CPGB immediately echoed Andreev's criticism in *Workers' Weekly*, 3 Sept. 1926: 'Sending delegates at decent intervals to sit at a table is not worth a brass farthing.'

87 Andreev's report in *Inprecorr* and *The Times*, 2 Sept. 1926. The AUCCTU's declaration of 7 June 1926 had been reprinted in *Trade Union Bulletin*, Nos. 7–8, 1 Aug. 1926.

88 *Kras. Int. Prof.* (1926), Nos. 9–10, pp. 410–11: appeal of Profintern to the AUCCTU and reply, 1 Sept. 1926. A meeting of the Moscow trade union organization showed the temporary *modus vivendi* between Tomsky and Lozovsky; see *Trud*, 9 Sept. 1926.

ARJAC survives reappraisal

In the initial stages of the trade union collaboration, the allies had been expected to fulfil both revolutionary and diplomatic tasks. However, the Russians' failure in Berlin to reach any tangible understanding with the General Council hastened the implementation of the new tactics of united front exclusively from below, inaugurated after the end of the general strike. In spite of this, apprehensions of an imminent rupture of Anglo-Soviet relations preserved ARJAC, an archetypal united front from above, from immediate liquidation.

In the Bournemouth TUC congress, held on 6–11 September, little of the solidarity and fraternal feelings shown towards Russia on previous occasions was discernible. On the contrary, it demonstrated the General Council's determination to circumscribe Russian meddling in TUC affairs. The General Council's decision not to raise the questions of either the general strike or the proceedings of ARJAC, combined with Joynson-Hicks' god-sent refusal of visas to the Russian delegation, left the congress with plain sailing. Pugh's single reference to the strike in his address, to the effect that the General Council did not intend 'to hold up life in the country', stood in sharp contrast with the Russian position.[89] Indeed, the Russians had contemplated taking the floor in the congress to reproach the General Council for its 'treacherous' activities. A speech by Tomsky destined for Bournemouth was instead delivered in an extraordinary meeting of the Moscow trade union organization. He spared no criticism of the General Council's refusal to recognize the political character of the strike and re-affirmed the AUCCTU's 'duty to "interfere"' in the national as well as international affairs of the British trade unions.[90] The main message of his speech was also included in a telegram to the TUC, which was regarded as a 'sensational

89 TUC, *Report of Proceedings at the Fifty-Eighth Annual Trades Union Congress* (London, 1926), pp. 71–73. Pugh's views were shared by Clynes, *Memoirs*, p. 96, who was convinced that political solutions were reached 'through the ballot-box, and not through violence or resistance'. Thomas' 'ballot-box' solution is in *My Story*, p. 108.

90 Meeting of 8 Sept. reported in *Izvestiya*, 18 and 19 Sept. 1926. Almost identical views were expressed by Lozovsky in *Mezh. Rabo. Dviz.*, No. 36, 6 Sept. 1926.

indictment' of the General Council.[91] It accused the General Council of sabotaging the miners' strike and of displaying a 'bend-the-knee' attitude towards the Government. Although it was not discussed by the congress, a short reply was adopted, condemning the 'ill-instructed and presumptuous' criticism.[92]

In view of the obvious setbacks suffered by the collaboration policy, the Russians were searching for a way of separating their diplomatic and revolutionary aims without admitting past mistakes. The CPGB, which had committed similar errors, was chosen as a scapegoat. Stalin's clash with Murphy over ARJAC in IKKI in July was used by the Russians to coerce the CPGB into a theatrical confession.[93] This was initiated immediately after Bournemouth by Murphy in Moscow, and was directed in the first place against the vacillating attitude of the CPGB towards the left wing in ARJAC. Murphy admitted that the Party held an 'insufficiently critical attitude' towards ARJAC, venerating it as a formal alliance of leaderships while it was in fact 'a straightforward organizational expression of a bloc between the Soviet and British proletariats'.[94] Following Murphy's example, the CPGB came to heel, condemning not only the General Council but also popular left-wing leaders such as Cook; it was suggested that the General Council had succeeded in 'harnessing Cook to their chariot'.[95]

To suggest that the self-accusations and the repudiation of the left wing in the General Council provoked heated controversy within the CPGB or between the Party and Comintern is to overlook the degree of submission of the CPGB to Moscow and the unpopularity of the collaboration policy in the CPGB

[91] So described in M. Cole (ed.), *Beatrice Webb's Diaries* (London, 1956), p. 118, but also correctly evaluated as a 'magnificent futility'.

[92] TUC library, HD 6350: copy of Tomsky's telegram and reply.

[93] This tendency was also discernible in the 7th plenum of IKKI; see *Puti Mirovoi Revolyutsii*, Vol. 1: Kuusinen, p. 129; Gallacher, p. 188.

[94] *Bol'shevik*, No. 18, 30 Sept. 1926, p. 8; *Komm. Int.* (1926), No. 2, pp. 8–9 and 12.

[95] Palme Dutt in *Inprecorr*, 23 Sept. 1926; *Workers' Weekly*, 17 Sept. 1926. See also *Workers' Weekly*, 24 Sept. and 1 Oct. 1926, for a dismissal of Purcell and others as 'active promoters and defenders of a policy of reaction'. The Russians refrained from fierce attacks on Cook until after it had become clear that the miners' strike was collapsing; see Lozovsky in *Pravda*, 26 Oct. 1926.

at any time.[96] Even the mild criticism levelled against the Party in the seventh plenum of IKKI was designed to vindicate the guidance provided by the Russians and Comintern in the establishment of a correct attitude towards the left wing. Otherwise Bukharin did not stint his praise of the Party for its impressive development, while Kuusinen referred to it as the 'most prized' section in Comintern.[97]

The radicalization of Russian policy in the trade unions was expressed in the controversy over the leadership. A message from Profintern to the NMM conference, at the end of August, called upon the NMM to purge the General Council of 'traitors, renegades and capitulators'. Profintern, finding itself free of the shackles previously imposed by the AUCCTU, announced a new era in which the NMM would replace the official leadership of the TUC by 'consolidating in an organizational form' its influence in the trade unions.[98]

The new militant policy was expressed clearly through the CPGB, bursting with confidence as a result of the sudden increase in its membership, during its conference which met on 16 and 17 October. Bell, presiding over the meeting, introduced the slogan 'Communism or Capitalism', excluding any alternatives. The conference adopted IKKI's thesis on 'opportunist errors' and on 'confusion within the Left Wing' and recognized the CPGB's role as that of providing through the NMM a new leadership for the TUC.[99]

In spite of the establishment of a clear line on the issue of leadership, Comintern's failure to produce a comprehensive British policy left two important questions in disarray: the attitude to the Labour Party and the future of the collaboration

96 For a representative view see Macfarlane, *The British Communist Party*, p. 175.

97 *Puti Mirovoi Revolyutsii*, Vol. II: resolution, p. 428; *ibid.*, Vol. I: Bukharin, p. 105, and Kuusinen, p. 129. See also review of plenum in *Komm. Int.* (1926), No. 15, pp. 4–6.

98 NMM, *Report of the Third Annual Conference, August 28th and 29th 1926* (London, 1926), p. 14. Zubok, sharing with Levin the direction of British affairs in Executive Bureau of Profintern, in *Mezh. Rabo. Dviz.*, No. 35, 2 Sept. 1926. See also Martin, *Communism and the British Trade Unions*, p. 73.

99 Bell's speech in *Workers' Weekly*, 22 Oct. 1926; IKKI's manifesto to the CPGB in *Pravda*, 27 Oct. 1926; *The English Congress of the CPGB*, pp. 67 and 73–79.

between the British and Soviet trade union movements. The ambivalent attitude towards Labour was apparent in the fact that the CPGB, faced with the alternative of the increasingly severe Conservative Government, regarded the installation of even a moderate Labour Government as an event of revolutionary significance.[100] This was by no means consistent with the CPGB's devastating attack on Labour, particularly for the conduct of its annual conference at Margate soon after the TUC had met.[101]

The uncertainty surrounding the future of ARJAC, however, was a weightier factor in Anglo-Soviet relations. At the TUC congress in Bournemouth it was admitted that the General Council had failed to come across 'any tangible evidence' that the IFTU had agreed to participate in a conference with the Russians. Purcell, certainly the most energetic supporter of the alliance in the General Council, nevertheless opposed Russian demands for a world congress, as this was likely 'to put International Trade Union unity many years off'. There was little dissent from Purcell's statement that the road should be made 'easy for the Russians to come in under the umbrella' of the IFTU.[102]

Tomsky had few hopes from Bournemouth. He realized that as a result of Russian absence from the congress the General Council would 'gain complete control and exert full influence' over the trade unions' international policy. However, despite the ideological conflict he remained convinced, as his message to the TUC stated, that the British working class, which had more than once 'held back the mailed fist of the British capitalists hanging over the Workers' State', would repeat this in the 'hour of trial'.[103] The Russians' confidence was partly based on the assumption that the NMM would exert sufficient pressure to uphold Soviet interests. Indeed, the NMM, less vulnerable than the CPGB to accusations of dependence on Moscow, demonstrated in its annual conference that the diplomatic aspects of trade

100 *Comm. Rev.* (Nov. 1926), p. 340; Murphy in *Pravda*, 2 Sept. 1926.

101 *Komm. Int.*, No. 7, 21 Oct. 1926, pp. 19–20; H. Pollitt in CPGB, *What Margate Means* (London, n.d.), pp. 4 and 10–12.

102 TUC, *Report of Proceedings at the Fifty-Eighth Annual Trades Union Congress:* report of the GC, p. 89; Purcell, pp. 437–39.

103 TUC library, HD 6350. See Tomsky interviewed in *Pravda*, *Izvestiya* and *Trud*, 5 Sept. 1926.

union unity were an integral part of its political programme. The consolidation of ARJAC was specifically cited as the correct means of counteracting the menace of new wars, 'but even more direct and sinister the danger of the Conservatives' attack on Russia'.[104]

Melnichansky's assertion that the General Council had throughout remained loyal to the AUCCTU but hostile to Profintern was a more realistic evaluation of the proceedings in Bournemouth.[105] The General Council's wish to continue and cultivate relations was based not so much on fraternal feelings or internationalist ideals as on practical domestic interests; these ironically coincided with the arguments which had tipped the scales against a rupture in Cabinet. Ideological affinity was steadily yielding to economic considerations. In Bournemouth this was reflected in Pugh's address, which praised the General Council's 'continual effort to further the development of economic relations' with Russia, which had always been recognized as vital for easing the soaring unemployment in England.[106]

The fifteenth conference of the CPSU, which met between 25 October and 3 November, shed light on the radicalization of Comintern's policies in Britain and on the new revolutionary outlook towards ARJAC. Bukharin, who had just succeeded Zinoviev as the head of Comintern,[107] admitted that ARJAC had been 'a most important feature of Soviet international policy' in the search for trade union unity. However, as a result of the sharpening class struggle, he called for the transfer of the temporary authority which the AUCCTU had enjoyed in this sphere to the accredited hands of Profintern. Bukharin's speech initiated a flood of letters from 'bewildered' delegates expressing concern over the apparent abandonment of ARJAC. Bukharin swiftly corrected this misconception, re-establishing the validity of united

[104] NMM, *Report of the Third Annual Conference*, pp. 32–33 and 68; Lozovsky in *Pravda*, 12 Sept. 1926.

[105] *Trud*, 22 Sept. 1926.

[106] *Report of 58th TUC*: report of GC, pp. 246–47; Pugh, p. 76. See also L. L. Lorwin, *Labor and Internationalism* (New York, 1929), p. 322, and Miller, *Socialism and Foreign Policy*, pp. 176–77.

[107] *KPSS v Rezolyutsiyakh i Resheniyakh*, Vol. 3, p. 361. According to J. Humbert-Droz, *De Lénine à Staline* (Neuchâtel, 1971), p. 266, Bukharin never achieved the title of president of Comintern which Zinoviev had held.

front tactics.[108] Lozovsky further attempted to smooth over the misunderstanding by describing the immediate tasks allotted to the committee: 'to gain influence over the English working-class movement' and to challenge its present leadership.

The new militancy received even fuller expression a month later in the plenum of Comintern when Profintern supplanted the AUCCTU. The NMM, defined as placed 'under the political leadership of the Communist Party', was called upon to give correct guidance to ARJAC.[109] Tomsky acknowledged the changing of the guard. The bulk of his report on the activities of the trade unions, a subject for long debate in the central committee, was devoted to the role of the unions in the industrialization of Russia and other domestic problems. He dealt only perfunctorily with the new objectives of ARJAC, stating that work in this field should proceed 'under the guidance' of the central committee of the Party. However, his scepticism about the ability of the British communists to gain the confidence of the masses was evident.[110]

The decision to give ARJAC a new face did not conceal from the opposition the underlying unchanged motives for its preservation. Bukharin's thesis on the 'unsteady and uneven' state of the stabilization of capitalism was seized upon by the opposition, which called for an intensification of revolutionary activities in the West; the dissolution of ARJAC would be a landmark in that direction. This sporadic criticism was dismissed by Mikoyan for its opportunism and its use as 'a weapon in the struggle against the party'.[111]

The priority given to the construction of socialism in Russia[112] fitted in well with the earlier discussion on the threat of new wars.

108 *XV Konferentsiya VKP*, pp. 38 and 95–96.

109 Lozovsky in *ibid.*, p. 313, and in *Puti Mirovoi Revolyutsii*, Vol. 1, p. 498. See also Murphy in *Puti Mirovoi Revolyutsii*, Vol. 1, p. 486.

110 On the discussion of Tomsky's thesis in the central committee of the CPSU see *Trud*, 22 Oct. 1926, and *Inprecorr*, 28 Oct. 1926; Tomsky's speech, *XV Konferentsiya VKP*, p. 295.

111 *XV Konferentsiya VKP*: Bukharin, pp. 5–6; Zinoviev, p. 565; Mikoyan, p. 683. In Party history the opposition is blamed for failing to recognize the 'uneven stabilization' and embarking instead on a '"revolutionary" position of adventures and putsches'; see N. V. Ruban, 'Bor′ba Partii Protiv Trotskistsko-Zinov′evskoi Oppozitsii', *Voprosy Istorii KPSS* (1958), No. 5, p. 133.

112 *XV Konferentsiya VKP*: Stalin, p. 440; resolution, pp. 815–16.

Manuilsky had introduced the topic with an appeal to Comintern to resist 'pacifist illusions', while Bukharin warned of external attempts to disturb the process of implementing socialism in Russia.[113] However, it was Stalin who gave the most lucid and candid explanation of Russian expectations from the Western workers in anticipating the danger of 'a military intervention': 'So far it is a fact that the workers of the capitalist countries are not in a position to support our revolution with a revolution against their own capitalists. Yet it is also a fact that the capitalists are unable to recruit "their" workers for a war against our Republic . . . On this sympathy now rests the international situation of our Republic. Without it we should now be facing constant new attempts at intervention and interruption of our construction work, without the benefits of our "breathing-space".'[114]

The meeting of the seventh plenum of IKKI, from 22 November to 16 December, represented a crossroads on the way towards a left-wing policy, recognized a year later as the 'third period' in Comintern.[115] However, with the opposition still lurking in the background the CPSU could not admit that the stabilization of capitalism had halted without contradicting the theoretical basis for the construction of socialism in Russia. In a long speech to the plenum, supplemented by an essay, Bukharin tried to reconcile the priority given to the Soviet Union with the radical international outlook prompted by the uneven stabilization of capitalism. The period was characterized by occasional eruptions of social unrest which were not irrelevant episodes but an

[113] *ibid.*: Manuilsky, pp. 51–54; Bukharin, p. 92.

[114] *ibid.*, pp. 440–41.

[115] B. C. Hopper, 'Narkomindel and Comintern', *Foreign Affairs* (July 1942), dates the turning-point as late as 1928 and ascribes it to Stalin. Degras, 'United Front Tactics', pp. 20–22, agrees on this date but rightly attributes the new policy to changing attitudes in the trade unions. Humbert-Droz, *De Lénine à Staline*, p. 281, overestimates Bukharin's role as the architect of the policy, totally ignoring Lozovsky. T. Draper, 'The Strange Case of Comintern', *Survey* (1972), Vol. 18, No. 3, thoroughly examines the origins of the period. He correctly dates them in mid-1926 but overlooks the impact of the general strike (pp. 102–103). He incorrectly suggests that the formula 'class against class' first appeared only in late 1927 (p. 111); this was coined by Lozovsky in the course of the general strike (see *supra*, pp. 155–56). Lozovsky repeated this epithet in IKKI's plenum; see *infra*, p. 206.

indication of the steady deterioration of capitalism. The task of the world proletariat was therefore to foster these revolutionary outbreaks whenever they occurred. At present Bukharin observed such situations in Britain and in China, but ranked them below the construction of a socialist economy in the Soviet Union. Russia was in the best position 'to curb the process of capitalist development'.[116]

Once the hierarchy of revolutionary aims had been fixed the plenum could indulge in panegyrics on the recent events in Britain. Lozovsky, who was perhaps more than anybody responsible for the sharp antagonism in the British trade unions after the general strike, went further than Bukharin in welcoming the new era. The strike had caused a regrouping of the class structure in Britain in which for the first time 'class stood against class'.[117] This was expanded in the resolution on the situation in Britain. As a result of the growing influence of the diehards among the Conservatives and the capitulation of the trade union bureaucracy, who were now 'siding with the capitalists', class-conscious workers were coalescing in the revolutionary organizations.[118]

For a time, however, the theoretical juggling left intact united front tactics in the trade unions. These were fully justified by both Stalin and Bukharin, who nevertheless stressed the prominent role of Profintern and the revolutionary unions in their implementation.[119] As in the previous Party conference, however, a more realistic interpretation was forthcoming. Lozovsky himself, reviewing the plenum, explained that tactics aimed at winning over the masses were essential so long as reaction was prevalent and posed a threat to the USSR.[120]

Significantly, in its opening session the plenum heard greetings from a communist member of the Moscow garrison. In reply, V. Kolarov, a Bulgarian member of the presidium, launched into

116 *Puti Mirovoi Revolyutsii*, Vol. I, pp. 28–29, 40 and 92–96.

117 *ibid.*, pp. 492–93.

118 *ibid.*, Vol. II, pp. 423–24. See also Gallacher's report for the CPGB in *ibid.*, Vol. I, p. 564.

119 *ibid.*: Bukharin, p. 104; *ibid.*, Vol. II: Stalin, pp. 21–22. Bell, *ibid.*, Vol. I, pp. 236–37, defined the tactics as 'tearing the workers from the influence of the Social Democrat organizations'.

120 *Mezh. Rabo. Dviz.*, No. 1, 6 Jan. 1927. For a discussion of the threat of war see pp. 231–40.

a description of the diplomatic blocs created in the West to crush the Soviet Union. It was the urgent duty of the world proletariat 'to repel any assault directed against the USSR'.[121] Stalin pursued the line he had expounded in the Party conference, maintaining that the construction of socialism in Russia would mean 'the improvement of the revolutionary position of the world proletariat in the struggle with capitalism'. Yet the prerequisite for this was the safety of the Soviet Union and the forestalling of new interventions.[122]

In the seventh congress of the Soviet trade unions, which overlapped the IKKI plenum in Moscow, it became apparent that the organization of world support was entrusted to Profintern while the AUCCTU's resources were directed to the domestic scene to ensure the acceleration of the implementation of socialism in Russia.[123] However, in view of the continuous talk of the danger of war, even Lozovsky devoted part of his speech to the validity of united front tactics and the need to continue with the collaboration policy.[124] Gallacher underlined Russia's prominence as the spearhead of the international trade unions and champion of solidarity. However, his statement that the British trade unions 'looked up to the Russians' and expressed a desire for close ties with them was not confirmed by relations with the General Council, which had become precarious.[125]

Early in April the General Council had been invited to send delegates to the Russian trade union congress. However, bearing in mind the strain which the first visit to Russia had introduced into their relations with Amsterdam, they declined the invitation. Two more attempts to persuade them, made at the peak of the estrangement after Bournemouth, were unsuccessful.[126] The Russians suffered yet another setback when informed of the General Council's intention to introduce changes in the constitution of ARJAC which would establish the sovereignty of each movement in its own country.[127]

121 *Puti Mirovoi Revolyutsii*, Vol. I, p. 16.
122 *ibid.*, Vol. II, pp. 12–13; resolution on these lines, p. 447.
123 See Dogadov's review of the congress in *Pravda*, 21 Dec. 1926.
124 *VII S'ezd Prof. Soyuzov*, pp. 254–55.
125 *ibid.*, pp. 17–18; resolution, p. 740.
126 TUC archives, *Minutes of GC, 1925–6*, p. 268, 28 Apr. 1926; *ibid.*, *Minutes of GC, 1926–7*, p. 5, 22 Sept. 1926, and p. 32, 24 Nov. 1926.
127 TUC archives, B. 113 8/2/45: Citrine to Melnichansky, 30 Nov. 1926.

Tomsky was fully aware of the fresh blow to the alliance. His report to the congress, which acknowledged once more the transfer of international affairs to the hands of Profintern, was bitterly critical of the General Council. In his characteristically metaphorical language Tomsky indicted the General Council for approaching the alliance against the capitalist offensive like someone who says: 'Let's have a scrap; only be careful not to tear my new shirt.' Still at one with Lozovsky, he advocated the consolidation of ARJAC as 'a symbol of the unity of Russian and British workers' rather than a bloc of leaders. In view of the fragility of ARJAC it was important to 'consolidate the basis of support [for the alliance] among the rank and file'.[128]

Lozovsky, obviously satisfied with the proceedings, contributed little to the discussion, although he augmented Tomsky's concluding observation. He reiterated his conviction that in return for the aid to the miners pressure would be exerted on the General Council to pursue a policy favourable to Russia.[129] Gallacher had suggested to IKKI's plenum that by offering a helping hand to the miners the Russians had secured safeguards against hostile activities. In the early stages of the trade union congress, Bukharin directed attention to the significant fact that although the General Council was absent the militant miners had acknowledged the Russian aid by sending their own delegation.[130] To illustrate this point Cook was now called to the platform, repeating the statement he had made upon his arrival in Russia that on no account would the miners 'allow Baldwin's Government to interfere in Russian affairs'.[131] Hardy even more outspokenly pledged the NMM's commitment to preventing deterioration in Anglo-Soviet relations. He clearly reflected the

[128] *VII S'ezd Prof. Soyuzov*, pp. 71–74; resolution, p. 737. Similar views were expressed in a leader in *Trud*, 15 Dec. 1926, reviewing the congress.

[129] *VII S'ezd Prof. Soyuzov*, p. 266.

[130] *Puti Mirovoi Revolyutsii*, Vol. 1, p. 6; *VII S'ezd Prof. Soyuzov*, pp. 19–20.

[131] *VII S'ezd Prof. Soyuzov*, p. 286; *Pravda*, 4 Dec. 1926. Hodgson in a dispatch to Chamberlain, F.O. 371 N4884/1687/38, 22 Oct. 1926, which like others on the subject was overlooked, suggested that the assistance to the miners and the attempts to create sub-committees under the auspices of the ARJAC were measures to preserve the alliance at all costs.

Russian point of view, stating that the support of the miners did more than the ties with the 'good-for-nothing, scheming' General Council in gaining for Russia the sympathy of the British workers. He concluded with an undertaking to continue the collaboration from below if the existence of ARJAC were to be prejudiced.[132]

The diplomatic justifications for preserving ARJAC, overtly pronounced in the trade union congress, were played down in the IKKI plenum.[133] This was apparently an attempt to disconcert the opposition, whose presence was more conspicuous there. Lozovsky touched only briefly on the future of ARJAC in the closing stages of his report to the plenum on Profintern's activities. His expectations were confined to a 'demonstration of unity' between the workers of the two countries, while differences with the General Council were described as 'irreconcilable'.[134]

The Serbian Vuiović, the only member of the secretariat of IKKI still aligned with Trotsky, unequivocally demanded that the Russians withdraw from the committee. He warned that by adhering to ARJAC, whose British delegates were responsible for the betrayal of the general strike, the Russians were cultivating illusions that the General Council would stand by Russia in the event of an intervention. Kamenev, the only other prominent member of the opposition to challenge Lozovsky, maintained that an alliance with the General Council would inevitably lead directly to the defeat of world revolution.[135]

The majority's supporters made only occasional remarks on the value of ARJAC as a buffer against intervention,[136] while

132 *VII S'ezd Prof. Soyuzov*, p. 293; greetings in the same spirit from Pollitt, Richardson and Lansbury, read to the congress, pp. 833–35; *ibid.*, p. 285: 61% of the assistance to the miners originated in Russia. The Russians clearly overestimated the effect this would have. The MFGB, *Annual Volume of Proceedings for the Year 1926*, pp. 1402–406, corroborated the size of the Russian contribution, but diverted attention away from it.

133 Both discussions of ARJAC took place on 10 and 11 December.

134 *Puti Mirovoi Revolyutsii*, Vol. I, pp. 541–43 and 545.

135 *ibid.*, Vol. II: Vuiović, pp. 180–82; Kamenev, p. 196. The opposition took the floor despite earlier pledges to the central committee of the CPSU not to do so. It was accused of intending 'to aggravate the factional struggle against the party and Comintern'; *Bol'shevik*, Nos. 23–24, 31 Dec. 1926, pp. 3–12.

136 See for instance Shatskin, representing IKKI, in *Puti Morovoi Revolyutsii*, Vol. II, p. 184.

most of their arguments stressed its value as a demonstration of solidarity with the British rank and file. It was best summed up by a Canadian delegate, who referred to ARJAC as a 'window on the British workers'.[137] The most vigorous supporter of ARJAC, however, was Kolarov, who had so vehemently defended Russian interests in earlier sessions. He was concerned that the break-up of the committee would be received by the 'wide masses with feelings of indignation and resentment'. He also warned that the dissolution of ARJAC would aid the insidious activities of 'the enemies of Comintern, Profintern and Russia'.[138]

ARJAC therefore lived to fight another day, despite its failure to fulfil its revolutionary tasks. The decision was vindicated as an example of the validity of united front tactics, but the diplomatic undercurrents were still powerful.

[137] *ibid.*, p. 223.

[138] *ibid.*, p. 274. The Russian majority had by that time established full control over Comintern. According to Humbert-Droz, *De Lénine à Staline*, pp. 266–67, Stalin had created a rival secretariat of IKKI which functioned under his exclusive direction.

6

The Rupture of Anglo-Soviet Relations

The British note: prelude to the breach

The diehards, after a short lull, renewed their vigorous campaign for the expulsion of the Russians from Britain at the beginning of 1927. Having exhausted the general strike's potential for rousing anti-Soviet sentiments, they now diverted attention to Russia's 'subversive activities' in China. By pointing out the Russians' association with the xenophobic movement in China at the end of 1926 they successfully inflamed passions and resuscitated the debate on the future of Anglo-Soviet relations.[1] The diehards failed, however, to force a rupture on this issue as the threat to British interests in China subsided considerably after Chiang Kai-shek's sudden change of heart towards the Russians.

The Chinese communists, influenced by the Russians to a large extent, had been pursuing united front policies with Kuomintang since 1923. Russian involvement was intensified by the collaboration of military advisers in Chiang Kai-shek's northern expedition, which aimed to unify China and curtail the influence of the imperialist powers. The opposition in Russia, however, had long felt doubts about the fragile nature of the alliance. Indeed on 14 April 1927, a month before the Anglo-Soviet rupture, Chiang Kai-shek suddenly turned against his communist allies, massacring many of them in Shanghai and later in Hankow.[2]

[1] On association of Russians with disturbances in China see Balfour papers, 49694/5–6: exchange of letters with Baldwin, 9 and 10 Jan. 1927, and 49704/165: memorandum prepared for Baldwin, 11 Jan. 1927. Arthur Balfour was the Lord President of the Council.

[2] B. Schwartz, *Chinese Communism and the Rise of Mao* (Cambridge, 1951) pp. 42–60; H. Isaacs, *The Tragedy of the Chinese Revolution* (London, 1938); G. Nollau, *International Communism and World Revolution* (London, 1961), pp. 98–104. A Soviet version is in Kapitsa, *Sovetsko-Kitaiskie Otnosheniya*, pp. 177–81.

Since the events in Shanghai in May 1925,[3] the British Government, though concerned at Soviet influence in Kuomintang, had refrained from intervening directly in the civil war, largely because of its inability to establish which side would emerge victorious. By the end of 1926, however, the decision had been taken to disregard the crumbling central Government. Negotiations with Chiang Kai-shek were initiated, together with a show of force: British troops were landed in Shanghai early in 1927 to defend the foreign settlement.[4]

The whole question of Anglo-Soviet relations was due for reconsideration at the beginning of 1927. The disturbances in China served the diehards as grounds for a resolution in Cabinet instructing Chamberlain to prepare a protest Note citing evidence of Russia's hostility towards Britain. In addition Hodgson was to be alerted to the possibility of a rupture.[5] Chamberlain, however, though increasingly less confident that the *status quo* could be preserved, had Baldwin's firm support in opposing any extreme action. The Prime Minister shared his view that a breach would endanger the pacification of Europe, but was even more concerned that it might bridge the widening gulf between extreme and moderate elements in the British labour movement.[6]

The Foreign Office had serious reservations about the wisdom of dispatching a Note, let alone severing relations. Gregory, who was assigned to the drafting of the protest, warned that it comprised a collection of 'slanderous rather than aggressive utterances' by Russian politicians; not only was it an insufficient pretext for representations, but it was likely to have a 'boomerang effect', provoking Russian protests against anti-Soviet speeches by British Ministers. It was bound to be dismissed in Moscow as a 'mild bombshell', and its effect would be confined to British internal affairs. While the drafting proceeded, the feeling crystallized that hovering between the alternatives of 'kicking the

[3] See above pp. 67–68.

[4] F.O. 371 12511 F6833/6833/10: memo by Newton, a senior official in the Far Eastern Department, on Soviet-Chinese relations 1921–27; F.O. 371 12403 F3041/2/10: memorandum on British policy towards the Nationalist Government.

[5] Cab. 23/54 2(27)1, 17 Jan. 1927.

[6] F.O. 371 12589 N209/209/38: minutes by Chamberlain, 15 and 16 Jan. 1927; Balfour papers, 49736/289–91: Chamberlain to Balfour, 22 Jan. 1927.

Bolsheviks out or leaving them alone altogether' was inadvisable.[7] The Office's observations were conveyed to the Cabinet in order to impress on it the unproductive nature of the proposed move.[8]

Chamberlain also supplemented Gregory's earlier memorandum against decisive action towards the Russians with one of his own which categorically opposed a rupture. A severance of relations, he believed, would demonstrate the Government's 'displeasure and indignation' but would not inflict a 'fatal or . . . even a serious blow' on the Soviet Government. His main concern was the effect of a crisis in Anglo-Soviet relations on Germany. It was likely to place Stresemann, who attached great importance to striking a balance in his relations with East and West, in an embarrassing position.[9]

Chamberlain's moderate stance was supported by communications from Ambassadors in the major European capitals, none of whom approved unreservedly of a rupture with Russia. Significantly, Lindsay, the newly-appointed Ambassador to Berlin, saw eye to eye with Chamberlain, reporting on German officials' apprehensions that any diplomatic representations to Russia might ignite 'an armed conflict of the old-fashioned sort'. The persistent rumours in Berlin that Britain contemplated severe measures induced Schubert, Secretary of State for Foreign Affairs, to warn that a rupture would put Germany in a position of 'gravest peril'.[10]

Hodgson remained a severe critic of the Government's policy towards Russia. During his leave in London in February, he realized even before Chamberlain that a protest Note, designed to placate the diehards, was in fact an irrevocable step towards terminating diplomatic relations with Russia. He seriously doubted what the Government was likely to gain from such a move apart from 'a moment of panic' and the 'encouragement of chauvinistic tendencies' in Russia.[11]

[7] F.O. 371 12589 N341/102/38: minutes by Gregory and Orde, 15 Jan. 1927; F.O. 371 12589 N342/209/38: minutes by Gregory and Tyrell, 24 Jan. 1927; F.O. 371 12589 N546/209/38: minute by Gregory, 8 Feb. 1927.

[8] Balfour papers, 49736/292: Chamberlain to Balfour, 26 Jan. 1927.

[9] Cab. 24/184 C.P. 25(27), 24 Jan. 1927.

[10] F.O. 371 12589 N551/209/38: Gregory to Chamberlain (views of heads of missions), 9 Feb. 1927; F.O. 371 12589 N793/209/38: Foreign Office memorandum presented to Cabinet, 16 Feb. 1927.

[11] F.O. 371 12589 N546/209/38: Hodgson to Chamberlain, 4 Feb. 1927;

The Russians maintained vigilant observation of British politics after Krasin's death, particularly in view of the anxiety evoked by events in China. Surprisingly, however, the inflated fear of British aggression which had overshadowed relations with Britain during 1925 and 1926 was gradually giving way to a more relaxed outlook. The traditional argument that only its unwillingness to 'defy the mood of the workers' prevented the British Government from confronting Russia was fast being replaced[12] by more realistic diplomatic calculations. This tendency reflected Litvinov's search for accommodation with the capitalist world through integration in the European community, and also his erroneous evaluation of the balance of power in the British Cabinet.

Successive statements by Litvinov at the beginning of the year initiated the confident approach. The first of these, on 5 February, revealed Litvinov's intention of driving a wedge between Chamberlain and the diehards. He dismissed the diehards' vigorous pressure on the question of China as an attempt to hold the Soviet Government 'responsible for their own mistakes, wishing to make it a scapegoat on the basis of fantastic legends'.[13] The Soviet Press condensed this statement into an appeal to Chamberlain to seize from Churchill 'the reins of British policy towards Russia'.[14] In order to assure Chamberlain of his good intentions, Litvinov called upon Hodgson on 11 February, impressing on him Russia's desire for peace as a prerequisite for the uninterrupted construction of a socialist economy in Russia.[15]

As Rosengoltz found out in an interview with Chamberlain a few days later, the Foreign Secretary certainly did not appreciate the moral support from Moscow in his clash with the diehards. Rosengoltz had to content himself with Chamberlain's reminder

F.O. 371 12589 N780/209/38: minute by Tyrrell on conversation with Hodgson, 18 Feb. 1927; F.O. 371 12589 N791/209/38: memorandum by Hodgson, 23 Feb. 1927.

12 The isolated traditional view quoted is in *Trud*, 5 Feb. 1927.

13 M. Litvinov, *Vneshnyaya Politika SSSR. Rechi i Zayavleniya 1927–1937* (Moscow, 1937), pp. 243–44.

14 'Cherchilliada', *Ekon. Zhzn.*, 6 Feb. 1927.

15 F.O. 371 12589 N753/209/38: Hodgson to Chamberlain, 11 Feb. 1927. Gascoigne, in the Northern Department, minuted on 22 Feb. that Litvinov appeared 'as reasonable and conciliatory' as could be expected (*ibid.*).

that the decision to maintain relations had been taken because the Government 'had thought fit to do so, and not for want of provocation or lack of justification for breaking off relations'.[16] Litvinov, however, was in no way discouraged from pursuing his overtures. In reply to a question addressed to him in the central executive committee of the Soviets on 21 February, he issued a disguised ultimatum: the continuance of mutually beneficial relations would depend on the establishment of 'real normal' communications. It was, as the Soviet Press clarified, 'a stiff protest against the growing anti-Soviet campaign in Britain'.[17]

Meanwhile the diehards were exploiting all measures at their disposal to coerce the Government into action. These included leaking to the *Daily Mail* information on the proceedings in Cabinet, published on 16 February with a demand that the Government should take a firm line.[18] Their case was put before Cabinet by Churchill on 18 February, when he suggested that events in China should form the central theme of the protest Note. If bloodshed followed an exacerbation of the conflict in China, he warned, public opinion in England would attribute it to Russian intrigues and 'would not tolerate the continuation of relations with them'.[19] Birkenhead, who heartily concurred, proposed that the Note should follow the lines of the Curzon ultimatum submitted to the Russians in 1923.

Reservations about such a move, however, had previously been laid before Cabinet in a memorandum by Steel-Maitland, the Minister of Labour. Describing the Note in its present form as 'a bolt from the blue', he feared that it would put the Government in an awkward position, in that the Note might lead to a rupture before the decision to sever relations had been taken.[20]

16 F.O. 371 12589 N662/209/38: Chamberlain to Hodgson on conversation with Rosengoltz, 14 Feb. 1927.

17 *Mezh. Zhzn.* (1927), No. 2, pp. 100–103; *Izvestiya*, 22 Feb. 1927.

18 F.O. 371 12589 N676/209/38: minute by C. M. Palairet, who replaced Gregory as the head of the Northern Department, 17 Feb. 1927.

19 Account of the meeting is based on Cab. 23/54 12(27)1, unless otherwise stated.

20 Cab. 24/84 C.P. 43(27), 8 Feb. 1927; Steel-Maitland papers, GD 193/223, notes for a speech. Steel-Maitland, a former critic of Labour's Russian policy (see above pp. 46–47), now believed that a diplomatic row would amount to 'cutting off their nose to spite our face'.

The dispassionate view of the President of the Board of Trade on the volume of trade between the two countries weakened the Foreign Office's arguments in defence of maintaining relations. His memorandum demonstrated beyond doubt that the Russians had been the beneficiaries from trade with Britain. It ruled out the placing of larger orders in Britain so long as the Russians failed to obtain substantial credits.[21]

Once again Chamberlain's insistence that a rupture would leave deep scars in Britain's relations with the rest of Europe gained him a majority. It was, however, recorded that if Russia continued with its provocative policy 'a breach of relations within the next few months was almost inevitable'.[22] The decision to proceed with the dispatch of the Note while deferring conclusive discussion on the whole question of Anglo-Soviet relations was mainly the result of Chamberlain's convincing arguments. It was also admitted that the lack of an incident of the 'Zinoviev letter' type made a breach unjustifiable; this admission presaged the search for such an incident by the diehards.

Chamberlain, uncomfortably isolated from ministers with whom he was usually aligned, was quickly succumbing to the pressure. Although he remained convinced that as Foreign Secretary he was obliged to 'think of consequences and to look far beyond [the diehards'] horizons', he met Churchill half way by introducing some significant amendments to the Note. In its new form it was regarded by Birkenhead as bound to 'lead things to a head one way or another'.[23]

The Note, handed to Rosengoltz on 23 February, nevertheless remained a pot-pourri of pettily vindictive Soviet published material. Perhaps the most representative was 'a grossly insulting and mendacious cartoon' from *Izvestiya* which depicted Chamberlain applauding the execution of Lithuanian communists. In essence, while the first draft described these utterances as an impediment to better relations, the final version was a clear warning to the Russians that unless they 'refrained from inter-

21 F.O. 371 12581 N619/9/38: copy of memorandum by President of BOT transmitted to Cabinet, 11 Feb. 1927.

22 Cabinet meeting of 2 Mar. reached same conclusions: Cab. 23/54 14(27)1.

23 Chamberlain papers, 35/1/19: exchange of letters with Churchill, 21 and 22 Feb. 1927; Birkenhead, *Life of F. E. Smith*, p. 537.

ference with purely British concerns' a breach would become inevitable.[24]

Litvinov apparently failed to reassess his newly-formulated policy in the light of the British Note. On the contrary, it was believed to bear out his earlier observations, thereby dulling Russia's senses on the eve of the rupture. The Russians, overlooking the real threat embodied in the Note, regarded it as a concession to extreme opinion, reflecting the climax of the previous months' campaign by the Press and the diehards.[25] Litvinov's reply, handed to Peters in Moscow on 26 February, fully justified the Foreign Office's apprehensions. A list of anti-Soviet speeches by Cabinet Ministers was produced to counter British charges. The accusations were viewed as an attempt to mollify the diehards and their vagueness was attributed to the lack of incriminating evidence.[26] Litvinov concluded by perfunctorily dismissing the threat of a rupture as unlikely to 'intimidate any one at all' in Russia. The commentary in the Soviet Press made its customary digest of the Russian Note: disciplinary action against the diehards was a prerequisite for regulating Anglo-Soviet relations.[27]

The warning contained in the British Note was not passed over by the whole of Narkomindel. Chicherin, now spending longer periods in Germany for medical treatment, expressed his disapproval in a letter to Stalin of the 'naïvety and self-delusion' of those who believed that the British move was 'a warning not only to us but also to the diehards'. He correctly read in it the surrender of the moderates in the British Cabinet to those who would be satisfied only with a rupture. The Note, he predicted to Rosengoltz, was 'only a beginning; British attacks on us will proliferate'.[28] Chicherin's warnings should have sounded the alarm in Russia. Events in Britain and in Geneva, where

[24] F.O. 371 12589 N805/209/38: Chamberlain to Rosengoltz.

[25] *Izvestiya*, 25 Feb. 1927.

[26] *Ekon. Zhzn.*, 25 Feb. 1927, characteristically declared: 'Hard evidence was not produced in the past and is not produced now.'

[27] F.O. 371 12589 N867/209/38: Peters to Chamberlain (Note from Narkomindel); leaders in *Izvestiya* and *Ekon. Zhzn.*, 27 Feb. 1927.

[28] Letter from Chicherin to Stalin and Rykov, 11 Mar. 1927, quoted in A. Gromyko, 'Diplomat Leninskoi Shkoly', *Izvestiya*, 5 Dec. 1962; *Dok. Vne. Pol.*, Vol. x, pp. 117–18, 18 Mar. 1927.

Chamberlain met his European colleagues in March, left little doubt that a severance of relations with Russia was impending.

Scant sympathy was shown towards Russia from either side of the House in the Parliamentary debate of 3 March on Anglo-Soviet relations. MacDonald, confining his criticism to the content of the Note, assured the Commons that had he been in office remonstrations would have been made to Moscow long before 1927.[29] The diehards added their customary invective, with Locker-Lampson proposing a simple solution to the Russian problem: 'For the anthropoid ape of the Bolshevik jungle give me the big stick, yes, and the bigger boot.' Compared with such utterances, Chamberlain's speech defending the cautious steps undertaken by the Government seemed moderate, although he did repeat that the Note was 'the last word' before breaking off trade and diplomatic relations.[30]

Chamberlain, like Chicherin, was fully aware that the Note was 'a stage further towards a breach'. Though disturbed by the 'deeply stirred' public opinion which lacked 'any conception of the finest shades of foreign policy', he hastened to prepare the European powers for such an eventuality.[31] Even before the debate in Parliament Chamberlain had summoned ambassadors to the Office to emphasize the 'uncertain character' of Anglo-Soviet relations, hinting that the possibility of a rupture could not be excluded.[32] Soon after the debate he attended a session of the Council of the League, where he found Stresemann and Briand perturbed by the latest British measures. They appeared to believe that military action would inevitably follow the termination of Anglo-Soviet relations. Throughout a week of energetic negotiations, Chamberlain constantly disavowed the

29 *Parl. Deb. H.C.*, Vol. 203, cols. 620–25. MacDonald expressed similar but stronger views in an interview in *Manchester Guardian*, 25 Feb. 1927.

30 *Parl. Deb. H.C.*, Vol. 203: Locker-Lampson, col. 650; Chamberlain, cols. 631–34.

31 On imminence of rupture see F.O. 800/260: Chamberlain to Lindsay, 1 Mar. 1927; F.O. 371 12590 N1279/209/38: Chamberlain to Sir Miles Lampson, British representative in Peking, 21 Mar. 1927.

32 F.O. 371 12589 N847/209/38: Chamberlain to Crewe on conversation with French Ambassador in London, 24 Feb. 1927; F.O. 371 12589 N984/209/38: minute by Chamberlain on conversation with Italian Ambassador, 1 Mar. 1927.

aggressive intentions attributed to Britain but pointed out the fragility of relations with the Russians.[33]

By mid-April Chamberlain noted that it 'might at any moment become impossible' to maintain the 'semblance of diplomatic relations with the Soviet Government'.[34] This reflected the mood in Cabinet. When the decision to make remonstrations to Russia had been taken, an incident of the 'Zinoviev letter' type had been sought to justify the expulsion of the Russians.[35] Such incidents were in fact forthcoming. Soon after the League meeting, the Attorney-General, Douglas Hogg, presented to the Cabinet alleged instructions from Comintern on interference in British domestic affairs. Only Chamberlain's graphic prediction of the ill effects in Europe of any extreme action temporarily postponed the confrontation.[36]

Chamberlain's warning in Parliament on 3 March had not been taken seriously by the Russians, who assumed that the Government maintained a passive policy of 'not severing relations – not embarking on fresh negotiations'. The explanation for this complacency seems to be a deep-rooted conviction that a rupture would inevitably lead to military intervention which without the support of either Germany or Poland would be impracticable.[37] Chicherin's tireless campaign since Locarno to convince Germany of its key role in determining Britain's inactivity or aggression struck a responsive chord in Berlin.[38]

While Anglo-Soviet relations were deteriorating, Germany, anxious to preserve its neutrality and prevent entanglement, was even considering bringing about a 'speedy compromise through pressure' on Moscow. It was felt that confrontation might be avoided if Narkomindel were to dissociate itself from Comintern's

[33] F.O. 800/260: Chamberlain to Tyrrell from Geneva, 9 Mar. 1927. An account of Stresemann's meeting with Chamberlain is in Sutton, *Gustave Stresemann*, Vol. III, pp. 116–26. Chamberlain issued in Geneva a *démenti* of the alleged British aggressive intentions, *The Times*, 9 Mar. 1927.

[34] Chamberlain papers, 54/331: Chamberlain to Ambassador in Oslo, 22 Apr. 1927.

[35] See above p. 16.

[36] Cab. 23/90B: confidential annexes to Cab. 14(27)1A and Cab. 17(27), 17 and 18 Mar. 1927, written in Hankey's own hand.

[37] *Izvestia*, 5 Mar. 1927; *Mezh. Zhzn.* (1927), No. 3, pp. 51–53.

[38] See observations by Peters in F.O. 371 12590 N1325/209/38, 11 Mar. 1927, and by Hodgson in F.O. 371 12589 N996/209/38: letter to Gregory (n.d. – early Mar. 1927?).

propaganda activities.[39] In view of this, Chamberlain's departure to Geneva was regarded by the Russians as an attempt to recruit the rest of the Locarno signatories to a crusade against Russia, while the more immediate danger of conventional diplomatic action was ignored. This miscalculation persisted despite the fact that shortly after the League's session Litvinov was informed by Stresemann that, while a rupture was more likely than ever because of the diehards' pressure, Chamberlain had undertaken not to pursue warlike measures against Russia 'even after a breach'.[40] Attention was diverted from Britain's transparent intentions by Narkomindel's constant suspicion that Germany had concluded secret agreements in Geneva concerning the passage of troops through its territory. The charges against Germany were criticized by Chicherin, who not only believed in Germany's goodwill but also reminded Narkomindel that Britain was the main enemy.[41] The final solution in April of the 'crisis of confidence' with Germany relaxed Russian vigilance.

The Russians' failure to perceive the gathering clouds in London was reinforced by their participation in the World Economic Conference in Geneva early in May. In an attempt to integrate themselves into the European system, the Russians expressed their desire for peaceful coexistence and stressed the significance of the Soviet economy in world markets. They were encouraged by the interest shown in the Soviet delegation and the contacts established with commercial circles. In the conference a new word was used for 'coexistence'; *sozhitel'stvo*, 'coexistence between people', was replaced by *sosushchestvovanie*, 'coexistence between states'.[42] Consequently, while the

39 H. L. Dyck, 'German-Soviet Relations and the Anglo-Soviet Break, 1927', pp. 72–75. For Germany's intention to mediate see F.O. 800/260: Lindsay to Chamberlain on conversation with Schubert, 26 Feb. 1927.

40 *Dok. Vne. Pol.*, Vol. x, pp. 108–109: N. Krestinsky, Soviet Ambassador in Berlin to Litvinov on conversation with Stresemann, 16 Mar. 1927. On Soviet suspicions see Rosenbaum, *Community of Fate*, pp. 242–46.

41 *Dok. Vne. Pol.*, Vol. x, pp. 116 and 118–20: Litvinov to Krestinsky, 17 and 19 Mar. 1927; Gromyko, 'Diplomat Leninskoi Shkoly', Nikonova, *Antisovetskaya Vneshnyava Politika*, pp. 171–74, still regards the meeting as an attempt to renew a *cordon sanitaire* around Russia.

42 Review of the conference in *Mezh. Khz. i Mezh. Pol.* (1927), No. 4, pp. 3–9; Miliutin, Vice-President of the Communist Academy, *ibid.* (1927), Nos. 5–6, pp. 61–66. On the economic prospects see L. M. Khinchuk, *K Istorii Anglo-Sovetskikh Otnoshenii* (Moscow, 1928),

diehards were leaving no stone unturned in their search for a pretext for expelling them, the unsuspecting Soviet diplomats in London were 'cheerful and optimistic', convinced of the imminence of a brighter future.[43]

The Arcos raid and the severance of relations

The event which precipitated the breach with Russia was the raid on 12 May by the Metropolitan Police on the premises jointly occupied by Arcos and the Soviet Trade Delegation in search of a missing War Office document. Although a rupture had become inevitable, the raid was not a deliberate act towards this end by Cabinet, which was presented with a *fait accompli*.[44] Chamberlain, who was consulted before the issue of the search warrant, overlooked the diplomatic implications of the action, which he preferred to regard as a purely judicial matter. Whether the raid was intentionally mounted by Joynson-Hicks to force the hand of the Government remains arguable.[45] The Home Secretary certainly encountered little criticism in Cabinet of the course he had adopted, despite the failure of the police to produce incriminating evidence and the series of blunders committed during the search. Even the violation of the 'immunity from arrest and search' which the chairman of the Trade Delegation enjoyed under the 1921 trade agreement was passed over.[46]

Late in the afternoon of 11 May, Joynson-Hicks had been

pp. 35–40. On coexistence see D. T. Lahey, 'Soviet Ideological Development of Coexistence: 1917–1927', *Canadian Slavonic Papers* (1964), Vol. VI, pp. 90–94.

43 Maisky, *Vospominaniya Sovetskogo Diplomata*, pp. 100–101.

44 The Chancellor of the Duchy of Lancaster, R. Cecil, in *A Great Experiment* (London, 1947), p. 183, claims that the Cabinet was consulted before the raid; his memory is certainly at fault.

45 Russian historians deduce this without hesitation; see V. I. Popov, *Anglo-Sovetskie Otnosheniya (1927–1929)* (Moscow, 1958), p. 57, and Volkov, *Anglo-Sovetskie Otnosheniya*, p. 298. Similar conclusions based on speculation and inconclusive evidence are made by R. D. Warth, 'The Arcos Raid and the Anglo-Soviet "Cold War" of the 1920's', *World Affairs Quarterly* (1958), Vol. XXIX, pp. 126–29. On Joynson-Hicks' undoubted satisfaction with the raid see H. A. Taylor, *Jix-Viscount Brentford*, pp. 235–39.

46 Article V of the agreement, reproduced in full in Ullman, *The Anglo-Soviet Accord*, pp. 474–78.

informed by the War Secretary of evidence obtained by Military Intelligence two days earlier. In January a British Army signals training pamphlet had been sighted by an English employee in Arcos, where photocopies of it were made. Despite the minimal significance of the document[47] and the time which had elapsed since January, the Home Secretary impulsively decided to raid 'Soviet House'. He immediately sought the advice of Chamberlain, but apparently failed to mention that the search would also include the premises of the Soviet Trade Delegation. After Joynson-Hicks had given an assurance that he would order a search of 'any *business* house in London entirely unconnected with Russia' in similar circumstances, Chamberlain gave his consent without second thoughts.[48]

The Soviet Embassy, after ignoring persistent rumours of the likelihood of a raid earlier in the year, was taken completely by surprise when it received news of the search on the afternoon of 12 May. After a quick appraisal of the situation, Bogomolov, the First Secretary, hastened to the Foreign Office for an explanation, only to find Palairet equally perplexed, since the Northern Department had not been briefed. While Bogomolov was ascertaining the extent of the search emergency steps were taken in the Office. Peters was informed by cable of the latest developments and authorized 'to take such precautions as occurred' to him to forestall Soviet retaliation.[49] Anxiety in the Soviet Embassy mounted when Bogomolov returned from 'Soviet

47 Home Office archives, file 144/8403 509413/1. The document, 'Description of and Instructions for Wireless Telegraph', marked 'Confidential', carried the lowest security rating. Two documents also marked 'Confidential' found in the course of the raid were dismissed by the Air Ministry as 'of no value'; see H.O. 144/8403 509413/17: minute by Scott, Home Office, 14 May 1927.

48 *Parl. Deb. H.C.*, Vol. 206: Joynson-Hicks, cols. 2229–303, and Chamberlain, col. 2261, 26 May 1927 (my italics). F.O. 372 2315 T6374/600/373: minute by Chamberlain, 17 May 1927, confirms this sequence of events. Childs, head of the Special Branch, in *Episodes and Reflections*, pp. 233–34, remembers being well aware of the Russian claim for immunity when informed by the Home Secretary of the decision to raid.

49 F.O. 372 2315 T6374/600/373: Palairet minuted on 17 May that he told Bogomolov 'in perfect truth' that he 'knew nothing about it'. F.O. 371 12590 N2309/209/38: Gregory to Peters. Events from the Russian viewpoint are recalled in Maisky, *Vospominaniya Sovetskogo Diplomata*, pp. 102–103.

House' with the alarming news that the police were not discriminating between Arcos and the Trade Delegation. Further attempts to persuade the Foreign Office to bring the raid to a halt proved unsuccessful. Rosengoltz had to content himself with a promise by Henderson to raise the issue in Parliament the next day.[50]

The next morning, however, Rosengoltz succeeded in seeing Chamberlain and left him a Note protesting against the violation of the 1921 trade agreement. The conversation which followed revealed that Chamberlain did not as yet fully comprehend the political implications of the raid. While he was willing to take up with the Home Office allegations of police misconduct during the search, he maintained that the raid was 'not an administrative act but a process of law taken in pursuance of a magistrate's warrant', and would have been undertaken 'in a similar case against any other company' established in Britain.[51]

Chamberlain presumably hoped that by allowing the Home Secretary a free hand he would avert confrontation with him and keep the issue out of the diplomatic arena. However, the contravention of the diplomatic privileges of the Trade Delegation made the Foreign Office's involvement inevitable. It was indeed apprehension about this question which induced Chamberlain to take the unusual step of visiting Joynson-Hicks at the Home Office shortly after Rosengoltz had left.[52] To his dismay Chamberlain found the Home Secretary examining a report by Childs which confirmed that the search had been extended to the entire premises, including the offices of the Trade Delegation. Childs, however, who was well aware of the Russian claim for immunity, had postponed the search of the head of the Delegation's office, marking all cupboards and safes: 'To be preserved for decision'. Yet even now Chamberlain appeared anxious not

[50] F.O. 372 2315 T6175/600/373: minute by Thompson, Metropolitan Police, on meeting with Bogomolov, 15 May 1927. For Rosengoltz's meeting with Henderson see *Parl. Deb. H.C.*, Vol. 206, col. 2292, 26 May 1927.

[51] Chamberlain papers, 50/332: Note by Rosengoltz, 12 May 1927; F.O. 372 2315 T6056/600/373: memorandum by Chamberlain on conversation with Rosengoltz, 13 May 1927.

[52] Bishop, *The Administration of British Foreign Relations*, pp. 310 ff., points out that all friction between the Foreign and Home Offices concerned individual aliens. The issue of Arcos was an exception.

to interfere in the Home Office's sphere. After handing over Rosengoltz's Note, he merely expressed the view that if the Russians' protest was justified it 'might be difficult to defend the issue'.[53]

Although the Northern Department was still not consulted, Warner, the head of the Treaty Department, was sent over to advise the Home Office on questions arising from the Russian claim of immunity. Warner found the Home Secretary eager to extract the utmost from the search. He was determined to disregard the question of immunity on the basis of police observations that the activities of the offices were so closely interconnected as to render a distinction impracticable. Joynson-Hicks had made up his mind that 'the complete answer to any protest' would be to instruct the police to search the Delegation's offices 'for evidence that they contained Arcos papers and were used by Arcos'. Chamberlain, briefed about the meeting, still showed no intention of standing in the way of Joynson-Hicks. He was even inclined to accept the view that the privileges accorded by the 1921 agreement did not permit the chairman of the delegation 'to cover with his cloak anything and everything which he chooses to claim when the search is in progress'.[54]

While the search continued uninterruptedly on Sunday 15 May, no further communication passed between the Foreign and Home Offices. On Monday an interdepartmental meeting took place in which Tyrrell, Gregory and Warner, representing the Foreign Office, acquiesced in the interpretation that the immunity enjoyed by the head of the Trade Delegation and his office did not extend to the whole Delegation. All parties, however, agreed that the difficulty in distinguishing between the various offices made it practically impossible to observe this immunity. This decision was conveyed to Parliament in its session by Joynson-

[53] H.O. 144/8403 509413/1: memorandum on meeting between Chamberlain and Joynson-Hicks and enclosed memorandum by Childs. Chamberlain was seriously disturbed by the 'fuss' which the raid provoked and full of mistrust of Childs; see Chamberlain papers, 5/418: letter to Ida, his sister.

[54] F.O. 372 2315 T6056/600/373: minutes by Warner, 13 May 1927, and Chamberlain, 14 May 1927. On 14 May a Home Office representative visited 'Soviet House' and instructed the police to 'endeavour to obtain evidence on the use of Arcos of the other "sacred" room'; see H.O. 144/8403 I 509413/17.

Hicks, who justified the extent of the search on the grounds that it was difficult to say where 'one building begins and the other ends'.[55]

Litvinov, like Chamberlain, did not fully comprehend the political consequences of the raid. Since Locarno, Soviet diplomacy had assumed that there was no immediate threat to Anglo-Soviet relations so long as Britain failed to create a European bloc with a clear-cut anti-Soviet orientation. The raid was seen as a limited action, possibly engineered by the diehards to put pressure on the Government. The only immediate fear was for the state of Anglo-Soviet trade relations.

The first reaction to the raid was to point out its similarity to a raid on part of the Soviet legation in Peking on 6 April, which the Russians suspected was carried out with British consent.[56] The London raid's timing and the choice of Arcos suggested that it was a desperate attempt to sabotage Russian achievements in the World Economic Conference and 'hamper the further developments of Anglo-Soviet commercial relations'.[57] Khinchuk's comment from Geneva on the search of his offices was that the diehards undoubtedly aimed at undermining 'the possibility of coexistence of two national economic systems (capitalist and socialist) as well as the improvement of relations with business circles in Britain'.[58] This was a clear reference to the breakthrough in the negotiations with the Midland Bank, which was considering a loan of £10 million to the Russians, the bulk of which was to be spent on the purchase of British industrial products. This agreement was immediately cited by the Soviet

[55] F.O. 372 2315 T6727/600/373: memorandum by Scott on interdepartmental meeting in the Home Office, 16 May 1927; *Parl. Deb. H.C.*, Vol. 206, col. 910.

[56] See 'Pekin–London', *Trud*, 14 May 1927, and identically titled leader in *Pravda*, 15 May 1927. Joynson-Hicks might have been inspired by the Peking raid, but the Cabinet certainly made no use in the present conflict of the incriminating material seized, which was received from Lampson only on 28 Oct. 1927. See F.O. 371 12502 F8322 and F8437/3241/10.

[57] Leader in *Izvestiya*, 14 May 1927. See also *Ekon. Zhzn.*, 14 and 24 May 1927.

[58] *Izvestiya*, 18 May 1927. It was later suggested in *Mezh. Zhzn.* (1929), No. 11, pp. 47–49, that the raid signalled the reimposition of the economic blockade.

Press as the major inspiration for the raid; to the diehards it was like 'the red rag to the bull'.[59]

A Note of protest had already been drawn up by Narkomindel by 14 May but was not submitted to Peters, replacing Hodgson who was on leave, until the evening of 17 May. Narkomindel presumably left the door open for a British explanation which would avert a full-scale conflict. The Note was strikingly similar to the representation made by the Russians in February. Litvinov, using Russia's commercial potential for Britain as a bargaining counter, emphasized that relations must not simply be preserved but must be regularized. He therefore again demanded from the British Government a clear declaration of their intentions. This was combined with a veiled threat: unless normal conditions for conducting relations were established Russia would withdraw orders from Britain.[60] To demonstrate that these were not empty words, the Soviet Government passed a decree confining trade to countries with which the Soviet Union enjoyed 'normal diplomatic relations' and which guaranteed 'unimpeded and normal conduct of commercial operations'.[61] Although it is tempting to assume that this was a last-ditch attempt to forestall a diplomatic crisis,[62] these measures had been contemplated earlier. They were incorporated in the Russian platform for the World Economic Conference to reinforce the monopoly of trade and prevent the crystallization of economic blocs against Russia.[63]

Litvinov's representations and the search's failure to yield results hastened the Foreign Office's embroilment in the affair. On Monday 16 May, the last day of the police occupation of 'Soviet House', Warner noted that 'unless the Police have made

[59] *Ekon. Zhzn.*, 17 May 1927. See also Mikoyan in *ibid.*, and leader in *Izvestiya*, 15 May 1927. An exchange of letters, however, between the Soviet Trade Delegation and the Midland Bank, 9 and 11 May, demonstrates that the agreement was not quite complete; see *Dok. Vne. Pol.*, Vol. x, pp. 191–93 and p. 634, note 41.

[60] F.O. 371 12591 N2532/209/38: Peters to Chamberlain (Note from Litvinov). The Soviet Press adopted the same attitude as in Feb. A leader in *Izvestiya*, 18 May 1927, called upon Chamberlain and Baldwin to recognize 'the intrigues of their Black Hundred colleagues'.

[61] The decree is in *Dok. Vne. Pol.*, Vol. x, pp. 220–21.

[62] Palairet certainly thought so; see his minute of 23 May 1927 in F.O. 371 12581 N2312/9/38.

[63] 'Monopoliya Vneshnei Torgovli i Kapitalisticheskie Okruzhenie', *Ekon. Zhzn.*, 29 Mar. 1927.

some startling discovery today perhaps a preliminary draft-reply to M. Rosengoltz should be prepared'.[64] Such a reply would have expressed regret at the search but dismissed the Russian claim for immunity. The only alternative to what was taken to be a degrading course seemed to be a rupture. It was apparently hoped that enough incriminating material would be turned up by the search to prove the implication of either Rosengoltz or the Soviet Government in propaganda activities.

When Scotland Yard actually produced the material in the Office on 18 May, Palairet admitted disappointedly that it provided only 'very flimsy reasons for breaking off diplomatic relations'.[65] While the energies of the Northern Department were harnessed to discussing the outcome of the raid, Chamberlain's eyes were still closed to the possibility that it might result in a breach. In a conversation on 18 May with Briand, who was accompanying the French President on a visit to Britain, Chamberlain restated the British policy towards Russia as pursued since February: although the Government possessed sufficient proof of hostile Soviet activities, concern for tranquillity in Europe dictated forbearance.

The views underwent a considerable change in the next twenty-four hours; when Chamberlain saw Briand off on the evening of 19 May, he intimated to him that action might be 'more imminent' than he had realized the day before.[66] The change followed intensive consultations in the Office throughout the day concerning Joynson-Hicks' draft statement to Parliament on the result of the search. The Note from Litvinov, which was received on the same morning, showed no intention of passing over the affair in silence. Chamberlain finally realized that the Home Secretary's statement, which presented the case 'in so weak a form as to amount practically to a confession of a failure', would leave him to face the consequences. Gregory's vehement arguments against half-measures like the expulsion of Rosengoltz, and in favour of 'indicting the whole gang' as the only 'dignified course', seem to have won the day.

Chamberlain, however, preoccupied with the French visitors,

[64] F.O. 372 2315 T6116/600/373.

[65] F.O. 371 12608 N2289/2187/38.

[66] F.O. 371 12637 W4715/4715/17: record of meetings by Chamberlain, 19 May 1927.

could not be present at the beginning of the Cabinet meeting which was due to discuss the affair that evening. He therefore conveyed to Baldwin his dissatisfaction at Joynson-Hicks' statement and promised to present one of his own which would afford a 'complete justification for our action – a justification indeed so complete that the only criticism to be made upon it is that it must almost certainly involve the dismissal of the Soviet Mission'.[67]

Neither statement, however, gained the complete support of Cabinet; a special committee was formed to draft a new one and to recommend a future pattern for Anglo-Soviet relations. While some moderate ministers, notably Balfour, still believed that a better means could be found to combat the 'sinister combination of legitimate trade with illegitimate propaganda', Chamberlain was now committed to the facile solution of a rupture.[68] On the night of the Cabinet meeting, Peters was informed that 'a severance of relations may take place early next week'.[69]

Chamberlain's primary objection to a rupture, on the grounds that it might produce a chain reaction in Europe and push Germany into Russia's arms, had by now lost much of its power. The warnings to Europe following the protest Note to Russia in February had prepared the scene for such a move. Still more significant were signs of a thaw in Franco-German relations. It seemed that the Germans were finally prepared to settle their differences with France and accept Briand's formula for the reduction of Allied occupation forces. Stresemann had also intimated to Chamberlain that he would adhere to his neutral position and maintain only 'passable terms' with Russia.[70]

Oddly enough the proposal of a rupture, which in the past

67 On the Foreign Office's deliberations see Chamberlain papers, 38/3/2: letter to Baldwin, 19 May 1927. Gregory's views are in F.O. 800/260: letter to Chamberlain, 19 May 1927. Palairet minuted at the end of the day that the reply to Litvinov's Note 'may be more "clear and unambiguous" than Moscow may like'; see F.O. 372 2315 T6374/600/373.

68 Balfour papers, 49736/302–304: Balfour to Chamberlain, 20 May 1927; Cab. 23/55 32(27)2.

69 F.O. 371 12590 N2309/209/38: Chamberlain to Peters.

70 F.O. 371 12598 N2117 and N2702/520/38: Lindsay to Chamberlain on conversations with Stresemann, 7 May and 5 June 1927; F.O. 371 12148 C4084/2050/18: Chamberlain to Lindsay, 16 May 1927.

had been a subject for serious reservations in the Foreign Office, had this time encountered little opposition. In fact this course seems to have been agreed on with such alacrity that some obvious anomalies had been overlooked. Shortly before the next Cabinet meeting it had to be pointed out to Chamberlain that the expulsion of the diplomatic mission would not entail that of Arcos, which was registered as a British firm. Further, the Government's interests in maintaining normal trade would be hampered by the abrogation of the trade agreement – the inescapable result of the Russians' alleged abuse of their privileges.[71]

These questions, however, were not tackled by the Cabinet meeting of 23 May, when Chamberlain raised the issue of a severance of relations. Although still sceptical about the advantages Britain would derive from such a course, he was satisfied that the 'ill effects, if any, on the general European situation would now be much less'. The serious admission by the committee appointed at the previous meeting that the Soviet Embassy's complicity in the propaganda activities in the Trade Delegation 'could not be completely substantiated from the documents seized' did not deter the overwhelming majority from pressing for a rupture. It was decided to select for this purpose other documents ironically not intercepted in connection with the raid.[72] The alternative material was chosen with reference to the conflict in China. It was confined to 'hostile' instructions passed by Rosengoltz to Borodin and evidence of anti-British propaganda schools in various parts in Russia. An announcement was then made that evidence had been obtained during the raid of espionage activities by the Trade Delegation, which served as a clearing house for subversive messages. This, together with the previously selected material, was brought before Parliament by Baldwin on 24 May to justify the Government's decision to break off relations with Russia. The draft Note to that effect was approved by Cabinet the next day.[73]

The Government's decision was endorsed by Parliament on 26 May by a majority of 357 to 111. Chamberlain, insisting that Russia was 'incorrigible', did not dwell on the events leading up

[71] F.O. 371 12590 N2309/209/38: Chamberlain to Gregory, 20 May 1927; minute by Gregory on meeting with Warner and Palairet, 21 May 1927.

[72] Cab. 23/55 33(27)1.

[73] *Parl. Deb. H.C.*, Vol. 206, cols. 1842–49; Cab. 23/55 34(27)1.

to the severance. The British Government, he maintained, had 'practised forbearance until forbearance was out-worn'. Very few speakers shared the diehards' exhilaration at the 'effective spring cleaning' stamping out 'the red rot which promised to spread everywhere and ruin us'.[74] Both Labour and Liberals pointedly argued that the Government had submitted to the pressure of an extreme minority in its midst and sacrificed the interests of foreign policy.[75]

The Note informing the Russians of the Cabinet's decision was handed to Rosengoltz on 26 May. It accused the Russian Government of continuing subversive activities through Comintern despite the warning embodied in the February Note. This defiance had culminated in the 'abuse of diplomatic privileges' granted by the 1921 trade agreement. The Russians were given to understand, however, that the Government did not wish to 'interfere with the ordinary course of legitimate Anglo-Russian trade'.[76]

On the day of Baldwin's announcement to Parliament of the decision to sever relations, *Izvestiya* was still predicting in a reassuring leader that the 'serious differences of opinion' which had prevented the Cabinet from reaching agreement in its first meeting would be solved in Russia's favour by the moderating influence of Chamberlain and Baldwin. When the surprising news reached Moscow, attempts to fathom the rationale behind the breach remained fruitless. The only hope was that the Labour movement and commercial circles would bring to bear last-minute pressure on the Government to reverse its decision. To encourage such moves Mikoyan rejected out of hand Baldwin's proposal to provide facilities for the maintenance of trade. Instead he threatened that Russia would immediately 'liquidate existing business' in Britain. This was accompanied by an announcement that orders withdrawn from Britain would be diverted to Germany and the USA.[77]

74 *Parl. Deb. H.C.*, Vol. 206; Chamberlain, col. 2217; Locker-Lampson, col. 2253.

75 *ibid.*: Clynes, cols. 2198–9, Henderson, col. 2298, and Ponsonby, col. 2256; Lloyd George, cols. 2218–2230. The Liberal *Manchester Guardian*, 27 May 1927, ascribed the decision to the 'tactical necessity of saving the face of the Home Secretary'.

76 F.O. 371 12591 N2461/209/38.

77 *Ekon. Zhzn.*, 25 May 1927. See also leaders in *Izvestiya* and *Pravda*

In these circumstances Litvinov's swift comment that the severance 'was not a fortuitous or unexpected event' was clearly intended to cover up Narkomindel's serious misjudgement of British intentions. Attention was diverted from the setback, probably because of the opposition's accusations in the current IKKI plenum of Government complacency,[78] by revitalizing the danger of war. Litvinov found an explanation for the breach in Britain's 'speeding up of preparation for war; any other interpretation should be discarded and would be absurd from the point of view of British interests'.[79] The Press took up Litvinov's arguments so forcibly as to precipitate a war scare. The rupture was presented as an irrational move, comprehensible only as an attempt to prevent the Russians from pursuing a policy of 'peaceful co-existence'; it was 'a forerunner of new wars and new interventions'.[80] A more realistic evaluation of the situation was, however, contained in the Note handed to Peters on 27 May. While repeating Litvinov's earlier statements, it dismissed the British action as an attempt to hush up the failure of the search and extricate Joynson-Hicks 'from the dreadful fix into which he had fallen'.[81]

War fever in Russia

The traumatic memory of the intervention, aggravated by the failure to spread the revolution beyond Russia's borders, had brought about a substantial revision of the Soviet concept of 'war'. In the days when world revolution had been the order of the day, a world war, expected to fragment into civil wars in its early stages, was contemplated with equanimity. However, the stabilization of capital, which afforded the long-term breathing space essential for the construction of a national socialist economy, had brought the Soviet view close to the conventional bourgeois concept of war as a totally destructive phenomenon. By 1927

of the same date and a statement by Khinchuk of 30 May 1927 in *K Istorii Anglo-Sovetskikh Otnoshenii*, pp. 133–34.

78 See below, pp. 243–245.

79 Litvinov's announcement is in *Anglo-Sovetskie Otnosheniya*, pp. 122–25. See also *Mezh. Zhzn.* (1927), No. 9, pp. 31–41.

80 'Maska Sorvana', *Izvestiya*, 27 May 1927. See similar leaders in *Pravda* and *Ekon. Zhzn.*, 28 May 1927.

81 F.O. 371 12591 N2463/209/38: Peters to Chamberlain.

the likelihood of a clash between the Western powers, or even of a war of liberation by the colonized peoples, seemed remote, while an eventual combined attack by the capitalist countries on Russia was still regarded as inevitable.[82]

The switching of emphasis to the *danger* of war was discernible in Soviet obsessions about the formation of potential anti-Soviet blocs, combined with diplomatic moves towards participation in the peace arrangements in Europe. The Russians, assuming that the key to European politics lay in London, were vigilant observers of the moves of British diplomacy. The war scare which followed the severance of relations was not an isolated incident but the climax of a series of similar events during the deterioration of Anglo-Soviet relations since the end of 1924 – notably during the negotiations at Locarno.[83] The current scare, however, was so thoroughly permeated by domestic political considerations as to make it impossible to determine decisively its genuineness.

A war scare on a minor scale had occurred at the end of 1926 in connection with the deterioration of Anglo-Soviet relations and growing speculations about British military intervention in China. The alarm sounded in the fifteenth conference of the CPSU was even more loudly echoed at the Party's district conferences early in 1927. Both Voroshilov and Bukharin depicted the international situation in such sombre colours that according to foreign observers 'people began to lay in stores of provisions and traders further raised the already high prices'.[84]

The Russians, however, were not referring to an imminent attack. N. Uglanov, the secretary of the Moscow party committee, provided an explanation for the scare: although nobody was yet 'treading on [their] toes' the workers should be on the alert and prepared to 'anticipate the danger'. Indeed, expert

82 See a discussion by Milyutin in *Mezh. Khz. i Mezh. Pol.* (1927), Nos. 5–6, pp. 3–6. A discussion of Marxist attitudes to war is in Carr, *The Bolshevik Revolution 1917–1923*, Vol. 3, pp. 541 ff. John P. Sontag, in 'The Soviet War Scare of 1926–27', *Russian Review* (Jan. 1975), Vol. 34, No. 1, pp. 66–67, understates the impact of the rupture on the ignition of the scare.

83 See above, pp. 78–80.

84 On the fifteenth conference, see pp. 203–205; reports of the district conferences are in *Izvestiya*, 14 Jan., 4 and 23 Feb. 1927. Observation on the scare from Riga are in *The Times*, 18 Feb. 1927, and *Manchester Guardian*, 25 Feb. 1927.

British observers were inclined to belittle the significance of the campaign. To Hodgson it announced the opening of the 'bull-frogs' chorus' season.[85] This short but intensive spell of apprehension soon subsided to give way to Litvinov's peace offensive and subsequently to complacency at the time of the rupture. The opposition, however, alarmed by the developments in China, continued to warn of the 'powerful groups of capitalists, deliberately and systematically preparing the ground for an imperialist united front against the Soviet Union'. Zinoviev's proposals for thwarting British aggression by strengthening the alliances with France and Germany coincided with Chicherin's recommendations but were disregarded in the Politburo. The changing fortunes in China precipitated some discussion on the issue, but this was confined mainly to Comintern.[86]

The outbreak of the war scare, as distinct from the constant fear of war, was closely interconnected with the struggle for power. The severance of Anglo-Soviet relations gave force to the opposition's demands, put before the current eighth plenum of IKKI, for discussion of the fragile state of peace in view of events in China. It was, however, relatively easy for the majority to turn the tables on the opposition. Both Litvinov, in his statements following the breach, and Stalin, in his speech to the plenum, appropriated the opposition's arguments and emerged as the prophets of approaching war, regardless of information to the contrary in their possession.[87]

Following the adoption by the IKKI plenum of a thesis on the

[85] F.O. 371 12588 N275 and N757/190/38: Hodgson to Chamberlain, 17 Jan. and 22 Feb. 1927.

[86] On the opposition see *Inprecorr*, 10 and 17 Feb. 1927; Zinoviev's proposals are in Trotsky archives, T–911, 'Nabrosok o Zadachakh Nashei Vneshnei Politiki pered Litsom Ukhudzheniya Mezhdunarodnogo Polozheniya SSSR'. On Comintern and developments in China see J. Humbert-Droz, '*L'Oeil de Moscou' à Paris* (Paris, 1964), pp. 250–55, and *The Communist* (Apr. 1927), pp. 121–24.

[87] For details of the information see p. 235. Deutscher, *The Prophet Unarmed*, p. 333, argues that the majority introduced the scare to create 'a state of public nervousness and national alarm in which it was all too easy to damn the Opposition as unpatriotic'. For views that the scare was spurious and exploited by Stalin and Trotsky alike see Daniels, *The Conscience of the Revolution*, p. 286, and Warth, 'The Arcos Raid and the Anglo-Soviet "Cold War" of the 1920's', pp. 134–40.

danger of war, Alexei Rykov, the chairman of the Council of Peoples' Commissars, launched the subject on a national scale. In a portentous speech to the plenum of the Moscow Soviet at the end of May, he dwelt on Britain's warlike intentions and substantiated these observations with intercepted correspondence of the British Embassy suggesting its involvement in espionage. These allegations served a double purpose: they balanced similar accusations made by the British after the raid as well as bringing home the gravity of the situation. A careful study of the speech nevertheless reveals that Rykov had in mind a hypothetical eventuality; at present Britain was still 'desperately searching for foreign hands' to execute its belligerent plans.[88]

The threat of an imminent war, however, which in the next fortnight pushed all other news from the front pages of the Soviet Press, incited an acute atmosphere of panic. British intentions were unequivocally depicted as the 'liquidation of the proletarian dictatorship, overthrow of the Soviet rule, annihilation of the Socialist structure, return to the old regime, and the transformation of the Soviet Union into a colony of British bankers, into an agrarian appendage of international imperialism'.[89] The dimensions of the scare and its far-reaching effects on the home front did not, however, lead to a departure from the principles of 'peaceful coexistence of two national economic systems' which had only recently received a new emphasis. This policy was still regarded as the best, if not the only, method of breaking out of the tightening capitalist encirclement led by Britain.[90]

In real terms it was made clear virtually from the moment of severance that while it had inflicted considerable damage to Soviet prestige in international affairs it posed no immediate threat to Russia's integrity. Chamberlain, who had gone out of his way to deny rumours of a British crusade following the dispatch of the February Note, now stood by his undertakings. The Germans, seriously alarmed that any move might tilt the balance of power, were assured shortly after Baldwin's announce-

[88] A. I. Rykov, *Angliya i SSSR* (Moscow, 1927), pp. 4–5, 21–31 and 36. Hodgson published a *démenti* in *The Times*, 13 June 1927.

[89] Leader in *Ekon. Zhzn.*, 1 June 1927. Almost identical leaders are in *Izvestiya*, 1 and 2 June 1927. The CPGB contributed to the build-up of the scare; see Palme Dutt in *Inprecorr*, 19 May 1927.

[90] Leader in *Izvestiya*, 5 June 1926.

ment of the breach that it was in no way 'the prelude to some wider policy'. Stresemann, however, seeking confirmation of this position, reiterated to the British Ambassador in Berlin his intention of fulfilling to the letter the Berlin Treaty of April 1926. Chamberlain's further disavowal of any aggressive designs convinced Stresemann that the British Government had no immediate military plans, although he still 'regretted their action'.[91]

Both France and Poland gave Chamberlain's policy a cool reception. The French promptly denied the possibility of similar diplomatic action on their part. A. Zaleski, Pilsudski's Foreign Minister, greeted with scepticism the circulating rumours of Britain's war preparations but took the cautious step of impressing on Chamberlain that Poland's common frontier with Russia necessitated correct Polish-Soviet relations.[92]

Narkomindel, *au courant* with the general frame of mind of the major powers, evaluated the breach as premature from the British point of view; there was no tangible evidence that Chamberlain was making progress towards the formation of an anti-Soviet bloc. Although the long-term effects of the breach were uncertain, Litvinov intimated to the Ambassador in Berlin, on the very day of the severance, his belief that Russia 'faced no danger in the near future'. This view was apparently shared by Chicherin who, when protesting against the inflated scare, was 'enlightened' by a colleague: 'Sh! We know. But we need this against Trotsky.'[93] Before returning to Russia, Chicherin had

[91] F.O. 371 12591 N2491/209/38: note by Gregory on conversation with counsellor of German Embassy, 25 May 1925; F.O. 371 12591 N2556/209/38: exchange of letters between Chamberlain and Lindsay, 30 and 31 May 1927; F.O. 371 12592 N2659/209/38: Lindsay to Chamberlain on conversation with Stresemann.

[92] F.O. 371 12584 N2425/47/38: Crewe (Paris) to Chamberlain, 26 May 1927; F.O. 371 12592 N2684/209/38: Muller on conversation with Zaleski, 30 May 1927. The Polish Ambassador in London conveyed to Chamberlain similar fears of a Russian expedition against Poland; see Chamberlain papers, 50/338.

[93] *Dok. Vne. Pol.*, Vol. x, p. 244: Litvinov to Krestinsky, 27 May 1927. For the admittance of Britain's failure to organize an anti-Soviet bloc see *Mezh. Zhzn.* (1927), No. 8, pp. 55–60, and *Mir. Khz. i Mir. Pol.* (1927), No. 9, pp. 14–16. On Chicherin's views see Fischer, *Men and Politics*, pp. 88–9. Murphy, the CPGB representative in Moscow at the time, suggests in *Stalin*, pp. 207–208, that Stalin was the architect of the scare and that Litvinov collaborated in propagating it.

received emphatic undertakings from Briand that France's Russian policy would remain independent from Britain's. Precisely the same words were echoed by Zaleski in conversation with Voikov, the Soviet Ambassador in Warsaw: Poland 'did not associate itself with the position held by Britain in relations with the USSR'.[94]

Still more significant from the Russian point of view were Stresemann's assurances to Chicherin in Baden-Baden that Germany would not be 'dragged into a struggle directed against the Soviet Union'. In two further meetings in Berlin, Stresemann categorically disclaimed the existence of 'any secret agreement concerning the passage of troops through Germany'.[95]

No attempt was made, however, to use this information to alleviate the tension introduced by the breach. On the contrary, the assassination of Voikov on 7 June by a White Russian émigré in Warsaw was immediately seized upon to stir up further agitation. Neither the frenzied diplomatic efforts by the Polish Government to clear itself of complicity nor the admission by Chicherin that the murder was a 'purely personal act' which had no 'political significance' diminished the scare.[96] An accusing finger was pointed at England as the brains behind this 'provocative act' and comparisons were drawn to the assassination of the Archduke Franz Ferdinand in Sarajevo, which had precipitated the outbreak of the First World War. The implication of Britain in the murder was reinforced two days later when the Soviet Government issued a statement attributing to it other hostile activities, ranging from alleged attempts on Bukharin's life earlier in the year to a series of bomb explosions in Leningrad. The unavoidable conclusion that Britain was 'urgently conducting

[94] *Dok. Vne. Pol.*, Vol. x, pp. 231–32: Chicherin to Litvinov, 24 May 1927; *ibid.*, pp. 260–62: P. Voikov, Soviet Ambassador in Warsaw, to Litvinov, 1 June 1926.

[95] *ibid.*, pp. 300–308: memorandum by Chicherin, 11 June 1927, on conversations with Stresemann, 6, 9 and 10 June 1927. According to Gromyko, 'Diplomat Leninskoi Shkoly', Chicherin disapproving of Stalin's conduct of foreign policy during 1927, submitted his resignation upon his return but was persuaded to withdraw it.

[96] On the Voikov affair see Korbel, *Poland between East and West*, pp. 218–21. On Chicherin's view as transmitted to Stresemann see F.O. 371 12592 N2923/203/38: memorandum by Chamberlain on conversation with Stresemann, 14 June 1927.

preparations for a war against the USSR' was widely circulated and intensified the prevailing trepidation.[97]

In the meeting of the Council of the League in Geneva shortly after the assassination of Voikov, Chamberlain finally succeeded in putting British policy towards Russia in its correct perspective. The meeting, however, had the reverse effect on Russia, where the war scare was becoming a permanent feature of both foreign and domestic politics.

Upon his arrival in Geneva, Stresemann, whose main concern was the prevention of German involvement, was encouraged to learn from Briand that France considered the British move a 'political blunder' and was determined to resist being 'stirred up into a war against Russia'.[98] He was further reassured by his meeting with Chamberlain, who left no doubt that the rupture was undertaken in 'self-defence' and denied current rumours of British aggressive intentions.[99]

In a meeting of the foreign ministers of the Locarno Treaty signatories, which took place on 14 June, Chamberlain surveyed the steps leading to the breach. He defined the act as 'a simple rupture of diplomatic relations' and ruled out any possibility of 'pursuing matters in a direction hostile to the Soviet Government'. Moreover, Chamberlain declined Briand's proposal that the League should pledge support to Poland in case of hostilities on the part of Russia.

In a subsequent meeting Briand communicated an undertaking by Pilsudski to the French Ambassador in Warsaw to do his utmost 'to settle the issue which had arisen with the Soviet Government peacefully and to calm the excitement in Russia'.[100] Zaleski had made similar declarations on the same day, and before leaving for London Chamberlain had yet another meeting

97 Leader in *Izvestiya*, 8 June 1927, and Government statement in *ibid.*, 9 June 1927. For reports on the atmosphere of the scare see *The Times*, 22 June 1927, Fischer, *The Soviets in World Affairs*, Vol. 2, pp. 741–42, and G. Hilger and A. Meyer, *The Incompatible Allies* (New York, 1953), pp. 215–16.

98 Sutton, *Gustave Stresemann*, Vol. III, p. 156.

99 F.O. 371 12592 N2923/209/38: memorandum by Chamberlain on meeting with Stresemann, 14 June 1927.

100 F.O. 371 12601 N2956/1606/38 and 12152 C5332/5294/18: Chamberlain to Tyrrell (notes by Selby, private secretary to Chamberlain), 16 and 17 June 1927.

with Stresemann in which he anxiously attempted to convince him that Britain was in no way engaged in the creation of an anti-Soviet bloc. Stresemann, who deplored the idea of a 'crusade against Russia', was persuaded of Chamberlain's sincerity and promised to use his influence with Chicherin to bring home to him the peaceful intentions of the Western powers.[101] Chamberlain certainly emerged from the session in Geneva with the firm conviction that because of Germany's delicate position it was essential for Britain to avoid the slightest suggestion of involvement in any anti-Soviet formation.[102]

In Russia the spontaneous alarm was gradually being transformed into a constant state of apprehension, justified by the Soviet Union's isolated position in the international arena as a result of the rupture. Voroshilov ushered in the new approach on 10 June, claiming that Britain had only temporarily failed to mobilize the rest of the European countries into an anti-Soviet combination. The Soviet people should prepare for the attack which might be launched 'in two years, one year, or possibly, though very unlikely, in a few months'. In a corresponding speech to the Leningrad Soviet, Tomsky announced the 'beginning of the end of the breathing space' which obliged the Soviet Union to make adequate preparations for a new war.[103]

The perpetuation of the threat of war in its new phase had little to do with the Anglo-Soviet rupture which had precipitated it. It was oriented towards stimulating the population into extensive industrial expansion.[104] It is highly plausible that it was primarily the need for national economic mobilization which had induced the leadership to sound the alarm in Russia following the severance of relations. Hardly had the break been announced

101 F.O. 371 12598 N3039/520/38: Chamberlain's record of conversation with Stresemann, 18 June 1927; Stresemann, *His Diaries*, Vol. III, pp. 161–69. Dyck, 'German-Soviet Relations and the Anglo-Soviet Break, 1927', p. 79, believes that the assumption by Germany of a mediatory role caused the 'erosion of Soviet confidence in Germany' and started the *real* war scare.

102 F.O. 371 12595 N3410/309/38: minute by Chamberlain, 15 July 1927.

103 Voroshilov, 11 June, and Tomsky, 12 June 1927, in *Izvestiya*, *Pravda* and *Trud*.

104 Brodovsky, reputed to be the strong man in the Soviet Embassy in Berlin, intimated to a German official that the scare was encouraged to overcome the apathetic 'nichevo-ist' attitude of the population; F.O. 371 12596 N4326/306/38: Lindsay to Chamberlain, 7 Sept. 1927.

when N. Bryukhanov, the Commissar for Finance, gave an interview to the Press in which he called for special efforts to stiffen defensive readiness 'not only on the military front, but most urgently on the economic front'.[105] Voroshilov's speech was followed up by the declaration of a 'defence week' on 17 June in which appeals for military preparedness and industrial efforts were interlocked. Slogans of the type it introduced – 'Our defence is extensive industrialization and reconstruction of the national economy' – became a common feature of the Soviet Press.[106]

The conversion of the war scare into an enduring atmosphere of anticipation of war found coherent expression through Stalin at the end of July. Stalin now introduced a 'conspiracy theory' which regarded the chain of incidents from the February Note to Voikov's murder, including the search of the Peking premises, the Arcos raid and the rupture, as a comprehensive British plan aimed at 'organizing war against Russia'. Between the lines appeared the two main objects of maintaining the scare, which corresponded to its two phases. The short-term aim was to discredit the opposition for its failure 'to rally around the party notwithstanding the external danger'. The long-term object was to develop urgently 'the national economy and expand both our military and civilian industries'.[107]

Bukharin echoed Stalin, warning party activists in Leningrad that one of the 'extreme difficulties' facing the country was the determination of the capitalist world 'to challenge the internal growth of the Soviet Union'. By the end of the year the

105 *Ekon. Zhzn.*, 28 May 1927. Similar views were expressed by Frumkin, his deputy, despite his reservations about accelerated industrialization; see E. H. Carr and R. W. Davies, *Foundations of a Planned Economy, 1926–1929*, Vol. I, pt. II, pp. 734–39. Tomsky also emphasized the productionist line against the background of the scare in *Pravda*, 27 May 1927, and *Trud*, 29 May 1927.

106 On the 'defence week' see L. Grigor'ev and S. Olenev, *Bor'ba SSSR za Mir i Bezopasnost' v Europe* (Moscow, 1956), pp. 58–63. Characteristic slogans are in *Ekon. Zhzn*, and *Pravda*, 10 July 1927. See also P. Shubin, *Chego Khotyat Lordy?* (Moscow, 1927), pp. 60–63.

107 Stalin, *Sochineniya*, Vol. 9, pp. 322–30; see also leader in *Pravda*, 29 July 1927. This theory was simultaneously introduced in Narkomindel's organ; see Maisky under the pseudonym of Taigin in *Mezh. Zhzn.* (1927), No. 7, pp. 3–12. The conspiracy theory provides a guideline for Soviet historians covering the period; see for example Volkov, *Anglo-Sovetskie Otnosheniya*, Chap. VII.

permanent nature of the threat was revealed by Kalinin, who admitted that the danger lay not in the possibility of the British Government's 'declaration of war tomorrow', but in its 'incessant and systematic preparation of such a war'. This could be forestalled by the rapid construction of socialist industry in Russia.[108]

The dissolution of ARJAC

The dilatory conduct of the general strike by the General Council had virtually debarred Comintern from bypassing the CPGB and converting the trade unions to communism *en masse* by means of an alliance with the left nucleus of their official leadership. Hopes of using the collaboration either to enroll the Soviet trade unions in Amsterdam or openly to challenge it had faded even earlier. With expectations from the collaboration running low, the setbacks inflicted on Soviet diplomacy in Britain in 1927 put ARJAC to an acid test.

The varying interpretations of the constitution of ARJAC had proved to be the main stumbling-block to the implementation of any of its resolutions. By the beginning of 1927 the Russians' violent abuse of the General Council for its handling of the general strike deterred the TUC's leaders even from seeking a comprehensive International, while priority was given to elucidating the nature of the Anglo-Soviet collaboration.[109] The hard-headed General Council, however, voted against the dissolution of ARJAC, which might encourage those who were 'agitating for a severance of diplomatic and trade relations' with Russia. To minimize further dissension, they approached the Russians at the end of November with a proposal for the addition to ARJAC's constitution of two clauses which would establish the 'definite recognition and observance of the complete authority and autonomy' of each movement in its own country.[110]

In spite of the IKKI plenum's resolutions affirming the duty of the Russian unions to 'interfere' in the domestic affairs of their

[108] Bukharin in *Pravda* and *Izvestiya*, 18 Aug. 1927; Kalinin in *Pravda*, 12 Oct. 1927.

[109] TUC archives, B 113 18/2/45: GC's memorandum on ARJAC, Sept. 1926.

[110] TUC archives, B 113 18/2/48: GC's memorandum on ARJAC, 16 Nov. 1926; *Minutes of IC, 1926–7*, Meeting 2, 23 Nov. 1926; B 113 18/2/45: Citrine to Melnichansky, 30 Nov. 1926.

British counterparts,[111] the AUCCTU was urgently seeking to avoid a head-on collision with the General Council. Melnichansky's reply to Citrine, which conveyed the resolution reached by the presidium of the AUCCTU on 5 January, abstained from the all too familiar vituperation of earlier communications. It expressed reservations about the proposed amendments but, with an eye on the future, contended that ARJAC should take appropriate measures to forestall the 'constantly developing political and economic offensive of capital'.[112] The General Council, strictly adhering to the advisory and temporary nature of the alliance, confined their commitment to helping the Russians to integrate within the available framework of the IFTU.

The chances of achieving this object, however, considerably diminished when the executive committee of the IFTU, in its meeting on 13 January, flatly refused to discuss the Russian issue, let alone the prospects of an international conference. After the rejection of the General Council's appeal for a reversal of the decision, the International Committee concluded that to break through the impasse the Russians should be advised to reconsider their decision not to join Amsterdam.[113]

In the meantime the Russians had been informed that, provided they 'distinctly understood' that the revision of ARJAC's constitution was the primary issue, the General Council was ready to call a meeting of the committee. By withholding such an undertaking, the Russians brought the alliance to its *nadir*. Following Bevin's advice, the General Council agreed to postpone any further meeting of ARJAC pending a thorough examination of the nature of the collaboration.[114] However, the swift deterioration of Anglo-Soviet relations, marked by the dispatch of Chamberlain's Note only a day after the General Council's decision, prolonged the death agonies of ARJAC. The General Council, adopting a more flexible outlook towards the Russians, agreed

111 *Puti Mirovoi Revolyutsii*, Vol. II, p. 414.

112 TUC archives, B 113 18/2/45: Melnichansky to Citrine, 7 Jan. 1927.

113 TUC archives, *Minutes of IC, 1926–7*, Meeting 4, 18 Jan. 1927; B 113 18/2/56: exchange of letters between the GC and the IFTU, 15 and 22 Feb. 1927.

114 TUC archives, B 113 18/2/45: Citrine to Melnichansky, 26 Jan. 1927; *Minutes of GC, 1926–7*, p. 56, 22 Feb. 1927. Bevin had earlier proposed a ballot in all unions to decide the future of ARJAC; see B 113 18/2/41, 3 Jan. 1927.

to convene ARJAC at the end of March to discuss all aspects of the capitalist offensive.[115]

At a different level, Profintern, adhering to the letter of the resolutions of the various congresses at the end of 1926, dissociated itself from attempts to patch up the feud with the TUC. A miniature conference of Profintern's executive bureau had reached agreement on the incompetence of the General Council to lead the unions and called for its overthrow. The final repudiation was deferred, however, pending the result of the TUC's executives' conference, due to meet on 20 January 1927 to debate the general strike.[116] The approval by this conference of the General Council's leadership of the strike provoked Profintern into a furious onslaught on the 'new junta' with the slogan: 'Absolutely no confidence in the present General Council'. Profintern, itching to abandon united front tactics in favour of a purely militant policy, declined yet another abortive debate in Amsterdam of the Russian question and instructed its adherents 'to give working-class unity a new lease of life against the will of reformist leaders and over their heads'.[117]

This eagerness to abandon united front tactics before they were totally discredited was not entirely shared by the NMM, which still regarded itself not as a 'separate trade organization endeavouring to fulfil the functions of a trade union, but as a body of active workers *inside* the existing trade union movement'. This, however, was hardly a matter of choice for the NMM, which at the beginning of 1927 was isolated by the General Council's stern measures preventing the affiliation to the TUC of individual NMM members and trades councils holding a dual allegiance.[118]

115 TUC archives, *Minutes of IC, 1926–7*, Meeting 6, 28 Feb. 1927; B 113 18/2/45: Citrine to Melnichansky, 1 Mar. 1927.

116 Meeting of executive bureau, 20, 21 and 23 Dec. 1926, in *Mezh. Rabo. Dviz.*, Nos. 51–52, 31 Dec. 1926. For Lozovsky's acrimonious approach to the GC after the collapse of the miners' strike see *Pravda*, 31 Oct. 1926.

117 Levin in *Mezh. Rabo. Dviz.*, Nos. 4 and 5, 27 Jan. and 3 Feb. 1927. On Lozovsky's call for total war with the General Council see preface to *Chetyre Dokumenta* (Moscow, 1927), pp. 4–13.

118 NMM, *Is Trade Unionism Played Out?* (London, n.d. – 1926?), p. 4. For a review of the TUC's measures to curtail the NMM's activities see Martin, *Communism and the British Trade Unions*, pp. 83–85 and 97–98, and *Mezh. Rabo. Dviz.*, Nos. 17–18, 5 May 1927. See also Bullock, *Ernest Bevin*, Vol. 1, p. 377.

On the eve of the breach, the position of the NMM had become untenable and frequent complaints were made about the difficulty of 'resisting splitting tendencies' within the movement. However, the clash between Profintern and the AUCCTU over expectations from the General Council had by now lost much of its ferocity, and differences of opinion lay in nuances rather than substance. It was obvious that the gulf between the British and Soviet trade unions had not narrowed and that the final parting was imminent.[119]

ARJAC's Berlin meeting between 29 March and 1 April produced, however, an unexpected truce. The British delegation, mostly concerned with the threat to trade posed by the fragile state of Anglo-Soviet relations, was prepared to make concessions in return for Russian acceptance of the proposed amendments to the constitution of ARJAC. A prolonged discussion in a small sub-committee culminated in a revised version of the clauses on mutual aid in which each movement undertook to respect the other's autonomy in domestic affairs. The Russians' reward came in an addendum which re-established ARJAC not merely as a step towards international unity but as the appropriate instrument to cope with the offensive of capitalism. The ill-defined nature of the offensive was clarified by reference to the menace of 'new and devastating wars'. A general consensus existed to the effect that ARJAC was 'particularly necessary in averting the danger of aggression against the Soviet Union'. However, the failure to draft a concrete plan to contain this threat was reminiscent of the incipient stages of the collaboration.[120]

ARJAC's new constitution was one of the major topics raised by the opposition in the April session of the central committee of the CPSU. Trotsky, drawing attention to the recent collapse of united front tactics in Kuomintang, predicted a similar future for the collaboration in Britain. In a proposed resolution he called

119 On complaints see Hardy in *Kras. Int. Prof.* (1927), No. 5, pp. 90–94, and in *Mezh. Rabo. Dviz.*, No. 24, 16 June 1927. Humbert-Droz, '*L'Oeil de Moscou' à Paris,* pp. 248–50, witnessed the still discernible animosity between Tomsky and Lozovsky in Comintern.

120 No stenographic record of the meeting seems to exist; the present survey is based on TUC archives, B 113 18/2/45: memorandum on ARJAC's meeting, and *Trade Union Bulletin* (Apr. 1927), No. 4.

for the immediate dissolution of ARJAC and the reprimanding of Tomsky for his handling of the Berlin meeting.[121]

The coincidence of the defeat in China with the concession made in Berlin was undoubtedly a source of embarrassment to the leadership. Unlike the publicity following previous meetings of ARJAC, information about both the proceedings in Berlin and the approval of the new constitution by the AUCCTU on 8 April was subdued. The exception was a long interview with Tomsky in which he explained the decision as 'defying the aspirations of the enemies of the working class' to eliminate the committee.[122]

The full support given to Tomsky in the central committee further revealed the diplomatic reasoning behind the decision taken in Berlin. Despite accusations of opportunism, the majority expressed its firm decision to preserve ARJAC: 'The English bourgeoisie was only waiting for the dissolution of ARJAC as a signal for severing diplomatic relations with the USSR.' In the presidium of IKKI on 11 May, Bukharin even more bluntly defined the diplomatic orientation of the Russian position in Berlin as aimed at 'forestalling an imperialist attack on Russia'.[123]

When a day later Arcos was raided without provoking a serious challenge from ARJAC, Trotsky threw down the gauntlet to Bukharin. In a memorandum submitted to the eighth plenum of IKKI, which met from 18 to 30 May, he attacked the collaboration on two counts. Firstly, he attributed the preservation of the committee to the political opportunism of the majority, which had hitherto been reluctant frankly to admit the diplomatic expectations from the alliance. 'Is it possible', asked

121 Trotsky archives, T-3046, 'Proekt Rezolyutsii po Voprosu ob Anglo-Russkom Komitete'. In *The Third International After Lenin*, pp. 131–133, he overestimates the GC's need to preserve ARJAC 'as its political screen from the masses'.

122 Précis of proceedings of AUCCTU's meeting, *Pravda*, 15 Apr. 1927; Tomsky's interview, *Trud*, 5 Apr. 1927. Petrovsky later provided the same explanation: the Russians, 'familiar with the train of thought of ARJAC's enemies', did not fall into the trap set for them in Berlin; see *Komm. Int.* (1927), No. 24, p. 31. See also NMM, *Peace but not with Capitalism* (London, 1927), p. 26.

123 The leader of *Trud*, 19 Apr. 1927, is in fact a report of the debate in the central committee. On Bukharin's speech see Trotsky archives, T-3058. Bukharin repeated similar views in IKKI's plenum; see *Inprecorr*, 30 June and 7 July 1927.

Trotsky rhetorically, 'to use the trade unions at one moment in the interests of international class policy, and at the next for some particular, allegedly diplomatic, purpose?' Secondly, he vigorously opposed the suggestion that the alliance could effectively hold off a British attack. Trotsky then drew up a detailed list of ARJAC's drawbacks, warning that if a rupture followed the raid the General Council, 'the ballast without which the ship of British imperialism could hardly be expected to stay afloat', should not be counted on for support.[124]

Stalin's reply to the opposition largely avoided reference to the British issue, concentrating on Comintern's policies in China and the increasing threat to world peace. However, towards the end he struck a dramatic note in breaking the news of the rupture to the plenum. The announcement provided him with an opportunity to draw parallels between the hostile attitudes of the British Government and the opposition: the former threatened the CPSU with 'war and intervention' while the latter menaced it with 'a split'. The plenum therefore, Stalin concluded, was witnessing 'the emergence of no less than a united front from Chamberlain to Trotsky'.[125]

Murphy, who as representative of the CPGB was less vulnerable to accusations of defending ARJAC in support of Soviet national interests, was allotted the task of justifying the collaboration. Basing his case on the acute danger of war, the issue which the opposition had introduced, he mercilessly attacked Trotsky for his destructive approach to ARJAC. Murphy believed that it could exercise a restraining influence on the approaching capitalist offensive. Trotsky himself was accused of opportunism in using the platform of Comintern to improve his political standing in the CPSU. Resorting to analogies similar to Stalin's, Murphy warned Trotsky that by pursuing the 'adventurist policy' of dissolving the committee, he seemed to be welcoming the breach

124 No protocol of this plenum has ever been published; the present account is based on several speeches, memoranda and reviews of the meeting. Trotsky archives, T–3058, 'Bor'ba Za Mir i Anglo-Russkii Komitet'. The 'Declaration of the 83', the opposition's doubts of the leadership's ability to guide the CPSU in the event of war, was submitted on 25 May, the day of the breach; see Daniels, *The Conscience of the Revolution*, p. 284.

125 Stalin, *Sochineniya*, Vol. 9, pp. 311–12.

'on the principle that the worse the situation is, the better it is for the revolution'.[126]

Yet another method of defusing the opposition's criticism of ARJAC was by underlining the inconsistency of their arguments. Particular emphasis was laid on Zinoviev's staunch support of the committee in its initial stage.[127] However, Murphy's position and a subsequent speech by P. Neumann, a prominent member of the KPD, serve to illustrate that Comintern had been relegated to an auxiliary function in Soviet foreign policy. Neumann's denunciations of Trotsky were bound up with a pledge of loyalty to the Soviet Union as the 'first victorious communist society of the world, the organizational centre of the proletarian revolution'.[128] Similar but even more pointed views were expressed by an editorial in Comintern's organ which presented the Anglo-Soviet confrontation as the focal point of the world class struggle: 'An assault on the Soviet Union is an attack on the working class. By defending the Soviet state, one defends oneself from the class enemy.'[129]

The crisis in Anglo-Soviet relations of May 1927 put the trade union collaboration to a double test: it remained to be seen whether ARJAC could be activated and, if so, whether a manifestation of solidarity between the workers of the two countries would register an impact on the British Government. Tomsky and Dogadov, bearing in mind these vital questions, urged the General Council on 14 May to summon ARJAC, calling for 'straining of all efforts of the working class' to withstand the anti-Soviet policy. Pollitt, the general secretary of the NMM, supplemented this with a specific proposal for an emergency

126 *Komm. Int.* (1927), No. 24, pp. 8–11. D. Petrovsky, *Uroki Maiskogo Plenuma Kominterna* (Leningrad, 1927), pp. 31–32, levelled similar accusations: Trotsky seized ARJAC as 'the ace of trumps, not in the struggle against the danger of war but in the struggle against Comintern'. Similar views are in 'Komintern na Postu', *Pravda*, 19 May 1927.

127 D. Petrovsky, *Das Anglo-russische Komitee und die Opposition in der KPSU* (Hamburg, 1927), pp. 46–49.

128 *Komm. Int.* (1927), No. 24, pp. 12–17. On the mobilization of the world proletariat in defence of Russia see also resolutions in *10 Let Kominterna*, pp. 258–60; on the condemnation of Trotsky's views on the threat of war see *10 Let Kominterna*, pp. 265–66.

129 *Komm. Int.* (1927), No. 22, pp. 3–6. This line was adopted by the CPGB; see Bell in *The Communist* (July 1927), pp. 246–51.

conference of the TUC's executives, which would 'prepare a General Strike to combat the obvious moves that are being made to force war on Soviet Russia'.[130]

The time, however, was by no means ripe for a resurrection of the 'Hands off Russia' campaign of the 1920s. By ill fortune the Arcos raid coincided with the publication in the British Press of Tomsky's criticism of the General Council for its meek acceptance of the Government's 'draconic' Trade Union Bill.[131] Despite the grave international situation, Citrine reproached Tomsky for his breach of the pledge taken in Berlin to refrain from interfering in the TUC's internal affairs. Tomsky minimized the significance of his criticism, which he insisted reflected only his personal views, but did not retract its substance: he did not believe 'in infallibility in general, not even of the Pope in Rome'.[132]

The acrimony in relations with the AUCCTU was noticeable when Citrine's minimal action of protesting to Baldwin on 13 May against the Home Office's measures was received with mixed feelings by the General Council. Citrine's protest, moreover, had only underlined Britain's economic interests; a severance of relations would endanger the trade essential to ease soaring unemployment. In a lively meeting of the International Committee, Thomas dissociated himself from the protest while Purcell himself admitted that a meeting of ARJAC could 'serve no object' at present.[133]

[130] TUC archives, B 114 947 D4: AUCCTU to Citrine; TUC archives, B 113 18/2/45: Pollitt to Citrine, 19 May 1927.

[131] Tomsky's interview in *Trud*, 8 May 1927, was reproduced in *Inprecorr*, 12 May 1927, and fully quoted in *The Times*, 14 May 1927. The Trade Disputes and Trade Unions Bill *inter alia* made illegal sympathy strikes which caused hardship to the community or exerted pressure on the Government; see Bullock, *Ernest Bevin*, Vol. 1, pp. 377–79.

[132] TUC archives, B 114 947 D4: exchange of letters, 13 May and 6 June 1927.

[133] Citrine's letter, *Report of Proceedings at the 59th Annual Trades Union Congress*, p. 213; TUC archives, *Minutes of IC, 1926–7*, Meeting 10, 23 May 1927. The campaign launched by the CPGB, 'moving to the head of its agenda the task of defending the Soviet Union', registered hardly any impact; see *Kommunisticheskii Internatsional pered Shestym Vsemirnym Kongressom* (Moscow–Leningrad, 1928), p. 102.

After the breach the Russians, attaching new importance to the collaboration, besought the General Council to convene the committee in view of the 'intention of the tories to thrust a war upon the USSR'. Once again it was the TUC's concern at 'the effect of the rupture on trade with Russia', and to a lesser degree their disapproval of Labour's vacillation on the issue, which resulted in consent for an informal meeting of the chairmen and secretaries of the Anglo-Soviet delegations.[134]

The unofficial nature of the meeting and its limited scope were a source of dissatisfaction to the Russians, who sought an open defiance of the Conservatives' action.[135] To divert attention from the petty recriminations which had passed between British and Soviet trade union leaders, extraordinary efforts were made to emphasize the anxiety of the Soviet trade unions' rank and file for a successful outcome to the meeting. It was made crystal clear that the Soviet delegation was departing for Berlin with the single object of organizing joint action with the TUC to 'dispel the threat of war'. However, there was growing fear that the results might confirm that the alliance was 'merely a scrap of paper'.[136]

The circumstances of the meeting did not permit the Russians' customary tactics of refusing to come to the point. Tomsky and Melnichansky, who owing to difficulties in obtaining visas arrived in Berlin only late in the evening of 18 June, pressed for an immediate session. From the outset they posited the permanent nature of the committee and underlined its urgent task of providing a 'safeguard against the dangers of aggression against Russia'. To demonstrate that matters of procedure were immaterial in this crisis, they readily gave way to Citrine's demand for a letter of explanation to the General Council on the harsh tone of the correspondence leading to the meeting. After warning that a delay in convening a full meeting at that juncture 'would be equivalent to passing sentence of death upon it', the Russians proceeded to spell out their expectations from ARJAC. They

134 TUC archives, B 113 18/2/45: Dogadov to Citrine, 3 June 1927; *Minutes of IC, 1926–7*, Meetings 11 and 12, 2 and 9 June 1927.

135 *Pravda*, 18 June 1927.

136 *Trud*, 18 June 1927. On rank-and-file feelings see also *Izvestiya*, 18 June 1927. The CPGB previewed the meeting with even greater pessimism; see *The Communist* (June 1927), pp. 198–201.

had in mind similar measures to those taken by the British workers in summer 1920 to prevent the Government from embarking on an anti-Soviet course.[137] As a first step, they wished ARJAC to appeal to the workers to 'refuse to manufacture or transport ammunitions'. The British representatives, however, aware of the General Council's stiffening attitude towards the AUCCTU and the TUC's precarious standing with the Government, had no intention of proceeding further than the protest letter handed to Baldwin. The meeting, therefore, ended in deadlock when the Russians were advised to approach the IFTU, 'the appropriate body' for such an action.[138]

A step towards the final breakdown of the committee, and with it effective opposition to the Government's policy towards Russia, was taken by the General Council shortly after the Berlin meeting. Although different opinions were still evident in the General Council when it met to consider the reappraisal of the alliance, the gap had considerably narrowed; not a single motion was tabled in favour of unconditional support of Russia. Thomas suggested the postponement of further communication until after a debate in the TUC congress, while Hicks, at the other end of the spectrum, proposed the summoning of ARJAC as a preliminary step towards the introduction of the issue into a conference under the auspices of the IFTU. Thomas finally won the upper hand when the Russians were informed of the General Council's unwillingness to call ARJAC.[139]

Disillusionment about ARJAC dominated an extraordinary

[137] Profintern expressed more confidence in the emergence of *spontaneous* councils of action; see *Kras. Int. Prof.* (1927), No. 7, pp. 43–44. The CPGB appealed for the formation of such councils in *Labour Monthly* (July 1927), p. 409.

[138] TUC archives, B 113 18/2/49: report of discussion on the proposed meeting of ARJAC; Tomsky's letter of explanation was sent from Berlin on 20 June and is in TUC archives B 114 18/2/23. On the 'procrastination tactics' of the GC see Lorwin, *Labour and Internationalism*, pp. 357–58.

[139] TUC archives, *Minutes of GC, 1926–7*, pp. 90–91 and 93, 22 June 1927. The stiffening attitude towards Russia was apparent in a resolution moved in the meeting expressing 'the fervent hope that the practice of executing persons for political offences, with or without trial, will cease'. Citrine also recollected this tendency in *Men at Work*, pp. 92–93, and *I Search for Truth in Russia* (London, 1936), pp. 300–301.

session of the AUCCTU, hastily convened on 28 June to discuss the fiasco of the Berlin session. It was clear from the outset that Tomsky, once the most vehement protagonist of the committee, had turned against it. Drawing up a balance sheet for the collaboration, he could not avoid the conclusion that the mismanagement of the revolutionary situation of 1926 by the British members of the committee had been aggravated by their failure to implement measures against imminent war. His speech expressed bitter disappointment in ARJAC, which had been 'established to struggle against the danger of war but had at a critical stage hidden its face in a cowardly fashion'. He contemptuously dismissed Citrine's protest to Baldwin as an 'impotent, drivelling, two-faced document'. However, the fact that the opposition had correctly predicted the ineffectiveness of the collaboration and the lack of a decisive evaluation of united front tactics seem to have inhibited the Russians from taking the initiative and withdrawing from the committee. While Tomsky expressed no intention of pursuing negotiations with the General Council, the resolution moved by the session provided for a resumption of talks if the British unilaterally adopted 'PRACTICAL measures to thwart the Conservative offensive'.[140]

Now the question was merely which movement would manoeuvre the other into secession from ARJAC. The General Council certainly showed no intention of giving way to the Russian demands; in a statement issued on 27 July, they returned to the Russians' abuse of the alliance and failure to abide by the amended constitution.[141]

Meanwhile the General Council made a last abortive attempt to dispose of the Russian question within the framework of Amsterdam by transferring it to the fourth congress of the IFTU, which met in Paris at the beginning of August. The British delegates themselves now exploited the threat of war to urge the IFTU to renew negotiations with the Russians. Their pleas, however, were totally rejected by the majority of the delegates, whose views were summed up by Stenhuis, a distinguished Dutch

[140] Review of the meeting and resolution in *Trud*, 29 June 1927; Tomsky's speech in *Trud*, 1 July 1927. This position was later endorsed by the central committee of the CPSU; see *KPSS v Rezolyutsiyakh i Resheniyakh*, Vol. 3, p. 471.

[141] *Report of 59th TUC*, pp. 203–207.

Social Democrat: the Russians had 'done nothing but heap insults upon us'.[142]

The Soviet reply to the General Council's statement of 27 July was postponed until 30 August, when it was approved by a session of the AUCCTU in connection with the impending TUC congress. In presenting it to the gathering, Dogadov went out of his way to outline differences of opinion with the British allies and repudiated the decision taken by ARJAC in April that each side should refrain from interfering in the other's affairs. The reply itself deplored the transformation of ARJAC into a 'committee for the interchange of documents' and described the General Council's statement as an attempt 'to give the collaboration a first-class funeral'. The AUCCTU, determined not to withdraw from the committee, provoked the General Council into doing so by maintaining their 'sacred right' of divulging the General Council's 'crimes committed against the working class'.[143]

This communication was a compensation for the Russian absence, for the second year running, from the TUC congress which met in Edinburgh between 5 and 10 September. It was reinforced by a telegram from Moscow which not only repeated previous accusations but declared that the General Council had formed an 'alliance' with the Conservative Government. Both communications undoubtedly encouraged the vacillating General Council to terminate the collaboration. The ambiguous attitude towards Russia was demonstrated by Hicks' presidential address. While voicing the TUC's 'great deal of resentment' against the Russians' 'crude arrogance', he praised the Russian achievement on the tenth anniversary of the revolution, pledging the TUC to defend the 'conquest of the Russian workers'.[144]

142 *Report of Proceedings at the Fourth Ordinary Congress of the IFTU* (Amsterdam, 1927): Purcell, p. 32; Hicks, pp. 46–47; Citrine, p. 512; Stenhuis and similar views, pp. 44–48 and 53–55. Unfriendly views towards Russia were incorporated in the report to the congress; see *Report on Activities during the Years 1924, 1925 and 1926*, pp. 53–58.

143 AUCCTU session in *Trud*, 3 Sept. 1927. *Pravda*, 3 Sept. 1927, claimed that the GC's statement reflected the 'contagious effect' of the diplomatic rupture. The British overtures to Amsterdam were dismissed by Profintern as 'throwing dust in the eyes of the workers'; see Levin in *Mezh. Rabo. Dviz.*, No. 34, 25 Aug. 1927. See also Lozovsky in *Trud*, 10 Aug. 1927.

144 *Report of 59th TUC*, pp. 69–70. On the GC's discussion of the Russian

The General Council's report gave a detailed account of developments in ARJAC throughout the year but left open the question of future relations. The proposed withdrawal from the committee was dramatically announced by Citrine shortly after the adoption of a resolution outlawing the NMM. Strongly condemning the Russians' continuous interference in the TUC's affairs, he insisted that it could no longer be treated as a 'subservient branch of the Communist Party'. So far as Russia's security was concerned, he rejected suggestions that ARJAC provided an effectual safeguard. British workers would find the proper means of providing help in the hour of need.[145] Clynes, Bromley, Thomas and Bevin, who followed Citrine on the rostrum, fully supported him. Oddly enough, the only reservations came from Cramp of the National Union of Railwaymen, who had opposed the alliance with the Russians in 1924. The resolution, he warned, would be interpreted as tacit support from the TUC of the rupture and would encourage the Government 'to go on with their warlike preparations'. This argument was unable to prevent a decisive victory for the supporters of dissolution. However, to restore the balance the congress deplored the rupture and particularly its economic consequences.[146]

Profintern's self-imposed restraint in criticizing the General Council following the severance had been relaxed after the miscarriage of the informal meeting in Berlin. The General Council was then accused of 'voluntarily serving as the direct tool of the most reactionary, most active imperialist Government in the world'. The General Council was not only accused of incompetence to lead the trade unions, but placed on a level with the Conservative Party – the antithesis of the Soviet regime. This offensive gathered momentum throughout July when explicit suggestions were made that the General Council was 'supporting Chamberlain in executing his bellicose policy against the USSR'.[147]

letter see TUC archives, *Minutes of GC, 1926–7*, p. 110, 5 Sept. 1927.

[145] *Report of 59th TUC*, pp. 358–60. On the coincidence of the repressive measures against the NMM and the dissolution see Braunthal, *History of the International*, pp. 306–307, and Pollitt, *Serving My Time*, pp. 180–87.

[146] *Report of 59th TUC*, pp. 367–71. The voting was 2,551,000 to 620,000.

[147] Lozovsky in *Pravda*, 29 June 1927; Zubok in *Mezh. Rabo. Dviz.*, No.

Profintern's unbridled criticism threw the NMM conference, which met shortly before the Edinburgh congress, into confusion. The conference, meeting amidst growing speculations about ARJAC's imminent dissolution, adopted a distinctly militant line which contributed much to the detachment of non-communists from the movement.[148] The abandonment of the sacred cow of the united front was justified on the grounds that the bureaucracy of the TUC had openly declared itself against class struggle and 'moved bag and baggage to Chamberlain's camp'.[149]

The dissolution of the committee may have contributed significantly to the implementation of the 'third period' of class against class in Comintern. It certainly demonstrated the futility of the long-standing hope that fraternal feelings could be channelled in support of the Soviet Union. The termination of the collaboration gained autonomy for Profintern in the conduct of international trade union relations. The definition of spheres of activity also relieved the tension and contradictions in Soviet foreign policy which had resulted from the frequent attempts to accommodate revolutionary ends with the attainment of national goals.[150]

The aftermath

The severance of relations had only a marginal impact on the course of Anglo-Soviet relations; rather than marking an innovation, it was a concrete expression of the state of relations over

27, 7 July 1927. See also 'Edinyi Front ot Chemberlena do Gensoveta', *Trud*, 29 July 1927; *Komm. Int.* (1927), No. 7, pp. 5–7; *Inprecorr*, 27 July 1927. Before long this became the official line of both Comintern and Narkomindel; see *Kommunisticheskii Internatsional pered Shestym Vsemirnym Kongressom*, pp. 96–97, and *Mir. Khz. i Mir. Pol.* (1928), No. 1, pp. 4–5.

148 *Kras. Int. Prof.* (1927), No. 11, pp. 504–507; Murphy in *Pravda*, 30 Sept. 1927. The dissociation was also reflected in the CPGB's dwindling membership; see *Inprecorr*, 20 Oct. 1927.

149 *Mezh. Rabo. Dviz.*, No. 3, 22 Sept. 1927; 'Gensovet na Sluzhbe u Imperializma', *Pravda*, 9 Sept. 1927. The CPGB aligned itself with Profintern. Pollitt accused the GC of 'playing Baldwin's game in the Trade Union movement' in *Labour Monthly* (Oct. 1927), pp. 592–93, and *The Communist* (Oct. 1927), pp. 101–105 and 115–19.

150 On the solution of the contradictions see F. Borkenau, 'The Comintern in Retrospect', *The Dublin Review* (Mar. 1943), pp. 43–44.

the past three years. Birkenhead probably reflected widespread feelings in Cabinet when he noted that by breaking off relations with Russia the Government had 'got rid of the hypocrisy of pretending to have friendly relations' with that country.[151]

The British Government, taking as their model Soviet-American relations, aimed to preserve normal trade relations while reducing diplomatic contacts to a minimum. In a statement to Parliament on 28 July, Chamberlain, after asserting that while the 'old abuse' continued relations could not be resumed, concluded: 'But trade may go on. We will do nothing to interfere with it, and we have no desire to push, and no intention of pushing, our differences any further.' Later in the year Baldwin in his Guildhall speech declared that if the Russians undertook to abstain from interference in British domestic affairs and from a 'policy of intrigue and hostility elsewhere' his Government would 'meet them in that spirit of liberty and good will' which inspired its foreign policy.[152]

These and similar utterances raised the Russians' faint hopes that relations, which they believed had been severed prematurely, would soon be resumed. They expected to hasten this outcome by threatening to divert orders originally destined for Britain to other countries and deprive Britain of essential Russian goods. Chicherin, reacting to current rumours that Britain was seeking to relax the tension, described the assumption that Anglo-Soviet trade could continue on the same scale in the absence of diplomatic relations as a 'profound error'.[153] This, however, was to a large extent an empty threat. Since 1925 Russian orders had already been diverted from Britain to Germany, where credit had proved easier to obtain. The volume of Anglo-Soviet trade did drop sharply in the period 1927–28, partly because of a shortage of grain for export, but it regained its previous proportions during the next year. In spite of their meagre reserves of foreign currency, the Russians could not afford to lose the only

[151] Birkenhead, *Life of F. E. Smith*, pp. 538–39. See also speeches reported in *The Times*, 6 June and 8 July 1927.

[152] *Parl. Deb. H.C.*, Vol. 209, col. 1530; *The Times*, 10 Nov. 1927.

[153] *Dok. Vne. Pol.*, Vol. x, pp. 349–50, 5 Aug. 1927. On the economic threat, see *Mezh. Khz. i Mezh. Pol.* (1927), No. 9. p. 5; Wise in *Manchester Guardian*, 23 May 1927; W. P. Coates, *The Tories and Russian Trade* (London, 1928), pp. 5 and 22–23.

commercial partner with whom they enjoyed a trading surplus.[154]

Baldwin's speech, warmly welcomed in Russia, emboldened Litvinov to put out feelers to ascertain the possibility of resuming relations. At the end of November the Foreign Office received several indirect Russian proposals for a meeting between Litvinov and Chamberlain in Geneva. These overtures, regarded by Chamberlain as a 'silly impertinence', were discussed by Cabinet, which was inclined to agree to a meeting; it was seen as an opportunity to promote commercial interests and dispel the Russians' fears of Britain's belligerent intentions. Chamberlain assured Cabinet, however, that he would be 'most careful not to commit H.M.G. to any change of policy'.[155]

The first direct contact since the rupture between the two parties took place in Geneva on 5 December 1927. Litvinov found Chamberlain politely unbending, holding the Soviet Government responsible for Comintern's subversive activities throughout the British Empire and refusing to initiate any further negotiations. The meeting thus dashed the remaining Russian hopes of reversing the course of relations with the Conservative Government.[156] The year 1928 indeed proved uneventful in

[154] E. H. Carr and R. W. Davies, *Foundations of a Planned Economy*, Vol. 2, pp. 712–16.

Soviet trade with its major partners, in percentages of total trade:

	1925–26		*1926–27*		*1927–28*	
	imp.	*exp.*	*imp.*	*exp.*	*imp.*	*exp.*
England	18.6	31.8	15.6	29.1	5.3	23.2
Germany	25.6	18.8	25.3	24.7	29.5	29.2
U.S.A.	17.8	14.3	23.0	2.5	22.1	3.5

Fluctuations in volume of Anglo-Soviet trade in £ millions:

1924–25	*1925–26*	*1926–27*	*1927–28*	*1928–29*
50.8	42.4	40.1	28.6	38.2

Tables based on *Voprosy Torgovli* (1930), No. 5, pp. 29–30, and *Mezh. Zhzn.* (1929), No. 11, p. 55.

[155] For the favourable reaction in Russia to Baldwin's speech, see Rykov in *Pravda*, 25 Nov. 1927; *Izvestiya*, 2 Dec. 1927. For Litvinov's overtures see F.O. 800/227: minute by Locker-Lampson, 28 Nov. 1927; F.O. 371 12593 N2650/209/38: Cadogan (Geneva) to Chamberlain, and minute by Chamberlain, 30 Nov. 1927; Cab. 23/55 59(27)2: Cabinet meeting of 30 Nov. 1927.

[156] F.O. 371 12593 N5796/209/38: Chamberlain to Tyrrell, 5 Dec. 1927.

Anglo-Soviet relations, with the sole exception of the sensational revival of the 'Zinoviev letter' affair. This was precipitated by Gregory's dismissal from the Foreign Office after his conviction for improperly speculating in francs.

At the beginning of 1929 the Government came under increasing pressure from groups of diverse political affinities to restore diplomatic relations with the Soviet Union in the interests of British trade. The programme of the Labour Party for the coming elections embodied a resolution to that effect.[157] The formation of a Labour Government in June 1929 did not, however, bring an immediate restoration of relations. Wise after their experience of 1924, the new Government conditioned a resumption on the solution of controversial issues, particularly that of propaganda. Preliminary negotiations dragged on until November, while ambassadors were exchanged a month later. A new trade agreement was eventually signed on 16 April 1930 but relations remained inimical and distrustful in character.[158]

157 For surveys of this period, see Coates, *A History of Anglo-Soviet Relations*, Chap. XII; Fischer, *The Soviets in World Affairs*, Vol. 2, pp. 694–98; Popov, *Anglo-Sovetskie Otnosheniya*, pp. 131–41.

158 D. N. Lammers, 'The Second Labour Government and the Restoration of Relations with Soviet Russia (1929)', *Bull. Inst. Hist. Res.* (May 1964), Vol. XXXVII, pp. 60–72; M. Beloff, *The Foreign Policy of Soviet Russia* (Oxford, 1952), Vol. I, pp. 16–18; *Mezh. Zhzn.* (1929), No. 11, pp. 47–62.

Conclusions

The Soviet Union's drive towards securing full recognition in Europe in the mid-1920s found its fullest expression in relations with Britain. During these years, the course of Anglo-Soviet relations, besides providing the criterion for the success of Soviet foreign policy, registered a vital impact on the general outlook of the Soviet Union. It reflected the gradual subordination of revolutionary proselytization to the more pressing need for acceptance on an equal footing by the Western nations. The transition, combined with a measure of success in reintegration into Europe, had far-reaching consequences in the domestic domain. In comparison relations with Russia had a marginal effect on Britain, whose main problem lay in communicating with a state which conformed to no existing category and appeared to pursue an unconventional foreign policy in defiance of international codes of behaviour. 'There are notoriously no precedents', complained Gregory, probably the leading authority on Russia in the Foreign Office, 'for dealing with a regime – one can hardly say a country – like the Soviets.'[1]

The enmity which marked these relations was on the whole not a continuation of the historical feud between Britain and Russia; this largely vanished when Curzon relinquished his post as Foreign Secretary at the end of 1923. The roots of the post-war friction lay in antagonism towards the perplexing new regime committed to crushing the world social order, and the failure to adopt an adequate policy towards it. Prior to recognition the dilemma was not yet acute. While the Russians still cherished hopes of spreading the revolution beyond Russia's borders, thereby overcoming their weakness and isolation, the British did not entirely abandon their expectations that the new regime would be ousted or, even more likely, collapse of its own accord. Recognition

[1] F.O. 800/260: Gregory to Chamberlain, 19 May 1927.

marked the turning-point in so far as it admitted that the Soviet Union had surmounted its initial obstacles and, against all odds, was likely to survive. The perfunctory nature of recognition left an ineradicable strain in the pattern of relations, which was discernible during the more turbulent years of the 1930s.

The purpose of this study has been to describe and explain two conflicting trends in Anglo-Soviet relations in the period under examination: the British indifference to the steady deterioration of relations after recognition and the Russians' desperate efforts to salvage them. The outstanding feature of Anglo-Soviet relations in the 1920s is the discrepancy between the prominence which Tsarist Russia had occupied in British foreign policy and the scanty attention paid to the Bolshevik state, whose weakness precluded it from serious consideration in the post-war regrouping of Europe. Against this background Britain, indisputably the more powerful partner, dictated the pace of Anglo-Soviet relations throughout the period. Britain's lack of a strong incentive for fostering relations and the consequent policy of aloofness frustrated Russia's tireless initiatives to improve relations and rendered a stalemate practically inevitable.

The divergence between the Labour and Conservative Governments in the formulation of policy towards the Soviet Union is not so wide as is commonly supposed. Although the Russians had a better opportunity for achieving *rapprochement* with Labour, neither British Government was willing to make allowances for the uniqueness of the Bolshevik regime, or to employ extraordinary measures in encounters with it. The formulation of both Labour and Conservative policy was based on a fundamentally similar outlook on foreign affairs. Ideological affiliations, however, which had little bearing on the basic concepts of policy, resulted in dissensions within the parties which exerted pressure on both Governments to modify their original intentions. The most striking overall similarity in the handling of the Russian issue is to be found in the grave suspicion of the Russians' explicit desire to regulate relations and the exaggeration of the ideological motives behind the Russian policies. While paying disproportionate attention to Comintern's revolutionary utterances and the threat it posed to the world order, the British overlooked the increasing subordination of revolutionary to diplomatic aims.

In this context the Anglo-Soviet trade union committee was regarded as a revolutionary expression while its diplomatic overtones were completely ignored.

Entrenched resentment against communism played a major role in Anglo-Soviet relations. The issue of propaganda became the focal point in relations despite the actual weak grip of the communists in Britain and their negligible influence throughout the Empire. Yet in countries like Germany and France, where the threat was much more real, communist activities only rarely affected relations with Russia. The Conservatives openly assumed the mission of preserving Britain from the 'evil' of communism at home and placed the blame for subversive activities squarely with Moscow. Propaganda, moreover, was an issue which linked rather than divided the successive Governments in Britain. MacDonald had evinced little sympathy for the Bolshevik state and was concerned to dissociate Labour's policies from those of the communists.

Both administrations gave priority to the organization of a new concert of Europe in which Britain would hold the balance of power. It was hoped that this would be achieved by reconciling France and Germany. MacDonald had laid the foundations for such a policy in the Allied Conference in July 1924 which regulated the question of war debts and reparations, while Chamberlain completed the task in the more spectacular, though less effective, conclusion of the Locarno treaty of guarantees. This diplomacy deliberately avoided arrangements in the East and drove a wedge between Russia and the countries of western Europe. However, the crowning achievement of Soviet diplomacy, the Rapallo Treaty of 1922, reinforced by the 1926 Berlin Treaty, compelled the British Government to take Russia into consideration. Upon taking office Chamberlain concurred with Ponsonby's belief that a severance of relations was likely to introduce disturbing elements in Europe. The possible effects on Germany of any hostile British move towards Russia proved to be a sufficiently strong argument in favour of maintaining correct relations. However, this by no means constituted an inducement to establish friendly relations. Several initiatives by Germany to reconcile Russia and Britain, in an attempt to avert the potential dilemma of alignment with East or West, elicited no response.

The market which Russia seemed to offer to British industry

in a period of economic recession united Labour and the Conservatives in moves to seek a certain measure of accommodation. Such considerations, however, were not overwhelming; they rather reflected prospects for the future. The Soviet economy, crippled by the war and lack of credit, produced only a small overall volume of trade which in addition was disadvantageous to Britain.

Labour's policy aimed to resolve the anomaly of relations with the Bolshevik regime through the regulation of outstanding questions. The choice of policy stemmed from a combination of expediency and a need to satisfy powerful pressures from the rank and file. It was far from providing a firm basis for reciprocal relations. Indeed, recognition was essentially a completion of the task undertaken by Lloyd George and reflected the universally-held view that the Soviet regime was stable enough to remain effectively in power. The reluctance with which recognition was granted by MacDonald and the incomplete nature of the move are discernible in the conditions attached to it and the decision to exchange *chargés d'affaires* instead of ambassadors, to the Russians' dismay. MacDonald displayed little interest in the negotiations of the Anglo-Soviet Treaty and vacillated before finally signing it. There is no better illustration of the half-heartedness with which Labour approached Russia than the clumsy handling of the 'Zinoviev letter' affair.

The Conservative Party returned to power determined to bring to an end the flirtation with Russia but resisted attempts by extremists within its own camp to provoke open antagonism. It assumed an indifferent attitude which, while certainly not friendly, fell short of the bloodthirsty character ascribed to it by the Russians.

The dividing line between the two policies lay in their execution. In the case of Labour, pressure was brought to bear on the Government by the trade unions and militant back-benchers calling for an explicit identification of Labour with the Soviet regime. In addition MacDonald entrusted the entire conduct of Russian affairs to Ponsonby, a close associate of the Labour back-benchers; distrustful of the Foreign Office, he was committed to the integration of Russia in European affairs. The conclusion of the Anglo-Soviet treaty of 1924 should be largely attributed to his personal handling of the negotiations. It was mainly in comparison with these negotiations that the Conservative policy of keeping the Soviet Union at arm's length was evaluated in Moscow as hostile.

With Chamberlain's appointment as Foreign Secretary, the formulation of policy towards Russia was returned to the Foreign Office, which despite its anti-Soviet posture maintained a remarkable degree of objectivity. The policy of 'reserve' pursued by the Conservatives until the rupture was said to spring from the conviction that isolating Russia would force it to resemble other European countries. However, it seems to have been to a great extent an *ad hoc* policy arrived at almost unconsciously in the absence of a concrete alternative. The lack of a coherent policy provoked continuous pressure from the diehards for a severance of relations. The eventual capitulation of the Cabinet to this pressure in 1927 was an unconcealed response to emotion rather than national interest.

The underlying assumption that the Government needed only to 'sit tight and await Russian developments'[2] was strongly contested by the Foreign Office's representatives in Moscow. Hodgson, the Chargé d'Affaires and one of the few British officials with a realistic view of the situation, tried repeatedly but in vain to convince Chamberlain that although the Soviet regime was committed to 'overthrow the present cosmos and replace it by a dictatorship of the proletariat' its overriding preoccupation was attaining and consolidating control over its own country. He resisted the policy of leaving Russia on the sidelines and regarding it as a 'dangerous plague'.[3] Though a moderating influence, Hodgson was unable substantially to alter the course of events. With his Consular Service background, he was not accorded by Chamberlain the respect due to a full-blown diplomat.

By 1924 Anglo-Soviet relations had become the cornerstone of Soviet diplomacy in view of the priority given to the recovery of the Soviet Union in the period of construction of socialism in one country. A fundamental re-evaluation had taken place since Trotsky had declared, when appointed as the first Commissar for Foreign Affairs, that the 'victorious revolution does not

[2] F.O. 800/227: minutes by Locker-Lampson and Chamberlain, 26 Feb. 1926.

[3] F.O. 371 N4229/53/38, 20 May 1926.

require recognition from the professional representatives of capitalist diplomacy'. The evolution of Soviet foreign policy was marked by a vigorous search for a *modus vivendi* with capitalism and an obsession with breaking out of isolation. It was realized that Russia's domestic policies must be to a large extent formulated and re-adjusted in reaction to the achievements in the international arena. Any move towards the restoration of the domestic economy could only be pursued under sufficient guarantees that the capitalist world, and particularly Britain, had abandoned its intention of annihilating the regime by force, and was prepared to grant full recognition to the Soviet Union. It was hoped that subsequently any possible anti-Soviet measures, notably an economic blockade, would be forestalled, and free communications ensured.

Once full relations had been established and outstanding issues regulated, the Russians hoped for a flow of foreign credit and technological assistance. The last object necessitated a certain degree of mutual confidence and close cooperation. To fulfil these objects Britain had to be convinced that commercial relations held advantages for both parties. However, the disproportionate attention devoted by the Soviet Union to Britain and the subdued response this evoked resulted in an unbalanced relationship.

The characteristic feature of Anglo-Soviet relations during 1924–27 is the dynamism of Soviet foreign policy in its efforts to gain manoeuvrability, in contrast with the inflexibility of British diplomacy. In the absence of compelling incentives behind their initiatives the Russians were forced to resort to varied methods in an attempt to break through the impasse. These overtures should be approached with a broad outlook, as they emerged from an interplay of political relations, domestic factors and revolutionary aspirations.

The uniqueness of Soviet diplomacy in the 1920s stems from the Soviet Union's claim to be the *avant-garde* of world revolution. Great pains were taken by the Russians to coordinate two inherently conflicting tendencies. This process took place in the context of Anglo-Soviet relations, which provide an unparalleled opportunity for following the order of priorities set by the Russians in which national interests gained the upper hand over international aspirations. This, however, did not imply the abandonment of revolutionary principles but marked the full identification of the welfare of the Soviet Union with the prospects of world revolution.

At the beginning of 1924 the reluctant admittance by Comintern of a period of 'stabilization of capitalism' indicated the slowing pace of world revolution. It posed for the Russians the problem of concentrating on the fulfilment of national aims while ensuring the minimum possible friction with international revolutionary policies.

Early attempts to strike the balance were executed under the assumption that Comintern could function as an aid rather than a hindrance to Soviet foreign policy and yet retain its international identity. The open-ended united front tactics which paved the way for alliances with non-communist workers found their fullest expression in Britain. The foundation of a minority movement in the trade unions under the auspices of Profintern was matched by the cultivation of relations between the Soviet trade unions and the leadership of the TUC. Both alliances, however, were inspired by strong diplomatic considerations. In their early stages they were well disguised, and theoretical juggling enabled their presentation as pure products of class solidarity. However, the turn of fortunes at the end of 1924 and the formation of a Conservative Government upset the delicate balance, and emphasis was placed on the united front from above with the TUC. This was in conflict with the orthodox theory of these tactics, which justified a united front from above only as a complementary measure to unity from below. The departure from orthodoxy was accompanied by pressure on the CPGB to approve the alliance and fully support the NMM regardless of the threat it posed to the Party's own existence by duplicating its functions. Moreover, on occasions when the NMM's militant policy clouded the collaboration between the Soviet and British trade unions it was instructed to moderate its policies. The apex of the diplomatic drive through the trade unions was the creation of the Anglo-Soviet trade union committee in April 1925. This was a product of expediency whose aims were vaguely defined in order not to contradict the basic concepts of Soviet foreign policy.

No less striking than the unorthodoxy of this diplomatic move is its singular ineffectiveness. It is difficult to understand the Russians' extraordinary belief that the trade unions would be able to exert direct pressure on the Conservative Government and influence its relations with Russia. However, the clue may lie in Russia's searing experiences between 1918 and 1920. While the British Government had led the intervention in the civil war, the British left had consistently opposed the dispatch of troops and munitions to Poland in 1920. The Russians' paranoiac fear of Britain's warlike intentions naturally led them to seek security in the British trade unions. However, by the mid-twenties they seriously overestimated both the danger of further British intervention and the assistance which the trade unions would render in such an event.

The necessity of cloaking fraternal relations with a heavy ideological overlay contributed, moreover, to the failure of the alliance to progress beyond its initial steps. Paradoxically the TUC, which had undergone significant organizational changes since 1920, now pursued a policy somewhat resembling that of the Government. Its primary aim with regard to the Soviet Union was on the one hand the economic recovery of the country, which could lead to the expansion of Anglo-Soviet trade, and on the other hand the enrolment of the Soviet unions into the IFTU as an antidote to the splitting tendencies encouraged by Profintern. The gulf between the Russians' hopes from the alliance and its actual development became conspicuous after the Scarborough TUC congress in autumn 1925 when it was realized that no substantial differences existed between Labour, labelled by Comintern as a 'third bourgeois party', and the TUC.

The situation was not critical so long as revolutionary and diplomatic measures did not clash. However, the dangers inherent in the double-edged weapon of the united front were revealed by the Russians' predicament during the general strike in May 1926. The news of the strike, declared by the General Council of the TUC which had only recently been discredited by the Russians, was received in Moscow with complete surprise. The Russians, by reluctantly fulfilling their obligation as the vanguard of world revolution and providing assistance to the strikers, compromised their diplomatic standing. Their uncomfortable position was further aggravated by their inevitable criticism of the TUC for repudiating the political nature of the strike and terminating it at its height. By admonishing the TUC the Russians inevitably introduced acrimony into the collaboration at a time when a demonstration of solidarity was urgently needed.

The threat of a severance of relations, however, restrained the Russians from withdrawing from ARJAC, thereby exposing their opportunist view of the collaboration. In addition desperate efforts were made to dissociate the Soviet state from the support of the miners, claiming rather that it was a spontaneous gesture by the Soviet trade unions, allegedly independent of the state. Pending reappraisal of the alliance the Russians resorted to the unworkable formula of invigorating the alliance while sustaining their critical approach. Yet the general strike had taught a clear lesson: Comintern, far from being a pillar of Soviet diplomacy, now appeared to be a thorn in its side.

Events in Britain figured prominently in the inner party struggle in 1926 and 1927. The gradual emergence by 1927 of Stalin as the undisputed leader helped to solve the dilemma which faced the Russians in 1926. The defeat of the internationalist opposition, who regarded permanent revolution as the *sine qua non* for the survival of the Soviet Union, accounted for the pragmatic approach that the basis for socialism could be independently laid in Russia. The emphasis was steadily shifting from international aspirations to the satisfaction of national necessities. It is not surprising therefore that the majority's victory coincided with the Russification of Comintern, thereby completing the identification of the world revolution with the bastion of socialism established in Russia.

The general strike and disillusionment with the TUC, culminating in the dismantling of ARJAC in 1927, initiated the slow transition towards the 'class against class' period in Comintern, which received official cachet only in 1928. The origins of this policy lay in the long-standing rivalry between Lozovsky, the head of Profintern and an opponent of unity with the social democrats, and Tomsky, a fervent advocate of the pragmatic alliance. The change of line was conceived against the background of events in Britain and had immediate consequences on the course of Anglo-Soviet relations. It encouraged the severance of the hitherto organic ties between Comintern and Soviet diplomacy. This process constituted a major landmark in the evolution towards moderation of Soviet diplomacy and relegated revolutionary activities to a lower place in the hierarchy.

Soviet diplomacy increasingly resembled that of the other European countries, although not occupying the same prominence as in other political systems.

Narkomindel's slow accumulation of authority was marked by Chicherin's gradual replacement by Litvinov as the effective head of the Commissariat shortly after the general strike. Chicherin, a confirmed Anglophobe, had been noted for his opposition to integration within the European system and his vigorous denunciation of the League of Nations as a nest of anti-Soviet plots. Litvinov's emergence was characterized by his tireless efforts to recover the damage inflicted on Anglo-Soviet relations, his drive for 'peaceful co-existence', and the placatory gestures which were made towards the League of Nations throughout 1927.

The change, however, came too late to prevent the breakdown in Anglo-Soviet relations, which had demonstrated the bankruptcy of Soviet foreign policy and even more strikingly the failure to rally the trade unions in support of the USSR. The war scare which followed the severance of relations exposed the Soviet Union's lack of real security. The rupture also contributed to the realization that with the failure to obtain foreign financial assistance the recovery of Russia depended largely on the exploitation of internal resources.

Although by 1927 most European countries had followed Britain's example in granting formal recognition, Russia's isolation was not substantially reduced. Anglo-Soviet relations were resumed at the end of 1929, but they retained a tension which was a legacy from the failures and misunderstandings of the earlier period.

Bibliography

I. MANUSCRIPT SOURCES

1. Records of Government Departments

Home Office Archives:

Home Office: selection of material concerning the 'Zinoviev letter' affair and the Arcos raid

Public Record Office:

Cabinet Conclusions (Cab. 23)

Cabinet Papers (Cab. 24)

Committee of Imperial Defence: minutes and memoranda (Cab. 2)

Foreign Office: General Correspondence, minutes and memoranda (F.O. 371)

Foreign Office: Private Correspondence of Austen Chamberlain, Eyre Crowe, Godfrey Locker-Lampson, Ramsay MacDonald, Arthur Ponsonby, William Tyrrell (F.O. 800)

Public Record Office, Ashridge:

Foreign Office, Treaty Department: minutes and memoranda (F.O. 372)

2. TUC Archives

Correspondence with Soviet trade unions

Correspondence with the IFTU

Minutes of General Council, International Committee, and Financial and General Purposes Committee of the TUC

Records of ARJAC's meetings

3. Collections of Private Papers

Baldwin, Stanley: University of Cambridge Library

Balfour, Arthur: British Museum

Chamberlain, Austen: University of Birmingham Library

Churchill, Winston: deposited with Mr M. Gilbert

Haldane, Viscount: National Library of Scotland, Edinburgh

Lansbury, George: London School of Economics and Political Science

Lloyd George, David: Beaverbrook Library, London

MacDonald, Ramsay: deposited with David Marquand, M.P.

Morel, E.D.: London School of Economics and Political Science

Ponsonby, Arthur: Bodleian Library and with Baron Ponsonby

Steel-Maitland, Arthur: Scottish Record Office, Edinburgh

Trevelyan, Charles: University of Newcastle Library

II. PRINTED SOURCES

A. Primary Sources

1. Protocols and Verbatim Reports

Comintern

Kommunisticheskii Internatsional pered Shestym Vsemirnym Kongressom (Moscow–Leningrad, 1928).

Otchet Ispolkoma Kominterna (Aprel' 1925-Yanvar' 1926) (Moscow–Leningrad, 1926).

Puti Mirovoi Revolyutsii. Sed'moi Rasshirennyi Plenum Isponitel'nogo Komiteta Kommunisticheskogo Internatsionala, 2 vols. (Moscow–Leningrad, 1927).

Pyatyi Vsemirnyi Kongress Kommunisticheskogo Internatsionala. Stenograficheskii Otchet, 2 vols. (Moscow, 1925).

Rasshirennyi Plenum Ispolkoma Kommunisticheskogo Internatsionala. Stenograficheskii Otchet (Moscow, 1925).

Shestoi Rasshirennyi Plenum Ispolkoma Kominterna. Stenograficheskii Otchet (Moscow–Leningrad, 1927).

Shestoi Rasshirennyi Plenum Ispolkoma Kominterna. Tezisy i Rezolyutsii (Moscow, 1927).

Tivel', A. and Kheimo, M. (ed.), *10 Let Kominterna* (Moscow–Leningrad, 1929).

Communist Party of the Soviet Union:

Chetyrnadtsataya Konferentsiya Rossiiskoi Kommunisticheskoi Partii (B). Stenograficheskii Otchet (Moscow, 1925).

XV Konferentsiya Vsesoyuznoi Kommunisticheskoi Partii (B). Stenograficheskii Otchet (Moscow–Leningrad, 1927).

XIV S'ezd Vsesoyuznoi Kommunisticheskoi Partii (B). Stenograficheskii Otchet (Moscow, 1926).

KPSS v Rezolyutsiyakh i Resheniyakh (Moscow, 1970), Vol. 3.

Trinadtsatyi S'ezd Rossiiskoi Kommunisticheskoi Partii (B) (Moscow, 1963).

Communist Party of Great Britain:

The Eighth Congress of the Communist Party of Great Britain: Papers, Theses, and Resolutions, 1926 (London, 1927).

Report of the Seventh Congress of the Communist Party of Great Britain (London, 1925).

Speeches and Documents of the Sixth Conference of the Communist Party of Great Britain (London, n.d.).

Hansard, 5th Series, *Parliamentary Debates, House of Commons, 1924–27.*

International Federation of Trade Unions:

The Activities of the IFTU, 1922–1924 (Amsterdam, 1927).

Report on Activities during the Years 1924, 1925 and 1926 (Amsterdam, 1927).

Report of Proceedings at the Fourth Ordinary Congress of the International Federation of Trade Unions (Amsterdam, 1927).

Miners' Federation of Great Britain, *Annual Volume of Proceedings for the Year 1926* (1927).

National Minority Movement:

Report of the National Minority Conference held on August 23rd and 24th 1924 (London, 1924).

Report of the Second Annual Conference of the N.M.M. (London, 1925).

Report of the Special National Conference of Action, March 21st 1926 (London, 1926).

Report of the Special Unity Conference Held on 25 January 1925 (London, 1925).

Report of the Third Annual Conference, August 28th and 29th 1926 (London, 1926).

Profintern:

Chetvertaya Sessiya Tsentral'nogo Soveta Krasnogo Internationala Profsoyuzov. Otchet (Moscow–Leningrad, 1927).

Desyat' Let Profinterna v Rezolyutsiyakh (Moscow, 1930).

III Kongress Krasnogo Internatsionala Profsoyuzov. Stenograficheskii Otchet (Moscow, 1924).

Soviet Trade Unions:

Sedmoi S'ezd Professional'nykh Soyuzov SSSR. Stenograficheskii Otchet (Moscow, 1927).

Shestoi S'ezd Professional'nykh Soyuzov, 1924. Stenograficheskii Otchet (Moscow, 1924).

Trades Union Congress, *Annual Congress Reports*, 1923–27.

2. Documentary Sources

Ministero Degli Affair Esteri, *I Documenti Diplomatici Italiani*, septima serie, vol. II (Rome, 1955).

Ministerstvo Inostrannykh Del SSSR:

Dobrov, A.F. (ed.), *Lokarnskaya Konferentsiya 1925g.* (Moscow, 1959).

Dokumenty Vneshnei Politiki SSSR, vols. VI–X (Moscow, 1962–65).

Narkomindel:

Anglo-Sovetskie Otnosheniya so Dnya Podpisaniya Torgovogo Soglosheniya do Razryva (1921–1927gg). (Moscow, 1927).

Antisovetskie Podlogi (Moscow–Leningrad, 1926).

Parliamentary Papers:

Command Paper 2253, 'Text of Draft of Proposed General Treaty between Great Britain and Northern Ireland and the Union of Socialist Republics'.

Command Paper 2260, 'General Treaty between Great Britain and Northern Ireland and the Union of Soviet Socialist Republics'.

Command Paper 2682, 'Communist Papers Seized during the Arrest of the Communist Leaders on 14 and 21 October, 1925'.

3. Newspapers and Periodicals

A.E.U. Monthly Journal (1926)
All Power (1924)
Bol'shevik
British Gazette (May 1926)
British Worker (May 1926)
The Communist (1927)
Communist Review (1924–26)
Daily Herald
Daily Mail
Ekonomicheskaya Zhizn'

International Press Correspondence
Izvestiya
Kommunisticheskii International
Krasnyi Internatsional Profsoyuzov
Labour Monthly
Manchester Guardian
Mezhdunarodnaya Letopis' (1924–25).
Mezhdunarodnaya Zhizn'
Mezhdunarodnoe Rabochee Dvizhenie
Mirovoe Khozyaistvo i Mirovaya Politika (1926–27)
Pravda
The Shop Assistant (1924–25)
Soviet Union Monthly (1926–27)
The Times
Trade Union Bulletin (1926–27)
Trade Union Unity (1925–26)
Trud
Workers' Weekly (1926)
Workers' Life (1927)

4. Contemporary Publications and Pamphlets

Andreev, A., *Anglo-Russkii Komitet* (Moscow–Leningrad, 1927).
Antoshkin, D. V., *Kratkii Ocherk Professional'nogo Dvizheniya v Rossii* (Moscow, 1928).
Bennett, A. J., *The General Council and the General Strike* (London, 1926).
Coates, W. P., *The Tories and Russian Trade* (London, 1928).
CPGB, *Orders from Moscow?* (London, Aug. 1926).
What Margate Means (London, n.d.).
Crisp, B., 'The Russian Treaty and the Liberals', *Foreign Affairs* (Oct. 1924).
Gal'sen, S., *Komintern i Profintern* (Moscow, 1926).
Grigor'ev, L., and Olenev, S., *Bor'ba SSSR za Mir i Bezopasnost' v Evrope* (Moscow, 1956).
Kamenev, L., *Anglo-Sovetskii Dogovor* (Leningrad, 1924).
Khinchuk, L. M., *K Istorii Anglo-Sovetskikh Otnoshenii* (Moscow, 1928).
Lozovsky, A., *Anglo-Sovetskaya Konferentsiya Professional'nykh Soyuzov* (Moscow, 1925).
British and Russian Workers (London, 1927).
Klass Protiv Klassa (Moscow–Leningrad, 1926).
Uroki Angliiskoi Zabastovki (Moscow–Leningrad, 1926).
The World's Trade Union Movement (London, 1925).
Za Edinstvo Mezhdunarodnogo Profdvizheniya (Moscow, 1925).
NMM, *Is Trade Unionism Played Out?* (London, n.d.).
Peace but not with Capitalism (London, 1927).
Pollitt's Reply to Citrine (London, 1928).
Petrovsky, D., *Das Anglo-russische Komitee und die Opposition in der KPSU* (Hamburg, 1927).
Uroki Maiskogo Plenuma Kominterna (Leningrad, 1927).
Radchenko, I., *Sovremennaya Angliya i Anglo-Sovetskii Dogovor* (Ekaterinslav, 1924).
Rakovsky, C., *Liga Natsii i SSSR* (Moscow, 1926).
'Moi Besedy s Chemberlenom', *Molodaya Gvardiya* (Nov. 1927).
Rykov, A. I., *Angliya i SSSR* (Moscow, 1927).
Shtein, B. E., *Gaagskaya Konferentsya* (Moscow, 1922).
Shubin, P., *Chego Khotyat Lordy?* (Moscow, 1927).

Taigin, I., *Angliya i SSSR* (Leningrad, 1926).
Tomsky, M. P., *Getting Together* (London, n.d.).
Profsoyuzy SSSR i ikh Otnoshenie k Kompartii i Sovetskomu Gosudarstvu (Moscow, 1928).
Trotsky, L., *Where is Britain Going?* (London, 1926).

5. *Memoirs, Diaries and Collected Works*
Balabanoff, A., *My Life as a Rebel* (London, 1938).
Boothby, R. J., *I Fight to Live* (London, 1947).
Cecil, R., *A Great Experiment* (London, 1947).
Chicherin, G. V., *Stat'i i Rechi po Voprosam Mezhdunarodnoi Politiki* (Moscow, 1961).
Childs, W., *Episodes and Reflections* (London, 1930).
Citrine, W., *I Search for Truth in Russia* (London, 1936).
Men and Work (London, 1964).
Clynes, J. R., *Memoirs* (London, 1937).
Cole, M. (ed.), *Beatrice Webb's Diaries* (London, 1956).
D'Abernon, Viscount, *The Diary of an Ambassador*, 3 vols. (New York, 1929–31).
Duff Cooper, A., *Old Men Forget* (London, 1953).
Fischer, R., *Stalin and German Communism* (Harvard, 1948).
Gregory, J. D., *On the Edge of Diplomacy* (London, 1928).
Hardy, G., *Those Stormy Years* (London, 1956).
Hastings, P., *Autobiography* (London, 1948).
Hodgson, R., 'Memoirs of an Official Agent', *History Today* (Aug. 1954).
Horner, A., *Incorrigible Rebel* (London, 1960).
Humbert-Droz, J., *De Lénine à Staline* (Neuchâtel, 1971).
'*L'Oeil de Moscou*' *à Paris* (Paris, 1964).
Litvinov, M., *Vneshnyaya Politika SSSR. Rechi i Zayavleniya 1927–1935* (Moscow, 1937).
Lockhart, B., *Ace of Spies* (London, 1967).
Maisky, I. M., 'Anglo-Sovetskoe Torgovoe Soglashenie', *Voprosy Istorii* (1957), No. 5.
'Iz Londonskikh Vospominanii', *Novyi Mir* (1968), No. 4.
Vospominaniya Sovetskogo Diplomata (Moscow, 1971).
Middlemas, K. (ed.), *Thomas Jones, Whitehall Diary* (Oxford, 1969).
Murphy, J. T., *New Horizons* (London, 1941).
Preparing for Power (London, 1934).
O'Malley, O., *The Phantom Caravan* (London, 1954).
Parmoor, Lord, *A Retrospect: Looking back over a Life of Eighty Years* (London, 1936).
Pollitt, H., *Serving My Time* (London, 1940).
Scheffer, P., *Seven Years in Soviet Russia* (London, 1931).
Serge, V., *Memoirs of a Revolutionary, 1901–1941* (Oxford, 1963).
Snowden, P., *An Autobiography*, 2 vols. (London, 1937).
Stalin, I. V. *Sochineniya* (Moscow, 1948), Vols. 8–9.
Strang, W., *Home and Abroad* (London, 1956).

Sutton, E. (ed.), *Gustave Stresemann, His Diaries, Letters, and Papers* (London, 1937), Vols. II and III.
Thomas, J. H., *My Story* (London, 1937).
Trotsky, L., *My Life* (London, 1930).

B. Secondary Sources

Abramov, B. A., 'Razgrom Trotskistsko-Zinov'eskogo Antipartiinogo Bloka', *Voprosy Istorii KPSS* (1959), No. 6.
Adibekov, G. M., 'K 50-Letiyu Profinterna', *Novaya i Noveishaya Istoriya* (1971), No. 4.
Allen, V. L., 'The Re-organization of the Trades Union Congress, 1918–1927', *British Journal of Sociology* (1960), Vol. 11.
Baykov, A., *The Development of the Soviet Economic System* (Cambridge, 1950).
Beloff, M., *The Foreign Policy of Soviet Russia* (Oxford, 1952), Vol. 1.
Birkenhead, Earl of, *F. E.: The Life of F. E. Smith, First Earl of Birkenhead* (London, 1959).
Bishop, D. G., *The Administration of British Foreign Relations* (Syracuse, 1961).
Borkenau, F., 'The Comintern in Retrospect', *The Dublin Review* (Mar. 1943).
Brand, C., *The British Labour Party* (Stanford, 1965).
Brandt, C., *Stalin's Failure in China 1924–1927* (Harvard, 1958).
Braunthal, J., *History of the International, 1914–1943* (London, 1967), Vol. II.
Bullock, A., *The Life and Times of Ernest Bevin* (London, 1960), Vol. 1.
Carr, E. H., *The Bolshevik Revolution 1917–1923* (London, 1953), Vol. 3.
Foundations of a Planned Economy 1926–1929 (London, 1971), Vol. 2.
The Interregnum 1923–1924 (London, 1954).
Socialism in One Country 1924–1926 (London, 1964), Vol. 3.
Carr E. H. and Davies, R. W., *Foundations of a Planned Economy 1926–1929* (London, 1969), Vol. 1.
Chester, L., Fay, S. and Young, H., *The Zinoviev Letter* (London, 1967).
Coates, W. P. and Z. K., *A History of Anglo-Soviet Relations* (London, 1943).
Cole, G. D. H., *British Trade Unionism To-Day* (London, 1945).
Craig, G. A. and Gilbert, F. (ed.), *The Diplomats, 1919–1939* (Princeton, 1953).
Crook, W. H., *Communism and the General Strike* (Connecticut, 1960).
The General Strike (Univ. of North Carolina, 1931).
Crowe, Sibyl, 'The Zinoviev Letter: A Reappraisal', *Journal of Contemporary History* (July, 1975), Vol. 10, No. 3.
Daniels, R. V., *The Conscience of the Revolution* (Harvard, 1960).
Debo, R. H., 'George Chicherin: Soviet Russia's Second Foreign Commissar' (Univ. of Nebraska Ph.D. thesis, 1964).
Degras, J., 'United Front Tactics in the Comintern 1921–1928', in Footman, D. (ed.), *International Communism.* St. Antony's Papers No. 9 (London, 1960).

Deutscher, I., *The Prophet Unarmed* (Oxford, 1970).
Soviet Trade Unions (London, 1950).
Draper, T., 'The Strange Case of Comintern', *Survey* (1972), Vol. 18, No. 5.
Dyck, H. L., 'German-Soviet Relations and the Anglo-Soviet Break, 1927', *Slavonic Review* (Mar. 1966), No. 1.
Weimar Germany and Soviet Russia 1926–1933 (London, 1966).
Fischer, L., *Men and Politics* (New York, 1966).
The Soviets in World Affairs, 1917–1929, 2 vols. (Princeton, 1951).
Flanders, A. D., *Trade Unions* (London, 1952).
Freund, G., *Unholy Alliance* (London, 1957).
Gasiorowski, Z. J., 'The Russian Overture to Germany of December 1924', *The Journal of Modern History* (June 1958), Vol. XXX.
'Stresemann and Poland before Locarno', *Journal of Central European Affairs* (Apr. 1958), Vol. XVIII.
Glenny, M. V., 'The Anglo-Soviet Trade Agreement, March 1921', *Journal of Contemporary History* (1970), Vol. 5, No. 2.
Grant, N., 'The "Zinoviev Letter" Case', *Soviet Studies* (1967), Vol. XIX, No. 2.
Graubard, S. R., *British Labour and the Russian Revolution 1917–1924* (Harvard, 1956).
Greaves, H. R. G., 'Complacency or Challenge?', *Political Quarterly* (Jan.-Mar. 1961).
Gromyko, A., 'Diplomat Leninskoi Shkoly', *Izvestiya*, 5 Dec. 1962.
Grün, A. G., 'Locarno: Idea and Reality', *International Affairs* (1955), Vol. XXXI.
Gurovich, P. V., *Vseobshchaya Stachka v Anglii 1926g.* (Moscow, 1959).
Higbie, C., 'The British Press in Selected Political Situations, 1924–1938' (London Univ. Ph.D. thesis).
Hilger, G. and Meyer, A., *The Incompatible Allies* (New York, 1953).
Hodgson, R., Obituary of Chicherin, *Slavic Review* (1937), Vol. XV.
Hopper, B. C., 'Narkomindel and Comintern', *Foreign Affairs* (July 1942).
Imam, Z., 'Soviet Russia's Policy towards India and its Effect on Anglo-Soviet Relations, 1917–1928' (London Univ. Ph.D. thesis, 1964).
Isaacs, H., *The Tragedy of the Chinese Revolution* (London, 1938).
James, R. R., *Memoirs of a Conservative* (London, 1969).
Jasny, N., *Soviet Economists of the Twenties* (Cambridge, 1972).
Johnstone, D., 'Austen Chamberlain and the Locarno Agreement', *University of Birmingham Historical Journal* (1961), Vol. VIII, No. 1.
Kapitsa, M. S., *Sovetsko-Kitaiskie Otnosheniya* (Moscow, 1958).
Karoi, L., *Velikobritaniya i Lokarno* (Moscow, 1961).
Karpova, R. F., *L. B. Krasin* (Moscow, 1962).
Klugmann, J., *A History of the Communist Party of Great Britain*, 2 vols. (London, 1968–69).
Korbel, J., *Poland between East and West* (Princeton, 1963).
Korey, W., 'Zinoviev on the Problem of World Revolution' (Columbia Univ. Ph.D. thesis, 1961).

Korey, W., 'Zinoviev's Critique of Stalin's Theory of Socialism in One Country, December 1925–December 1926', *The American Slavonic and East European Review* (Dec. 1950).

Lahey, D. T., 'Soviet Ideological Development of Coexistence: 1917–1927', *Canadian Slavonic Papers* (1964), Vol. VI.

Lammers, D. N., 'The Second Labour Government and the Restoration of Relations with Soviet Russia (1929)', *Bull. Inst. Hist. Res.* (May 1964), Vol. XXXVII.

Lorwin, L. L., *Labour and Internationalism* (New York, 1929).

Lyman, R. W., *The First Labour Government, 1924* (London, 1957).

Macfarlane, L. J., *The British Communist Party* (London, 1966).

'"Hands off Russia" – British Labour and the Russo-Polish War 1920', *Past and Present* (1968), No. 38.

Martin, R., *Communism and the British Trade Unions, 1924–1933* (Oxford, 1969).

McKenzie, K., *Comintern and World Revolution, 1928–1943* (Columbia, 1964).

Middlemas, K. and Barnes, J., *Baldwin* (London, 1969).

Miliband, R., *Parliamentary Socialism* (London, 1964).

Miller, K. E., *Socialism and Foreign Policy* (The Hague, 1967).

Morgan, R. P., 'The Political Significance of the German-Soviet Trade Negotiations 1922–25', *The Historical Journal* (1963), No. VI.

Mowat, C. L., *Britain between the Wars, 1918–1940* (London, 1955).

Great Britain since 1914 (London, 1971).

Nicolson, H., *King George the Fifth: His Life and Reign* (London, 1952).

Nikonova, S. B., *Antisovetskaya Vneshnyaya Politika Angliiskikh Konservatorov, 1924–1927* (Moscow, 1963).

Nollau, G., *International Communism and World Revolution* (London, 1961).

Nove, A., *An Economic History of the U.S.S.R.* (London, 1969).

Ostoya-Ovsynyi, J. D., *Leninskaya Diplomatiya Mira i Sotrudnichestva* (Moscow, 1965).

Pelling, H., *The British Communist Party* (London, 1958).

'Governing without Power', *Political Quarterly* (Jan.–Mar. 1961).

Popov, V. I., *Anglo-Sovetskie Otnosheniya (1927–1929)* (Moscow, 1958).

Rosenbaum, K., *Community of Fate: German-Soviet Diplomatic Relations 1922–1928* (Syracuse, 1965).

Ruban, N. V., 'Bor′ba Partii Protiv Trotskistsko-Zinov′evskoi Oppozitsii', *Voprosy Istorii KPSS* (1958), No. 5.

Ryzhikov, V. A., *Zigzagi Diplomatii Londona* (Moscow, 1973).

Sayers, M., and Kahn, A. E., *The Great Conspiracy against Russia* (New York, 1946).

Schapiro, L., *The Communist Party of the Soviet Union* (London, 1960).

Schram, S., 'Christian Rakovskij et le Premier Rapprochement Franco-Soviétique', *Cahiers du Monde Russe et Soviétique* (1960), No. 4.

Schwartz, B., *Chinese Communism and the Rise of Mao* (Cambridge, 1951).

Seymons, J., *The General Strike* (London, 1957).

Shishkin, V. A., *Sovetskoe Gosudarstvo i Strany Zapada v 1917–1923gg.* (Leningrad, 1969).
Solov'ev, O. F., 'Iz Istorii Bor'by Sovetskogo Pravitel'stva za Mirnoe Sosushchestvovanie s Angliei', *Voprosy Istorii* (1965), No. 2.
Sontag, John P., 'The Soviet War Scare of 1926–27', *The Russian Review* (Jan. 1975), Vol. 34, No. 1.
Taylor, A. J. P. *English History 1914–1945* (Oxford, 1965).
Taylor, H. A., *Jix–Viscount Brentford* (London, 1933).
The Third International After Lenin (New York, 1970).
Trotsky, L., *The Revolution Betrayed* (London, 1937).
Trukhanovskii, V. G., *Noveishaya Istoriya Anglii* (Moscow, 1958).
Turok, V. M., 'Anglo-Frantsuzskie Peregovory o "Zapadnom Bloke"', *Seriya Istorii i Filosofii* (1948), No. 4.
Ullman, R. H., *The Anglo-Soviet Accord* (Princeton, 1972).
Britain and the Russian Civil War (Princeton, 1968).
Viktorov, Ya., 'Tri Chemberlena', *Bol'shevik* (1940), No. 8.
Volkov, F. D., *Anglo-Sovetskie Otnosheniya, 1924–1929gg.* (Moscow, 1958).
Vygodskii, S. Ya., *Vneshnyaya Politika SSSR 1924–1929* (Moscow, 1963).
Warth, R. D., 'The Arcos Raid and the Anglo-Soviet "Cold War" of the 1920's, *World Affairs Quarterly* (1958), Vol. XXIX.
'The Mystery of the Zinoviev Letter', *South Atlantic Quarterly* (Oct. 1950), Vol. XLIX.
Webb, S., 'The First Labour Government', *The Political Quarterly* (Jan.–Mar. 1961).
Weir, L. M., *The Tragedy of Ramsay MacDonald* (London, 1938).
Woodhouse, M. G., 'Rank and File Movements among the Miners of South Wales, 1910–1926' (Oxford Univ. D.Phil. thesis, 1969).
Zarnitskii, S. V. and Segreev, A., *Chicherin* (Moscow, 1966).
Zarnitskii, S. V. and Trofimova, L. M., *Krasin, Sovetskoi Strany Diplomat* (Moscow, 1968).

Index